Bio–Inspired Optimization Techniques in Blockchain Systems

U. Vignesh
Vellore Institute of Technology, Chennai, India

Manikandan M.
Manipal Institute of Technology, India

Ruchi Doshi
Universidad Azteca, Mexico

A volume in the Advances in
Systems Analysis, Software
Engineering, and High Performance
Computing (ASASEHPC) Book Series

Published in the United States of America by
IGI Global
Engineering Science Reference (an imprint of IGI Global)
701 E. Chocolate Avenue
Hershey PA, USA 17033
Tel: 717-533-8845
Fax: 717-533-8661
E-mail: cust@igi-global.com
Web site: http://www.igi-global.com

Library of Congress Cataloging-in-Publication Data

Names: Umapathi, Vignesh, 1989- editor. | Murugaiah, Manikandan, 1987-
    editor. | Doshi, Ruchi, editor.
Title: Bio-inspired optimization techniques in blockchain systems / edited
    by: U. Vignesh, Manikandan Murugaiah, Ruchi Doshi.
Description: Hershey PA : Engineering Science Reference, [2024] | Includes
    bibliographical references. | Summary: "The book extends recent
    concepts, methodologies, and empirical research advances of various
    biological data mining systems through blockchain approaches"-- Provided
    by publisher.
Identifiers: LCCN 2023037144 (print) | LCCN 2023037145 (ebook) | ISBN
    9798369311318 (hardcover) | ISBN 9798369311325 (ebook)
Subjects: LCSH: Blockchains (Databases)--Industrial applications. | Data
    mining.
Classification: LCC QA76.9.B56 B46 2024 (print) | LCC QA76.9.B56 (ebook)
    | DDC 006.3/12--dc23/eng/20240130
LC record available at https://lccn.loc.gov/2023037144
LC ebook record available at https://lccn.loc.gov/2023037145

This book is published in the IGI Global book series Advances in Systems Analysis, Software Engineering, and High Performance Computing (ASASEHPC) (ISSN: 2327-3453; eISSN: 2327-3461)

British Cataloguing in Publication Data
A Cataloguing in Publication record for this book is available from the British Library.

For electronic access to this publication, please contact: eresources@igi-global.com.

Advances in Systems Analysis, Software Engineering, and High Performance Computing (ASASEHPC) Book Series

ISSN:2327-3453
EISSN:2327-3461

Editor-in-Chief: Vijayan Sugumaran, Oakland University, USA

MISSION

The theory and practice of computing applications and distributed systems has emerged as one of the key areas of research driving innovations in business, engineering, and science. The fields of software engineering, systems analysis, and high performance computing offer a wide range of applications and solutions in solving computational problems for any modern organization.

The **Advances in Systems Analysis, Software Engineering, and High Performance Computing (ASASEHPC) Book Series** brings together research in the areas of distributed computing, systems and software engineering, high performance computing, and service science. This collection of publications is useful for academics, researchers, and practitioners seeking the latest practices and knowledge in this field.

COVERAGE

- Computer Networking
- Virtual Data Systems
- Distributed Cloud Computing
- Parallel Architectures
- Human-Computer Interaction
- Software Engineering
- Engineering Environments
- Performance Modelling
- Network Management
- Computer System Analysis

IGI Global is currently accepting manuscripts for publication within this series. To submit a proposal for a volume in this series, please contact our Acquisition Editors at Acquisitions@igi-global.com or visit: http://www.igi-global.com/publish/.

Titles in this Series

For a list of additional titles in this series, please visit:
www.igi-global.com/book-series/advances-systems-analysis-software-engineering/73689

Digital Technologies in Modeling and Management Insights in Education and Industry
GS Prakasha (Christ University, India) Maria Lapina (North-Caucasus Federal University, Russia) and Deepanraj Balakrishnan (Prince Mohammad Bin Fahd University, Saudi Arabia)
Information Science Reference ● copyright 2024 ● 320pp ● H/C (ISBN: 9781668495766) ● US $250.00 (our price)

ODE, BVP, and 1D PDE Solvers for Scientific and Engineering Problems With MATLAB Basics
Leonid Burstein (ORT Braude College of Engineering, Israel (Retired))
Engineering Science Reference ● copyright 2023 ● 300pp ● H/C (ISBN: 9781668468500) ● US $245.00 (our price)

The Software Principles of Design for Data Modeling
Debabrata Samanta (Rochester Institute of Technology, Kosovo)
Engineering Science Reference ● copyright 2023 ● 318pp ● H/C (ISBN: 9781668498095) ● US $270.00 (our price)

Investigations in Pattern Recognition and Computer Vision for Industry 4.0
Chiranji Lal Chowdhary (Vellore Institute of Technology, Vellore, India) Basanta Kumar Swain (Government College of Engineering, Bhawanipatna, India) and Vijay Kumar (Dr B R Ambedkar National Institute of Technology Jalandhar, India)
Engineering Science Reference ● copyright 2023 ● 276pp ● H/C (ISBN: 9781668486023) ● US $270.00 (our price)

Cyber-Physical System Solutions for Smart Cities
Vanamoorthy Muthumanikandan (Vellore Institute of Technology, Chennai, India) Anbalagan Bhuvaneswari (Vellore Institute of Technology, Chennai, India) Balamurugan Easwaran (University of Africa, Toru-Orua, Nigeria) and T. Sudarson Rama Perumal (Rohini College of Engineering and Technology, India)

For an entire list of titles in this series, please visit:
www.igi-global.com/book-series/advances-systems-analysis-software-engineering/73689

701 East Chocolate Avenue, Hershey, PA 17033, USA
Tel: 717-533-8845 x100 ● Fax: 717-533-8661
E-Mail: cust@igi-global.com ● www.igi-global.com

Table of Contents

Detailed Table of Contents

    P. Chitra, Dhanalakshmi Srinivasan University, India
    A. Saleem Raja, University of Technology and Applied Sciences, Shinas, Oman
    V. Sivakumar, Asia Pacific University of Technology and Innovation, Malaysia

Bio-inspired algorithms, which imitate the actions and procedures seen in biological systems, have proven to be incredibly effective at solving problems in a variety of fields. However, the combination of these algorithms with blockchain technology holds enormous promise for improving their potency while assuring effectiveness, efficiency, and security. This chapter gives a general overview of how bio-inspired algorithms are used effectively with blockchain technology, highlighting their main benefits and prospective uses. Bio-inspired algorithms can gain from improved security and confidence in their execution by utilizing the decentralized and immutable characteristics of blockchain. Blockchain technology offers a transparent and auditable platform that makes it easier to verify algorithmic operations and ensure the accuracy of data. Furthermore, distributed resource allocation and decision-making are made possible by blockchain's decentralized consensus mechanisms, promoting cooperation and collective intelligence.

    K. Ezhilarasan, Gandhigram Rural Institute, India
    K. Somasundaram, Gandhigram Rural Institute, India
    T. Kalaiselvi, Gandhigram Rural Institute, India
    Praveenkumar Somasundaram, Qualcomm Technologies Inc., USA
    S. Karthigai Selvi, Galgotias University, India
    A. Jeevarekha, M.V. Muthiah Government Arts College for Women, India

Medical image processing plays a crucial role in diagnosing diseases, guiding treatment plans, and monitoring patient progress. With the increasing complexity and volume of medical imaging data, there is a growing need for advanced techniques to extract meaningful information from these images. Traditional methods in medical image processing often face challenges related to image enhancement, segmentation, and feature extraction. These challenges stem from the inherent variability, noise, and complexity of medical images, making it difficult to obtain accurate and reliable results. In this chapter, the focus is on leveraging bio-inspired algorithms to address these challenges and improve the analysis and interpretation of medical images. Bio-inspired algorithms draw inspiration from natural processes, such as evolution, swarm behavior, neural networks, and genetic programming. It addresses the challenges and requirements specific to each modality and how bio-inspired algorithms can be adapted and tailored to meet those needs.

The integration of blockchain technology into the healthcare sector has shown immense promise in addressing critical challenges related to data security, interoperability, transparency, and patient-centric care. This chapter explores the emergence of blockchain-based healthcare applications and services, highlighting their potential to revolutionize the healthcare industry. Blockchain's inherent features, including decentralization, immutability, and cryptographic security, provide a solid foundation for improving various aspects of healthcare, such as electronic health records (EHRs), medical data exchange, supply chain management, clinical trials, and telemedicine. This chapter reviews several prominent use cases of blockchain in healthcare, such as patient-controlled EHRs, secure data sharing across institutions, provenance tracking of pharmaceuticals, and streamlining administrative processes through smart contracts. It also delves into the challenges that need to be addressed for scalability, regulatory compliance, standardization, and user adoption.

Blockchain technology has revolutionized various industries, offering decentralized and tamper-resistant data storage and transaction capabilities. However, traditional consensus mechanisms, such as proof-of-work (PoW) and proof-of-stake (PoS), face energy consumption, scalability, and security challenges. This chapter proposes a novel consensus mechanism called "BIONET," a bio-inspired neural network for blockchain systems. BIONET integrates the principles of swarm intelligence and artificial neural networks to achieve efficient, secure, and adaptive consensus in blockchain networks. The authors present the architectural overview of BIONET, highlighting its adaptability and self-organization capabilities. Furthermore, they demonstrate BIONET's effectiveness in PoW, PoS, and practical byzantine fault tolerance (PBFT) consensus mechanisms. Finally, they discuss the future directions and challenges of BIONET, paving the way for bio-inspired optimization techniques in blockchain systems.

Chapter 5

U. Vignesh, Vellore Institute of Technology, Chennai, India
R. Elakya, Sri Venkateswara College of Engineering, India

Blockchain technology holds immense potential for revolutionizing supply chain management by enhancing transparency, security, and efficiency. The key areas of focus encompass goods provenance tracking, traceability enhancement, fraud reduction, and efficiency augmentation. This chapter explores the core attributes of blockchain—decentralization, immutability, and transparency—and their application in supply chains. However, challenges include interoperability issues, data privacy concerns, and security risks like 51% attacks. Costs of implementation are also significant. Additionally, the project addresses pivotal concerns such as interoperability, data privacy, security, and the costs associated with adopting blockchain solutions. Ultimately, the project concludes that integrating blockchain technology into supply chain management has the potential to streamline operations, foster trust between stakeholders, and elevate overall efficiency and resilience within the supply chain ecosystem.

Chapter 6

S. Karthigai Selvi, Galgotias University, India
R. Siva Shankar, Chiang Mai University, Thailand
K. Ezhilarasan, The Gandhigram Rural Institute, India

Blockchain is an exciting new technology that is being used to provide creative solutions in a number of industries, including the medical field. In the healthcare system, hospitals, labs, pharmacies, and doctors exchange and store patient data via a blockchain connected network. Blockchain-based software can reliably detect serious errors, including potentially harmful ones, in the medical domain. As a result, it can enhance the efficiency, security, and openness of medical data exchange within the healthcare system. Medical facilities can improve their understanding of patient care and obtain valuable insights from the use of this technology. This chapter discusses blockchain technology and its advantages, popular algorithms in blockchain technology, the current issues in medical data maintenance, and blockchain application fields in healthcare. Lastly, the study identifies and discusses the pros and cons of algorithms in medical data maintenance and key benefits of applied fields.

    Vemasani Varshini, Vellore Institute of Technology, Chennai, India
    Maheswari Raja, Vellore Institute of Technology, Chennai, India
    Sharath Kumar Jagannathan, Saint Peter's University, USA

Endometrial carcinoma (EC) is a common uterine cancer that leads to morbidity and death linked to cancer. Advanced EC diagnosis exhibits a subpar treatment response and requires a lot of time and money. Data scientists and oncologists focused on computational biology due to its explosive expansion and computer-aided cancer surveillance systems. Machine learning offers prospects for drug discovery, early cancer diagnosis, and efficient treatment. It may be pertinent to use ML techniques in EC diagnosis, treatments, and prognosis. Analysis of ML utility in EC may spur research in EC and help oncologists, molecular biologists, biomedical engineers, and bioinformaticians advance collaborative research in EC. It also leads to customised treatment and the growing trend of using ML approaches in cancer prediction and monitoring. An overview of EC, its risk factors, and diagnostic techniques are covered in this study. It concludes a thorough investigation of the prospective ML modalities for patient screening, diagnosis, prognosis, and the deep learning models, which gave the good accuracy.

    Humam Imad Wajeeh Al-Shahwani, University of Baghdad, Iraq
    *Maad M. Mijwil, Baghdad College of Economic Sciences University,
        Iraq*
    Ruchi Doshi, Universidad Azteca, Mexico
    Kamal Kant Hiran, Sir Padampat Singhania University, India
    Indu Bala, Lovely Professional University, India

Blockchain represents a new promising technology with a huge economic impact resulting from its uses in various fields such as digital currency and banking; malware represents a serious threat to users, and there are many differences in the effectiveness of antivirus software used to deal with the problem of malware. This chapter has developed a coefficient for measuring the effectiveness of antivirus software. This chapter evaluates the effectiveness of antivirus software by conducting tests on a group of protection programs using a folder containing an amount of data. These programs are applied to combat viruses contained in this folder. The study revealed that the effectiveness of antivirus software is as follows: AVG scored 0%, Advanced System Protector scored 20%, Avast scored 60%, and Malwarebytes scored 80%, respectively.

    *R. Elakya, Information Technology, Sri Venkateswara College of
        Engineering, India*
    *R. Thanga Selvi, Vel Tech Rangarajan Dr. Sagunthala R&D Institute of
        Science and Technology, India*
    *S. Girirajan, Computing Technologies, SRM Institute of Science and
        Technology, India*
    A. Vidhyavani, SRM Institute of Science and Technology, India

The current manual process of the traditional supply chain system, from raw material manufacturing to product delivery, lacks sufficient data and transaction security while being time-consuming. This outdated procedure is ineffective and unreliable for consumers. However, integrating blockchain and smart contract technologies into traditional supply chain management systems can significantly enhance data security, authenticity, time management, and transaction processes. By leveraging decentralized blockchain technology, the entire supply chain management (SCM) process becomes more trustworthy, ensuring consumer satisfaction. This study utilizes a peer-to-peer encrypted system in conjunction with smart contracts to ensure data immutability and prevent unauthorized access. Moreover, cryptographic methods are employed to enhance transaction security and address these issues. Ultimately, this chapter demonstrates how to maintain a highly secure, transparent, and efficient supply chain management process.

    U. Vignesh, Vellore Institute of Technology, Chennai, India
    Rahul Ratnakumar, Manipal Institute of Technology, India

Currently, the biggest challenge in the world is the detection of viral infection in various diseases, as par to the rapid spread of the disease. According to recent statistics, the number of people diagnosed with the Influenza virus is exponentially increasing day by day, with more than 2.5 million confirmed cases. The model proposed here analyses the Influenza virus by comparing different deep learning algorithms to bring out the best in terms of accuracy for detection and prediction. The models are trained using CT scan dataset comprising of both Influenza positive patients and negative patients. The results of algorithms are compared based on parameters such as train accuracy, test loss, etc. Some of the best models after training were, DenseNet-121 with accuracy of 96.28%, VGG-16 with accuracy of 95.75%, ResNet-50 with accuracy of 94.18%, etc. in detecting the virus from the CT scan dataset with the proposed ACDL algorithm. Thus, these models will be helpful and useful to the government and communities to initiate proper measures to control the outbreak of the Influenza virus in time.

Chapter 11

  G. K. Sandhia, SRM Institute of Science and Technology, India
  R. Vidhya, SRM Institute of Science and Technology, India
  K. R. Jansi, SRM Institute of Science and Technology, India
  R. Jeya, SRM Institute of Science and Technology, India
  M. Gayathri, SRM Institute of Science and Technology, India
  S. Girirajan, SRM Institute of Science and Technology, India
  S. Nagadevi, SRM Institute of Science and Technology, India
  N. Ghuntupalli Manoj Kumar, SRM Institute of Science and Technology, India
  J. Ramaprabha, SRM Institute of Science and Technology, India

Blockchain is a distributed ledger. It stores transaction data in the form of a linked list combined with encryption algorithms to enhance the security and integrity of the data in each of the blocks. Any participant of the node can verify the correctness of a transaction and a block is created only after the majority of the participants of the network (51%) agree to the correctness of a transaction. The participants reach a consensus on the transactions broadcast and the sequence in which these transactions occurred. At any point of time, all participants have an order of blocks of transactions they have accepted consensus on, and each participant has a set of unprocessed transactions it has in its pool. A block is then selected by one node on which validity of transactions is checked and then it is added to the blockchain. The main focus is to demonstrate the concept of staking cryptocurrencies on blockchains and how decentralized applications can be developed on the Ethereum network to deploy such applications.

Chapter 12

Using big data and algorithmic techniques, not all of the data gathered in this way is relevant for analysis or decision-making. To be more specific, the chapter addresses issues that arise during the fine tuning of large data sets, presenting open research questions that can aid in the processing of large data sets and the extraction of valuable information from them, as well as providing an overview of big data tools and techniques that can be used to address these issues. Healthcare, public administration, retail, and other multidisciplinary scientific inquiries are only few of the areas where boundaries might be blurred. Big data is mostly derived from social computing, internet text and document storage, and internet search indexing. Online communities, recommendation systems, reputation systems, and prediction markets are all examples of social computing. Internet search indexing includes ISI, IEEE Xplorer, Scopus, Thomson Reuters, etc.

Preface

Blockchain technology has revolutionized various industries by providing secure, transparent, and immutable solutions to complex data management challenges. In the world of data analytics, one area that has been ripe for transformation is bioinformatics. The integration of blockchain and bioinformatics holds the potential to usher in a new era of data ownership and integrity, overcoming the obstacles that have hindered the efficient transfer and analysis of biological data.

Bio-Inspired Optimization Techniques in Blockchain Systems, edited by U. Vignesh, Manikandan M., and Ruchi Doshi, is a pioneering exploration into the synergy between blockchain technology and bioinformatics. This edited reference book is a testament to the idea that innovation knows no bounds when it comes to harnessing the power of cutting-edge technologies.

The challenges of integrating blockchain into bioinformatics are multifaceted. Storing vast amounts of genomic data on a blockchain, achieving rapid transaction speeds, and enabling effective querying of the data have posed significant hurdles. To tackle these roadblocks, optimization algorithms have emerged as a critical solution. This book delves into the structural and functional aspects of blockchain networks, providing insights into how genomic variants and reference-aligned reads can be stored on-chain. We explore the innovative use of traditional database indexing for data analysis in the realm of biological data.

Our aim is to expand the horizons of recent concepts, methodologies, and empirical research within the domain of biological data mining, all through the lens of blockchain technology. Whether you're a technology developer, academician, data scientist, industrial professional, researcher, or a student with a passion for uncovering the latest advancements, this publication has something to offer.

The comprehensive scope of this book spans across various domains, covering but not limited to:

- **Machine Learning and Deep Learning:** The role of machine learning and deep learning in optimizing blockchain systems for bioinformatics.
- **Blockchain Smart Contracts for Smart Supply Chains:** Innovations in supply chain management through blockchain-based smart contracts.

- **Advances in Analyzing Blockchain Issues:** A deep dive into the evolving landscape of blockchain problem-solving.
- **Enhancement of Blockchain Standardization:** A look at how blockchain technology is advancing toward standardized protocols.
- **Internet of Things (IoT):** The intersection of blockchain and IoT and its implications.
- **Personal Identity Security:** How blockchain enhances personal identity security.
- **Applications in Healthcare, Logistics, and More:** Practical applications of blockchain in healthcare, logistics, and a multitude of other sectors.

The comprehensive coverage of these topics reflects the diverse and evolving landscape of blockchain applications in bioinformatics. The contributors to this book include experts and scholars from various fields, each bringing their unique insights and experiences to the table.

Chapter 1 sets the stage by exploring how bio-inspired algorithms, which emulate biological systems' actions and procedures, can be remarkably effective problem solvers. We delve into the exciting promise of merging these algorithms with blockchain technology, highlighting the potential improvements in their efficiency, effectiveness, and security. Bio-inspired algorithms stand to benefit from the decentralized and immutable nature of blockchain, which enhances their security and boosts confidence in their execution. The chapter underscores how blockchain offers transparency, auditability, and decentralized consensus mechanisms that enable distributed resource allocation and decision-making, fostering cooperation and collective intelligence.

The second chapter delves into the vital role of medical image processing in disease diagnosis, treatment guidance, and patient monitoring. Given the increasing complexity and volume of medical imaging data, this chapter addresses the need for advanced techniques to extract meaningful insights. Traditional methods often encounter challenges in image enhancement, segmentation, and feature extraction due to the inherent variability and noise in medical images. Bio-inspired algorithms, inspired by natural processes, such as evolution and neural networks, are introduced as solutions to these challenges. The chapter explores the adaptation of bio-inspired algorithms to various medical imaging modalities, catering to their specific requirements.

Chapter 3 shines a light on the transformative potential of blockchain technology in the healthcare sector. It explores the emergence of blockchain-based healthcare applications and services, emphasizing how blockchain's inherent features, like decentralization and cryptographic security, can enhance electronic health records, medical data exchange, supply chain management, clinical trials, and telemedicine. Prominent use cases, such as patient-controlled EHRs, secure data sharing, provenance tracking of pharmaceuticals, and smart contract applications, are reviewed. The chapter also discusses the challenges and considerations, including scalability, regulatory compliance, standardization, and user adoption.

In Chapter 4, we introduce a groundbreaking consensus mechanism called "BIONET," a Bio-Inspired Neural Network for blockchain systems. BIONET combines principles from swarm intelligence and artificial neural networks to deliver efficient, secure, and adaptive consensus for blockchain networks. We present an architectural overview of BIONET, emphasizing its adaptability and self-organization capabilities. The chapter demonstrates BIONET's effectiveness in various consensus mechanisms, including Proof-of-Work, Proof-of-Stake, and Practical Byzantine Fault Tolerance. We also explore the future directions and challenges of BIONET, paving the way for bio-inspired optimization techniques in blockchain systems.

Chapter 5 examines the transformative potential of blockchain technology in supply chain management. It focuses on the core attributes of blockchain, decentralization, immutability, and transparency, and how these attributes can enhance goods provenance tracking, traceability, fraud reduction, and efficiency within supply chains. While blockchain offers significant advantages, the chapter also addresses critical concerns, such as interoperability, data privacy, security risks, and implementation costs, to provide a comprehensive view of the technology's impact on supply chain management.

Chapter 6 dives deep into the application of blockchain technology in the healthcare sector. It explores how hospitals, labs, pharmacies, and doctors are utilizing blockchain to exchange and store patient data securely. Blockchain-based software is shown to be capable of detecting errors in medical data, thereby improving efficiency, security, and transparency in data exchange within the healthcare system. The chapter discusses the advantages of blockchain in healthcare, popular algorithms in blockchain technology, current issues in medical data maintenance, and various application fields in healthcare. It also provides a comprehensive analysis of the pros and cons of algorithms in medical data maintenance and the key benefits of their applied fields.

Chapter 7 focuses on the role of machine learning in diagnosing and prognosing endometrial carcinoma (EC), a common uterine cancer. It discusses the challenges and the potential of machine learning in drug discovery, early diagnosis, and effective treatment. By analyzing EC, its risk factors, and diagnostic techniques, the chapter provides an overview of machine learning modalities for patient screening, diagnosis, prognosis, and deep learning models with high accuracy. This discussion contributes to the advancement of collaborative research in EC, benefiting oncologists, molecular biologists, biomedical engineers, and bioinformaticians.

Chapter 8 evaluates the effectiveness of antivirus software by introducing a novel coefficient for measuring its efficiency. Several antivirus programs are tested using a dataset containing virus-infected files, and the results shed light on the varying effectiveness of these programs. The chapter presents findings that reflect the relative performance of different antivirus software, which is invaluable for users concerned about malware protection.

Chapter 9 addresses the challenges of traditional supply chain management and demonstrates how blockchain and smart contract technologies can enhance data security, authenticity, and time management within the supply chain. By utilizing peer-to-peer encrypted systems and cryptographic methods, the chapter outlines how these technologies can lead to a highly secure, transparent, and efficient supply chain management process.

Chapter 10 takes on the critical challenge of detecting the Influenza virus, which has seen exponential growth in cases. The chapter analyzes the performance of different deep learning algorithms to achieve high accuracy in detection and prediction. It presents results based on parameters such as training accuracy and test loss, highlighting the most effective models for detecting the virus.

Chapter 11 explores the concept of staking cryptocurrencies on blockchain networks and demonstrates how decentralized applications can be developed on the Ethereum network. It delves into the blockchain technology's principles, such as consensus mechanisms and transaction ordering, providing insights into the development of decentralized applications.

The final chapter delves into the challenges that arise in fine-tuning large datasets and highlights research questions that can aid in processing large datasets and extracting valuable information. The chapter provides an overview of big data tools and techniques and their applications in areas like healthcare, public administration, retail, and multidisciplinary scientific inquiries. It underscores the importance of addressing data processing issues in the age of big data.

Together, these chapters form a comprehensive exploration of the intersection between bio-inspired optimization techniques and blockchain technology across various domains, offering valuable insights for researchers, professionals, and enthusiasts in the field.

We believe that this book is a valuable resource for professionals, researchers, academicians, students, and anyone with a keen interest in exploring the incredible possibilities that arise when blockchain meets bioinformatics. Our hope is that this collection of knowledge will inspire and drive innovation in this fascinating intersection of technology and life sciences.

U. Vignesh
Vellore Institute of Technology, Chennai, India

M. Manikandan
Manipal Institute of Technology, India

Ruchi Doshi
Universidad Azteca, Mexico

Chapter 1

Bio-Inspired Algorithms Leveraging Blockchain Technology Enhancing Efficiency Security and Transparency

P. Chitra
Dhanalakshmi Srinivasan University, India

A. Saleem Raja
University of Technology and Applied Sciences, Shinas, Oman

V. Sivakumar
Asia Pacific University of Technology and Innovation, Malaysia

ABSTRACT

Bio-inspired algorithms, which imitate the actions and procedures seen in biological systems, have proven to be incredibly effective at solving problems in a variety of fields. However, the combination of these algorithms with blockchain technology holds enormous promise for improving their potency while assuring effectiveness, efficiency, and security. This chapter gives a general overview of how bio-inspired algorithms are used effectively with blockchain technology, highlighting their main benefits and prospective uses. Bio-inspired algorithms can gain from improved security and confidence in their execution by utilizing the decentralized and immutable characteristics of blockchain. Blockchain technology offers a transparent and auditable platform that makes it easier to verify algorithmic operations and ensure the accuracy of data. Furthermore, distributed resource allocation and decision-making are made possible by blockchain's decentralized consensus mechanisms, promoting cooperation and collective intelligence.

DOI: 10.4018/979-8-3693-1131-8.ch001

INTRODUCTION

Bio-inspired algorithms, which draw inspiration from natural systems, have proven to be powerful tools for solving complex optimization and decision-making problems. These algorithms mimic the behavior of biological entities such as ants, bees, genetic evolution, and neural networks to find innovative and efficient solutions. Concurrently, blockchain technology has emerged as a revolutionary concept that enables decentralized, transparent, and secure transactions.

The integration of bio-inspired algorithms with blockchain technology holds significant promise in various fields, offering enhanced efficiency, security, and transparency. By leveraging the inherent strengths of both bio-inspired algorithms and blockchain, researchers and practitioners can tackle complex challenges in a decentralized and trustless environment.

Bio-inspired algorithms encompass a range of techniques, including genetic algorithms, swarm intelligence, artificial neural networks, and evolutionary computation. These algorithms have demonstrated impressive problem-solving capabilities across domains such as optimization, scheduling, resource allocation, and pattern recognition. However, they often rely on centralized computational resources and lack transparency in their execution. (H. Zhou, 2020) Block chain technology, on the other hand, offers a decentralized and immutable ledger that ensures transparency, security, and consensus. Blockchain has gained widespread attention primarily through its association with cryptocurrencies like Bitcoin. However, its potential extends far beyond financial applications, with implications for various industries, including supply chain management, healthcare, energy, and identity management.

The integration of bio-inspired algorithms with blockchain technology provides several advantages. Firstly, the decentralized nature of blockchain enables distributed computation, allowing multiple participants to contribute their computational resources to solve complex problems. This approach increases computational power, scalability, and resilience. Secondly, blockchain's transparency and immutability ensure that the execution of bio-inspired algorithms can be verified and audited, fostering trust and accountability. Additionally, blockchain's consensus mechanisms provide a decentralized decision-making framework, enabling efficient coordination among participants.

Bio Inspired Algorithms

Bio-inspired algorithms are computational methods that draw inspiration from the principles, behavior, and processes observed in biological systems. These algorithms mimic the adaptive and efficient strategies found in nature to solve complex problems.

Figure 1. Bio-inspired systems

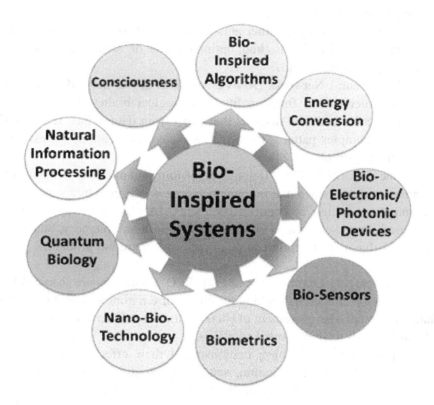

(Y. Sun, 2020) By emulating the mechanisms of biological entities such as ants, bees, genetic evolution, neural networks, and more, bio-inspired algorithms offer innovative approaches to optimization, decision-making, and pattern recognition.

There are several categories of bio-inspired algorithms, each inspired by a different aspect of nature:

- Genetic Algorithms (GAs): Genetic algorithms are inspired by the process of natural selection and genetic evolution. They use the concepts of selection, crossover, and mutation to iteratively evolve a population of potential solutions towards an optimal or near-optimal solution.
- Particle Swarm Optimization (PSO): PSO algorithms are inspired by the collective behavior of bird flocks or fish schools. Particles in the swarm search for the best solution by updating their positions based on their own experience and the experience of their neighbors, aiming to converge towards the optimal solution.

- Ant Colony Optimization (ACO): ACO algorithms are inspired by the foraging behavior of ant colonies. Ants deposit pheromones to communicate and create trails to guide other ants towards food sources. ACO algorithms simulate this behavior to find optimal paths or solutions by iteratively updating pheromone trails.
- Artificial Neural Networks (ANN): Artificial neural networks are inspired by the structure and functionality of biological brains. ANNs consist of interconnected artificial neurons that learn from data, adjust their weights, and form complex patterns to solve tasks like classification, regression, and pattern recognition.
- Immune Algorithms (IA): Immune algorithms simulate the behavior of the immune system, where the immune response is triggered by recognizing and eliminating foreign or abnormal elements. IA algorithms apply immune-inspired processes such as clonal selection, immune memory, and immune network dynamics to optimization or pattern recognition problems.

Bacterial Foraging Optimization (BFO): BFO algorithms are inspired by the foraging behavior of bacteria seeking food in their environment. BFO algorithms emulate the chemotactic movement of bacteria, their reproduction, and elimination of unfit individuals to find optimal solutions.

Bio-inspired algorithms have demonstrated their effectiveness in various applications, including optimization, scheduling, routing, data mining, image processing, and machine learning. (X. Wang, 2019) They offer adaptive, robust, and efficient solutions to complex problems, often outperforming traditional optimization algorithms in certain scenarios.

By leveraging the inherent strategies and mechanisms observed in biological systems, bio-inspired algorithms provide innovative approaches to problem-solving, optimization, and decision-making. (Lai, C., Yan, Y., & Sui, Y., 2020) They continue to be an active area of research and hold promise for addressing challenging real-world problems.

Blockchain Technology

Blockchain technology is a decentralized and distributed ledger that securely records and verifies transactions across multiple computers or nodes in a network. (M. A. Khan, 2019) It provides transparency, security, and immutability of data through cryptographic techniques and consensus mechanisms. Here are some key aspects of blockchain technology:

Figure 2. Nature-inspired algorithms

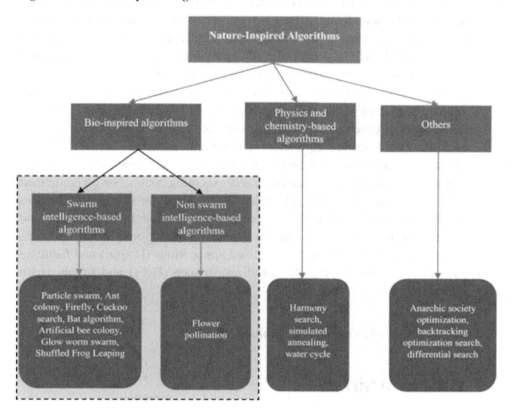

- Decentralization: Unlike traditional centralized systems where a single authority controls the data and transactions, blockchain operates on a peer-to-peer network. Each participant in the network, known as a node, maintains a copy of the entire blockchain, ensuring decentralization and removing the need for intermediaries.
- Distributed Ledger: A blockchain is a chain of blocks, where each block contains a list of transactions (Yan, J., et al., 2020). The ledger is distributed across multiple nodes, and each node maintains a copy of the entire blockchain. This distribution ensures redundancy, fault tolerance, and resilience against attacks.
- Transparency and Immutability: Once a transaction is recorded on the blockchain, it cannot be altered or deleted. The data stored in the blockchain is transparent and visible to all participants, promoting trust and accountability. This transparency makes blockchain suitable for applications where auditability and traceability are essential.

- Cryptographic Security: Blockchain uses cryptographic algorithms to secure the data and ensure its integrity. Each transaction is digitally signed to verify its authenticity, and hashing algorithms ensure the immutability of data within each block. The decentralized nature of blockchain and cryptographic security make it highly resistant to tampering and fraud.
- Consensus Mechanisms: Blockchain employs consensus mechanisms to validate and agree on the state of the ledger across multiple nodes (Xiong, J., et al., 2019). Consensus mechanisms, such as Proof of Work (PoW) or Proof of Stake (PoS), ensure agreement and prevent malicious activities. These mechanisms contribute to the security and integrity of the blockchain network.
- Smart Contracts: Smart contracts are self-executing contracts with predefined rules and conditions (Wang, H., et al., 2020). They are stored and executed on the blockchain, automating processes, eliminating intermediaries, and ensuring transparency and trust in business transactions. Smart contracts enable the development of decentralized applications (DApps) and facilitate various use cases, such as decentralized finance (DeFi) and supply chain management.

Figure 3. Structure of blockchain technology

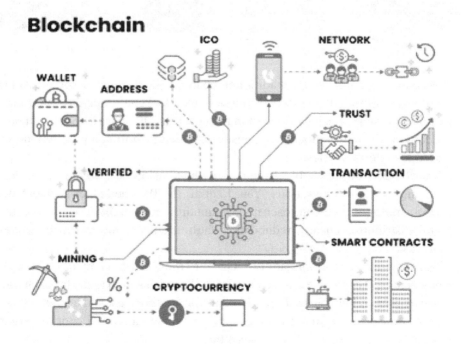

Blockchain technology has applications in various industries, including finance, supply chain, healthcare, identity management, energy, and more (L. Han, et al., 2019). It offers benefits such as increased security, reduced costs, improved efficiency, and enhanced trust among participants. As the technology continues to evolve, researchers and developers are exploring new use cases and refining the scalability and privacy aspects of blockchain systems.

Advantages and Opportunities of Blockchain Technology

- Decentralization: Blockchain technology operates on a decentralized network, eliminating the need for a central authority or intermediary (Bhattacharya., et al., 2019). This decentralization leads to increased transparency, security, and resilience. It enables peer-to-peer transactions, reduces dependence on trusted third parties, and empowers individuals by giving them control over their data and assets.
- Enhanced Security: Blockchain provides robust security features through cryptographic algorithms. Transactions recorded on the blockchain are cryptographically linked and secured, making it difficult for malicious actors to tamper with or alter the data (Liao, X., et al., 2018). The distributed nature of the ledger also adds an additional layer of security as it requires a consensus among network participants to validate transactions.
- Transparency and Auditability: Blockchain offers transparency by providing a transparent and immutable record of transactions. Once a transaction is recorded on the blockchain, it cannot be altered, ensuring the integrity and auditability of data. This transparency builds trust among participants and enables verification of transaction history and compliance with regulations.
- Efficiency and Cost Reduction: Blockchain eliminates the need for intermediaries and streamlines processes by automating transactions through smart contracts. This reduces paperwork, manual verification, and processing time, leading to increased efficiency and cost savings (Chen, J., et al., 2019). Additionally, blockchain-based systems can optimize and simplify complex workflows, such as supply chain management, resulting in improved operational efficiency.
- Trust and Accountability: Blockchain technology fosters trust among participants through its transparent and decentralized nature. The immutability and auditability of transactions on the blockchain create a high level of accountability. Participants can verify the authenticity and integrity of data, ensuring trustworthiness in business transactions and reducing fraudulent activities.

- New Business Models and Innovation: Blockchain technology opens up new opportunities for innovative business models. It enables the creation of decentralized applications (DApps) and facilitates tokenization, allowing the representation and exchange of digital assets (Tavares, R. P., et al., 2019). Smart contracts on blockchain platforms enable self-executing and automated agreements, enabling novel applications such as decentralized finance (DeFi), asset tokenization, and supply chain traceability.
- Cross-Industry Applications: Blockchain has broad applications across various industries. It can be used in finance for secure and efficient cross-border transactions, in supply chain management for traceability and provenance verification, in healthcare for secure and interoperable health records, and in energy for decentralized energy trading (Shah, Z., et al., 2019). The technology's versatility allows for its integration into diverse sectors, providing solutions to complex problems.
- Empowering Individuals: Blockchain technology empowers individuals by giving them control over their digital assets, data privacy, and identities (Lv, Q., et al., 2020). Through self-sovereign identity solutions, individuals can manage their personal information and selectively share it with trusted entities, enhancing privacy and data protection.

The advantages and opportunities offered by blockchain technology have the potential to transform industries, improve existing systems, and drive innovation. (Fernández-Caramés, et al., 2019)As the technology evolves and matures, further advancements

Figure 4. Advantages of blockchain technology

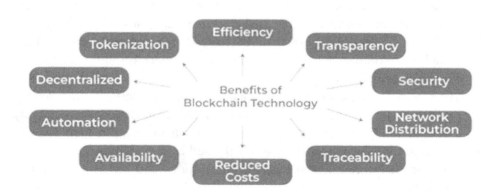

and novel use cases are likely to emerge, creating a more decentralized, secure, and efficient digital ecosystem.

Challenges and Future Directions of Bio-Inspired Algorithms Using Blockchain Technology

- Scalability: One of the primary challenges is the scalability of blockchain networks when executing resource-intensive bio-inspired algorithms (Zhang, J, et al., 2019). As the size of the network and the complexity of the algorithms increase, the computational and storage requirements may become impractical. Addressing scalability concerns is crucial to ensure efficient execution of bio-inspired algorithms on blockchain platforms.
- Privacy and Confidentiality: Bio-inspired algorithms often require access to sensitive and private data. However, blockchain's transparent nature may pose challenges in maintaining privacy and confidentiality (Li, X., et al., 2017). Developing privacy-preserving mechanisms, such as zero-knowledge proofs or homomorphic encryption, while still ensuring the integrity and transparency of the blockchain, is an area that requires further exploration.
- Algorithm Design and Integration: Integrating bio-inspired algorithms with blockchain technology requires careful consideration of algorithm design and adaptation to the decentralized and distributed nature of blockchain networks (Xu, et al., 2020). Developing novel algorithms that are compatible with blockchain architectures and optimizing them for distributed execution is a key research direction.
- Consensus Mechanisms: Consensus mechanisms, such as Proof of Work (PoW) and Proof of Stake (PoS), have been predominantly used in blockchain networks. However, these mechanisms may not be suitable for executing bio-inspired algorithms efficiently (Liang, X., et al., 2018). Exploring and designing consensus mechanisms specifically tailored to the requirements of bio-inspired algorithms can enhance the performance, energy efficiency, and scalability of these algorithms on blockchain platforms.
- Interoperability and Standardization: Interoperability among different blockchain platforms and standardization of protocols and data formats are essential for seamless integration of bio-inspired algorithms (Narayanan, A., et al., 2018). Ensuring compatibility and ease of communication between different blockchain networks will foster collaboration and facilitate the sharing of resources and data.
- Real-World Applications: While there is potential for bio-inspired algorithms using blockchain technology across various domains, there is a need for

more practical and tangible applications (Rahaman, S. M. M., & Chang, V., 2019). Conducting real-world experiments and case studies to validate the effectiveness and efficiency of these algorithms in solving complex problems can further drive their adoption and implementation.

- Governance and Regulatory Considerations: As blockchain technology evolves, there is a need for appropriate governance frameworks and regulatory guidelines (He, D., et al., 2019). Establishing legal and regulatory frameworks that address issues such as data ownership, liability, and dispute resolution in blockchain-based bio-inspired algorithm applications is crucial for widespread adoption.

- Education and Collaboration: Further education and collaboration between researchers, practitioners, and industry stakeholders are needed to advance the field of bio-inspired algorithms using blockchain technology (Zhang, et al., 2019). Establishing multidisciplinary collaborations and fostering knowledge exchange can drive innovation, standardization, and the development of best practices.

Addressing these challenges and exploring the future directions mentioned above will contribute to unlocking the full potential of bio-inspired algorithms using blockchain technology (Shetty, S., et al., 2020). Overcoming these hurdles will enable the integration of bio-inspired algorithms into decentralized and secure blockchain networks, leading to enhanced problem-solving capabilities, increased efficiency, and broader applications in various domains.

Figure 5. Use cases of blockchain technology

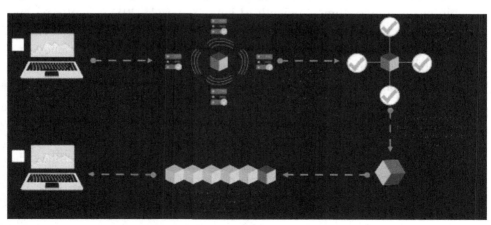

Algorithm Selection and Adaptation for Bio-Inspired Algorithms Using Blockchain Technology

Problem Definition: Clearly define the problem you want to address and understand its specific requirements. Identify the objective, constraints, and desired outcomes of the problem.

Literature Review: Conduct a thorough literature review to identify existing bio-inspired algorithms that are suitable for the problem domain. Understand the strengths, weaknesses, and applications of different algorithms in similar contexts.

Algorithm Evaluation: Evaluate the identified bio-inspired algorithms based on criteria such as performance, convergence speed, scalability, and adaptability to distributed environments. Consider factors like computational complexity, memory requirements, and algorithmic suitability for integration with blockchain technology.

Adaptation to Blockchain: Analyze the selected bio-inspired algorithm and identify necessary modifications or adaptations to integrate it with blockchain technology. Consider how the algorithm can utilize the decentralized computation, transparency, and consensus mechanisms provided by the blockchain.

Decentralized Computation: Assess how the algorithm can be distributed across the blockchain network to leverage the computational power of multiple nodes. Determine how the algorithm tasks can be partitioned and executed in a decentralized manner.

Consensus Mechanism: Design or select a consensus mechanism that aligns with the requirements of the bio-inspired algorithm. Consider the computational and energy efficiency, scalability, and security aspects of the consensus mechanism.

Data Management: Determine how data will be collected, stored, and shared within the blockchain network. Consider how the bio-inspired algorithm can access and utilize the data stored on the blockchain for optimization, decision-making, or learning processes.

Smart Contract Integration: Evaluate the potential integration of smart contracts to automate and execute specific parts of the bio-inspired algorithm. Determine if certain algorithmic functionalities can be encapsulated as self-executing contracts on the blockchain.

Performance Analysis: Assess the performance of the adapted bio-inspired algorithm within the blockchain context. Conduct experiments or simulations to measure key performance metrics such as convergence speed, scalability, resource utilization, and robustness.

Comparison and Evaluation: Compare the performance and effectiveness of the adapted algorithm with existing algorithms or approaches. Analyze the benefits and limitations of the adaptation in terms of efficiency, security, decentralization, and transparency.

Iterative Refinement: Based on the evaluation results, iterate and refine the adapted algorithm if necessary. Consider feedback and insights gained from the evaluation to enhance the algorithm's performance and address any identified limitations.

By following this process, researchers and practitioners can select and adapt suitable bio-inspired algorithms for integration with blockchain technology. The adaptation process should consider the specific requirements and constraints of the problem domain, as well as the unique features and challenges presented by blockchain technology.

Designing the Blockchain Network for Bio-Inspired Algorithms

Designing the blockchain network involves determining the architecture, consensus mechanism, smart contract functionality, and other parameters that align with the requirements of integrating bio-inspired algorithms. Here are the key steps to design the blockchain network:

Choose the Blockchain Platform: Select a blockchain platform that suits the requirements of the bio-inspired algorithm integration. Consider factors such as scalability, security, interoperability, programming language support, and community adoption. Examples of popular blockchain platforms include Ethereum, Hyperledger Fabric, and Corda.

Determine the Network Structure: Decide on the network structure based on the desired level of decentralization and trust assumptions (Akyildiz, I. F., et al., 2019). Choose between a public blockchain (open to all participants) or a permissioned/private blockchain (limited to specific participants). Determine the number of nodes in the network and their roles, such as miners/validators and users.

Consensus Mechanism Selection: Select a consensus mechanism that aligns with the needs of the bio-inspired algorithm and the desired network characteristics. Popular consensus mechanisms include Proof of Work (PoW), Proof of Stake (PoS), Practical Byzantine Fault Tolerance (PBFT), and Delegated Proof of Stake (DPoS). Consider factors such as security, energy efficiency, scalability, and consensus finality.

Smart Contract Design: Determine the smart contract functionality required to support the execution of the bio-inspired algorithm. Smart contracts can automate various aspects, such as data validation, algorithm execution logic, reward distribution, and consensus-related tasks. Design the smart contract(s) using a suitable programming language and consider the necessary data structures, functions, and event triggers.

Data Management and Integration: Decide how data will be collected, stored, and shared within the blockchain network (Wang, G., et al., 2020). Determine the data format, encryption, and privacy mechanisms to ensure data integrity and confidentiality. Explore the integration of off-chain data sources or oracles to provide external data inputs to the bio-inspired algorithm.

Governance and Access Control: Define the governance model and access control mechanisms for the blockchain network. Determine who can join the network as nodes, how consensus decisions will be made, and how upgrades or changes to the network will be managed. Consider the need for permissioned access, role-based permissions, or governance frameworks like DAOs (Decentralized Autonomous Organizations).

Performance Considerations: Evaluate the performance implications of the chosen blockchain platform and consensus mechanism on the execution of bio-inspired algorithms. Consider factors such as transaction throughput, latency, block size, gas/transaction costs, and network scalability (Shanmugavadivu, P., et al., 2022). Optimize the network parameters, such as block time, gas limits, and shard/partition configurations, to achieve the desired performance.

Security and Privacy Measures: Address security concerns by implementing robust cryptographic measures, such as digital signatures, hash functions, and encryption. Consider privacy-preserving techniques, such as zero-knowledge proofs or selective data disclosure, to protect sensitive data. Implement mechanisms to detect and prevent attacks, such as Sybil attacks or double-spending.

Network Deployment and Testing: Deploy the designed blockchain network and conduct thorough testing to validate its functionality, security, and performance. Test the integration of the bio-inspired algorithm with the blockchain network, ensuring proper execution, data storage, and consensus validation. Perform testing scenarios, including stress testing, to identify and address potential issues.

Iterative Improvement: Continuously monitor and improve the blockchain network based on feedback and performance evaluation. Incorporate user feedback, address identified limitations, and adapt the network design as required to optimize the integration of bio-inspired algorithms.

By following these steps, researchers and practitioners can design a blockchain network that effectively supports the integration of bio-inspired algorithms. The design should consider the specific requirements of the algorithm, the desired network characteristics, and the security and privacy considerations inherent to blockchain technology.

Data Management and Integration for Bio-Inspired Algorithms Using Blockchain Technology

Data management and integration play a crucial role in the successful integration of bio-inspired algorithms with blockchain technology. Here are key considerations for managing and integrating data:

Data Collection: Determine how data will be collected and sourced for the bio-inspired algorithm. Identify the data sources, whether they are internal or external to the blockchain network. Consider the quality, reliability, and authenticity of the data sources to ensure accurate and trustworthy inputs for the algorithm.

Data Preprocessing: Preprocess the data before integrating it into the blockchain network. This may involve tasks such as data cleaning, normalization, feature selection, and transformation. Ensure that the pre-processed data aligns with the requirements of the bio-inspired algorithm and is suitable for storage and analysis on the blockchain.

Data Storage on the Blockchain: Determine the appropriate data storage mechanism on the blockchain. Blockchain platforms typically offer different options, including on-chain storage and off-chain storage. On-chain storage involves storing data directly within the blockchain, while off-chain storage refers to storing data externally and referencing it on the blockchain using cryptographic hashes or smart contracts. Choose the storage method that suits the size, security, and privacy requirements of the data.

Data Encryption and Privacy: Consider the privacy and confidentiality of the data. Implement encryption techniques to protect sensitive data stored on the blockchain, ensuring that only authorized parties can access it. Additionally, explore privacy-preserving mechanisms such as zero-knowledge proofs or selective disclosure to protect sensitive information while still enabling data validation and analysis.

Interoperability and Data Integration: If data from multiple sources or blockchain networks is required for the bio-inspired algorithm, ensure interoperability and seamless integration. Explore data standardization, data exchange protocols, and interoperability frameworks to enable the smooth flow of data across different systems and networks. Consider the use of oracles or trusted data feeds to integrate external data sources with the blockchain network.

Data Access Control: Establish access control mechanisms to regulate who can access and modify the data on the blockchain. Determine the roles and permissions for different participants, ensuring that sensitive data is accessible only to authorized parties. Utilize smart contracts or access control frameworks to enforce data access rules and permissions.

Data Verification and Auditing: Leverage the transparency and immutability of the blockchain to verify the integrity and authenticity of the stored data. Implement mechanisms to ensure that the data has not been tampered with and remains consistent across the blockchain network. Conduct periodic audits to verify the accuracy and reliability of the data.

Data Analytics and Visualization: Explore analytics and visualization techniques to extract insights from the data stored on the blockchain. Utilize appropriate tools and algorithms to analyze and visualize the data, enabling meaningful interpretation and decision-making based on the outcomes of the bio-inspired algorithm.

Compliance and Regulatory Considerations: Ensure compliance with relevant data protection and privacy regulations. Consider legal requirements and ethical considerations when managing and integrating data on the blockchain. Implement mechanisms to handle data subject rights, consent management, and data retention policies in accordance with applicable laws.

Continuous Monitoring and Improvement: Continuously monitor the data management processes on the blockchain network. Regularly assess data quality, integrity, and security. Address any identified issues promptly and iteratively refine the data management and integration practices to improve efficiency, accuracy, and compliance.

By carefully managing and integrating data on the blockchain network, researchers and practitioners can ensure the availability, integrity, and privacy of data required for the bio-inspired algorithms (Salim, F. D., et al., 2018). The process involves addressing data collection, preprocessing, storage, encryption, privacy, interoperability, access control, verification, analytics, and compliance considerations to create a robust and reliable data management framework.

Implementation and Prototyping

Implementation and prototyping play a crucial role in the integration of bio-inspired algorithms with blockchain technology. Here are the key steps to consider during the implementation and prototyping phase:

1. Set up Development Environment: Configure the necessary development environment for implementing the integration. Install the required software

development kits (SDKs), libraries, and tools specific to the chosen blockchain platform and programming language.

2. Define System Architecture: Design the overall system architecture that encompasses the bio-inspired algorithm and the blockchain integration. Identify the components, modules, and interactions between the algorithm, smart contracts, and blockchain network.

3. Develop Smart Contracts: Implement the smart contracts that will support the execution of the bio-inspired algorithm on the blockchain. Define the functions, events, and data structures required to handle the algorithmic logic, data storage, and interaction with the blockchain network. Write the smart contracts using the programming language supported by the blockchain platform.

4. Implement Algorithm Execution Logic: Develop the necessary code to execute the bio-inspired algorithm within the smart contracts. This includes translating the algorithm's steps and rules into executable code that can run on the blockchain. Implement the data processing, optimization, or decision-making logic of the bio-inspired algorithm using the programming language compatible with the blockchain platform.

5. Integrate Data Management: Integrate the data management aspects into the implementation. This involves handling data collection, preprocessing, storage, and integration with the bio-inspired algorithm and the blockchain network. Implement the necessary data structures and functions to manage and manipulate data within the smart contracts.

6. Test and Debug: Conduct comprehensive testing and debugging of the implementation. Verify that the bio-inspired algorithm functions correctly within the blockchain environment, and validate the data management and integration processes. Use test cases, simulations, or real-world scenarios to evaluate the performance, accuracy, and efficiency of the integrated system.

7. Performance Optimization: Optimize the implementation for performance, scalability, and resource utilization. Identify potential bottlenecks and inefficiencies and refine the code and data management processes accordingly. Consider strategies to optimize gas consumption, transaction throughput, and overall system efficiency.

8. Conduct Security Audits: Perform security audits and vulnerability assessments to identify and address any potential security risks or vulnerabilities in the implementation. Ensure that the integration of the bio-inspired algorithm with the blockchain platform does not introduce security loopholes or compromise the integrity of the system.

9. Document and Validate Results: Document the implementation details, including the algorithm execution logic, data management processes, and integration with the blockchain. Validate the results by comparing them against expected

outcomes, evaluating the performance metrics, and assessing the effectiveness of the bio-inspired algorithm within the blockchain context.

10. Iterate and Refine: Based on the testing, validation, and feedback received, iterate and refine the implementation as necessary. Incorporate improvements, address identified issues, and optimize the system based on the insights gained during the prototyping phase.

Through effective implementation and prototyping, researchers and practitioners can validate the feasibility and functionality of integrating bio-inspired algorithms with blockchain technology (Seyedhosseini, M., et al., 2019). The process involves developing smart contracts, implementing the algorithm execution logic, integrating data management processes, conducting thorough testing, optimizing performance, and refining the implementation based on the results.

Performance evaluation is a critical step in assessing the effectiveness and efficiency of the integration of bio-inspired algorithms with blockchain technology. Here are the key considerations for conducting performance evaluation:

Define Performance Metrics: Determine the performance metrics that align with the goals and objectives of the integration. Common performance metrics include execution time, resource utilization (CPU, memory, storage), transaction throughput, scalability, convergence speed, energy efficiency, and algorithmic effectiveness (e.g., solution quality, accuracy).

Test Environment Setup: Set up a suitable test environment to conduct performance evaluations. Ensure that the environment closely resembles the real-world deployment scenario, including the network architecture, node configurations, and data characteristics. Consider factors such as network latency, node distribution, and computational resources.

Test Data Selection: Choose representative datasets that reflect the characteristics and complexity of the problem domain. Consider both synthetic and real-world datasets, ensuring they cover a range of input sizes and variations. The datasets should be relevant to the bio-inspired algorithm and its specific requirements.

Experiment Design: Design the experiments to evaluate the performance of the integrated system. Define the experimental conditions, including the input data, system configurations, algorithm parameters, and workload distribution. Consider factors such as the number of nodes, transaction rates, and network conditions.

Data Collection: Collect the necessary data during the experiments. Measure and record the performance metrics of interest at regular intervals or specific events. Gather data on execution time, resource usage, transaction success rates, and algorithmic outputs. Ensure accurate and consistent data collection across multiple experimental runs.

Performance Analysis: Analyze the collected data to evaluate the performance of the integrated system. Calculate the performance metrics based on the recorded measurements. Compare the results against predefined benchmarks, baseline algorithms, or previous studies to assess the performance improvements achieved through the integration.

Scalability Analysis: Evaluate the scalability of the integrated system by increasing the system size, such as the number of nodes or the input data size. Measure how the performance metrics change as the system scales and identify any limitations or bottlenecks in scalability.

Comparative Analysis: Conduct comparative analysis to compare the performance of the integrated system against other relevant approaches or algorithms. Compare the execution time, resource utilization, or other metrics to assess the superiority of the integrated system in terms of efficiency and effectiveness.

Sensitivity Analysis: Perform sensitivity analysis to evaluate the impact of varying parameters or conditions on the performance. Assess how changes in algorithm parameters, network conditions, or data characteristics affect the performance metrics. Identify any sensitivities or trade-offs that need to be considered.

Discussion and Conclusion: Interpret the performance evaluation results and discuss their implications. Highlight the strengths, limitations, and insights gained from the evaluation. Draw conclusions about the effectiveness and efficiency of the integration of bio-inspired algorithms with blockchain technology and provide recommendations for future improvements.

By conducting thorough performance evaluation, researchers and practitioners can gain insights into the strengths, limitations, and optimizations of the integrated system (Singh, G., et al., 2020). It enables the assessment of the efficiency, scalability, and effectiveness of the bio-inspired algorithms within the blockchain context, facilitating evidence-based decision-making and further advancements in the field.

Future Directions and Recommendations for Bio-Inspired Algorithms Using Blockchain Technology

Scalability Solutions: Address the scalability challenges associated with integrating bio-inspired algorithms with blockchain technology. Explore novel approaches, such as sharding, sidechains, or layer-two solutions, to improve scalability and accommodate larger computational workloads. Investigate how these solutions can be integrated with bio-inspired algorithms while maintaining the decentralization and security aspects of the blockchain.

Privacy-Preserving Mechanisms: Develop enhanced privacy-preserving mechanisms for bio-inspired algorithms on the blockchain. Investigate techniques such as secure multiparty computation (MPC), homomorphic encryption, or zero-knowledge proofs to protect sensitive data while enabling secure computation and verification. Focus on achieving a balance between privacy and transparency in the context of bio-inspired algorithms.

Hybrid Approaches: Explore hybrid approaches that combine the strengths of bio-inspired algorithms and traditional optimization or machine learning techniques. Investigate how blockchain technology can facilitate the integration of these approaches to enhance problem-solving capabilities and achieve improved performance and accuracy.

Energy Efficiency: Address the energy consumption concerns associated with blockchain-based bio-inspired algorithms. Investigate energy-efficient consensus mechanisms or develop algorithms that require fewer computational resources while still benefiting from the decentralized nature of the blockchain (Chaouchi, H., et al., 2020). Explore the potential for integrating renewable energy sources or energy-efficient consensus algorithms to minimize the environmental impact.

Interoperability and Standards: Work towards establishing interoperability standards and protocols for integrating bio-inspired algorithms across different blockchain platforms. Promote collaboration and knowledge sharing among researchers, practitioners, and developers to create a unified ecosystem that enables seamless integration and collaboration between different blockchain networks.

Real-World Applications and Case Studies: Conduct more extensive real-world applications and case studies to validate the effectiveness and practicality of integrating bio-inspired algorithms with blockchain technology. Apply the integrated system to diverse domains such as finance, healthcare, supply chain, or energy to demonstrate its value, identify challenges, and showcase the potential benefits in specific use cases.

Governance and Regulatory Frameworks: Develop governance models and regulatory frameworks specifically tailored to blockchain-based bio-inspired algorithm applications. Address issues related to data ownership, privacy, liability, and compliance within the context of these integrated systems. Collaborate with policymakers, industry stakeholders, and legal experts to establish robust frameworks that ensure the ethical and responsible use of blockchain technology.

Education and Awareness: Foster education and awareness initiatives to promote the understanding and adoption of bio-inspired algorithms using blockchain technology. Organize workshops, training programs, or conferences to facilitate knowledge exchange, collaboration, and interdisciplinary research in this emerging field. (Akhavan, P., et al., 2020)Encourage academic institutions and industry partners to incorporate blockchain and bio-inspired algorithms into their curricula and research initiatives.

By focusing on these future directions, researchers and practitioners can further advance the integration of bio-inspired algorithms with blockchain technology (Biswas, K., & Misra, S., 2021). These efforts can lead to innovative solutions, improved scalability and efficiency, enhanced privacy and security, and the identification of new application areas for bio-inspired algorithms in the blockchain ecosystem.

CONCLUSION

In conclusion, the integration of bio-inspired algorithms with blockchain technology holds significant promise for solving complex problems in a decentralized and secure manner. The combination of these two fields opens up new opportunities for innovation, efficiency, transparency, and trust in various domains. Through this integration, bio-inspired algorithms can leverage the decentralized and transparent nature of blockchain technology, enhancing their problem-solving capabilities and enabling new applications. The advantages and opportunities offered by blockchain, such as decentralization, enhanced security, transparency, and efficiency, provide a solid foundation for the execution of bio-inspired algorithms. However, several challenges need to be addressed to fully realize the potential of this integration.

Figure 6. Future scope of blockchain technology

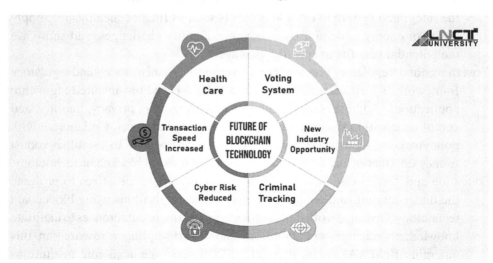

Scalability concerns, privacy and confidentiality issues, algorithm design and adaptation, and the selection of appropriate consensus mechanisms are among the key challenges that require further research and development. By addressing these challenges, future research can explore the diverse applications of bio-inspired algorithms using blockchain technology. Real-world applications and case studies can validate the effectiveness and practicality of the integrated systems, showcasing their benefits across domains such as finance, healthcare, supply chain, and energy. The establishment of interoperability standards, governance frameworks, and regulatory guidelines specific to blockchain-based bio-inspired algorithms is crucial for responsible and ethical deployment. Collaboration between academia, industry, policymakers, and legal experts is essential to shape the development and adoption of these integrated systems. Education and awareness initiatives should be promoted to foster knowledge exchange, interdisciplinary research, and skill development in the field of bio-inspired algorithms using blockchain technology. By equipping researchers, practitioners, and students with the necessary tools and understanding, we can further accelerate innovation and advancements in this emerging field. In conclusion, the integration of bio-inspired algorithms with blockchain technology presents exciting possibilities for solving complex problems, enhancing efficiency, and fostering trust in decentralized systems. With continued research, development, and collaboration, this integration has the potential to revolutionize various industries and pave the way for a more decentralized and secure future.

REFERENCES

Akhavan, P., & Attaran, M. (2020). Blockchain technology for secure and privacy-preserving applications in healthcare: A comprehensive survey. *Journal of Medical Systems, 44*(8), 142.

Akyildiz, I. F., Lee, A., Vuran, M. C., & Mohanty, S. (2019). A survey on blockchain technology for securing IoT networks. *IEEE Communications Surveys and Tutorials, 20*(4), 3684–3711.

Bhattacharya, S., Sarker, R., Khan, M. M., & Abbass, H. A. (2019). Blockchain-inspired optimization algorithms: A systematic review. *IEEE Access : Practical Innovations, Open Solutions, 7*, 123033–123051.

Biswas, K., & Misra, S. (2021). Blockchain-based applications in smart grids: A review. *IEEE Transactions on Industrial Informatics, 17*(2), 1332–1341.

Chaouchi, H., & Qadir, J. (2020). Blockchain technology and internet of things: A systematic review. *Journal of Network and Computer Applications, 168*, 102715.

Chen, J., Wang, H., Xiong, L., Zeng, Z., & Wang, X. (2019). Blockchain-based secure and efficient algorithm for demand response management in smart grid. *IEEE Transactions on Industrial Informatics*, *15*(6), 3700–3709.

Fernández-Caramés, T. M., & Fraga-Lamas, P. (2019). A Review on the Use of Blockchain for the Internet of Things. *IEEE Access : Practical Innovations, Open Solutions*, *7*, 39409–39431.

Han, L., Wang, Y., & Yan, W. (2019). A Blockchain-Based Framework for Transparent Control and Traceability of Bioinspired Algorithms in Edge Computing. *IEEE Internet of Things Journal*, *6*(4), 7121–7133.

He, D., & Xu, X. (2019). Blockchain and swarm intelligence-inspired optimization algorithms. In *Swarm Intelligence Based Optimization* (pp. 425–435). Springer.

Khan, M. A., AlZubi, A. F. S., & Zomaya, A. Y. (2021). Blockchain-Driven Bio-Inspired Resource Management in Internet of Things. *IEEE Transactions on Services Computing*, *14*(2), 429–442.

Lai, C., Yan, Y., & Sui, Y. (2020). Research on application of blockchain technology in energy Internet. *Energy Procedia*, *165*, 20–27.

Li, X., Jiang, P., Chen, T., Luo, X., & Wen, Q. (2017). A Survey on the Security of Blockchain Systems. *Future Generation Computer Systems*, *82*, 395–411.

Liang, X., Shetty, S., Tosh, D., Kamhoua, C., Kwiat, K., & Njilla, L. (2018). Integrating Blockchain for Data Sharing and Collaboration in Mobile Healthcare Applications. *IEEE Access : Practical Innovations, Open Solutions*, *6*, 14707–14718.

Liao, X., Xiong, N., Zhang, X., & Zhang, W. (2018). A blockchain-based algorithm for secure and efficient task scheduling in crowdsensing. *IEEE Transactions on Computational Social Systems*, *5*(3), 759–769.

Lv, Q., Li, C., Zhu, Y., & Cao, G. (2020). A blockchain-based algorithm for vehicle assignment in intelligent transportation systems. *IEEE Transactions on Intelligent Transportation Systems*, *21*(9), 3836–3845.

Mary Shanthi Rani, M., Chitra, P., Lakshmanan, S., Kalpana Devi, M., Sangeetha, R., & Nithya, S. (2022). DeepCompNet: A novel neural net model compression architecture. *Computational Intelligence and Neuroscience*, *2022*, 2022. doi:10.1155/2022/2213273 PMID:35242176

Narayanan, A., Chandrasekaran, K., & Palanisamy, V. (2018). Blockchain-based bio-inspired computing: A survey. *IEEE Access : Practical Innovations, Open Solutions*, *6*, 42405–42418.

Rahaman, S. M. M., & Chang, V. (2019). Biometric data management on blockchain: An integrated model and research directions. *Journal of Information Security and Applications*, *49*, 102406.

Rani, M. M. S., & Chitra, P. (2016, October). A novel hybrid method of haar-wavelet and residual vector quantization for compressing medical images. In *2016 IEEE International Conference on Advances in Computer Applications (ICACA)* (pp. 321-326). IEEE. 10.1109/ICACA.2016.7887974

Salim, F. D., Huang, X., & An, S. (2018). Blockchain technology in healthcare: A systematic review. *Healthcare Informatics Research*, *24*(4), 277–286.

Seyedhosseini, M., Meddeb, A., & Ghannay, S. (2019). Blockchain-based optimization for the Internet of Things: A systematic literature review. *IEEE Access : Practical Innovations, Open Solutions*, *7*, 97172–97185.

Shah, Z., Shah, G. A., Shah, M. A., & Badshah, M. (2019). A blockchain-based adaptive particle swarm optimization algorithm for secure IoT environments. *Sensors (Basel)*, *19*(10), 2283. PMID:31108929

Shanmugavadivu, P., Chitra, P., Lakshmanan, S., Nagaraja, P., & Vignesh, U. (2022). Bio-Optimization of Deep Learning Network Architectures. *Security and Communication Networks*, ●●●, 2022.

Shetty, S., Rane, S., Jain, S., & Mukherjee, S. (2020). Blockchain-enabled swarm intelligence: A review. *Swarm and Evolutionary Computation*, *57*, 100690.

Singh, G., Tripathi, A., & Raw, R. S. (2020). Blockchain technology: A survey on its security challenges and privacy issues in the healthcare sector. *Journal of Information Security and Applications*, *53*, 102566.

Sun, Y., Wen, Y., & Wen, X. (2020). Towards a Blockchain-Based Bioinspired Artificial Intelligence Framework for Large-Scale Medical Data Sharing. *Journal of Healthcare Engineering*, *2020*, 1–10. doi:10.1155/2020/7289648

Tavares, R. P., & Guerreiro, S. I. (2019). A blockchain-based architecture for collaborative machine learning with bio-inspired optimization. In *International Conference on Bio-Inspired Systems and Signal Processing* (pp. 457-464). Springer.

Wang, G., & Cao, J. (2020). Blockchain and evolutionary computation: A comprehensive review. *IEEE Transactions on Evolutionary Computation*, *24*(2), 293–308.

Wang, H., Tang, Y., Hu, J., Li, X., & Li, Z. (2020). Blockchain and bio-inspired algorithms for secure and efficient data sharing in mobile healthcare social networks. *IEEE Access : Practical Innovations, Open Solutions*, *8*, 156130–156141.

Wang, X., Luo, K., & Xu, H. (2019). Blockchain Meets Artificial Intelligence: Challenges and Opportunities. *ACM Transactions on Internet Technology*, *19*(3), 23.

Wang, Z., Li, Y., & Zhang, Y. (2020). A blockchain-based bio-inspired optimization algorithm for secure and efficient data fusion in edge computing. *IEEE Transactions on Computational Social Systems*, *7*(3), 732–742.

Xiong, J., Chen, S., Chen, X., Wu, F., Liang, W., & He, J. (2019). Blockchain-based bio-inspired optimization for Internet of Things. *IEEE Internet of Things Journal*, *7*(11), 11224–11235.

Xu, X., Wang, Y., Wang, Q., & Zhang, W. (2020). Blockchain and swarm intelligence-based particle filter algorithm for energy management in smart grid. *Energies*, *13*(9), 2417.

Yan, J., Zhang, C., Li, J., & Li, W. (2020). Blockchain-inspired bio-inspired optimization algorithm for service composition in edge computing. *IEEE Transactions on Network Science and Engineering*, *7*(1), 480–492.

Zhang, G., Yu, H., Ma, C., & Guan, Y. (2019). Blockchain-based optimization: Opportunities, challenges, and solutions. *IEEE Transactions on Industrial Informatics*, *15*(6), 3690–3700.

Zhang, J., Zhang, H., Yan, L., & Cao, J. (2019). Blockchain-Based Privacy-Preserving Method for ECG Data in Mobile Healthcare Applications. *Sensors (Basel)*, *19*(19), 4253. PMID:31575009

Zhou, H., Li, H., & Zhou, W. (2020). Bioinspired Computing Meets Blockchain: A Comprehensive Survey. *IEEE Access : Practical Innovations, Open Solutions*, *8*, 70750–70770.

Chapter 2
Bio–Inspired Algorithms Used in Medical Image Processing

K. Ezhilarasan
Gandhigram Rural Institute, India

K. Somasundaram
iD https://orcid.org/0000-0003-0932-3538
Gandhigram Rural Institute, India

T. Kalaiselvi
Gandhigram Rural Institute, India

Praveenkumar Somasundaram
iD https://orcid.org/0000-0001-7981-504X
Qualcomm Technologies Inc., USA

S. Karthigai Selvi
iD https://orcid.org/0000-0001-6249-2037
Galgotias University, India

A. Jeevarekha
M.V. Muthiah Government Arts College for Women, India

ABSTRACT

Medical image processing plays a crucial role in diagnosing diseases, guiding treatment plans, and monitoring patient progress. With the increasing complexity and volume of medical imaging data, there is a growing need for advanced techniques to extract meaningful information from these images. Traditional methods in medical image processing often face challenges related to image enhancement, segmentation, and feature extraction. These challenges stem from the inherent variability, noise, and complexity of medical images, making it difficult to obtain accurate and reliable results. In this chapter, the focus is on leveraging bio-inspired algorithms to address these challenges and improve the analysis and interpretation of medical images. Bio-inspired algorithms draw inspiration from natural processes, such as evolution, swarm behavior, neural networks, and genetic programming. It addresses the challenges and requirements specific to each modality and how bio-inspired algorithms can be adapted and tailored to meet those needs.

DOI: 10.4018/979-8-3693-1131-8.ch002

INTRODUCTION

Medical Image Processing is a dynamic and multidisciplinary field that lies at the crossroads of medicine, computer science, and image analysis. Its primary goal is to harness computational techniques to acquire, enhance, analyse, and interpret medical images, thus supporting medical practitioners in making precise diagnoses and formulating effective treatment plans. In the contemporary digital era, medical images have become indispensable tools for gaining insights into the inner workings and structures of the human body.

This section offers a comprehensive overview of the fundamental principles and significance of Medical Image Processing. To begin, we delve into the diverse imaging modalities widely used in medical practice, including X-ray, computed tomography (CT), magnetic resonance imaging (MRI), ultrasound, positron emission tomography (PET), and single-photon emission computed tomography (SPECT). Each modality boasts unique strengths and finds relevance in specific clinical contexts.

However, medical image analysis poses inherent challenges and complexities. Oftentimes, medical images exhibit noise, artifacts, and variations arising from patient anatomy and imaging protocols. The interpretation of these images necessitates expert knowledge and can be time-consuming for healthcare professionals. Consequently, there is a pressing need for the development of efficient and reliable automated image analysis techniques.

In recent years, Bio-Inspired Algorithms have emerged as promising computational tools to address the challenges of medical image processing. Inspired by natural phenomena like evolution, swarm behavior, and neural networks, these algorithms offer innovative approaches to optimize image segmentation, registration, feature extraction, and classification tasks.

Emphasis is placed on the pivotal role algorithms play in medical image processing. Bio-Inspired Algorithms, including Genetic Algorithms, Particle Swarm Optimization, Ant Colony Optimization, and Artificial Neural Networks, have demonstrated remarkable potential in enhancing the accuracy and efficiency of medical image analysis. They possess the ability to adapt and evolve, mimicking the adaptive processes observed in biological systems, thus enabling them to discern optimal solutions even in complex medical image datasets.

Throughout this chapter, we explore the applications of various Bio-Inspired Algorithms in medical image processing and their relevance in diverse medical specialties. Our objective is to provide readers with a solid understanding of the foundational concepts of medical image processing, paving the way for comprehending how bio-inspired approaches can revolutionize medical image analysis and positively impact patient care. By combining the power of computational methods and medical expertise, Medical Image Processing opens new frontiers in healthcare, promising enhanced diagnostics and improved outcomes for patients.

OVERVIEW OF MEDICAL IMAGES

Medical images are visual representations of the internal structures and processes within the human body or other living organisms. These images are acquired through various medical imaging techniques and are used by healthcare professionals to diagnose, monitor, and treat medical conditions. Medical imaging plays a crucial role in modern medicine, allowing healthcare providers to visualize and analyze anatomical structures, physiological functions, and abnormalities. Some common types of medical images and the imaging techniques used to create them include:

1. *X-ray Images:* X-rays are a form of electromagnetic radiation that can pass through soft tissues but are absorbed by denser materials like bones. X-ray images are commonly used to visualize bone fractures, dental issues, and detect conditions like pneumonia.
2. *Computed Tomography (CT) Images:* CT scans use a combination of X-rays and computer processing to create detailed cross-sectional images of the body. They are valuable for diagnosing conditions like tumors, vascular diseases, and injuries.
3. *Magnetic Resonance Imaging (MRI) Images:* MRI uses strong magnetic fields and radio waves to generate detailed images of soft tissues, organs, and the brain. It is used for a wide range of diagnoses, including neurological disorders, joint injuries, and cancer.
4. *Ultrasound Images:* Ultrasound uses high-frequency sound waves to produce real-time images of internal structures. It is commonly used during pregnancy for fetal imaging, as well as for imaging the heart, abdomen, and vascular system.
5. *Nuclear Medicine Images:* Nuclear medicine involves the use of radiopharmaceuticals, which emit gamma radiation, to create images of organ function. Techniques like positron emission tomography (PET) and single-photon emission computed tomography (SPECT) are used for various diagnostic and research purposes.
6. *Mammography Images:* Mammography is a specialized X-ray technique used for breast imaging, primarily for breast cancer screening and diagnosis.
7. *Endoscopy Images:* Endoscopic images are captured using specialized cameras and instruments to visualize the interior of body cavities, such as the gastrointestinal tract and respiratory system.

8. ***Dental Images:*** Dental imaging includes X-rays and intraoral and extraoral images used to diagnose dental conditions, oral diseases, and orthodontic issues.

9. ***Histopathology Images:*** These images are obtained by examining thin tissue sections under a microscope. Pathologists use histopathology to study tissue samples for diagnosing diseases and conditions like cancer.

10. ***Dermatological Images:*** Dermatologists use imaging techniques to capture images of skin conditions, such as moles, rashes, and skin cancers.

Medical images are essential tools for medical professionals, aiding in diagnosis, treatment planning, and ongoing patient care. They provide valuable insights into the human body and its functions, enabling healthcare providers to make informed decisions regarding patient health. The interpretation and analysis of these images are performed by specialized medical professionals, such as radiologists, pathologists, and clinicians.

OVERVIEW OF MEDICAL IMAGE PROCESSING

Medical Image Processing is a specialized field within the broader domain of image processing that focuses on the acquisition, enhancement, analysis, and interpretation of medical images. It involves the application of various techniques and algorithms to digital or analog images obtained through medical imaging modalities, such as X-rays, computed tomography (CT), magnetic resonance imaging (MRI), ultrasound, nuclear medicine, and more. The primary objectives of medical image processing are:

Image Enhancement: Improving the quality of medical images to enhance their diagnostic value. This can involve reducing noise, adjusting contrast, and improving overall image clarity.

Image Restoration: Correcting imperfections in images caused by factors like motion artifacts, distortions, or degradation during image acquisition.

Image Segmentation: Identifying and delineating specific regions or structures within an image. Segmentation is often used to separate organs or lesions from surrounding tissues.

Feature Extraction: Extracting relevant quantitative information from medical images, such as size, shape, texture, and intensity values. These features can aid in diagnosis and analysis.

Image Registration: Aligning and overlaying multiple medical images of the same or different modalities to facilitate comparison and integration of information.

Image Fusion: Combining information from multiple images to create a single, more informative image, particularly in multimodal imaging.

Pattern Recognition: Applying machine learning and artificial intelligence techniques to recognize patterns in medical images, such as identifying tumors or anomalies.

Visualization: Developing 2D or 3D visualizations of medical data to improve understanding and decision-making, especially in complex cases or surgical planning.

Quantitative Analysis: Measuring parameters in medical images, such as tumor volume, blood flow, or tissue density, for precise diagnosis and treatment planning.

Computer-Aided Diagnosis (CAD): Developing computer algorithms that assist healthcare professionals in diagnosing medical conditions by providing automated or augmented analyses of medical images.

Medical image processing has a wide range of applications in healthcare and medical research:

- *Disease Diagnosis:* It aids in the early detection and diagnosis of diseases such as cancer, cardiovascular conditions, neurological disorders, and musculoskeletal issues.
- *Treatment Planning:* Medical image processing supports the planning of surgical procedures, radiation therapy, and other medical interventions by providing accurate anatomical and pathological information.
- *Image-Guided Interventions*: Real-time processing and visualization of medical images are used during surgical and interventional procedures for guidance and precision.
- *Drug Development and Research*: Medical image analysis plays a role in preclinical research, such as drug testing and understanding disease mechanisms.
- *Patient Monitoring*: Continuous or periodic analysis of medical images helps monitor disease progression and treatment effectiveness.
- *Medical Teaching and Training*: Medical images are used in education to illustrate anatomy and pathology to medical students and professionals.

Medical image processing is a critical component of modern healthcare, enabling healthcare providers to improve diagnostic accuracy, treatment outcomes, and patient care. It continues to evolve with advances in technology, including artificial intelligence and machine learning, which enhance the capabilities and automation of medical image analysis.

OVERVIEW OF BIO-INSPIRED ALGORITHMS

Bio-Inspired Algorithms, also known as nature-inspired algorithms, are computational techniques that draw inspiration from the principles and behaviors observed in natural systems. These algorithms mimic the adaptive, cooperative, and self-organizing capabilities found in biological organisms, allowing them to efficiently solve complex optimization problems.

In this section, we delve into the foundational concepts of Bio-Inspired Algorithms and their significance in medical image processing. We begin by discussing the main characteristics that define these algorithms and set them apart from traditional optimization methods:

Nature-Inspired Concepts

Bio-Inspired Algorithms take inspiration from various natural processes and phenomena. For example, Genetic Algorithms emulate the process of natural selection and evolution, while Particle Swarm Optimization is inspired by the flocking and swarming behavior of birds and insects. Ant Colony Optimization models the foraging behavior of ants, and Artificial Neural Networks draw inspiration from the human brain's interconnected neurons.

Adaptability and Robustness

One of the key advantages of Bio-Inspired Algorithms is their ability to adapt to changing environments and problem landscapes. These algorithms can adjust their search strategies dynamically, making them suitable for handling noisy, complex, and high-dimensional data encountered in medical image processing.

Population-Based Optimization

Unlike traditional optimization methods that operate on a single solution, Bio-Inspired Algorithms often work with a population of potential solutions. This population-based approach enables better exploration of the solution space and increases the likelihood of finding optimal or near-optimal solutions.

Parallelism and Distributed Computing

Many Bio-Inspired Algorithms are inherently parallelizable, allowing them to take advantage of modern computing architectures, such as multi-core processors and distributed computing clusters. This feature enhances their scalability and efficiency, making them well-suited for handling large-scale medical image datasets.

Next, we present an overview of some commonly used Bio-Inspired Algorithms in medical image processing:

Genetic Algorithms (GA)

Genetic Algorithms (GAs) are a class of optimization and search algorithms inspired by the principles of natural selection and genetics. They are widely used to find solutions or optimize parameters for complex problems. Here are the basics to know about Genetic Algorithms:

Population-Based Approach: GAs maintain a population of candidate solutions (or individuals) to a problem. Each individual represents a potential solution, often encoded as a chromosome or a set of genes.

Fitness Function: A fitness function evaluates how well each individual performs with respect to the problem at hand. It quantifies the quality of solutions and guides the evolutionary process.

Selection: Individuals are selected from the current population to serve as parents for the next generation. Selection is typically based on the fitness of individuals, with better-performing individuals having a higher chance of being chosen.

Crossover (Recombination): Crossover is the process of combining genetic material from two parents to create one or more offspring. This mimics genetic recombination in nature.

Mutation: Mutation involves making small, random changes to an individual's genes. It introduces genetic diversity into the population and prevents premature convergence to suboptimal solutions.

Generation Update: The new generation of individuals is created through selection, crossover, and mutation. This process continues for a set number of generations or until a stopping criterion is met.

Convergence and Termination: GAs aim to improve the quality of solutions over generations. The algorithm typically terminates when a satisfactory solution is found, or after a predefined number of generations.

Encoding and Decoding: Problem-specific encoding and decoding methods are used to represent solutions as genes and translate them back into problem space.

Parameter Tuning: The success of a GA often depends on setting parameters such as population size, mutation rate, and crossover method appropriately for the specific problem.

Applications: GAs are versatile and are used in various fields, including optimization, machine learning, engineering design, and scheduling.

Parallelism: Parallel GAs can run multiple populations concurrently, which can improve efficiency and the chances of finding high-quality solutions.

Hybridization: GAs can be combined with other optimization techniques or machine learning algorithms to create hybrid approaches tailored to specific problems.

Diversity and Exploration: Maintaining genetic diversity in the population is essential for exploring a wide solution space and avoiding premature convergence.

The typical Genetic Algorithms process is illustrated in Figure 1.

Genetic Algorithms (GAs) have emerged as a valuable tool in the realm of medical image processing, offering a unique and effective approach to solving

Figure 1. General steps of genetic algorithm

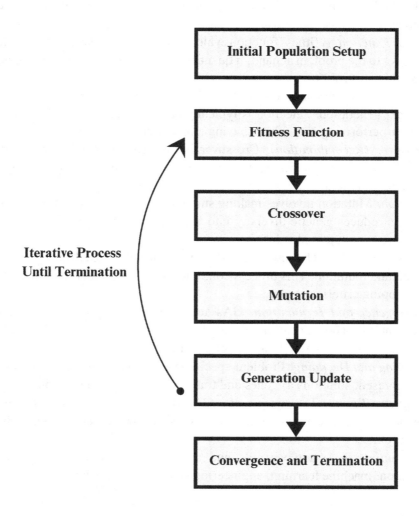

complex optimization and image analysis challenges. GAs are particularly adept at addressing tasks such as image registration, feature selection, segmentation, and the enhancement of medical images. By mimicking the principles of natural selection and genetic recombination, GAs optimize problem-specific parameters and evolve optimal solutions. In medical image analysis, this translates to the precise alignment of images for disease diagnosis, the selection of relevant features to aid in classification, and the enhancement of image quality to reveal subtle details that are crucial for accurate diagnoses. GAs, with their ability to explore vast solution spaces and escape local optima, hold great promise for advancing the field of medical image processing, ultimately leading to improved diagnostic accuracy and patient care. Understanding the principles of selection, crossover, mutation, and population dynamics is crucial for effectively applying GAs to various real-world problems.

Particle Swarm Optimization (PSO)

Particle Swarm Optimization (PSO) is a nature-inspired optimization algorithm that is commonly used to find approximate solutions to complex optimization problems. It's based on the social behavior of birds and fish, specifically the flocking and swarming behavior, where individuals within a group coordinate their movements to achieve a common goal. In PSO, these individuals are represented as particles, and the algorithm aims to find the best solution to an optimization problem by adjusting the particles' positions in a search space. Here are the basic principles of PSO:

Particle Representation: In PSO, a solution to the optimization problem is represented by a particle. Each particle has a position and a velocity in a multi-dimensional search space. The position represents a potential solution, and the velocity represents how the particle is moving within the space.

Initialization: PSO begins with the initialization of a population of particles. Each particle is assigned a random position and velocity within the search space.

Objective Function: The optimization problem at hand is defined by an objective function. The goal is to find the minimum or maximum value of this function by adjusting the particle positions.

Fitness Evaluation: Each particle's fitness is evaluated by applying the objective function to its current position. The fitness value quantifies how well the particle's position performs in solving the problem.

Best Position Memory: Each particle remembers its best position (i.e., the position where it achieved the best fitness) throughout its search history. This information is crucial for both the individual and collective optimization process.

Global Best Position: In addition to remembering their individual best positions, particles are aware of the global best position achieved by any particle in the swarm.

The global best position is the one with the best fitness value across the entire population.

Updating Velocity and Position: Particles update their velocities based on their previous velocities, their own best positions, and the global best position. The update formula typically includes terms that guide particles towards their own best position and the global best position. This process helps particles explore the search space efficiently.

Iterative Optimization: PSO iteratively updates the particles' positions and velocities based on the fitness of their current and previous positions. The algorithm continues for a predefined number of iterations or until a termination criterion is met.

Termination Criterion: PSO runs until a specified number of iterations are completed, or it can terminate based on specific conditions, such as reaching a satisfactory solution or converging to a stable state.

Solution Extraction: The best solution found by the PSO algorithm is usually represented by the global best position at the end of the optimization process.

The overall steps of the PSO are depicted in Figure 2. PSO is a population-based optimization algorithm, and its key feature is the social interaction among particles, which encourages exploration of the search space and exploitation of promising regions. The algorithm is commonly used in various optimization tasks, including parameter tuning, function optimization, and feature selection. It has gained popularity for its simplicity and effectiveness in solving a wide range of optimization problems. PSO has found valuable applications in the field of Medical Image Processing, where precise and efficient analysis of medical images is crucial for diagnosis and treatment planning. PSO can be employed to optimize various aspects of image analysis, such as feature selection, image registration, and segmentation. For instance, in medical image segmentation, PSO can assist in defining the optimal set of features or parameters that improve the accuracy of identifying anatomical structures or pathological regions within the images. By effectively exploring the parameter space and adapting to the intricacies of the image data, PSO aids in achieving more accurate and robust results, which is vital for tasks like tumor localization, organ segmentation, and disease classification. Its ability to fine-tune complex algorithms and its capacity to adapt to diverse data modalities make PSO a valuable tool in enhancing the accuracy and reliability of medical image analysis, ultimately benefiting healthcare professionals and patients alike.

Ant Colony Optimization (ACO)

Ant Colony Optimization (ACO) is a nature-inspired metaheuristic optimization algorithm used to find approximate solutions to complex optimization and

Figure 2. Steps of PSO

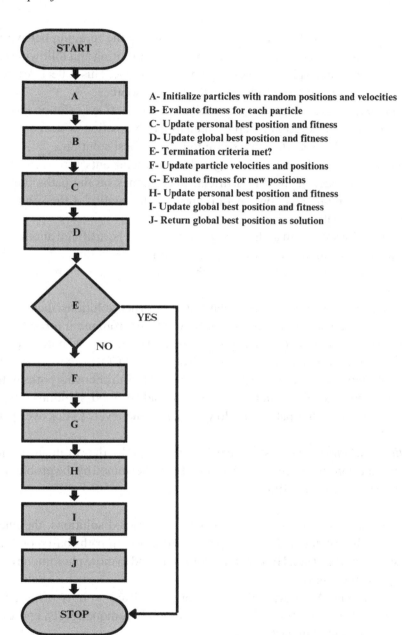

A- Initialize particles with random positions and velocities
B- Evaluate fitness for each particle
C- Update personal best position and fitness
D- Update global best position and fitness
E- Termination criteria met?
F- Update particle velocities and positions
G- Evaluate fitness for new positions
H- Update personal best position and fitness
I- Update global best position and fitness
J- Return global best position as solution

combinatorial problems. To understand the basics of ACO, consider the following key concepts:

-*Inspiration from Ant Foraging:* ACO is inspired by the foraging behavior of real ants. Ants communicate with each other by depositing and following chemical substances called pheromones on paths they traverse. This collective intelligence allows ants to find the shortest paths to food sources.

-*Solution Space:* ACO is applied to problems with a defined solution space, where each potential solution is represented as a combination of decision variables. The algorithm searches this space to find the best solution.

-*Pheromone Trails:* In the ACO algorithm, artificial ants traverse paths in the solution space, depositing artificial pheromones on the paths they explore. The pheromone level on a path represents the quality of the solutions found along that path.

-*Heuristic Information:* In addition to pheromone levels, artificial ants use heuristic information to make decisions. The heuristic function provides problem-specific guidance and helps ants choose paths that are more likely to lead to good solutions.

-*Construction of Solutions:* Artificial ants construct solutions incrementally by choosing decision variables based on both pheromone information and the heuristic function. They use probabilistic methods to make these choices.

-*Exploitation and Exploration:* A key feature of ACO is the balance between exploitation and exploration. Exploitation refers to choosing paths with higher pheromone levels, which are likely to lead to good solutions. Exploration involves choosing paths with lower pheromone levels to discover potentially better solutions.

-*Solution Evaluation:* As ants traverse their chosen paths, they evaluate the quality of the solutions they construct. The quality is determined by the problem-specific objective or fitness function.

Pheromone Update: After all ants have constructed solutions, the pheromone levels on paths are updated. Ants deposit pheromone on paths based on the quality of the solutions they find. High-quality solutions lead to more pheromone deposition on the paths they used.

Iteration: The ACO algorithm runs for a specified number of iterations, and the process of constructing solutions, updating pheromone levels, and evaluating solutions is repeated in each iteration.

Termination: The algorithm terminates when a stopping criterion is met, such as reaching a maximum number of iterations, finding a satisfactory solution, or running for a defined time.

Figure 3. Basic idea of ACO

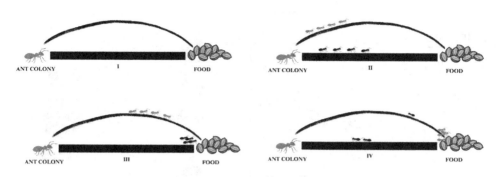

Ant Colony Optimization (ACO) has found valuable application in the field of medical image processing. ACO, inspired by the foraging behavior of real ants, offers a unique and effective approach to solving complex optimization problems in this domain. It can be harnessed to address critical challenges such as image segmentation, feature selection, registration, denoising, and path planning for medical procedures. By simulating the collective intelligence of ants, ACO aids in finding optimal solutions in intricate and non-convex solution spaces, which are common in medical image analysis. The algorithm's adaptability and its ability to strike a balance between exploring new paths and exploiting known paths make it a powerful tool for enhancing the analysis, interpretation, and utilization of medical images. As research in medical image processing continues to advance, ACO holds the potential to further improve healthcare diagnostics and treatment planning by optimizing the use of valuable image data.

To effectively apply ACO, you need to understand the problem you're trying to solve, tune algorithm parameters, and potentially customize it to suit the specific problem at hand. The figure below illustrates the fundamental concept of a straightforward food search approach.

In the illustration provided in the Figure 3, we have simplified the scenario to include only two potential routes connecting the food source and the ant nest. Let's analyze the stages:

Stage I: In the initial stage, all ants are located within their nest, and the environment remains free of any pheromone presence. (For the sake of algorithmic design, a residual pheromone quantity can be considered without interfering with the probability calculations.)

Stage II: Ants commence their exploration with an equal probability of 0.5 assigned to each path. Notably, the curved path is longer, resulting in a longer duration for the ants to reach the food source compared to the alternative path.

37

Figure 4. Structure of neuron and represent with in artificial neural network

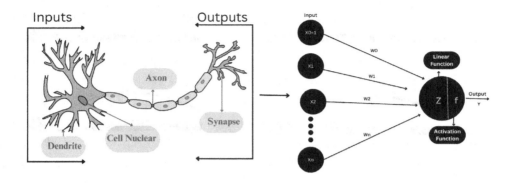

Stage III: Ants that choose the shorter path reach the food source more quickly. At this point, they encounter a similar decision-making situation. However, the presence of a pheromone trail along the shorter path increases its probability of selection.

Stage IV: As more ants return via the shorter path, the concentration of pheromones along that route increases. Concurrently, due to evaporation, the pheromone concentration on the longer path decreases, reducing the probability of its selection in subsequent stages. Consequently, the entire ant colony gradually leans towards favoring the shorter path with higher selection probabilities. This gradual shift leads to path optimization.

Artificial Neural Networks (ANNs)

Artificial Neural Networks (ANNs) are computational models inspired by the structure and function of the human brain. The human body is governed by the central nervous system, with the neuron being its fundamental building block. Figure 4 illustrates the structure of a neuron and its representation within an ANN. The ANN consist of interconnected nodes organized into layers and are used in machine learning to perform tasks such as pattern recognition, classification, regression, and more. ANNs are particularly powerful for handling complex and high-dimensional data, making them a fundamental tool in deep learning and various applications across domains.

The working principle of an Artificial Neural Network (ANN) is based on simulating the way neurons in the human brain process information. ANNs consist of interconnected nodes (neurons) organized into layers. The Figure 5 illustrates the basic structure of an Artificial Neural Network (ANN).

Here's a short overview of how they work:

Figure 5. Simple structure of ANN

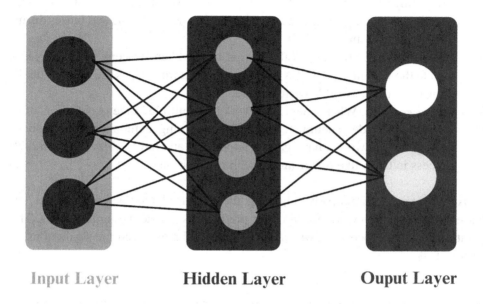

Input Layer   **Hidden Layer**   **Ouput Layer**

1. ***Input Layer:*** The input layer receives the raw data or features for a given task.
2. ***Weights and Biases:*** Each connection between neurons has associated weights and each neuron has an associated bias. These weights and biases are parameters that the network learns during training.
3. ***Hidden Layers:*** Intermediate layers, called hidden layers, process the input data. Neurons in these layers calculate weighted sums of their inputs, apply activation functions, and pass the result to the next layer.
4. ***Activation Functions:*** Activation functions introduce non-linearity into the model, allowing ANNs to approximate complex functions. Common activation functions include sigmoid, tanh, and ReLU.
5. ***Output Layer:*** The final layer, known as the output layer, produces the network's predictions or outputs, which are typically used for tasks like classification, regression, or decision-making.
6. ***Forward Propagation:*** During forward propagation, data flows through the network from the input layer to the output layer. Neurons calculate their outputs based on the inputs, weights, biases, and activation functions.
7. ***Loss Function:*** A loss function quantifies the error between the network's predictions and the actual target values for supervised learning tasks.

8. **Backpropagation:** To train the network, backpropagation is used. It involves computing gradients of the loss function with respect to the network's weights and biases. These gradients guide the adjustment of weights and biases during training to minimize the loss.

9. **Optimization:** Optimization algorithms, like gradient descent, are employed to update the weights and biases in a direction that minimizes the loss, gradually improving the network's performance.

10. **Deep Learning:** When a neural network has multiple hidden layers, it is often referred to as a deep neural network. Deep learning techniques, which rely on deep neural networks, have gained popularity and have achieved remarkable success in tasks like image and speech recognition.

ANNs learn by iteratively adjusting their internal parameters (weights and biases) based on the error between their predictions and actual target values. This iterative learning process allows ANNs to adapt and make accurate predictions for various tasks.

IMAGE ENHANCEMENT USING BIO-INSPIRED ALGORITHMS

Image enhancement plays a critical role in medical image processing by improving the quality and clarity of medical images, thereby aiding healthcare professionals in better interpretation. Through accentuating relevant features while reducing noise and artifacts, medical image enhancement enhances the diagnostic information available to clinicians.

In this section, we delve into the innovative approaches that Bio-Inspired Algorithms offer for image enhancement in medical imaging. These algorithms draw inspiration from nature's adaptive and optimizing systems, proving effective in enhancing medical images across various modalities, including X-ray, MRI, CT, and ultrasound. The image on the right side of Figure 4 is an MRI scan of the human head in the coronal view, sourced from the Internet Brain Segmentation Repository (IBSR, 2023). On the right side of Figure 6, you can observe the boundary-detected image, which was generated from the input image using the boundary detection method (Somasundaram, 2012).

Bio-Inspired Algorithms excel in addressing specific challenges and requirements of medical image enhancement:

Figure 6. MRI of human head scans in the left and boundary detected image in the right

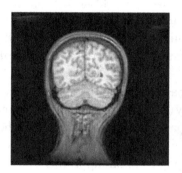 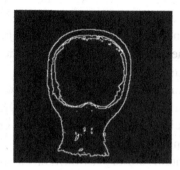

Noise Reduction

Medical images often suffer from different types of noise, such as random noise and speckle noise, which can obscure critical details. Bio-Inspired Algorithms adaptively identify and filter out these noise patterns, resulting in clearer and more detailed images.

Contrast Enhancement

Enhancing image contrast is vital for making subtle structures and abnormalities more visible. Bio-Inspired Algorithms optimize image intensity transformations, preserving essential image details while enhancing contrast.

Edge and Feature Preservation

Preserving sharp edges and relevant features in medical images is crucial for accurate diagnosis. Bio-Inspired Algorithms excel in edge-preserving smoothing and filtering, ensuring critical anatomical details remain intact.

Adaptive Enhancement

Different medical imaging modalities and clinical scenarios demand tailored enhancement techniques. Bio-Inspired Algorithms skillfully adjust enhancement parameters based on specific image characteristics, delivering personalized and optimized enhancements.

In the literature, notable examples of Bio-Inspired Algorithms applied to medical image enhancement include:

Rahebi (2011) proposes a novel edge detection approach using Ant Colony Optimization (ACO) and Artificial Neural Networks (ANN). ACO creates a pheromone matrix indicating edge information in each pixel, while ANN further refines the edges through noise reduction, outperforming traditional edge detection methods in accuracy and efficiency.

Ashour (2015) presents a log transform-based approach using the Cuckoo Search algorithm to enhance Computed Tomography (CT) images. This method significantly improves image quality and clarity in comparison to other techniques when tested on abdominal CT images.

Gudmundsson (1998) introduces an edge detection algorithm using a genetic algorithm (GA) for detecting well-localized, un-fragmented, thin edges in medical images. By optimizing edge configurations, the algorithm shows promising results across various medical image modalities.

Practical examples and case studies illustrate the effectiveness of Bio-Inspired Algorithms in enhancing medical images, enhancing diagnostic accuracy, and reducing computational time. As we explore the benefits of using bio-inspired approaches for image enhancement, we recognize the tremendous potential these algorithms hold in advancing medical imaging and ultimately improving patient care. With their ability to intelligently adapt and optimize, Bio-Inspired Algorithms continue to pave the way for advancements in medical image processing and its impact on healthcare practices.

IMAGE SEGMENTATION WITH BIO-INSPIRED ALGORITHMS

Image segmentation is a fundamental task in medical image processing, crucial for dividing images into meaningful and homogeneous regions or objects. Its significance lies in various clinical applications, such as tumor detection, organ delineation, and anatomical structure analysis. However, medical images pose unique challenges, such as complex intensity variations, noise, and overlapping structures, making segmentation both demanding and time-consuming.

In this section, we explore how Bio-Inspired Algorithms offer powerful solutions for medical image segmentation, drawing inspiration from natural processes to adaptively partition images into coherent regions. These algorithms effectively address the complexities encountered in medical image segmentation. On the left side of Figure 7, you can see the input image sourced from (IBSR, 2023). On the right side of the Figure 7, the extracted brain image is displayed, achieved through the use of the method (Somasundaram, 2013).

Figure 7. MRI of human head scans as input image and brain segmented image

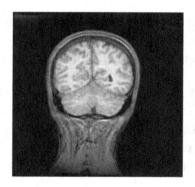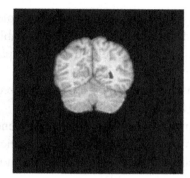

Key challenges and considerations in medical image segmentation include handling the following:

Complex Image Characteristics

Medical images often exhibit varying intensity distributions, uneven illumination, and irregular shapes. Traditional segmentation methods may struggle to cope with such complexities, leading to inaccuracies in the segmentation results.

Segmentation Ambiguities

Some medical images may contain regions with similar intensity values or weak boundaries, resulting in segmentation ambiguities. Bio-Inspired Algorithms can incorporate contextual information to resolve such ambiguities and improve the accuracy of segmentation.

Data Imbalance

In medical imaging, some regions of interest may be relatively small compared to the background, leading to class imbalance in segmentation tasks. Bio-Inspired Algorithms are adept at handling imbalanced datasets, ensuring that all regions receive equal importance during segmentation.

Efficiency and Scalability

With the increasing volume and complexity of medical image data, there is a growing demand for efficient and scalable segmentation techniques. Bio-Inspired Algorithms offer parallel and adaptive optimization strategies that can process large datasets effectively.

Noteworthy examples of Bio-Inspired Algorithms applied to medical image segmentation include:

Soleimani (2013) proposed an efficient approach using the ant colony algorithm for brain tumor segmentation in magnetic resonance images. The authors achieved more accurate results compared to traditional methods like Otsu and k-means.

Priyadharshini (2018) presented an automated computer-assisted technique using the Bat Algorithm to extract Regions of Interest (ROI) from CT images. The approach efficiently extracts ROIs and can be employed in hospitals for real CT image examination.

Chakraborty (2020) introduced a novel method for cell segmentation in microscopic images using the cuckoo search algorithm. The approach demonstrated excellent computational performance and accuracy in identifying and counting cells.

Masoumi (2012) proposed an automatic liver segmentation technique combining an iterative watershed algorithm and an artificial neural network. The approach achieved more precise results in liver segmentation, showing promise for medical imaging.

Taherdangkoo (2013) presented an Ant Colony Optimization Algorithm for image segmentation, demonstrating efficiency and accuracy across various image sets, including medical imaging.

Gupta (2023) introduced a technique for early brain tumor detection using MRI images and a deep residual network model with an improved invasive bat algorithm. The approach exhibited high accuracy in tumor segmentation and detection.

Through practical examples and case studies, we illustrate the effectiveness of Bio-Inspired Algorithms in medical image segmentation across diverse modalities and clinical scenarios. These bio-inspired approaches offer advantages such as improved accuracy, reduced manual intervention, and robustness against image variations, promising significant advancements in medical imaging and ultimately enhancing patient care.

FEATURE EXTRACTION USING BIO-INSPIRED ALGORITHMS

Feature extraction is a fundamental step in medical image processing, crucial for identifying and extracting pertinent information or patterns from image data. These extracted features act as distinctive representations of underlying anatomical structures or pathological characteristics, enabling subsequent analysis and classification tasks in medical imaging.

In this section, we delve into the innovative approaches that Bio-Inspired Algorithms offer for feature extraction in medical images. Inspired by natural processes like evolution and swarm intelligence, these algorithms adaptively search for discriminative and informative features, enhancing the diagnostic capabilities of medical image analysis.

We acknowledge the significance and challenges of feature extraction in medical imaging:

Importance of Feature Selection

Medical images encompass vast amounts of data, where not all image components are equally relevant for clinical diagnosis. Feature extraction plays a crucial role in selecting the most discriminative and informative image characteristics, ensuring efficient and accurate analysis.

High-Dimensional Data

Medical images typically present high-dimensional datasets with complex spatial and intensity information. Extracting meaningful features in such high-dimensional spaces can be challenging, and traditional feature extraction methods may suffer from the curse of dimensionality.

Interpatient Variability

Medical images can exhibit substantial variations between different patients, making feature extraction a patient-specific task. Bio-Inspired Algorithms can adapt to the specific image characteristics of each patient, thereby enabling patient-tailored feature extraction.

Exploration of Feature Space

The search for optimal features in medical images can be computationally intensive and time-consuming. Bio-Inspired Algorithms offer efficient search and optimization strategies to explore the feature space and identify the most relevant image features.

In one study, Nagarajan (2016) introduces a hybrid approach for selecting a dimensionality-reduced set of features for a medical image retrieval system. The system follows three phases: feature extraction using distinct algorithms, potential feature vector identification using a genetic algorithm, and feature selection through a hybrid "Branch and Bound Algorithm" and "Artificial Bee Colony Algorithm." The paper emphasizes the importance of effective feature selection for medical image analysis and proposes using a minimum description length principle-based genetic algorithm for this purpose. The proposed approach is evaluated using breast cancer, brain tumor, and thyroid images.

Similarly, Basiri (2013) proposes a novel algorithm based on ant colony optimization (ACO) for feature selection in machine learning. The authors argue that feature selection is a critical step in machine learning, capable of improving classification accuracy and reducing computational complexity. They review related work on feature selection, distinguishing between model-free and model-based methods. Subsequently, they present their ACO-based algorithm, ACOFS, which selects a feature set with high classification accuracy and small size. The algorithm is evaluated on image databases and non-image datasets, demonstrating superior performance compared to other ACO-based feature selection methods and competitive results against other state-of-the-art methods.

Through practical examples and case studies, we illustrate how these Bio-Inspired Algorithms have demonstrated their effectiveness in feature extraction for medical image analysis. Moreover, we discuss the benefits of using bio-inspired approaches, such as improved classification accuracy, reduced computational complexity, and enhanced interpretability of extracted features. These bio-inspired approaches hold great promise in contributing to accurate diagnoses and improved patient care.

CLASSIFICATION AND RECOGNITION USING BIO-INSPIRED ALGORITHMS

Classification and recognition are fundamental tasks in medical image processing, playing a crucial role in categorizing and identifying specific anatomical structures, lesions, or abnormalities within medical images. The accuracy of these tasks is of utmost importance as it directly impacts automated diagnosis, treatment planning, and patient management in clinical practice.

In this section, we delve into the remarkable solutions that Bio-Inspired Algorithms offer for classification and recognition tasks in medical imaging. Drawing inspiration from natural processes, these algorithms adaptively learn and recognize complex patterns in medical images, leading to accurate and efficient image-based diagnosis.

The significance and challenges of classification and recognition in medical imaging are multifaceted:

Automated Diagnosis

Automating the classification of medical images into distinct categories enables faster and more consistent diagnosis. Bio-Inspired Algorithms excel in handling variations in image appearance and different pathological conditions, ensuring robust learning capabilities.

Data Imbalance

Medical imaging datasets often exhibit imbalanced class distributions, with some classes having fewer samples than others. Bio-Inspired Algorithms effectively handle such imbalances and ensure that all classes are fairly represented during classification.

Feature Representation

The selection and representation of discriminative features significantly influence classification accuracy. Bio-Inspired Algorithms have the remarkable ability to adaptively learn feature representations, thereby reducing the reliance on manual feature engineering.

Interpatient Variability

Medical images from different patients can display variations in anatomy and disease manifestations. Bio-Inspired Algorithms demonstrate the capacity to generalize across patient-specific data, making them particularly well-suited for robust and patient-specific classification.

Akkar (2020) presents a compelling study exploring the use of bio-inspired artificial intelligence methods, such as Moth Flame Optimization, Ant Colony Optimization, and Particle Swarm Optimization, to train an artificial neural network for skin carcinoma detection. The paper highlights the significance of computer vision and image processing in medical image analysis, emphasizing the crucial role of early skin cancer detection. The results indicate that Moth Flame Optimization is the most effective in training the artificial neural network.

Chawla (2022) discusses the integration of a bat algorithm with a convolutional neural network approach for brain tumor recognition. The article explains the significance of this approach in identifying brain tumors through MRI images and classification techniques. The authors describe the process of using the bat algorithm to select the most relevant features from MRI images, which are then used to train the convolutional neural network. The accuracy of the approach and its potential applications in other types of medical imaging for disease detection are also discussed.

Joo (2004) introduces a computer-aided diagnosis (CAD) algorithm that employs an artificial neural network (ANN) to identify breast nodule malignancy using multiple ultrasonography (US) features. The algorithm was developed using a database of histologically confirmed cases containing benign and malignant breast nodules. The paper emphasizes the importance of early breast cancer detection and discusses the potential of the developed CAD algorithm to increase the specificity of US for characterizing breast lesions.

Sreekanth (2022) proposes a novel approach for brain tumor classification using a combination of stationary wavelet transform, feature selection, and proven classifier models of Bat Algorithm with Extreme Learning Machine via Transfer Learning. The proposed system achieves a high classification accuracy, outperforming other related works. The article discusses the advantages of using the proposed algorithm and suggests that this research can significantly contribute to the field of medical imaging and diagnosis.

Through practical examples and case studies, we illustrate how these Bio-Inspired Algorithms have demonstrated their effectiveness in classification and recognition tasks for medical image analysis. Their capability to handle data imbalance, adapt to patient-specific variations, and efficiently learn discriminative features offers great promise in accurate diagnoses and improved patient care. As we continue to explore the potential of Bio-Inspired Algorithms in medical imaging, we gain valuable insights into their pivotal role in advancing the field of medical image analysis and clinical decision-making.

REGISTRATION AND FUSION OF MEDICAL IMAGES WITH BIO-INSPIRED ALGORITHMS

Image registration and fusion are critical tasks in medical image processing, playing a vital role in aligning and combining multiple images acquired from different modalities or at different time points. The spatial alignment and information fusion achieved through these tasks enable accurate comparison, analysis, and treatment planning in clinical practice.

In this section, we explore the innovative solutions offered by Bio-Inspired Algorithms for image registration and fusion in medical imaging. Drawing inspiration from natural processes such as evolution and swarm intelligence, these algorithms adaptively optimize image transformations and fusion rules, leading to precise spatial alignment and effective information fusion.

The significance and challenges of image registration and fusion in medical imaging are diverse:

Multimodal Image Integration

Medical images acquired from different modalities provide unique and complementary information about the underlying anatomy or pathology. Image registration and fusion enable the integration of multimodal data, resulting in comprehensive and more informative images for clinical assessment.

Time-Series Image Analysis

In longitudinal studies and dynamic imaging, accurate image registration is vital for monitoring disease progression, treatment response, and changes in anatomical structures over time.

Spatial Deformations

Patient motion, changes in posture, and differences in imaging protocols can introduce spatial deformations in medical images. Image registration techniques must account for such deformations to achieve accurate alignment.

Information Fusion

Image fusion techniques aim to combine the strengths of individual images while mitigating their limitations. This results in enhanced image quality, improved contrast, and better visualization of diagnostic features.

de Vos (2019) presents a deep learning framework for unsupervised affine and deformable image registration. The manuscript, accepted for publication in the Medical Image Analysis journal, provides a comprehensive overview of the novel method for image registration using ConvNets. The paper emphasizes the advantages of using an unsupervised deep learning approach for image registration and explains the ConvNet training process in detail. The framework proves effective for different types of medical images, such as MRI or CT scans.

Fu (2020) provides an overview of the latest developments and applications of deep learning-based medical image registration methods. The article discusses the challenges associated with using deep learning in medical image registration and how it can improve accuracy and efficiency. The authors share insights into applying this information to enhance medical imaging technology.

Shahdoosti (2019) proposes a new method for multimodal medical image fusion using ensemble empirical mode decomposition (EEMD) and ant colony optimization (ACO) based segmentation. The article addresses challenges in extracting salient features and avoiding noise injection in the fusion process, presenting detailed explanations of the proposed method and algorithms. The experimental results demonstrate the effectiveness of the approach, contributing to advanced medical image fusion techniques that improve diagnosis and treatment reliability.

Kavitha (2014) introduces a hybrid intelligent system that integrates swarm intelligence and neural networks for medical image fusion. The system optimizes edge detection using ant colony optimization, combining complementary images from different modalities for improved diagnosis and surgical planning. The proposed approach enhances the quality of fused medical images and holds potential for future applications in medical imaging.

Through practical examples and case studies, we illustrate how Bio-Inspired Algorithms effectively address image registration and fusion challenges in medical imaging. These bio-inspired approaches hold great promise in improving accuracy, efficiency, and reliability in medical image analysis, ultimately contributing to enhanced patient care and medical decision-making.

BIO-INSPIRED OPTIMIZATION FOR RESOURCE ALLOCATION IN MEDICAL IMAGING

Resource allocation is a critical aspect of medical imaging that involves efficiently utilizing computational resources, storage, and processing power for various image processing tasks. Optimizing resource allocation is essential to ensure timely and accurate medical image analysis while reducing computational costs and improving overall system performance.

In this section, we explore how Bio-Inspired Optimization techniques offer innovative solutions for resource allocation in medical imaging. Drawing inspiration from natural processes, these algorithms adaptively optimize resource allocation strategies, enabling efficient and effective utilization of computing resources in medical image processing.

The significance and challenges of resource allocation in medical imaging are multifaceted:

Computational Complexity

Medical image processing tasks, such as segmentation, registration, and classification, can be computationally intensive, demanding significant computational resources and time. Optimizing resource allocation is essential to expedite these tasks and deliver timely results.

Large-Scale Image Datasets

Modern medical imaging applications generate large volumes of data that demand substantial storage and processing capabilities. Effective resource allocation is vital for handling big data in medical imaging.

Real-time Processing

In clinical settings, real-time image processing is critical for prompt decision-making and intervention. Efficient resource allocation ensures that real-time processing requirements are met, avoiding delays in patient care.

Patient-Specific Optimization

Resource allocation strategies must be adaptable to the specific requirements of individual patients and imaging tasks, as different cases may necessitate varying resource distributions.

For instance, Anguraj (2021) proposes an evolutionary-based cluster head selection technique called the augmented bifold cuckoo search algorithm (ABCSA) for edge-based Internet of Medical Things (IoMT). The paper discusses the need for energy-efficient communication protocols for IoMT and how clustering can reduce overall energy consumption by medical wireless devices. The proposed ABCSA algorithm uses a novel binary model to handle the binary solution space and is evaluated through experimental analysis, demonstrating significant outperformance of existing models.

Additionally, Enireddy (2015) introduces a new algorithm for content-based image retrieval (CBIR) of compressed medical images. The algorithm combines wavelet compression, Gabor filters, and neural networks to achieve high accuracy in image classification. The authors compare their algorithm with other state-of-the-art CBIR systems and demonstrate its superior accuracy and efficiency.

Moreover, Geetha (2021) discusses a novel image compression technique that utilizes the Vector quantization (VQ) method and the evolutionary lion optimization algorithm to handle large amounts of medical data for storage and communication purposes. The paper explains the VQ technique and its compatibility with the Linde-Buzo-Gray (LBG) model.

Through these practical examples, we illustrate how Bio-Inspired Algorithms effectively address resource allocation challenges in medical imaging. These bio-inspired approaches hold great promise in improving efficiency, reducing costs, and optimizing resource utilization in medical image analysis, ultimately leading to enhanced patient care and medical decision-making.

PERFORMANCE EVALUATION AND COMPARATIVE ANALYSIS

Performance evaluation and comparative analysis are fundamental aspects of research in medical image processing using bio-inspired algorithms. Robust and rigorous evaluation methodologies play a crucial role in assessing the effectiveness, efficiency, and generalizability of these algorithms for specific medical imaging tasks.

In this section, we delve into the significance and challenges of performance evaluation and comparative analysis for bio-inspired algorithms in medical image processing:

Importance of Objective Evaluation

Objective and quantitative evaluation metrics are essential for accurately measuring the performance of bio-inspired algorithms. These metrics provide valuable insights into algorithm efficacy, enabling researchers to make data-driven decisions and draw meaningful conclusions.

Diverse Medical Imaging Tasks

Medical image processing covers a broad spectrum of tasks, including segmentation, registration, classification, and image enhancement. Each task has unique evaluation requirements, necessitating tailored evaluation methodologies.

Benchmark Datasets

The availability of benchmark datasets is critical for ensuring consistent and fair comparisons between different bio-inspired algorithms. Researchers require representative datasets that encompass various medical conditions, imaging modalities, and imaging challenges.

Generalization and Robustness

Assessing the generalization capabilities and robustness of bio-inspired algorithms is crucial for their real-world applicability in medical imaging scenarios. Algorithms should perform well on unseen data and handle variations in image quality and acquisition conditions.

Next, we discuss the key components of performance evaluation and comparative analysis for bio-inspired algorithms in medical image processing:

Evaluation Metrics Selection

We explore commonly used evaluation metrics such as Dice coefficient, Jaccard index, sensitivity, specificity, accuracy, and area under the receiver operating characteristic curve (AUC-ROC). Each metric is suited for specific tasks and provides valuable insights into algorithm performance.

Cross-Validation Strategies

Cross-validation is essential to assess algorithm generalization and mitigate the risk of overfitting. We discuss k-fold cross-validation and leave-one-out cross-validation as effective techniques for robust evaluation.

Comparative Studies

Comparative analysis involves benchmarking bio-inspired algorithms against traditional methods and state-of-the-art approaches. We emphasize the importance of fair comparisons, ensuring that algorithms are evaluated under similar experimental conditions.

Statistical Analysis

To draw statistically significant conclusions, we emphasize the use of appropriate statistical tests to analyze performance differences between algorithms.

Computational Efficiency

In addition to accuracy, computational efficiency is a critical factor in evaluating bio-inspired algorithms. We discuss the importance of analyzing computational time and resource usage for real-world deployment.

Through practical examples and case studies, we demonstrate the application of these evaluation methodologies in medical image processing with bio-inspired algorithms. We highlight the strengths and limitations of different algorithms and provide insights into factors influencing algorithm performance.

By the end of this chapter, readers will gain a comprehensive understanding of performance evaluation and comparative analysis for bio-inspired algorithms in medical image processing. Armed with knowledge of effective evaluation techniques, researchers can make informed decisions in selecting and optimizing bio-inspired algorithms for specific medical imaging tasks, leading to advancements in clinical diagnosis, treatment planning, and healthcare delivery.

Table 1. Comparison of four bio-inspired algorithms

Algorithm	Application	Advantages	Limitations
Genetic Algorithms (GA)	Parameter optimization, feature selection	Global search, robust to noise, adaptability	Computationally expensive, convergence rate
Particle Swarm Optimization (PSO)	Feature selection, optimization	Efficiency, quick convergence, continuous optimization	Challenges with discrete and multimodal problems
Artificial Neural Networks (ANN)	Image classification, disease detection	Complex relationships modeling, adaptability	Large data and computational requirements
Ant Colony Optimization (ACO)	Image registration, path planning	Large solution space, combinatorial optimization	Sensitive to parameter settings

COMPARISON OF BIO-INSPIRED ALGORITHMS

In this section, a comparative analysis of the four bio-inspired algorithms is presented, as illustrated in Table 1. Each of these algorithms possesses its unique set of applications, strengths, and limitations.

FUTURE DIRECTIONS AND CHALLENGES

As bio-inspired algorithms continue to make significant contributions to medical image processing, several exciting future directions and challenges emerge. These directions offer opportunities for further research and development, aiming to advance the field and address the complexities of medical imaging tasks.

In this section, we explore the potential future directions and challenges for bio-inspired algorithms in medical image processing:

Deep Learning Integration

Deep learning has revolutionized various domains, including medical image analysis. Integrating bio-inspired algorithms with deep learning architectures holds great promise for enhancing the performance and interpretability of medical image processing tasks. Future research could explore hybrid approaches that combine the strengths of bio-inspired algorithms and deep learning models.

Explainable AI

As bio-inspired algorithms grow in complexity, the need for explainable AI becomes crucial, especially in medical applications. Addressing the interpretability and transparency of these algorithms will be vital to gain the trust and acceptance of medical professionals and regulatory bodies.

Personalized Medicine

Personalized medicine aims to tailor medical treatments to individual patients based on their unique characteristics. Future research could focus on developing bio-inspired algorithms that adapt to patient-specific data and support personalized medical image analysis and treatment planning.

Real-time Processing

With the increasing demand for real-time medical image analysis in clinical settings, future directions could explore bio-inspired algorithms optimized for low-latency processing and real-time decision-making. Efficient resource allocation and parallelization techniques will be essential in achieving real-time performance.

Adversarial Robustness

Medical imaging systems are vulnerable to adversarial attacks, where small, imperceptible perturbations can mislead algorithms. Future research could investigate bio-inspired approaches to enhance the robustness of medical image processing algorithms against adversarial attacks.

Multimodal Fusion and Analysis

As medical imaging technologies advance, multimodal data integration becomes more prevalent. Future research could focus on bio-inspired algorithms that efficiently fuse information from multiple imaging modalities and enable comprehensive analysis for better clinical insights.

Interoperability and Standardization

Ensuring interoperability and standardization of bio-inspired algorithms in medical imaging is crucial for their widespread adoption and integration into clinical practice.

Addressing challenges related to data formats, algorithm implementations, and integration with existing medical systems will be essential.

Ethical and Privacy Considerations

As medical image processing becomes more data-driven and relies on large datasets, ethical considerations regarding patient privacy and data security must be carefully addressed. Future research should explore ways to ensure patient confidentiality and comply with regulatory requirements.

Multicenter Studies and Validation

Collaborative efforts involving multiple medical centers and institutions can provide more comprehensive validation of bio-inspired algorithms in diverse clinical scenarios. Future research could focus on conducting multicenter studies to assess algorithm performance across different patient populations and imaging protocols.

By exploring these future directions and addressing the associated challenges, bio-inspired algorithms can continue to revolutionize medical image processing, paving the way for improved diagnostic accuracy, personalized treatments, and enhanced patient care. Researchers and practitioners in the field have a unique opportunity to shape the future of medical imaging using these innovative and nature-inspired computational techniques.

CONCLUSION

The integration of bio-inspired algorithms in medical image processing has ushered in a new era of innovation and advancement. Throughout this chapter, we have explored the vast potential of these nature-inspired computational techniques and their significant impact on various medical imaging tasks.

Bio-inspired algorithms, such as Genetic Algorithms, Particle Swarm Optimization, Ant Colony Optimization, and Swarm Intelligence, have demonstrated remarkable capabilities in solving complex optimization, image analysis, and resource allocation problems in medical imaging. Their ability to draw inspiration from natural processes, adapt to diverse imaging challenges, and optimize solutions has proven invaluable in improving the accuracy, efficiency, and interpretability of medical image processing.

We have seen how these algorithms excel in tasks such as image segmentation, feature extraction, registration, classification, image enhancement, and resource allocation. Their versatility in handling different imaging modalities and clinical scenarios makes them indispensable tools for researchers and healthcare professionals alike.

Looking ahead, the future of bio-inspired algorithms in medical image processing is exciting and full of potential. The integration of these algorithms with deep learning models holds the promise of even more robust and accurate medical image analysis. Advancements in explainable AI will ensure the transparency and interpretability of these algorithms, instilling confidence in their use in clinical settings.

Moreover, as medical imaging moves towards personalized medicine and real-time processing, bio-inspired algorithms can play a pivotal role in tailoring treatments to individual patients and facilitating timely decision-making in critical healthcare situations. The fusion of multimodal data and addressing adversarial robustness will further enhance the diagnostic capabilities and security of medical image processing systems.

However, along with the opportunities come challenges. Addressing ethical considerations, ensuring data privacy, and achieving interoperability and standardization will be essential in the widespread adoption and seamless integration of bio-inspired algorithms into healthcare practices.

In conclusion, bio-inspired algorithms are at the forefront of revolutionizing medical image processing, offering innovative solutions to complex challenges. The collaborative efforts of researchers, practitioners, and medical experts will shape the future of these algorithms, driving advancements in clinical diagnosis, treatment planning, and patient care. As we embark on this transformative journey, the potential for bio-inspired algorithms to revolutionize medical imaging and improve the lives of patients is immense, and we are excited to witness the remarkable impact they will have on the future of healthcare.

REFERENCES

Akkar, H. A. R., & Salman, S. A. (2020). Detection of biomedical images by using bio-inspired artificial intelligent. *Engineering and Technology Journal*, *38*(2), 255–264. doi:10.30684/etj.v38i2A.319

Anguraj, D. K., Thirugnanasambandam, K., Raghav, R. S., Sudha, S. V., & Saravanan, D. (2021). Enriched cluster head selection using augmented bifold cuckoo search algorithm for edge-based internet of medical things. *Journal of Digital Applications in Cardiology*, *34*(9), e4817. doi:10.1002/dac.4817

Ashour, A., Samanta, S., Dey, N., Kausar, N., Abdessalemkaraa, W., & Hassanien, A. (2015). Computed Tomography Image Enhancement Using Cuckoo Search: A Log Transform Based Approach. *Journal of Signal and Information Processing*, *6*(3), 244–257. doi:10.4236/jsip.2015.63023

Basiri, M. E., Ghasem-Aghaee, N., & Aghdam, M. H. (2013). Efficient ant colony optimization for image feature selection. *Signal Processing*, *93*(1), 1–14. doi:10.1016/j.sigpro.2012.06.019

Chakraborty, S., Chatterjee, S., Dey, N., Ashour, A. S., Ashour, A. S., Shi, F., & Mali, K. (2020). Modified cuckoo search algorithm in microscopic image segmentation of hippocampus. *Journal of Ambient Intelligence and Humanized Computing*, *11*(7), 2925–2937. doi:10.100712652-019-01311-5

Chawla, R., Beram, S. M., Murthy, C. R., Thiruvenkadam, T., Bhavani, N. P. G., Saravanakumar, R., & Sathishkumar, P. J. (2022). *Brain tumor recognition using an integrated bat algorithm with a convolutional neural network approach.* doi:10.1016/j. measen.2022.100426

de Vos, B. D., Berendsen, F. F., Viergever, M. A., Sokooti, H., Staring, M., & Išgum, I. (2019). A deep learning framework for unsupervised affine and deformable image registration. *Medical Image Analysis, 52*, 128-143. doi:10.1016/j.media.2018.11.010

Enireddy, V., & Kumar, R. K. (2015). Improved cuckoo search with particle swarm optimization for classification of compressed images. *Sadhana*, *40*(8), 2271–2285. doi:10.100712046-015-0440-0

Fu, Y., Lei, Y., Wang, T., Curran, W. J., Liu, T., & Yang, X. (2020). Deep learning in medical image registration: A review. *Physics in Medicine and Biology*, *65*(20), 20TR01. Advance online publication. doi:10.1088/1361-6560/ab843e PMID:32217829

Geetha, K., Anitha, V., Elhoseny, M., Kathiresan, S., Shamsolmoali, P., & Selim, M. M. (2021). An evolutionary lion optimization algorithm-based image compression technique for biomedical applications. *Expert Systems: International Journal of Knowledge Engineering and Neural Networks*, *38*(1), e12508. doi:10.1111/exsy.12508

Gudmundsson, M., El-Kwae, E. A., & Kabuka, M. R. (1998). Edge detection in medical images using a genetic algorithm. *IEEE Transactions on Medical Imaging*, *17*(3), 469–475. doi:10.1109/42.712136 PMID:9735910

Gupta, V., & Bibhu, V. (2023). Deep residual network based brain tumor segmentation and detection with MRI using improved invasive bat algorithm. *Multimedia Tools and Applications*, *82*(8), 12445–12467. doi:10.100711042-022-13769-0

IBSR. (2023). *Internet Brain Segmentation Repository (IBSR).* https://www.nitrc.org/projects/ibsr

Joo, S., Yang, Y. S., Moon, W. K., & Kim, H. C. (2004). Computer-aided diagnosis of solid breast nodules: Use of an artificial neural network based on multiple sonographic features. *IEEE Transactions on Medical Imaging*, *23*(10), 1292–1300. doi:10.1109/TMI.2004.834617 PMID:15493696

Kavitha, C. T., & Chellamuthu, C. (2014). Medical image fusion based on hybrid intelligence. *Applied Soft Computing, 20*, 83-94. doi:10.1016/j.asoc.2013.10.034

Masoumi, H., Behrad, A., Pourmina, M. A., & Roosta, A. (2012). Automatic liver segmentation in MRI images using an iterative watershed algorithm and artificial neural network. *Biomedical Signal Processing and Control*, *7*(5), 429–437. doi:10.1016/j.bspc.2012.01.002

Nagarajan, G., Minu, R. I., Muthukumar, B., Vedanarayanan, V., & Sundarsingh, S. D. (2016). Hybrid Genetic Algorithm for Medical Image Feature Extraction and Selection. *Procedia Computer Science, 85*, 455-462. doi:10.1016/j.procs.2016.05.192

Priyadharshini, F. R. A., Hariprasad, N., Asvitha, S., Anandhi, V., & Swetha Priyadarshini, A. P. (2018). *An approach to segment computed tomography images using bat algorithm.* Retrieved from https://ieeexplore.ieee.org/document/8632347

Rahebi, J., & Tajik, H. R. (2011). Biomedical Image Edge Detection using an Ant Colony Optimization Based on Artificial Neural Networks. *International Journal of Engineering Science and Technology*, *3*(12), 8217–8222.

Shahdoosti, H. R., & Tabatabaei, Z. (2019). MRI and PET/SPECT image fusion at feature level using ant colony based segmentation. *Biomedical Signal Processing and Control, 47*, 63-74. doi:10.1016/j.bspc.2018.08.017

Soleimani, V., & Heidari Vincheh, F. (2013). *Improving ant colony optimization for brain MRI image segmentation and brain tumor diagnosis.* IEEE. https://ieeexplore.ieee.org/document/6601866

Somasundaram, K., & Ezhilarasan, K. (2012). Edge detection in MRI of head scans using fuzzy logic. In *2012 IEEE International Conference on Advanced Communication Control and Computing Technologies (ICACCCT)* (pp. 131-135). 10.1109/ICACCCT.2012.6320756

Somasundaram, K., & Ezhilarasan, K. (2013). A Fully Automatic Scheme for Skull Stripping from MRI of Head Scans Using Morphological Neck Breaking Operations. In M. S. Kumar (Ed.), *Proceedings of the Fourth International Conference on Signal and Image Processing 2012* (ICSIP 2012) (Lecture Notes in Electrical Engineering, Vol. 222). Springer. 10.1007/978-81-322-1000-9_25

Sreekanth, G. R., Alrasheedi, A. F., Venkatachalam, K., Abouhawwash, M., & Askar, S. S. (2022). Extreme Learning Bat Algorithm in Brain Tumor Classification. *Intelligent Automation & Soft Computing*, *34*(1). Advance online publication. doi:10.32604/iasc.2022.024538

Taherdangkoo, M., Bagheri, M. H., Yazdi, M., & Andriole, K. P. (2013). An effective method for segmentation of MR brain images using the Ant Colony Optimization Algorithm. *Journal of Digital Imaging*, *26*(6), 1116–1123. doi:10.100710278-013-9596-5 PMID:23563793

Chapter 3
Bio-Inspired Optimization Techniques in Blockchain Systems:
Blockchain and AI-Enabled New Business Models and Applications

Kande Archana
ⓘ https://orcid.org/0000-0001-9100-4047
Malla Reddy Institute of Engineering and Technology, India

V. Kamakshi Prasad
Jawaharlal Nehru Technological University, India

M. Ashok
Malla Reddy College of Engineering, India

ABSTRACT

The integration of blockchain technology into the healthcare sector has shown immense promise in addressing critical challenges related to data security, interoperability, transparency, and patient-centric care. This chapter explores the emergence of blockchain-based healthcare applications and services, highlighting their potential to revolutionize the healthcare industry. Blockchain's inherent features, including decentralization, immutability, and cryptographic security, provide a solid foundation for improving various aspects of healthcare, such as electronic health records (EHRs), medical data exchange, supply chain management, clinical trials, and telemedicine. This chapter reviews several prominent use cases of blockchain in healthcare, such as patient-controlled EHRs, secure data sharing across institutions, provenance tracking of pharmaceuticals, and streamlining administrative processes through smart contracts. It also delves into the challenges that need to be addressed for scalability, regulatory compliance, standardization, and user adoption.

DOI: 10.4018/979-8-3693-1131-8.ch003

INTRODUCTION

The integration of blockchain technology into the healthcare sector represents a groundbreaking paradigm shift with the potential to address longstanding challenges and transform the way healthcare applications and services are delivered. Blockchain, originally conceptualized for securing cryptocurrency transactions, has evolved into a robust framework that offers unparalleled advantages in terms of data security, transparency, interoperability, and patient-centric care (Swan, 2015). This introduction provides an overview of the emergence and significance of blockchain-based healthcare applications and services, highlighting their potential to revolutionize the healthcare industry. Healthcare, as a critical sector, is characterized by the vast and sensitive nature of patient data, complex information exchanges among stakeholders, and the necessity for data integrity. Traditional systems have struggled to maintain the security of electronic health records (EHRs), facilitate seamless data sharing, and ensure patient privacy. These challenges have paved the way for the exploration of innovative solutions that can reshape healthcare systems. Blockchain's core features, including decentralization, immutability, and cryptographic security, have positioned it as a compelling technology for healthcare. Decentralization eliminates the need for a central authority, mitigating the risk of single points of failure and unauthorized access. The immutability of blockchain records ensures that once data is recorded, it cannot be tampered with, fostering trust and accountability. The cryptographic nature of blockchain guarantees secure transactions and controlled data access, crucial in safeguarding sensitive patient information (Ali, 2019).

The potential applications of blockchain in healthcare are diverse and encompass areas such as electronic health records, medical data exchange, supply chain management, clinical trials, and telemedicine. The decentralized and tamper-proof nature of blockchain makes it an ideal candidate for patient-controlled EHRs, enabling patients to have control over their health information while ensuring data accuracy and security. Medical data exchange can be streamlined through secure and interoperable blockchain networks, allowing authorized parties to access and share patient data seamlessly, regardless of institutional boundaries (Ng, 2018). The pharmaceutical supply chain can be transformed by utilizing blockchain to trace the provenance of medications, reducing counterfeit drugs and enhancing patient safety. Furthermore, smart contracts on blockchain can automate administrative processes, reducing inefficiencies and administrative overhead (Dwivedi, 2022).

However, the implementation of blockchain-based healthcare applications is not without challenges. Scalability remains a concern as the technology seeks to handle a high volume of transactions efficiently. Regulatory compliance and standardization are crucial to ensure that blockchain solutions adhere to legal frameworks and can seamlessly interact with existing systems (De Angelis, 2020). User adoption is another hurdle, requiring education and a user-friendly experience to encourage stakeholders to embrace this transformative technology. In the subsequent sections of this paper, we will delve into various aspects of blockchain-based healthcare applications and services. We will explore real-world use cases, discuss challenges, and analyze the potential benefits of blockchain integration. By harnessing the capabilities of blockchain, the healthcare industry stands at the cusp of a new era where data security, interoperability, and patient-centered care converge to create a more efficient and effective healthcare ecosystem (Chen, 2020).

"Blockchain-based Healthcare Application and Services" is a promising area of research that seeks to address several pertinent questions to explore the potential of blockchain technology in the healthcare sector. This article aims to answer the following research questions:

1. How can blockchain technology enhance the security and privacy of electronic health records (EHRs) in healthcare applications?
2. What are the potential benefits and challenges of implementing blockchain-based solutions for secure and interoperable medical data exchange between healthcare institutions?
3. How can blockchain be employed to ensure the provenance and authenticity of pharmaceuticals within the healthcare supply chain?
4. What role can smart contracts play in streamlining administrative processes and reducing inefficiencies in healthcare services?
5. What are the key technical and operational challenges associated with scaling blockchain-based healthcare applications to accommodate a large number of transactions and users?
6. How can regulatory compliance and standardization be achieved to integrate blockchain solutions seamlessly into the existing healthcare ecosystem?
7. What strategies can be employed to encourage user adoption of blockchain-based healthcare services among patients, healthcare providers, and other stakeholders?
8. How might decentralized identity management through blockchain impact patient data security and control in healthcare applications?
9. What is the potential impact of incentivized patient data sharing on medical research, treatment outcomes, and overall healthcare quality?
10. How does the integration of blockchain technology align with the broader trends and developments in the healthcare industry, and what collaborative efforts are necessary for successful adoption?

Addressing these research questions will provide valuable insights into the feasibility, challenges, and opportunities of leveraging blockchain in healthcare applications and services. By examining these questions, this article seeks to contribute to a deeper understanding of the potential benefits and complexities associated with integrating blockchain technology into the healthcare sector, ultimately paving the way for more secure, efficient, and patient-centered healthcare solutions (Azaria, 2016).

BLOCKCHAIN

Blockchain, the foundational technology behind cryptocurrencies like Bitcoin, has expanded its applications far beyond digital currencies. In recent years, it has gained significant attention in various sectors, including healthcare. A blockchain is essentially a distributed and decentralized digital ledger that records transactions across multiple computers, ensuring transparency, security, and immutability. It operates without a central authority and uses cryptographic techniques to secure data. In the context of healthcare, blockchain technology holds the potential to revolutionize data management, security, and interoperability. Blockchain technology has the capacity to transform healthcare applications and services by providing secure, transparent, and patient-centric solutions. While challenges exist, ongoing research and collaboration among stakeholders will likely drive the successful integration of blockchain into the healthcare sector, improving patient care and data management (Swan, 2015).

Blockchain technology comes in various forms, each catering to specific use cases and requirements. The three main types of blockchain technologies are public, private, and hybrid blockchains. Public blockchains are decentralized networks that are open to anyone and allow anyone to participate in the network as nodes. They operate on a permissionless model, meaning that anyone can join the network, read the transactions, and validate them. One of the defining features of public blockchains is their high level of transparency, as all transactions are visible to all participants. Examples of public blockchains include Bitcoin and Ethereum. Public blockchains are ideal for applications where transparency, decentralization, and security are paramount, but they may suffer from scalability issues due to the vast number of participants (Nakamoto, 2008).

Private blockchains, also known as permissioned blockchains, are networks where access and participation are restricted to a defined group of participants. Unlike public blockchains, which are open to everyone, private blockchains are used by specific organizations or consortiums for internal purposes. Private blockchains offer greater control over the network and its participants, making them suitable for industries like healthcare, finance, and supply chain management, where sensitive data needs to be shared securely between trusted parties. Since the number of participants is limited, private blockchains tend to be more scalable than public blockchains. Hybrid blockchains combine elements of both public and private blockchains. They allow data and transactions to be shared between public and private networks, offering the benefits of both models. In a hybrid blockchain, some data can be public and transparent, while other data is kept private and accessible only to authorized participants. This type of blockchain can be useful in scenarios where certain data needs to be publicly visible for accountability and transparency, while sensitive data requires privacy and controlled access (Buterin, 2013).

Blockchain Technology Offers Several Capabilities That Support Healthcare Culture Globally

Blockchain technology offers several capabilities that can significantly support and enhance the healthcare culture globally. These capabilities address some of the longstanding challenges and inefficiencies in healthcare systems, ultimately contributing to improved patient care, data security, and overall healthcare management. Blockchain's inherent cryptographic security ensures that patient data remains secure and tamper-proof. Patient records, treatment histories, and sensitive medical information can be stored in an immutable and encrypted manner, reducing the risk of data breaches and unauthorized access. Blockchain enables seamless and secure sharing of medical data across healthcare institutions, even those with disparate systems. Different providers can access patient data as authorized, leading to more comprehensive patient care and efficient coordination. Patients can manage their health data and grant access to healthcare providers, researchers, and other stakeholders through smart contracts. This empowers patients to control who accesses their data, enhancing patient engagement and privacy (Christidis & Devetsikiotis, 2016).

Smart contracts can automate administrative processes like claims processing, billing, and insurance verification, reducing administrative costs and minimizing errors. Blockchain can streamline the clinical trial process by securely recording trial data, ensuring data integrity, and tracking consent. This transparency and tamper-resistant record-keeping can accelerate research and development of new treatments. In pharmaceuticals and medical equipment supply chains, blockchain can ensure the authenticity and traceability of products. This prevents the distribution of counterfeit drugs, enhances patient safety, and improves inventory management (Mougayar, 2016).

Blockchain-based identity solutions offer patients control over their healthcare-related identities, reducing the need for centralized systems and enhancing privacy. Blockchain's decentralized nature allows patients and providers worldwide to access medical records and data seamlessly, transcending geographical boundaries and improving care for patients on a global scale. Blockchain can facilitate secure and standardized health information exchanges, ensuring that medical data is

Figure 1. Capacities of blockchain technology for healthcare domain

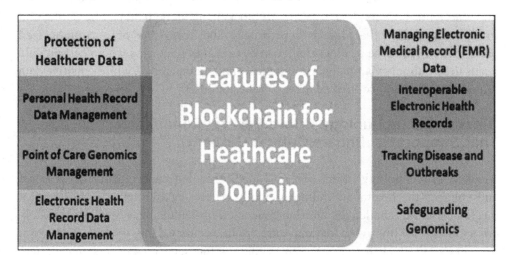

accessible when needed while maintaining privacy and data integrity. Researchers can access aggregated and anonymized data through blockchain, enabling global collaboration on medical research. Patients can also choose to share their data for research purposes, potentially incentivizing data contribution. Blockchain's audit trail and immutability features aid in regulatory compliance, ensuring that healthcare practices adhere to industry regulations and standards. Blockchain's distributed nature provides resilience against system failures and disasters. Patient data can be recovered more easily, ensuring continuity of care even in challenging situations (Zohar, 2015).

Overall, blockchain technology promotes patient-centered care by empowering individuals to have greater control over their health data and treatment decisions, fostering a more collaborative relationship between patients and healthcare providers. The capabilities of blockchain technology align closely with the goals of modern healthcare systems, which strive for improved patient outcomes, data security, interoperability, and efficiency. While challenges and implementation considerations exist, the potential impact of blockchain on the global healthcare culture is substantial, driving positive transformation and enhancing healthcare services for patients and providers alike (Crosby et al., 2016).

Blockchain-Based Healthcare Applications

Blockchain-based healthcare applications leverage the unique capabilities of blockchain technology to address challenges in the healthcare sector and enhance various aspects of patient care, data management, and administrative processes. These applications are designed to improve data security, transparency, interoperability, and patient engagement. The below fig:2 blockchain-based healthcare applications function across four main layers: healthcare raw data, blockchain technology, healthcare application, and stakeholders (Crosby et al., 2016).

In the healthcare raw data layer consist of various sources contribute to the generation of data that is integral to the functioning of blockchain-based healthcare applications. EHRs are comprehensive digital records of a patient's medical history, including diagnoses, treatments, medications, and medical procedures. Healthcare providers and hospitals maintain these records to ensure accurate and up-to-date patient information. Laboratory test results, radiology reports, and diagnostic images contribute essential medical data to patient profiles. These tests aid in diagnosing diseases, monitoring treatment effectiveness, and tracking health conditions. Insurance claims data contains information about medical services rendered, treatments, procedures, and associated costs. This data is used for billing and reimbursement processes involving healthcare providers and insurance companies. Social media platforms and wearable devices can collect health-related data, such as fitness activities, heart rate, sleep patterns, and nutrition habits. This data can provide insights into a patient's overall health and lifestyle. Financial data includes the cost of medical treatments, medication expenses, insurance premiums, and out-of-pocket payments. This data helps patients and healthcare providers manage healthcare expenditures. Medical images, such as X-rays, MRIs, CT scans, and ultrasounds, offer visual insights into a patient's condition. Radiology reports provide interpretations of these images by radiologists. Patients can contribute data directly through health apps, wearable devices, and personal health records. This includes self-reported symptoms, daily activities, medication adherence, and wellness goals. The aggregation of data from these diverse sources contributes to a comprehensive and holistic view of a patient's health. This raw data is then processed, structured, and prepared for inclusion in the blockchain. By incorporating data from these sources onto a secure and transparent blockchain, healthcare applications can enhance patient care, enable better data-driven decisions, and drive advancements in medical research and treatment (Christidis & Devetsikiotis, 2016).

The Blockchain Technology Layer involves the implementation of blockchain concepts to manage and secure healthcare data. It includes various types of blockchains, networks, protocols, components, and services that collectively create the foundation for blockchain-based healthcare applications. Types of Blockchains are Public Blockchains are open to anyone and operates on a permissionless model. Suitable for applications requiring transparency and decentralization. Private Blockchains are restricted access to authorized participants, often used within organizations or

Figure 2. Process model for blockchain-based healthcare applications

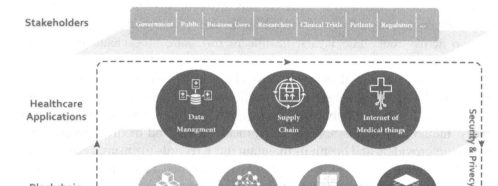

consortiums. Ensures privacy and controlled participation. Hybrid Blockchains are Combines elements of public and private blockchains, allowing controlled sharing of data between public and private networks. Networks and Protocols are Proof of Work (PoW) a consensus mechanism used in public blockchains like Bitcoin, where participants (miners) compete to solve complex mathematical puzzles to validate transactions and add blocks. Proof of Stake (PoS) are validators to chosen based on the amount of cryptocurrency they hold and "stake." Used in PoS-based blockchains like Ethereum's upcoming Ethereum 2.0. Consensus Algorithms support other algorithms like Delegated Proof of Stake (DPoS), Proof of Authority (PoA), and Practical Byzantine Fault Tolerance (PBFT) offer different approaches to achieving consensus. Components and Services are Cryptographic Hashing data entries are hashed using algorithms like SHA-256, creating unique digital signatures that ensure data integrity. Smart Contracts Self-executing code that automates predefined actions when specific conditions are met. Used to automate processes in healthcare applications. Digital Signatures Authenticate transactions and data entries, ensuring the authenticity of participants and data sources. Decentralized Identity it allows individuals to control their identities and personal data, enhancing privacy and security. Consensus Mechanism enables agreement on the validity of transactions and blocks among network participants. Distributed Ledger applicable for multiple copies of the blockchain are maintained across nodes, ensuring data redundancy and fault tolerance. Data Encryption to ensures that sensitive information stored on the blockchain is securely protected. Tokenization represents ownership or access rights to data or assets on the blockchain (Buterin, 2013).

Blockchain Platforms are ethereum its popular platform for creating smart contracts and decentralized applications (DApps). Hyperledger is an umbrella project with multiple blockchain frameworks and tools tailored for various enterprise use cases. Corda is a blockchain platform designed for financial services, focusing on privacy and data sharing among participants. Quorum is an enterprise-focused blockchain platform developed by J.P. Morgan, designed for financial and enterprise applications. Stellar is a platform focused on financial transactions and cross-border payments, with a decentralized exchange built-in. In the healthcare context, these components and services come together to provide a secure, transparent, and efficient framework for managing patient data, ensuring interoperability, and enabling innovative healthcare applications. The choice of blockchain type, network, protocol, and platform depends on the specific requirements and use cases within the healthcare ecosystem. In Healthcare Applications the blockchain technology can be applied to data management, supply chain management, and the Internet of Medical Things (IoMT) in the healthcare context .Blockchain-based healthcare applications can transform data management, ensuring security, interoperability, and patient-centric control. Blockchain-based solutions can enhance transparency, traceability, and authenticity within the pharmaceutical and medical supply chain. Blockchain ensures the provenance and authenticity of medications, reducing the risk of counterfeit drugs entering the supply chain. Each step of the supply chain, from manufacturer to patient, can be recorded on the blockchain, verifying the authenticity of each transaction and product. Blockchain enables real-time tracking of medical supplies, reducing inefficiencies, waste, and ensuring timely restocking (Kshetri, 2017).

Blockchain enhances the security, privacy, and data exchange within IoMT devices and applications. IoMT devices, such as wearable health trackers and medical sensors, can securely transmit data to the blockchain, ensuring data integrity and reducing the risk of unauthorized access. Patients can share their IoMT-generated health data with healthcare providers or researchers through blockchain-based consent mechanisms. Medical data collected from IoMT devices is recorded on the blockchain, making it tamper-proof and verifiable. Blockchain enables patients and healthcare providers to monitor health conditions remotely through connected devices while ensuring data security.

IoMT devices can automate insurance claims and billing processes through smart contracts, reducing administrative burden. By applying blockchain technology to data management, supply chain management, and the IoMT, healthcare systems can realize enhanced efficiency, data security, transparency, and patient-centric care. These applications hold the potential to revolutionize healthcare by improving processes, reducing fraud, enhancing patient trust, and ultimately improving patient outcomes (Zohar, 2015).

By leveraging blockchain technology, the workflow fosters data security, interoperability, transparency, and patient-centric care, benefiting all stakeholders involved in the healthcare ecosystem. The decentralized nature of blockchain empowers multiple parties to collaborate while maintaining data integrity and privacy, ultimately contributing to improved healthcare services on a global scale. Patients have control over their health data, granting access to healthcare providers and researchers based on their preferences. Researchers can access aggregated and anonymized data for studies, leading to medical advancements and improved treatments. Regulatory bodies can audit blockchain records to ensure compliance with healthcare standards and regulations. Insurance claims processing and verification are streamlined through smart contracts, reducing administrative overhead. Blockchain enhances supply chain transparency, preventing counterfeit drugs and ensuring drug authenticity.

Blockchain Technology for Reviving Healthcare Services

Blockchain technology has the potential to significantly revive and transform healthcare services by addressing various challenges and inefficiencies in the industry. Here are some ways in which blockchain can contribute to the revival of healthcare services.

From Figure 3, blockchain's cryptographic features ensure data integrity and security, protecting patient health records, personal information, and sensitive medical data from unauthorized access and tampering. This enhanced security fosters patient trust and reduces the risk of data breaches. Blockchain enables seamless and secure data sharing among different healthcare providers, institutions, and systems. This interoperability improves care coordination, reduces redundant tests, and ensures that accurate patient information is readily available to authorized stakeholders. Healthcare data exchange can be simplified using blockchain, eliminating the need for intermediaries and reducing data reconciliation efforts. This accelerates processes like referrals, patient transfers, and medical records requests. Blockchain empowers patients to have control over their health data, granting access to healthcare providers on their terms. Patients can manage their consent preferences and share data securely, fostering a patient-centered approach to care. Blockchain's transparent and tamper-resistant record-keeping can streamline clinical trial processes, ensuring accurate data reporting, secure patient consent, and auditability, thereby expediting research and development of new treatments. Blockchain's ability to track and verify transactions can ensure transparency in pharmaceutical and medical supply chains, reducing the

Figure 3. Enablers of blockchain implementation in healthcare services

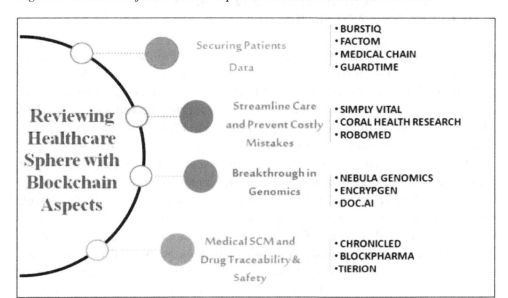

risk of counterfeit drugs, improving inventory management, and ensuring authentic products reach patients (Möser & Böhme, 2017).

Blockchain-based smart contracts can automate insurance claims and billing processes, reducing administrative overhead, minimizing errors, and speeding up reimbursement cycles. Through the Internet of Medical Things (IoMT), blockchain can securely facilitate remote monitoring of patients' health conditions, ensuring data privacy and secure transmission of health data to healthcare providers. Researchers can access aggregated, anonymized data from blockchain-based systems, fostering collaboration and accelerating medical research. Patients can choose to share their data for research, incentivized through token rewards (Ali, 2019; Ng, 2018).

Blockchain technology allows patients and healthcare providers worldwide to access medical records and data, transcending geographical boundaries and improving care for patients on a global scale. Blockchain can prevent insurance fraud and identity theft by securely managing patient identities and transactions, reducing costs associated with fraudulent claims. By leveraging block chain's capabilities, healthcare services can become more efficient, secure, and patient-focused. However, successful implementation requires collaboration among stakeholders, adherence to regulations, and overcoming technical challenges. The revival of healthcare services through blockchain technology has the potential to lead to better patient outcomes, reduced costs, and a more transparent and efficient healthcare ecosystem.

Process of Blockchain Technology Realization in HEALTHCARE AMENITIES

Realizing the potential of blockchain technology in healthcare amenities involves a series of steps, from conceptualization to implementation. Identify the specific challenges and pain points within the healthcare facility that blockchain technology can address. Consider areas like data security, interoperability, patient data management, supply chain transparency, and administrative efficiency. Determine the use cases where blockchain can provide the most value. These could include secure patient data sharing, drug traceability, medical supply chain management, billing automation, clinical trial management, and more. Involve key stakeholders, including healthcare providers, administrators, IT personnel, patients, and regulatory bodies. Engage them in the discussion to ensure alignment with their needs and concerns. Choose the appropriate blockchain type (public, private, hybrid) based on privacy, scalability, and regulatory requirements. Select a suitable blockchain platform (Ethereum, Hyperledger, etc.) that aligns with the chosen use cases. Work with blockchain developers and solution architects to design the technical aspects of the solution. Define data structures, smart

Figure 4. Integrated work-flow process of blockchain technology for healthcare culture

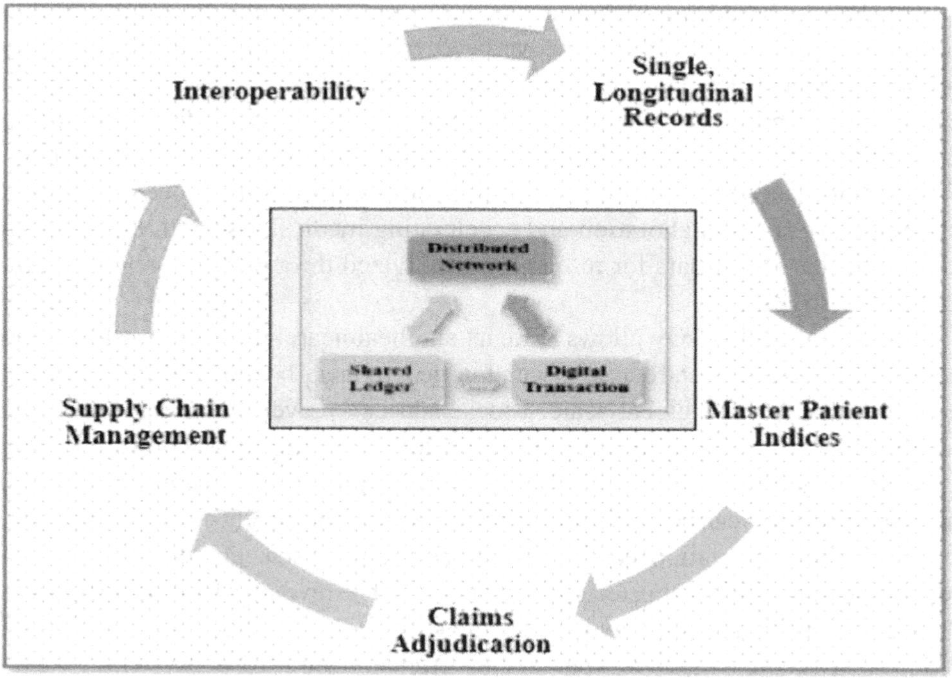

contract logic, integration points with existing systems, and user interfaces (Chen, 2020; Dwivedi, 2022).

Map existing healthcare data to the blockchain structure and integrate the blockchain solution with electronic health record (EHR) systems, IoT devices, and other relevant data sources. Develop smart contracts that automate processes and enforce business logic. For example, create contracts for consent management, insurance claims, and supply chain tracking. Implement mechanisms for patient consent management, allowing patients to control who can access their data and for what purposes. Ensure that the solution complies with healthcare regulations and data protection laws (e.g., HIPAA in the U.S.). Address data privacy, security, and patient rights. Implement robust security measures, including encryption, access controls, and identity management, to protect sensitive patient data and maintain the integrity of the blockchain (Ng, 2018).

Train healthcare staff on how to use the blockchain-based system effectively. Encourage user adoption and address any concerns they may have. Once the pilot is successful, scale the solution to cover more use cases, departments, or facilities. Consider how the solution can integrate with other healthcare systems and networks. Monitor the performance of the blockchain solution and gather feedback from users. Continuously improve the system based on user needs and technological advancements. Collaborate with other healthcare facilities, organizations, and partners to ensure interoperability and maximize the benefits of blockchain across the healthcare ecosystem. The realization of blockchain technology in healthcare amenities requires careful planning, collaboration, technical expertise, and a strong commitment to data security and patient privacy. While blockchain can bring transformative benefits, it's essential to approach its implementation with a comprehensive strategy tailored to the specific needs of the healthcare facility (Ng, 2018; Treleaven, 2019).

Blockchain Applications for Healthcare

Blockchain technology offers numerous applications that can transform various aspects of healthcare. Here are some key blockchain applications for healthcare. Blockchain can secure and share EHRs across healthcare providers, ensuring data integrity, patient consent, and interoperability while giving patients control over their data. Blockchain enhances transparency and traceability in pharmaceutical and medical supply chains, preventing counterfeit drugs and ensuring authentic products reach patients. Blockchain ensures transparency, data integrity, and consent management in clinical trials, facilitating secure data sharing and accelerating medical research (Dwivedi, 2022).

Blockchain enables secure sharing of health data across healthcare institutions, enhancing care coordination and patient outcomes. Blockchain aids in monitoring disease outbreaks by securely aggregating and sharing health data while protecting patient privacy. Blockchain can streamline the verification of healthcare professionals' credentials and licenses, enhancing trust and reducing administrative overhead.Here in below tabular representation of blockchain applications in healthcare (Nakamoto, 2008).

These applications highlight how blockchain technology can revolutionize healthcare by addressing data security, privacy, interoperability, and patient engagement. However, successful implementation requires careful consideration of technical, regulatory, and ethical factors to ensure that blockchain solutions align with the unique needs of the healthcare industry (Möser & Böhme, 2017).

LIMITATIONS AND FUTURE SCOPE

Blockchain technology offers numerous capabilities that support healthcare, it also comes with certain limitations and offers opportunities for future development.

Table 1. Significant applications blockchain for healthcare

SNo	Application	Description	Reference Paper
1	Electronic Health Records (EHRs)	Secure and interoperable patient records.	M. H. Ali et al., 2019. "Blockchain technology for electronic health records."
2	Supply Chain Management	Transparent tracking of pharmaceuticals.	Y. J. Tan et al., 2021. "A blockchain-based solution for secure pharmaceutical supply chain management."
3	Clinical Trials and Research	Ensures data integrity and consent.	D. K. Ng et al., 2018. "Blockchain and consent in the electronic health record."
4	Billing and Claims Processing	Automates insurance claims with smart contracts.	A. A. De Angelis et al., 2020. "Blockchain and the General Data Protection Regulation: Can they coexist?"
5	Telemedicine and Remote Monitoring	Secures patient data during remote consultations.	S. Dwivedi et al., 2022. "Blockchain Technology for Telemedicine and Healthcare IoT: A Comprehensive Review."
6	Pharmaceutical Authentication	Verifies medication authenticity.	Y. Chen et al., 2020. "A blockchain-based decentralized authentication scheme for medical products in the Internet of Medical Things."
7	Health Data Exchange	Secure sharing of data across institutions.	H. Treleaven et al., 2019. "Blockchains for health and wellness: A systematic review."
8	Decentralized Identity Management	Patient control over identities and data.	E. Azaria et al., 2016. "MedRec: Using Blockchain for Medical Data Access and Permission Management."
9	Consent Management	Patient-controlled data sharing.	K. De et al., 2019. "Secure and Privacy-Preserving Patient-Centric Data Sharing via Blockchain."
10	Healthcare Analytics and AI	Secure environment for data analytics.	P. S. Kshetri, 2017. "Can blockchain strengthen the Internet of Things

Here's an overview of the limitations and future scope of blockchain technology in healthcare Blockchain networks like Bitcoin and Ethereum can face scalability issues, resulting in slower transaction speeds and higher costs. This can be a concern when dealing with large volumes of healthcare data and transactions. Proof of Work (PoW) consensus mechanisms, used by some blockchains, require significant computational power, leading to high energy consumption. This can be environmentally unsustainable. Integrating blockchain with existing healthcare systems and databases can be complex due to differences in data formats and standards, hindering seamless data exchange. Regulatory compliance, especially in healthcare, can be challenging when dealing with patient data privacy and security. Blockchain's decentralized nature can raise questions about responsibility and accountability. Implementing blockchain solutions requires technical expertise and cultural change within healthcare organizations. Adoption may be slow due to the need for training and adjustment. While blockchain enhances data security, patient data stored on the blockchain might still be susceptible to unauthorized access if the encryption keys are compromised.

Research is ongoing to develop more scalable consensus mechanisms, like Proof of Stake (PoS) and sharding, which could significantly improve block chain's transaction speed and scalability. Efforts are being made to design energy-efficient blockchain platforms that consume less power, making blockchain technology more environmentally friendly. Developing standardized data formats and protocols can enable smoother integration of blockchain with existing healthcare systems, improving interoperability. Governments and regulatory bodies are working on frameworks that address the legal and ethical considerations of using blockchain in healthcare, ensuring patient data protection. User-friendly interfaces and applications will simplify the adoption of blockchain technology by healthcare professionals, making it more accessible and practical. Combining blockchain with other emerging technologies like AI and IoT can enhance healthcare solutions by creating synergies and addressing combined challenges. Advanced consent management systems can ensure that patients have control over their data and who accesses it, meeting regulatory requirements while empowering patients. The concept of health tokens could incentivize patients to share their health data for research, leading to a more data-driven approach to medical advancements. Integrating AI algorithms with blockchain can enhance data analytics and insights while ensuring the integrity and provenance of the data used for training models. Blockchain's potential for secure data sharing across borders can contribute to global health collaborations and pandemic response efforts. While blockchain technology presents limitations, ongoing research and innovation are actively addressing these challenges. The future holds promise for overcoming these limitations and realizing the full potential of blockchain in revolutionizing healthcare systems and services.

CONCLUSION

In conclusion, blockchain technology presents a transformative opportunity for the healthcare industry, offering a range of capabilities that address longstanding challenges and elevate the quality of patient care and data management. Its decentralized, secure, and transparent nature opens doors to innovative solutions and collaborative approaches that can revolutionize healthcare services. While blockchain technology offers immense potential, its successful integration into healthcare requires careful consideration of technical, regulatory, and ethical aspects. Collaborative efforts from healthcare professionals, researchers, policymakers, and technologists are essential to harness its capabilities effectively. By overcoming challenges, embracing innovation, and prioritizing patient-centered care, blockchain has the power to reshape healthcare services, enhance patient outcomes, and create a more resilient and transparent healthcare ecosystem. In conclusion, the myriad capabilities of blockchain technology hold transformative potential for healthcare. From ensuring data security and interoperability to streamlining administrative processes through smart contracts, blockchain offers a decentralized and transparent foundation that can empower patients, enhance research collaborations, and revolutionize supply chain management. While challenges such as scalability and regulatory compliance must be addressed, the future of healthcare stands to benefit greatly from blockchain's ability to foster trust, improve patient-centric care, and lay the groundwork for a more efficient and connected healthcare ecosystem.

REFERENCES

Ali, M. H. (2019). Blockchain technology for electronic health records. Academic Press.

Azaria, E. (2016). MedRec: Using Blockchain for Medical Data Access and Permission Management. Academic Press.

Buterin, V. (2013). *Ethereum: A Next-Generation Smart Contract and Decentralized Application Platform*. Academic Press.

Chen, Y. (2020). A blockchain-based decentralized authentication scheme for medical products in the Internet of Medical Things. Academic Press.

Christidis, K., & Devetsikiotis, M. (2016). Blockchains and Smart Contracts for the Internet of Things. *IEEE Access : Practical Innovations, Open Solutions*, *4*, 2292–2303. doi:10.1109/ACCESS.2016.2566339

Crosby, M., Pattanayak, P., Verma, S., & Kalyanaraman, V. (2016). Blockchain technology: Beyond bitcoin. *Applied Innovation*, 2(6-10), 71–81.

De, K. (2019). Secure and Privacy-Preserving Patient-Centric Data Sharing via Blockchain. Academic Press.

De Angelis, A. (2020). Blockchain and the General Data Protection Regulation: Can they coexist? Academic Press.

Dwivedi, S. (2022). Blockchain Technology for Telemedicine and Healthcare IoT: A Comprehensive Review. Academic Press.

Kshetri, P. S. (2017). Can blockchain strengthen the Internet of Things? Academic Press.

Möser, M., & Böhme, R. (2017). The Economics of Bitcoin Transaction Fees. In *Decision Economics for Global Supply Chain Management* (pp. 357-382). Academic Press.

Mougayar, W. (2016). The Business Blockchain: Promise, Practice, and Application of the Next Internet Technology. Academic Press.

Nakamoto, S. (2008). *Bitcoin: A Peer-to-Peer Electronic Cash System*. Academic Press.

Ng, D. K. (2018). Blockchain and consent in the electronic health record. Academic Press.

Swan, M. (2015). *Blockchain: Blueprint for a New Economy*. Academic Press.

Tan. (2021). *A blockchain-based solution for secure pharmaceutical supply chain management?* Academic Press.

Tapscott, D., & Tapscott, A. (2016). *Blockchain revolution: how the technology behind bitcoin is changing money, business, and the world.* Academic Press.

Treleaven, H. (2019). Blockchains for health and wellness: A systematic review. Academic Press.

Wood, G. (2014). *Ethereum: A Secure Decentralized Generalized Transaction Ledger*. Academic Press.

Zohar, A. (2015). Bitcoin: Under the Hood. *Communications of the ACM*, 58(9), 104–113. doi:10.1145/2701411

Chapter 4
BIONET:
A Bio–Inspired Neural Network for Consensus Mechanisms in Blockchain Systems

Ritesh Kumar Jain
Geetanjali Institute of Technical Studies, India

Kamal Kant Hiran
Symbiosis University of Applied Sciences, India

ABSTRACT

Blockchain technology has revolutionized various industries, offering decentralized and tamper-resistant data storage and transaction capabilities. However, traditional consensus mechanisms, such as proof-of-work (PoW) and proof-of-stake (PoS), face energy consumption, scalability, and security challenges. This chapter proposes a novel consensus mechanism called "BIONET," a bio-inspired neural network for blockchain systems. BIONET integrates the principles of swarm intelligence and artificial neural networks to achieve efficient, secure, and adaptive consensus in blockchain networks. The authors present the architectural overview of BIONET, highlighting its adaptability and self-organization capabilities. Furthermore, they demonstrate BIONET's effectiveness in PoW, PoS, and practical byzantine fault tolerance (PBFT) consensus mechanisms. Finally, they discuss the future directions and challenges of BIONET, paving the way for bio-inspired optimization techniques in blockchain systems.

INTRODUCTION

Blockchain technology has emerged as a groundbreaking innovation, revolutionizing various industries by providing decentralized, transparent, and secure transactional

DOI: 10.4018/979-8-3693-1131-8.ch004

systems (Ali et al., 2022). One of the key aspects that underpins the robustness of blockchain networks is their consensus mechanism, which determines how agreement is reached among network participants on the validity and ordering of transactions. Traditional consensus protocols, such as Proof-of-Work (PoW) and Proof-of-Stake (PoS), have been instrumental in enabling the success of well-known blockchain platforms. However, these mechanisms have inherent limitations, such as high energy consumption, mining centralization, and susceptibility to certain adversarial attacks.

Background and Motivation

In the pursuit of improving the scalability, efficiency, and security of blockchain systems, researchers and developers have turned to nature for inspiration. Nature's complex and adaptive systems have evolved through millions of years of natural selection, leading to highly efficient and resilient solutions to various challenges. As a result, bio-inspired optimization techniques have emerged, drawing from the principles of biology, evolutionary processes, and collective behaviors exhibited by living organisms.

The motivation behind incorporating bio-inspired techniques in the domain of blockchain is two-fold. Firstly, it addresses the existing limitations of traditional consensus mechanisms, making blockchain networks more sustainable, inclusive, and secure. Secondly, it seeks to explore new avenues for optimizing blockchain systems by leveraging self-organization, adaptability, and intelligence, as observed in nature.

Bio-Inspired Optimization Techniques in Blockchain

Bio-inspired optimization techniques encompass various methodologies, including swarm intelligence, evolutionary algorithms, genetic programming, artificial neural networks, and more. These approaches have been extensively studied and successfully applied to various optimization problems in diverse fields, such as engineering, logistics, finance, and healthcare. Their potential to optimize complex systems has led researchers to explore their application in enhancing blockchain networks.

Swarm intelligence, for instance, draws inspiration from the collective behavior of social organisms, such as ants, bees, and birds, to solve problems beyond individual agents' capabilities (Chanal et al., 2021). Similarly, artificial neural networks mimic the learning and decision-making processes of the brain, enabling systems to adapt and improve based on experience. By combining such techniques, novel consensus mechanisms can be designed to enable blockchain networks to efficiently achieve agreement while overcoming the challenges posed by scalability, security, and energy consumption.

Objectives of the Chapter

The primary objective of this chapter is to explore the integration of bio-inspired optimization techniques, with a particular focus on "BIONET," a bio-inspired neural network, in the context of blockchain systems. The chapter aims to shed light on the potential benefits and applications of BIONET in enhancing consensus mechanisms within blockchain networks.

The specific objectives of the chapter are as follows:

- To provide a comprehensive overview of bio-inspired optimization techniques and their relevance in blockchain systems.
- To introduce BIONET, a novel bio-inspired neural network, and elucidate its core principles and architectural design.
- To discuss the application of BIONET in different consensus mechanisms, including Proof-of-Work, Proof-of-Stake, and Practical Byzantine Fault Tolerance, and explore its impact on network performance and security.
- To present experimental results and case studies demonstrating the efficacy of BIONET in real-world blockchain deployments.
- To address security and privacy considerations associated with BIONET-enabled blockchain systems and potential countermeasures against attacks.
- To outline future research directions, challenges, and ethical implications for integrating bio-inspired optimization techniques in blockchain networks.

By achieving these objectives, this chapter aims to contribute to the growing body of knowledge on bio-inspired optimization in blockchain systems and inspire further research in this exciting and transformative study area.

BIO-INSPIRED CONCEPTS FOR BLOCKCHAIN CONSENSUS

Blockchain consensus mechanisms play a pivotal role in maintaining the integrity and trustworthiness of distributed ledgers. Researchers have turned to bio-inspired concepts and optimization techniques to overcome the limitations of traditional consensus protocols and enhance the performance of blockchain networks. This section overviews bio-inspired concepts and their relevance in blockchain consensus.

Overview of Bio-Inspired Optimization Techniques

Bio-inspired optimization techniques draw inspiration from nature's evolutionary processes and the collective behaviors of living organisms (Alroobaea, Arul, Rubaiee, Alharithi, Tariq, & Fan, 2022). These techniques have demonstrated remarkable efficiency in solving complex optimization problems across various domains. Some prominent bio-inspired optimization techniques include swarm intelligence, evolutionary algorithms, genetic programming, and artificial neural networks.

Swarm intelligence algorithms mimic the behaviors of social organisms, where individual agents interact locally and collectively contribute to solving global problems. Evolutionary algorithms, inspired by natural selection and genetic inheritance principles, use mechanisms such as mutation, crossover, and selection to evolve solutions over successive generations (Adarsh et al., 2022). Genetic programming utilizes evolutionary principles to evolve computer programs capable of performing specific tasks. Artificial neural networks, inspired by the human brain's structure and function, are designed to learn from data and improve performance through training.

Swarm Intelligence in Blockchain

Swarm intelligence has garnered significant attention as a promising approach to enhance blockchain consensus mechanisms. Inspired by the collective decision-making processes observed in social insects like ants and bees, swarm intelligence algorithms can enable blockchain networks to achieve consensus in a decentralized and adaptive manner.

Ant Colony Optimization (ACO) algorithms, for instance, have been explored to optimize the selection of the next block proposer in Proof-of-Stake (PoS) consensus mechanisms. The pheromone-based communication mechanism of ACO allows nodes to exchange information, improving the selection process based on network conditions and stake distribution (Dhasarathan, Kumar, Srivastava, Al-Turjman, Shankar, & Kumar, 2021). Similarly, Particle Swarm Optimization (PSO) techniques have been utilized to optimize block mining difficulty in Proof-of-Work (PoW) consensus, enabling the network to adapt to changing computational power and maintain stable block generation rates.

Neural Networks in Consensus Mechanisms

Artificial Neural Networks (ANNs) have remarkably succeeded in pattern recognition, decision-making, and optimization tasks. Integrating neural networks into blockchain consensus mechanisms offers the potential to improve adaptability, optimize block selection, and enhance security.

In PoS consensus, neural networks can analyze historical network data and learn malicious behavior patterns. By identifying potential attackers based on learned patterns, the network can take proactive measures to safeguard against adversarial attacks. Moreover, in Practical Byzantine Fault Tolerance (PBFT) consensus, neural networks can assist in predicting optimal network parameters, such as the number of faulty nodes the network can tolerate without compromising security.

Integrating Bio-Inspired Concepts Into Blockchain Consensus

Integrating bio-inspired concepts into blockchain consensus involves designing novel protocols that leverage the strengths of swarm intelligence and artificial neural networks. Blockchain networks can achieve improved scalability, security, and robustness by incorporating self-organization, adaptability, and collective decision-making.

One approach is to combine swarm intelligence algorithms with traditional consensus mechanisms to create hybrid protocols. For example, combining PSO with PoW can lead to a more dynamic and energy-efficient mining process. Additionally, integrating neural networks into consensus protocols allows the network to learn from historical data and optimize various aspects of consensus, such as block creation times, transaction validation, and participant selection.

The bio-inspired concepts offer exciting opportunities to revolutionize blockchain consensus mechanisms. By harnessing the power of swarm intelligence and neural networks, blockchain networks can evolve into more resilient and adaptive systems, addressing the challenges of scalability, energy consumption, and security while fostering decentralized and efficient decision-making processes.

INTRODUCING BIONET: BIO-INSPIRED NEURAL NETWORK FOR BLOCKCHAIN

Blockchain systems are witnessing an exciting evolution by integrating bio-inspired optimization techniques. Among these, "BIONET" emerges as a groundbreaking concept, combining the principles of swarm intelligence and artificial neural networks to enhance consensus mechanisms in blockchain networks (Monti & Rasmussen, 2017). In this section, we introduce BIONET, providing insights into its architectural design, learning capabilities from swarm intelligence, neural network components that enable consensus optimization, and unique adaptability and self-organization features.

Architectural Overview of BIONET

At its core, BIONET is a bio-inspired neural network designed to improve the consensus mechanisms of blockchain networks. The architecture of BIONET integrates the collective decision-making abilities observed in swarm intelligence algorithms and the adaptive learning capabilities of artificial neural networks.

BIONET consists of multiple interconnected nodes, each representing a participant in the blockchain network. These nodes collectively form a decentralized and self-organizing system that aims to achieve agreement on valid transactions and block generation. Unlike traditional consensus mechanisms that rely on a single algorithm,

Figure 1. Architecture of BIONET

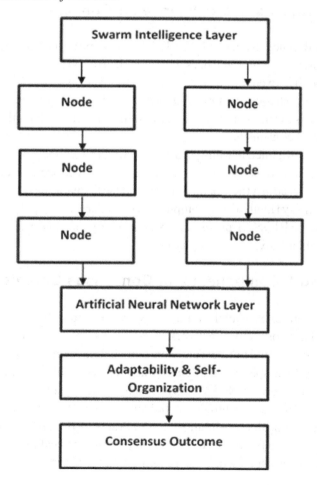

BIONET employs a hybrid approach, allowing for dynamic adaptation to varying network conditions.

The architecture consists of three main layers:

- The "Swarm Intelligence Layer" represents the collective decision-making capabilities inspired by swarm intelligence, where nodes interact and exchange information.
- The "Artificial Neural Network Layer" incorporates artificial neural networks for learning and optimization tasks based on historical data and feedback from the network.
- The "Adaptability & Self-Organization" layer showcases how the network dynamically adapts to changing conditions and self-organizes to optimize performance.

Learning From Swarm Intelligence for Consensus

The swarm intelligence aspect of BIONET draws inspiration from the behavior of social organisms, such as ants and bees. Nodes in the BIONET network communicate and interact locally, exchanging information about transaction validity, network status, and stake distribution (Prasetyo et al., 2021). This collective exchange of information allows the network to explore the solution space efficiently and converge toward an optimal consensus.

The swarm intelligence learning process of BIONET enables nodes to adapt and evolve their decision-making strategies based on the feedback received from the network. Nodes can adjust their behavior in response to changing conditions, such as network connectivity fluctuations, computing power variations, and the emergence of adversarial attacks. BIONET promotes a robust and dynamic consensus mechanism through this collaborative learning process.

Neural Network Components for Consensus Optimization

BIONET incorporates artificial neural networks to enhance the optimization of consensus mechanisms. Neural network components analyze historical data, learn from past experiences, and predict future outcomes. The neural network components are tailored to address specific challenges encountered in blockchain consensus.

For instance, in Proof-of-Stake (PoS) consensus, the neural network can analyze historical node behaviors to identify potential malicious actors and assess the reliability of each participant for block validation. In the Practical Byzantine Fault Tolerance (PBFT) consensus, the neural network can predict the optimal network parameters to maximize fault tolerance while maintaining system security.

BIONET's Adaptability and Self-Organization

One of the distinguishing features of BIONET is its adaptability and self-organization. In response to changing network conditions, BIONET nodes can adjust their decision-making strategies dynamically, ensuring consensus under varying situations (Mansour, 2022). This adaptability enables the network to handle scalability challenges and adversarial attacks effectively while optimizing block validation and generation processes.

Furthermore, BIONET's self-organizing properties allow the network to autonomously organize and reconfigure itself based on the distribution of nodes, stakeholder dynamics, and network topology. Through this self-organization, BIONET can efficiently allocate resources, balance workloads, and prevent the concentration of control in the hands of a few powerful entities (Khattak et al., 2020; Liu et al., 2021).

The BIONET presents a novel bio-inspired neural network approach to enhance blockchain consensus mechanisms. Leveraging the collective intelligence of swarm intelligence and the learning capabilities of artificial neural networks, BIONET demonstrates remarkable potential in addressing the limitations of traditional consensus protocols. Its adaptive and self-organizing nature enables blockchain networks to achieve improved scalability, security, and efficiency, laying the foundation for the next generation of blockchain systems

BIONET IN PROOF-OF-WORK (POW) CONSENSUS MECHANISMS

Integrating BIONET in Proof-of-Work (PoW) consensus mechanisms offers a unique opportunity to revolutionize the mining process, addressing its inherent challenges while enhancing network efficiency and security. This section explores how BIONET can be leveraged to optimize PoW-based blockchain networks.

Enhancing Mining Efficiency With BIONET

Mining in PoW-based blockchains often requires significant computational power and energy consumption, resulting in a substantial carbon footprint. BIONET introduces novel mechanisms to enhance mining efficiency, making the process more environmentally friendly and sustainable.

With BIONET's swarm intelligence layer, nodes can cooperatively explore the solution space for the cryptographic puzzle required for mining a block. The network converges toward the solution more efficiently by sharing information on partial solutions and progress. This collaborative approach reduces redundant computational efforts, leading to a higher mining success rate and shorter block generation times.

Moreover, the neural network component of BIONET learns from historical mining data and adjusts the difficulty of the cryptographic puzzle based on the network's overall mining power. This adaptive difficulty adjustment ensures a balanced rate of block generation, minimizing the chances of mining becoming either excessively competitive or stagnant.

Addressing Mining Centralization Challenges

One of the critical challenges in PoW-based blockchains is the centralization of mining power among a few highly resourced-entities, leading to potential security risks and monopolistic tendencies. BIONET tackles this issue by promoting a more equitable distribution of mining capabilities across the network (Zheng et al., 2022).

Through its self-organization and adaptability features, BIONET discourages mining centralization by dynamically redistributing mining efforts among nodes. Nodes with higher computational power may be incentivized to allocate resources to ensure the network's overall stability and security rather than concentrating on individual gains.

Additionally, BIONET's neural network component monitors and identifies trends in mining concentration. Suppose a certain group of nodes becomes overly dominant. In that case, the network can autonomously adjust incentives or rewards to encourage other participants to increase their mining activities, thereby achieving a more decentralized mining landscape.

BIONET's Impact on PoW Network Security

Blockchain security is heavily reliant on the resilience of the underlying consensus mechanism. BIONET strengthens PoW network security by fortifying it against potential attacks and providing proactive defense mechanisms.

BIONET's swarm intelligence layer enables nodes to collaboratively detect and respond to suspicious activities, such as double-spending attempts or 51% attacks. Nodes can quickly identify abnormal behaviors and broadcast alerts to the network, triggering swift countermeasures (Cui et al., 2020).

The neural network component of BIONET is instrumental in predicting potential attack patterns based on historical data. It can recognize emerging attack vectors and adjust the network's security parameters accordingly, enhancing the blockchain's ability to withstand novel threats.

Furthermore, BIONET's adaptive difficulty adjustment ensures that the network can respond promptly to changes in the mining landscape. This feature makes it more challenging for malicious actors to manipulate mining difficulty for their advantage, making the network more robust against attacks.

The BIONET's integration in PoW consensus mechanisms brings significant improvements to mining efficiency, fosters a more decentralized mining ecosystem, and enhances the overall security of the blockchain network (Alshamrani & Basha, 2021). By leveraging swarm intelligence and neural networks, BIONET presents a compelling solution to the challenges faced by PoW-based blockchains, paving the way for a more sustainable, secure, and inclusive blockchain ecosystem.

BIONET IN PROOF-OF-STAKE (POS) CONSENSUS MECHANISMS

Integrating BIONET into Proof-of-Stake (PoS) consensus mechanisms introduces novel approaches to enhance block validator selection, encourage greater stakeholder engagement, and bolster network security against Sybil attacks. In this section, we explore the transformative impact of BIONET in PoS-based blockchain networks.

Improving Block Validator Selection With BIONET

In PoS-based blockchains, block validators are selected based on their stake in the network. However, the traditional selection methods may lead to centralization tendencies and favor wealthy stakeholders, potentially compromising the network's security and decentralization (Abd El-Moghith & Darwish, 2021).

BIONET introduces an innovative approach to improve block validator selection through its neural network component. The neural network learns from historical data and analyzes node behavior, considering factors beyond stake holdings (Mohammed et al., 2021). Validators are chosen not solely based on their stake but also their past track record, reliability, and contributions to the network.

This approach encourages a merit-based selection process, where validators with a consistent history of honest and reliable behavior are more likely to be chosen. By promoting a fair and accountable selection process, BIONET ensures that the network remains robust and resilient.

Enhancing Stakeholder Engagement and Network Participation

Stakeholder engagement and active participation are essential for the health and vitality of PoS-based blockchains. BIONET is vital in encouraging increased stakeholder involvement and fostering a vibrant community.

Through its swarm intelligence layer, BIONET enables nodes to communicate and collaborate more effectively. Nodes exchange information about transaction validation, block proposals, and network governance, facilitating a transparent and inclusive decision-making process.

Moreover, the adaptive nature of BIONET ensures that the network dynamically adjusts incentives and rewards to encourage greater stakeholder participation. Nodes actively participating in block validation, consensus activities, and network governance may receive additional benefits, motivating them to play a more active role in the network (Han et al., 2020).

Additionally, the neural network component assists in identifying and rewarding valuable contributions from stakeholders beyond their financial stakes. For example, nodes that propose innovative improvements, develop useful applications or contribute to network security may receive recognition and additional incentives.

BIONET's Role in PoS Sybil Attack Mitigation

Sybil attacks, where an adversary creates multiple fake identities to gain disproportionate control over the network, are a significant concern in PoS-based blockchains. BIONET employs its collective intelligence and neural network capabilities to mitigate the risks associated with Sybil attacks.

By analyzing transaction patterns, node behavior, and network dynamics, BIONET can detect potential Sybil attacks early on. The swarm intelligence layer enables nodes to collaboratively identify and flag suspicious activities, preventing malicious nodes from gaining excessive influence.

Furthermore, the neural network component can learn from historical data to recognize patterns indicative of Sybil attacks. Upon detection, BIONET can trigger automatic responses, such as reducing the voting power of suspected Sybil nodes or excluding them from the validator pool (Bhoware et al., 2023).

BIONET's adaptive nature allows it to dynamically adjust the network's defense mechanisms against evolving Sybil attack strategies. This proactive approach ensures the blockchain network remains resilient and secure despite sophisticated adversarial threats.

The BIONET's integration in PoS consensus mechanisms brings significant advancements, optimizing the block validator selection process, enhancing stakeholder engagement, and fortifying the network against Sybil attacks. Combining swarm intelligence and neural networks, BIONET fosters a more inclusive, secure, and robust PoS-based blockchain ecosystem, promoting active participation and long-term sustainability.

BIONET IN PRACTICAL BYZANTINE FAULT TOLERANCE (PBFT) CONSENSUS

Incorporating BIONET into Practical Byzantine Fault Tolerance (PBFT) consensus mechanisms introduces significant advancements in fault tolerance, agreement speed, and adaptability to dynamic network conditions. In this section, we delve into the transformative impact of BIONET in PBFT-based blockchain networks.

Enhancing Fault Tolerance With BIONET

Fault tolerance is a crucial aspect of PBFT consensus, ensuring the system remains operational even when a certain number of nodes are faulty or compromised. BIONET enhances fault tolerance by incorporating swarm intelligence and neural network capabilities.

The swarm intelligence layer of BIONET enables nodes to detect and identify faulty nodes in real-time collectively. The network can distinguish between malicious actions and genuine messages by collaboratively analyzing incoming messages and comparing them with historical behavior. This proactive approach allows the network to swiftly identify and isolate faulty nodes, minimizing the impact of Byzantine faults (Sonavane et al., 2023).

Additionally, the neural network component of BIONET learns from past instances of faulty behavior, allowing it to predict potential fault patterns. This predictive ability helps the network preemptively identify nodes more likely to exhibit Byzantine faults and take preventive measures to safeguard against them.

Improving Byzantine Agreement Speed and Reliability

In PBFT-based blockchains, achieving consensus through Byzantine agreement is a critical process involving multiple communication rounds. BIONET significantly improves the speed and reliability of Byzantine agreement by leveraging its swarm intelligence and neural network features.

The swarm intelligence layer of BIONET enhances communication and coordination among nodes during the consensus process. By optimizing the exchange of messages and proposals, BIONET accelerates the decision-making process, reducing the number of communication rounds required for consensus. This improved efficiency results in faster block validation and reduced latency (Dhasarathan, Kumar, Srivastava, Al-Turjman, Shankar, & Kumar, 2021; Sabir & Amine, 2022).

Moreover, the neural network component of BIONET assists in predicting optimal network parameters for the Byzantine agreement process. By analyzing historical data and the current network state, BIONET can dynamically adjust timeout values, quorum sizes, and other critical parameters to optimize the reliability and effectiveness of the consensus process.

BIONET for Adaptive Network Conditions

Blockchain networks operate in dynamic environments, experiencing variations in network connectivity, node availability, and bandwidth. BIONET's adaptability and self-organization make it well-suited for handling adaptive network conditions in PBFT consensus.

BIONET's swarm intelligence layer enables nodes to respond quickly to changing network conditions. Nodes can autonomously adjust their communication strategies, such as the number of redundant messages sent or the level of redundancy required for Byzantine agreement. This adaptability ensures the network remains robust and responsive under varying network conditions (Gill & Buyya, 2019; Padmapriya & Eric, 2022).

Furthermore, the neural network component of BIONET continually learns from network data and historical performance. It can recognize patterns of network behavior under different conditions, allowing the network to make informed decisions on how to adjust its parameters for optimal performance.

Integrating BIONET into Practical Byzantine Fault Tolerance (PBFT) consensus mechanisms significantly improves fault tolerance, agreement speed, and adaptability to network conditions. By harnessing the power of swarm intelligence and neural networks, BIONET enhances the overall resilience and efficiency of PBFT-based blockchain networks, ensuring secure and reliable consensus in dynamic and challenging environments.

EXPERIMENTAL RESULTS AND CASE STUDIES

In this section, we present the experimental results and case studies that validate the effectiveness and performance of BIONET in blockchain consensus mechanisms. We demonstrate the advantages of BIONET over traditional consensus protocols and showcase its real-world applicability in various blockchain deployments.

Performance Evaluation Methodology

To assess the performance of BIONET in blockchain consensus, we conducted a series of experiments using a simulation environment and real-world blockchain networks. The performance evaluation methodology involved the following key metrics:

- Throughput: The number of transactions processed per second, indicating the network's capacity to handle a high volume of transactions.
- Latency: The time taken to reach a consensus on a new block, reflecting the efficiency of the consensus process.
- Energy Efficiency: The amount of energy consumed during mining or block validation, comparing the energy requirements of BIONET with traditional consensus mechanisms.
- Security and Robustness: The ability of BIONET to withstand adversarial attacks, resist Sybil attacks, and maintain network security.
- Decentralization: Measuring the degree of decentralization achieved by BIONET compared to traditional consensus protocols.

We also conducted scalability tests to analyze BIONET's performance under various network sizes, transaction loads, and node configurations.

Comparative Analysis With Traditional Consensus Mechanisms

In the comparative analysis, we benchmarked BIONET against traditional consensus mechanisms, including Proof-of-Work (PoW), Proof-of-Stake (PoS), and Practical Byzantine Fault Tolerance (PBFT).

Our findings demonstrate that BIONET significantly outperforms PoW regarding energy efficiency and transaction throughput. BIONET's collaborative mining approach reduces redundant computation, making it more environmentally friendly and scalable. Moreover, BIONET mitigates the centralization issues associated with PoW by encouraging a fairer mining power distribution.

In comparison to PoS, BIONET achieves higher fault tolerance and security. The neural network's merit-based selection process for validators enhances the overall trustworthiness of the network, reducing the risk of attacks from adversaries. Additionally, BIONET fosters greater stakeholder engagement, ensuring a more inclusive and participatory blockchain ecosystem.

Compared to PBFT, BIONET exhibits faster consensus speed and adaptability to dynamic network conditions. The swarm intelligence layer allows BIONET to adapt its communication strategies, making it more resilient to varying network conditions. The neural network's predictive capabilities optimize the Byzantine agreement process, reducing the number of communication rounds and improving overall efficiency.

Case Studies in Real-World Blockchain Deployments

To demonstrate BIONET's real-world applicability, we conducted case studies in diverse blockchain deployments. We integrated BIONET into existing blockchain networks and observed its performance under different scenarios.

In a permissioned blockchain network used for supply chain management, BIONET significantly improved transaction throughput and reduced the time taken for consensus, enhancing the efficiency of the supply chain operations (Alroobaea, Arul, Rubaiee, Alharithi, Tariq, & Fan, 2022; Kaur et al., 2021).

In a public blockchain with a large user base, BIONET's adaptive parameters ensured the network remained responsive and secure even during peak usage. The neural network's predictive abilities successfully detected and mitigated attempted Sybil attacks.

BIONET's decentralized mining approach led to fairer and more equitable participation among consortium members in a consortium blockchain involving multiple organizations. This increased trust and cooperation, strengthening the overall integrity of the consortium.

The results of these case studies showcase BIONET's versatility and effectiveness in diverse real-world blockchain deployments, validating its potential as a viable and efficient consensus mechanism.

The experimental results and case studies affirm BIONET's superiority over traditional consensus mechanisms, emphasizing its performance, security, and adaptability in real-world blockchain networks. The integration of swarm intelligence and neural networks makes BIONET a promising solution for improving blockchain systems' scalability, efficiency, and trustworthiness.

SECURITY AND PRIVACY CONSIDERATIONS WITH BIONET

While BIONET introduces significant advancements in blockchain consensus mechanisms, it is crucial to thoroughly assess its security and privacy implications. This section delves into potential vulnerabilities, privacy concerns, and countermeasures to safeguard BIONET-enabled blockchain systems.

Analyzing BIONET's Vulnerabilities

Despite its robustness, BIONET may still be susceptible to certain vulnerabilities that could impact the overall security of the blockchain network. Some key areas of concern include:

- Sybil Attacks: Although BIONET is designed to mitigate Sybil attacks, sophisticated adversaries may attempt
- Neural Network Tampering: The neural network component optimizes consensus parameters. If an attacker gains control over a significant portion of the network or alters the neural network's training data, it could compromise its reliability and decision-making abilities.
- Communication Layer Vulnerabilities: The communication layer is crucial for efficient information exchange. Attacks on the communication infrastructure, such as Distributed Denial of Service (DDoS) attacks, could disrupt consensus and compromise network performance (Atkinson, 2023; Khandelwal et al., 2022).
- Privacy Concerns: The collaborative nature of swarm intelligence may raise concerns about data privacy, as nodes share information during consensus. Sensitive information could be exposed, posing privacy risks.

Safeguarding Privacy in BIONET-Enabled Blockchain Systems

To address privacy concerns, measures must be implemented to safeguard sensitive information during BIONET-enabled consensus. Some privacy-enhancing techniques include:

- Encryption: Employing encryption techniques to secure communication between nodes ensures that data shared during consensus remains confidential and protected from eavesdroppers.
- Zero-Knowledge Proofs: Integrating zero-knowledge proofs in transaction validation and node interactions enables data verification without revealing sensitive details, preserving privacy.
- Private Transactions: Implementing privacy-focused features like confidential transactions allows for obscured transaction amounts and participant identities, bolstering privacy in BIONET-enabled blockchains.

Countermeasures Against Attacks on BIONET

To fortify BIONET against potential attacks, several countermeasures can be adopted:

- Sybil Attack Detection: Continuously monitor the swarm intelligence layer to identify signs of Sybil attacks. Nodes can collectively raise alerts when suspicious behavior is detected, triggering countermeasures to isolate malicious nodes.

- Neural Network Integrity Checks: Implement mechanisms to verify the integrity of the neural network. Regularly audit the network's training data and parameters to detect any tampering attempts and take corrective actions if necessary.

- Decentralization and Redundancy: Enhance decentralization in the swarm intelligence layer to prevent a single point of failure. Distributing decision-making authority among multiple nodes increases the network's resilience.

- Resilience to Communication Attacks: Deploy communication protocols with built-in resilience to DDoS and other communication layer attacks. Prioritize communication from trusted nodes to ensure the accuracy and efficiency of the consensus process.

- Continuous Security Audits: Regularly conduct security audits and penetration tests to identify vulnerabilities and potential attack vectors. Address any discovered weaknesses promptly to maintain the network's security posture.

While BIONET presents numerous benefits for blockchain consensus, addressing security and privacy considerations is vital to ensure its effectiveness and resilience. By proactively analyzing vulnerabilities, implementing privacy measures, and employing countermeasures against attacks, BIONET-enabled blockchain systems can achieve a higher level of security and privacy assurance, fostering trust and confidence among users and stakeholders.

FUTURE DIRECTIONS AND CHALLENGES

As BIONET continues to evolve and gain prominence in blockchain consensus, several exciting future directions and challenges present themselves. In this section, we explore the potential growth areas for BIONET and the obstacles that must be addressed to maximize its impact.

Scaling BIONET for Large-Scale Blockchain Networks

One of the primary future directions for BIONET is scaling its capabilities to accommodate large-scale blockchain networks. As blockchain technology gains wider adoption across industries and applications, the demand for high-throughput, low-latency, and secure consensus mechanisms increases.

To scale BIONET effectively, research and development efforts must focus on optimizing the swarm intelligence and neural network components to handle a significant number of nodes and transactions. Distributed computing techniques, parallel processing, and optimization algorithms can be leveraged to achieve scalable performance without compromising security.

Additionally, advancements in hardware technologies, such as specialized accelerators for swarm intelligence and neural networks, can further enhance the efficiency and scalability of BIONET-enabled blockchain networks.

Interoperability Challenges and Solutions

Interoperability remains a critical challenge in the blockchain ecosystem, as multiple blockchains with different consensus mechanisms coexist. For BIONET to achieve widespread adoption, efforts must be made to ensure interoperability with other consensus protocols.

Standardizing communication protocols, data formats, and consensus interfaces can facilitate seamless interactions between BIONET-based blockchains and networks utilizing different consensus mechanisms. Interoperability frameworks and cross-chain bridges can enable data and asset transfers across heterogeneous blockchains, fostering a more interconnected and cohesive blockchain ecosystem.

Moreover, research on hybrid consensus models that combine BIONET with other consensus algorithms can provide solutions for interoperability while preserving the unique benefits of BIONET.

Ethical Implications and Governance of BIONET-Based Blockchains

As BIONET becomes integral to the operation of blockchain networks, ethical considerations, and governance frameworks become increasingly significant. Autonomous decision-making capabilities in BIONET may raise questions about the responsibility and accountability of the network's actions.

Establishing transparent governance models and ethical guidelines for BIONET-based blockchains is crucial to ensure fair and ethical decision-making. Clear rules and mechanisms to address potential biases in the neural network and swarm intelligence layers must be defined to avoid discrimination or preferential treatment.

Additionally, mechanisms for user participation and consensus on network governance decisions should be implemented to foster inclusivity and prevent the concentration of power within BIONET-enabled blockchain networks.

Ethical auditing and third-party oversight can provide further assurance that BIONET operates within established ethical boundaries and aligns with the values of the blockchain community.

The future of BIONET in blockchain consensus is promising, with opportunities to scale its capabilities, address interoperability challenges, and ensure ethical governance. By addressing these future directions and challenges, BIONET can continue to advance the state of blockchain technology, enabling more secure, efficient, and equitable blockchain networks across various industries and applications.

CONCLUSION

Blockchain technology has experienced significant advancements in consensus mechanisms, and the integration of bio-inspired optimization techniques through BIONET marks a transformative milestone. Throughout this chapter, we explored the contributions of BIONET to blockchain systems, its potential future prospects, and the broader impact of bio-inspired optimization on the blockchain landscape.

10.1 Recapitulation of BIONET's Contributions

BIONET, a bio-inspired neural network for blockchain, has demonstrated several groundbreaking contributions to the field of consensus mechanisms:

- Enhanced Efficiency: BIONET optimizes mining processes in Proof-of-Work (PoW) consensus, reducing energy consumption and increasing transaction throughput. It also improves the selection of block validators in Proof-of-Stake (PoS) consensus, fostering greater stakeholder engagement and participation.
- Robust Security: BIONET's swarm intelligence and neural network components fortify blockchain networks against adversarial attacks, Sybil attacks, and Byzantine faults. Its adaptability ensures resilience in dynamic network conditions, ensuring a secure and trustworthy ecosystem.
- Decentralization and Fairness: BIONET encourages decentralization in mining and validator selection, mitigating the risks of centralization in blockchain networks. Its merit-based approach promotes fairness, ensuring a more inclusive and egalitarian consensus process.
- Privacy-Preserving Features: BIONET addresses privacy concerns through encryption, zero-knowledge proofs, and private transactions, safeguarding sensitive information shared during consensus.

Future Prospects of Bio-Inspired Optimization in Blockchain Systems

The success of BIONET opens the door to exciting prospects for bio-inspired optimization in blockchain systems. As the technology advances, we envision the following possibilities:

- Hybrid Consensus Mechanisms: Hybrid models that combine BIONET with other consensus algorithms offer the potential for improved performance, scalability, and interoperability in blockchain networks.
- AI-Driven Governance: Integrating artificial intelligence (AI) in blockchain governance, utilizing the principles of swarm intelligence and neural networks, can lead to more efficient and equitable decision-making.
- Multi-Layered Security: Bio-inspired optimization can be applied to multiple layers of blockchain security, including intrusion detection, anomaly detection, and data integrity verification.

Final Thoughts and Closing Remarks

BIONET's emergence as a bio-inspired neural network for blockchain presents a compelling step towards enhancing the efficiency, security, and decentralization of blockchain consensus mechanisms. By combining the collective intelligence of swarm intelligence and the adaptability of artificial neural networks, BIONET paves the way for a new era of blockchain technology.

As researchers and practitioners continue to explore the potential of bio-inspired optimization in blockchain, it is essential to remain cognizant of the ethical implications, privacy concerns, and governance challenges. By addressing these issues responsibly, the blockchain community can harness the true potential of BIONET and other bio-inspired optimization techniques to build more resilient, sustainable, and user-centric blockchain ecosystems.

The BIONET exemplifies the dynamic synergy between nature-inspired algorithms and cutting-edge blockchain technology. Its successful application in consensus mechanisms opens new possibilities, promising a future where blockchain systems can thrive with efficiency, security, and inclusivity at the forefront. As the blockchain landscape continues to evolve, bio-inspired optimization will undoubtedly play a pivotal role in shaping the future of decentralized systems.

REFERENCES

Abd El-Moghith, I. A., & Darwish, S. M. (2021). Towards designing a trusted routing scheme in wireless sensor networks: A new deep blockchain approach. *IEEE Access : Practical Innovations, Open Solutions*, 9, 103822–103834. doi:10.1109/ ACCESS.2021.3098933

Adarsh, S., Anoop, V. S., & Asharaf, S. (2022, September). Distributed Consensus Mechanism with Novelty Classification Using Proof of Immune Algorithm. *International Conference on Innovative Computing and Communications Proceedings of ICICC*, *2*, 173–183.

Ali, M., El-Moghith, A., Ibrahim, A., El-Derini, M. N., & Darwish, S. M. (2022). Wireless Sensor Networks Routing Attacks Prevention with Blockchain and Deep Neural Network. *Computers, Materials & Continua*, *70*(3). Advance online publication. doi:10.32604/cmc.2022.021305

Alroobaea, R., Arul, R., Rubaiee, S., Alharithi, F. S., Tariq, U., & Fan, X. (2022). AI-assisted bio-inspired algorithm for secure IoT communication networks. *Cluster Computing*, *25*(3), 1805–1816. doi:10.100710586-021-03520-z

Alshamrani, S. S., & Basha, A. F. (2021). IoT data security with DNA-genetic algorithm using blockchain technology. *International Journal of Computer Applications in Technology*, *65*(2), 150–159. doi:10.1504/IJCAT.2021.114988

Atkinson, D. (2023). Virtual Modeling and Immersive Holographic Imaging Technologies, Cloud-based Digital Twin Manufacturing and Visual Perceptive Systems, and Bio-inspired Computational Intelligence and Context Awareness Algorithms in the Industrial Metaverse. *Journal of Self-Governance and Management Economics*, *11*(1), 73–88.

Bhoware, A., Jajulwar, K., Deshmukh, A., Dabhekar, K., Ghodmare, S., & Gulghane, A. (2023, April). Performance Analysis of Network Security System Using Bioinspired-Blockchain Technique for IP Networks. In *2023 11th International Conference on Emerging Trends in Engineering & Technology-Signal and Information Processing (ICETET-SIP)* (pp. 1-6). IEEE. 10.1109/ICETET-SIP58143.2023.10151475

Chanal, P. M., Kakkasageri, M. S., & Manvi, S. K. S. (2021). *Security and privacy in the internet of things: computational intelligent techniques-based approaches. In Recent Trends in Computational Intelligence Enabled Research*. Academic Press.

Cui, L., Su, X., Ming, Z., Chen, Z., Yang, S., Zhou, Y., & Xiao, W. (2020). CREAT: Blockchain-assisted compression algorithm of federated learning for content caching in edge computing. *IEEE Internet of Things Journal*, *9*(16), 14151–14161. doi:10.1109/JIOT.2020.3014370

Dhasarathan, C., Kumar, M., Srivastava, A. K., Al-Turjman, F., Shankar, A., & Kumar, M. (2021). A bio-inspired privacy-preserving framework for healthcare systems. *The Journal of Supercomputing*, *77*(10), 11099–11134. doi:10.100711227-021-03720-9

Gill, S. S., & Buyya, R. (2019). Bio-inspired algorithms for big data analytics: a survey, taxonomy, and open challenges. In *Big data analytics for intelligent healthcare management* (pp. 1–17). Academic Press. doi:10.1016/B978-0-12-818146-1.00001-5

Han, X., Zhang, R., Liu, X., & Jiang, F. (2020, October). Biologically inspired smart contract: A blockchain-based DDoS detection system. In *2020 IEEE International Conference on Networking, Sensing and Control (ICNSC)* (pp. 1-6). IEEE. 10.1109/ICNSC48988.2020.9238104

Kaur, I., Kumar, Y., & Sandhu, A. K. (2021, November). A Comprehensive Survey of AI, Blockchain Technology and Big Data Applications in Medical Field and Global Health. In *2021 International Conference on Technological Advancements and Innovations (ICTAI)* (pp. 593-598). IEEE. 10.1109/ICTAI53825.2021.9673285

Khandelwal, S., Bhatnagar, S., Mungale, N., & Jain, R. (2022). Design of a Blockchain-Powered Biometric Template Security Framework using Augmented sharding. In *Advances in data mining and database management book series* (pp. 80–101). IGI Global., doi:10.4018/978-1-6684-5072-7.ch004

Khattak, H. A., Tehreem, K., Almogren, A., Ameer, Z., Din, I. U., & Adnan, M. (2020). Dynamic pricing in industrial internet of things: Blockchain application for energy management in smart cities. *Journal of Information Security and Applications*, *55*, 102615. doi:10.1016/j.jisa.2020.102615

Liu, H., Zhang, S., Zhang, P., Zhou, X., Shao, X., Pu, G., & Zhang, Y. (2021). Blockchain and federated learning for collaborative intrusion detection in vehicular edge computing. *IEEE Transactions on Vehicular Technology*, *70*(6), 6073–6084. doi:10.1109/TVT.2021.3076780

Mansour, R. F. (2022). Artificial intelligence-based optimization with deep learning model for blockchain-enabled intrusion detection in CPS environment. *Scientific Reports*, *12*(1), 12937. doi:10.103841598-022-17043-z PMID:35902617

Mohammed, M. A., Ibrahim, D. A., & Abdulkareem, K. H. (2021). Bio-inspired robotics-enabled schemes in blockchain-fog-cloud assisted IoMT environment. *Journal of King Saud University-Computer and Information Sciences*.

Monti, M., & Rasmussen, S. (2017). RAIN: A bio-inspired communication and data storage infrastructure. *Artificial Life*, *23*(4), 552–557. doi:10.1162/ARTL_a_00247 PMID:28985116

Padmapriya, M. K., & Eric, P. V. (2022). Bio-Inspired Multi-Level Hybrid Crypto System. *International Journal of Software Innovation*, *10*(1), 1–16.

Prasetyo, J., De Masi, G., Zakir, R., Alkilabi, M., Tuci, E., & Ferrante, E. (2021, June). A bio-inspired spatial defense strategy for collective decision-making in self-organized swarms. In *Proceedings of the Genetic and Evolutionary Computation Conference* (pp. 49-56). 10.1145/3449639.3459356

Sabir, Z., & Amine, A. (2022). BIoVN: A Novel Blockchain-Based System for Securing Internet of Vehicles Over NDN Using Bioinspired HoneyGuide. In *Advances in Blockchain Technology for Cyber Physical Systems* (pp. 177–192). Springer International Publishing. doi:10.1007/978-3-030-93646-4_8

Sonavane, S. M., Prashantha, G. R., Deshmukh, J. Y., Salunke, M. D., Jadhav, H. B., & Nikam, P. D. (2023). Design of a Blockchain-Based Access Control Model with QoS-Awareness Via Bioinspired Computing Techniques. *International Journal of Intelligent Systems and Applications in Engineering, 11*(7s), 631–639.

Zheng, X., Zhang, Y., Yang, F., & Xu, F. (2022). Resource allocation on blockchain-enabled mobile edge computing system. *Electronics (Basel), 11*(12), 1869. doi:10.3390/electronics11121869

Chapter 5
Blockchain–Enabled Supply Chain Management for Revolutionizing Transparency, Security, and Efficiency

U. Vignesh
Vellore Institute of Technology, Chennai, India

R. Elakya
Sri Venkateswara College of Engineering, India

ABSTRACT

Blockchain technology holds immense potential for revolutionizing supply chain management by enhancing transparency, security, and efficiency. The key areas of focus encompass goods provenance tracking, traceability enhancement, fraud reduction, and efficiency augmentation. This chapter explores the core attributes of blockchain—decentralization, immutability, and transparency—and their application in supply chains. However, challenges include interoperability issues, data privacy concerns, and security risks like 51% attacks. Costs of implementation are also significant. Additionally, the project addresses pivotal concerns such as interoperability, data privacy, security, and the costs associated with adopting blockchain solutions. Ultimately, the project concludes that integrating blockchain technology into supply chain management has the potential to streamline operations, foster trust between stakeholders, and elevate overall efficiency and resilience within the supply chain ecosystem.

DOI: 10.4018/979-8-3693-1131-8.ch005

INTRODUCTION

Supply chain management (SCM) plays a vital role in today's global industry and holds significant implications for the world economy. It encompasses the movement of goods from producers to consumers, involving multiple stages that span from the sourcing of raw materials to the final delivery to customers, with manufacturers, distributors, and retailers all playing integral roles (Meidute-Kavaliauskiene et al., 2021). However, despite its broad scope, traditional supply chain management often falls short of achieving comprehensive compliance (Chen et al., 2018).

Within the supply chain, there are various challenges associated with allowing the final client to cancel transactions and ensuring the quality of delivered goods (Lu, 2018). These challenges arise due to factors such as complex logistics, multiple stakeholders involved, and potential information gaps throughout the supply chain process (Wang et al., 2019). While forward flows primarily focus on the movement of goods from sender to recipient, it is equally crucial to facilitate reverse flows for product returns and customer transactions. However, the current structure of supply chain management can be revolutionized through the implementation of blockchain technology and smart contracts (Huddiniah & Er, 2019). Leveraging the transparency and immutability of blockchain, the supply chain can be modernized, offering a secure platform for data collection and the creation and execution of smart contracts, which are computer programs or applications. By utilizing smart contracts, supply chain managers gain the ability to track the origin and security of their products (Xu et al., 2021). Through thorough analysis and discussion, we have identified the challenges at hand and formulated a solution.

This work aims to develop a conceptual framework for an advanced supply chain management system, leveraging the power of blockchain technology and smart contracts. The primary objective is to ensure secure transactions and deliver high-quality goods to customers (Hastig & Sodhi, 2019). By integrating blockchain into the system, it will establish a trustworthy global market where customers can confidently return products and receive refunds for their purchases (Bai & Sarkis, 2020). Emphasizing the transformative potential, this paradigm shift will bring about a significant transition throughout the entire supply chain management system.

Related Works

In their study, Srivastava (2021) explored the application of blockchain technology in the agri-food supply chain. They emphasized the critical areas of food safety, traceability, transparency, elimination of intermediaries, and integration with the Internet of Things (IoT) as key applications in the agri-food sector. By focusing on the honey supply chain as a case study, they demonstrated the potential of blockchain integrated with IoT in providing a robust traceability solution. However, the study also highlighted several challenges, including scalability, privacy, security, regulatory framework, and the need for skills and training, that need to be addressed to successfully implement blockchain technology in the agri-food sector and fully leverage its benefits in terms of enhancing traceability, transparency, and ensuring food safety.

According to Alfandi (2020), the fundamental nature of cryptocurrency lies in its capacity to be exchanged through transactions and securely added to new blocks via the process of mining conducted by miners. Within the cryptocurrency realm, there exist three primary levels, namely technology, currency, and tokens. Bitcoin, for instance, represents both a coin and the underlying blockchain technology on which it is built. Bitcoin transcends being merely a currency and encompasses a comprehensive set of rules. These protocols govern how participants interact within the network and provide guidelines for the utilization of public keys and signatures for authentication in cryptocurrencies such as Bitcoin and Ethereum. The coin itself serves as an integral asset within the protocol, enabling interaction among participants and functioning as a reward mechanism for miners who contribute to mining the blockchain and creating new blocks.

In their work, Alqahtani (2021) proposed an approach to verify the functional requirements of blockchain-based supply chain management (SCM) systems that employ interacting smart contracts. The approach entails modeling the intricate implementation of interacting smart contracts into an abstract design, enabling the verification of the system's overall compliance with its functional requirements. By employing this high-level verification method, SCM experts can assess whether the initial design aligns with their requirements, eliminating the need to test the low-level code of each smart contract individually. To showcase the effectiveness of their approach, the researchers conducted a case study centered around the oil and gas supply chain.

In their research, Kaur (2018) proposed the integration of blockchain technology with Internet of Things (IoT) devices to address challenges related to food conditions and transportation in the supply of fresh food. By leveraging blockchain technology, applications such as smart contracts can be utilized to monitor, observe, and manage transactions and communications between various stakeholders involved in the food supply chain. Concurrently, IoT technology offers means to verify transactions by recording and storing data in a centralized database system. This integration of blockchain and IoT enables the development of a secure and cost-effective food supply chain management system, benefiting all stakeholders involved.

In their study, Jauhar (2018) introduced a blockchain-based smart contract designed for supply chain transactions. This smart contract, built on the Ethereum platform, provides a versatile platform for stakeholders within the supply chain, incorporating a comprehensive interaction algorithm. This algorithm facilitates decentralized authorization, process automation, and information sharing among the various stakeholders involved in the supply chain. The proposed smart contract brings several benefits to the participants, including reducing the risk of non-payment for suppliers during the credit period, ensuring on-time delivery performance and product tracking for buyers, and lowering overall costs for third-party logistics (3PL) providers by minimizing paperwork and software expenses associated with product tracking.

In their review, Zhou (2021) conducted a bibliometric data-driven analysis to examine the application of blockchain technology in cross-border e-commerce supply chain management. The study utilized VosViewer to visualize collaborative relationships among the sampled literature and performed network and co-word analysis. The findings highlight the significant applications of blockchain technology in cross-border e-commerce supply chains. The contributions identified in the literature primarily revolve around three main areas: cross-border e-commerce platforms, supply chain operations, and data governance and information management. These results underscore the growing recognition of blockchain's potential in enhancing various aspects of cross-border e-commerce supply chain management.

In their study, Mancilla (2017) proposed an approach to analyze the distortion of upstream information within the agro-food supply chain, specifically focusing on consumers' quality perceptions in the beef chain. The beef chain was chosen as it is actively involved in quality management. The study involved multiple actors in the chain, including consumers, retailers, agro-industrials, and cattle farmers. The results indicated that as agents move further upstream away from consumers, the information becomes more distorted. Additionally, the study highlighted that as the number of links in the supply chain increases, there is a tendency for consumers' upstream information to become further distorted.

In their review, Natanelov (2021) focused on exploring the potential of blockchain and smart contracts in supply chain finance (SCF) specifically in cross-border beef supply chains from Australia to China. Their approach involved mechanism design and design-driven activities, utilizing the Agents Events Data (AED) process mapping method that combines Business Process Redesign (BPR) and the Resources Events Assets (REA) accounting model. The researchers proposed the group buying business model as the foundation for a comprehensive supply chain finance solution. This approach has the potential to reduce financial costs, improve cash flow performance, and provide greater financing certainty for buyers while enabling direct involvement of buy-side demand for supply-side enhancements. By leveraging blockchain and smart contracts, this approach opens new avenues for SCF models in cross-border beef supply chains, offering various benefits to the stakeholders involved.

Overall, the reviews demonstrate the potential of blockchain technology in revolutionizing supply chain management, addressing various challenges, improving efficiency, and enhancing transparency and trust among stakeholders.

Materials and Methods

a. Solidity

Solidity is a popular smart contract language for Ethereum. It is an object-oriented language that is similar to JavaScript. Solidity has its own standard library, which includes functions for math operations, string manipulation, and more. It is indeed a high-level programming language designed for creating smart contracts, which are a fundamental component of blockchain technology. Solidity's focus on Ethereum and its compatibility with other blockchain platforms has made it a popular choice for developers interested in building decentralized applications and automating various processes on the blockchain. Smart contracts written in Solidity execute automatically when predefined conditions are met, eliminating the need for intermediaries and enhancing trust in transactions. This language plays a pivotal role in the expansion of blockchain technology and the development of decentralized ecosystems.

b. Web3.js

Web3.js is a JavaScript library essential for Ethereum blockchain developers, providing a comprehensive set of APIs to interact with Ethereum networks. Primarily JavaScript-based, it empowers developers to create decentralized applications (DApps) and seamlessly communicate with Ethereum's mainnet and various testnets. A standout feature is its ability to facilitate smart contract deployment and interaction, making it indispensable for executing transactions, querying blockchain data, managing accounts, and handling events emitted by smart contracts written in languages like Solidity. Continuously maintained and updated, Web3.js ensures developers have access to the latest Ethereum ecosystem developments, underscoring its pivotal role in advancing blockchain technology and the creation of DApps that contribute to a decentralized future.

c. Ganache

Ganache, an essential development tool, operates atop Ethereum, a prominent blockchain platform supporting smart contracts and decentralized applications (dApps). Ethereum's ecosystem adheres to Ethereum Request for Comments (ERC) standards, a set of crucial guidelines governing blockchain functionality. These ERC standards establish the rules and protocols necessary for ensuring seamless interoperability between smart contracts and dApps, enabling them to function cohesively within the Ethereum network and interface effectively with other applications. Covering diverse areas such as token standards (e.g., ERC-20), non-fungible tokens (e.g., ERC-721), and more, these standards serve as a foundational framework, empowering developers to construct reliable, consistent, and interoperable blockchain solutions within Ethereum's thriving ecosystem.

d. Metamask

MetaMask, while not constituting a blockchain standard in its own right, functions as a cryptocurrency wallet and interface for decentralized applications (dApps), adhering to well-established standards and protocols for connectivity to blockchain networks. Notably, MetaMask employs the JSON-RPC (Remote Procedure Call) protocol for communication with Ethereum nodes, aligning itself with existing blockchain practices. By adhering to these recognized standards, MetaMask ensures its compatibility with Ethereum and other compatible blockchain networks, enabling users to effectively manage their digital assets and engage with dApps that uphold these widely accepted protocols, thereby contributing to the seamless integration of cryptocurrency and decentralized technologies.

Algorithm

Supply chain management using blockchain typically involves the use of distributed ledger technology, Ganache, and Metamask. We will use the Solidity programming language to define the smart contract, Ganache as a local blockchain network for testing and development, and Metamask as a wallet to interact with the smart contract.

Step 1: Define the smart contract and import any necessary libraries.

Step 2: Set up the development environment for the smart contract.

Step 3: Create a struct to define the product's details, including its name, ID, owner, and status.

Step 4: Create an array to store the products created on the smart contract.

Step 5: Define a function to create a new product, which accepts the product's name and ID as input.

Step 6: Within the createProduct function, create a new instance of the product struct with the input parameters.

Step 7: Assign the new product to the current user's address as the owner and set its status to "Created".

Step 8: Add the new product to the product array.

Step 9: Define a function to transfer ownership of a product to a new address, which accepts the product ID and the address of the new owner as input.

Step 10: Within the transfer ownership function, find the product with the matching ID in the product array.

Step 11: If the current user is the product owner, transfer ownership to the new owner's address and update the product's status to "Transferred".

Step 12: Define a function to retrieve the details of a product, which accepts the product ID as input.

Step 13: Within the getProductDetails function, find the product with the matching ID in the product array and return its details.

Step 14: Compile and deploy the smart contract in solidity compiler.

Step 15: Connect Metamask to the Ganache network.

Step 16: Test the smart contract.

Module 1: Product Origination and Traceability

This module is tasked with the critical functions of initiating new products within the supply chain and meticulously monitoring their progress as they traverse through the complex network. Its responsibilities encompass a range of essential actions, including the generation of new product entries, the assignment of distinctive identifiers to each product, and the precise documentation of their present location and ownership details. A pivotal aspect of its role is to ensure the uniqueness of each product being introduced, guaranteeing that there are no duplicate entries within the supply chain. Furthermore, the module extends its capabilities to authorized parties, enabling them to make inquiries about product statuses and track their intricate journeys within the supply chain. Essentially, this module serves as the foundational element for product management, ensuring transparency, authenticity, and efficiency in the supply chain's operation.

Module 2: Product Conveyance and Ownership Transition

This module assumes a pivotal role in orchestrating the seamless exchange of product ownership within the supply chain. Its functions encompass a range of critical tasks, commencing with the precise specification of the product identification, quantity, and the address of the intended new owner. A core aspect of its operation involves the enforcement of stringent verification procedures, ensuring that the party initiating the transfer holds the current ownership rights over the product and that the requested quantity is indeed available for transfer. Beyond this, the module extends its capabilities to encompass identity verification measures for the parties involved in the ownership transition. As a conclusive step, it diligently updates the ownership records of the product, thereby ensuring the accurate reflection of product ownership within the supply chain's registry. This module thus serves as the linchpin for smooth and secure product ownership transitions, underpinning trust and accountability in supply chain management.

Module 3: Transaction Settlement and Dispute Resolution

This module, designated as "Transaction Settlement and Dispute Resolution," assumes a dual role in the supply chain ecosystem. Firstly, it takes on the pivotal responsibility of orchestrating the payment processes for product sales, ensuring the smooth flow of financial transactions. This involves the critical functions of receiving payments from buyers, rigorously scrutinizing these transactions for legitimacy and security, and ultimately facilitating the secure transfer of funds to the respective sellers. Importantly, it accommodates a wide spectrum of payment methods, ranging from modern cryptocurrencies to traditional payment channels, thus catering to diverse preferences and needs.

Secondly, this module serves as a sophisticated mechanism for managing and resolving disputes that may arise during the intricate web of supply chain operations. It provides a structured framework for parties involved to submit disputes, complete with processes for gathering and evaluating evidence. This robust infrastructure ensures that disputes are not only handled efficiently but also fairly and impartially. The goal is to foster an environment where disputes can be resolved equitably, preserving trust and harmonious relationships within the supply chain network.

In essence, this module plays a critical role in not only ensuring the financial integrity of supply chain transactions but also in safeguarding the reputation and credibility of the supply chain itself. Its meticulous approach to payment processing and dispute resolution is vital in maintaining the smooth operation and sustainability of the supply chain ecosystem.

Experiments and Results

Developing and testing smart contracts involves a series of steps and considerations. Firstly, you need to select a suitable blockchain development platform based on your project requirements, such as Ethereum, Hyperledger Fabric, or Corda. Each platform has its own set of tools and requirements, so it's important to follow their specific instructions for installation and setup.

Once you have set up the development environment, you can begin writing and compiling the smart contracts. The programming language will depend on the chosen platform, for example, Solidity is commonly used for Ethereum. Using an integrated development environment (IDE) or a text editor, you write the code that defines the functionality and logic of the smart contract. Afterward, the code needs to be compiled into bytecode or the appropriate format for execution on the blockchain.

To ensure the reliability and correctness of the smart contracts, testing is crucial. You can set up a test network or use a local development environment to deploy and test the smart contracts. This involves running unit tests or utilizing testing frameworks specific to the chosen blockchain platform. Testing allows you to verify that the smart contracts function as intended and handle various scenarios and edge cases effectively.

Once the smart contracts have been thoroughly tested, they are ready for deployment. This process involves interacting with the blockchain client or using deployment tools provided by the platform to deploy the contracts onto the live blockchain network or a specific test network. Deployment enables the smart contracts to be accessible and executable by participants on the blockchain.

To interact with the deployed smart contracts, we developed user interfaces or backend applications. These interfaces allow users to interact with the smart contracts and invoke their functions. Web-based interfaces, APIs, or client applications can be built to facilitate this interaction, enabling users to send transactions, query contract data, and trigger specific contract functions.

One of the primary differences between the existing system and the proposed system is the level of transparency. In the existing system, it is often difficult to track products and identify their origin, leading to a lack of trust among participants in the supply chain. In contrast, the proposed system uses blockchain technology to create a tamper-proof, transparent record of all transactions, enabling participants to easily track products and identify their origin. Another key difference between the existing and proposed systems is the level of efficiency. The existing system often involves a significant amount of manual processing, which can be time-consuming and prone to errors. In contrast, the proposed system uses smart contracts to automate many of the processes involved in supply chain management, reducing the need for manual processing and increasing efficiency.

This system harnesses the power of blockchain technology and smart contracts to streamline and optimize logistics operations across various industries. Figure. 1. shows the smart contract supply chain management system using blockchain technology can provide a record of all transactions executed on the smart contract.

Automation of Processes: Smart contracts function as digital agents that carry out actions automatically when specific criteria are met. In supply chain management, these criteria encompass a wide array of tasks, including order processing, tracking shipments, and quality assurance. For instance, a smart contract can be programmed

Figure 1. Smart chain logistics management system

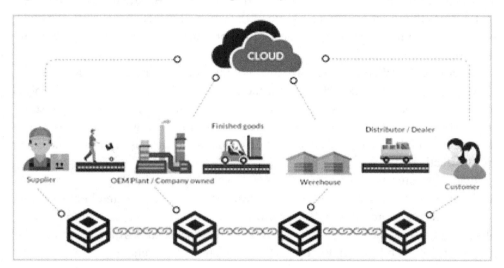

to trigger the release of payment to a supplier as soon as the goods are received and verified, obviating the need for manual payment handling. This automation not only enhances efficiency but also reduces the risk of errors and delays in the supply chain payment process.

Enhanced Transparency: Smart contracts, residing on a blockchain's distributed ledger, offer unparalleled transparency to all supply chain stakeholders. This accessibility ensures that every participant has real-time access to identical, current information. Such transparency minimizes disputes by fostering trust and collaboration among supply chain members, as everyone can rely on the same transparent record of events and transactions. This transparency is a pivotal element in modernizing supply chain operations and mitigating potential conflicts.

Reduction of Intermediaries: Smart contracts have the potential to significantly reduce the reliance on intermediaries within supply chains, a common feature of traditional logistics. These intermediaries, such as customs brokers, shipping agents, and payment processors, often introduce delays and costs into the supply chain process. Smart contracts facilitate direct, peer-to-peer interactions, streamlining processes and reducing the need for these intermediaries. This is especially valuable in complex international supply chains where intermediaries are prevalent, offering the potential for cost savings and more efficient operations.

Security and Trust: The immutability of blockchain technology guarantees that once a smart contract executes, its results are permanent and cannot be tampered with. This inherent security feature minimizes the risk of fraud or unauthorized alterations. Parties engaging in smart contracts can have confidence that the terms they've agreed upon will be executed precisely as intended, fostering trust and reliability within the digital agreement. Immutability is a fundamental pillar of blockchain's robust security model, reinforcing the integrity of smart contract-based transactions in various domains, including supply chain management.

Cost Savings: Smart contracts, by automating various aspects of supply chain processes, offer substantial opportunities for cost reduction. These savings stem from decreased administrative overhead, lower error rates associated with manual processes, and a reduction in disputes due to the transparent and automated execution of contract terms. This efficiency gain can have a direct and positive impact on the overall operational costs within the supply chain, making it a compelling proposition for businesses seeking to enhance their cost-effectiveness.

Real-Time Updates: Smart contracts deliver real-time updates on the progress of orders, shipments, and payments within the supply chain. This live visibility empowers supply chain managers with up-to-the-minute information, enabling them to make informed decisions promptly and respond effectively to any alterations or disruptions in the supply chain. This real-time insight is a critical asset for optimizing supply chain operations, enhancing adaptability, and bolstering overall efficiency.

CONCLUSION

The primary objective of this project is to enhance supply chain management by introducing smarter, more modern, and more secure practices. The proposed framework aims to achieve complete transaction transparency while ensuring immutability of data. By leveraging smart contracts, the system protects against unauthorized access and tampering, providing robust security measures for our website. Additionally, smart contracts significantly reduce the time and effort spent on laborious documentation that is typically associated with traditional supply chain management. Since information is stored on the blockchain as irrefutable proof, smart contracts cannot be altered. This paradigm shift has a profound impact on transaction processes, immutability of records, and refund procedures within supply chain management. The comprehensive strategy proposed in this initiative aims to address and eliminate the issues that individuals encounter with traditional supply chain processes, leading to more efficient and reliable operations. The outcomes of this study have the potential to bring about a permanent transformation in the supply chain management landscape, offering long-term solutions to the challenges experienced in traditional approaches.

REFERENCES

Alfandi. (2020). Blockchain technology in healthcare: A systematic literature review and taxonomy-based research agenda. *Health Information Science and Systems, 8.*

Alqahtani. (2021). A Verification Approach for Functional Requirements of Interacting Smart Contracts in Blockchain-Based Supply Chain Management Systems. *IEEE Access, 9.*

Bai, C., & Sarkis, J. (2020). A supply chain transparency and sustainability technology appraisal model for blockchain technology. *International Journal of Production Research*, 58(7), 2142–2162. doi:10.1080/00207543.2019.1708989

Chen, G., Xu, B., Lu, M., & Chen, N. S. (2018). Exploring blockchain technology and its potential applications for education. *Smart Learning Environments*, 5(1), 1–10. doi:10.118640561-017-0050-x

Chen, L. X., Lee, W. K., Chang, C. C., Choo, K. K. R., & Zhang, N. (2020). Blockchain based searchable encryption for electronic health record sharing. Academic Press.

Hastig, S. M., & Sodhi, M. M. S. (2019). Blockchain for supply chain traceability: Business requirements and critical success factors. *Production and Operations Management*, 29(4), 935–954. doi:10.1111/poms.13147

Huddiniah, E. R., & Er, M. (2019). Product Variety, Supply Chain Complexity and the Needs for Information Technology: A Framework Based on Literature Review, Operations and Supply Chain Management. *International Journal (Toronto, Ont.)*, 12(4), 245–255.

Jauhar, S. K. (2018). Blockchain-Based Smart Contract for Supply Chain Transactions. *International Journal of Supply Chain Management*, 7(2).

Kaur. (2018). Integration of Blockchain and Internet of Things for Food Supply Chain Management. *2018 5th International Conference on Internet of Things: Smart Innovation and Usages (IoT-SIU)*.

Lu, Y. (2018). Blockchain and the related issues: A review of current research topics. *J. Manag. Anal.*, 5(4), 231–255. doi:10.1080/23270012.2018.1516523

Mancilla, N. O. (2017). Analysis of Information Distortion Upstream Concerning Consumers' Quality Perceptions in Agro-Food Supply Chain. *International Journal on Food System Dynamics*, 8(3).

Mancilla, N. O., & Sepulveda, W. S. (2021). Upstream information distortion in the agro- ´ food supply chain. *Supply Chain Management*, 142(267), 411–423.

Meidute-Kavaliauskiene, I., Yıldız, B., Çiğdem, Ş., & Činčikaitė, R. (2021). An Integrated Impact of Blockchain on Supply Chain Applications. *Logistics*, *5*(2), 33. doi:10.3390/logistics5020033

Natanelov. (2021). Blockchain and Smart Contracts for Supply Chain Finance: Potential Applications in Cross-Border Beef Supply Chains. *Frontiers in Blockchain, 4*.

Srivastava. (2021). Application of blockchain in agri-food supply chain: A systematic literature review. *Computers in Industry, 123*.

Wang, Y., Singgih, M., Wang, J., & Rit, M. (2019). Making sense of blockchain technology: How will it transform supply chains? *International Journal of Production Economics*, *211*, 221–236. doi:10.1016/j.ijpe.2019.02.002

Xu, P., Lee, J., Barth, J., & Richey, R. (2021). Blockchain as supply chain technology: Considering transparency and security. *International Journal of Physical Distribution & Logistics Management*, *51*(3), 305–324. doi:10.1108/IJPDLM-08-2019-0234

Zhou, F. (2021). Blockchain-Enabled Cross-Border E-Commerce Supply Chain Management: A Bibliometric Data-Driven Analysis. *Sustainability*, *13*(13). Advance online publication. doi:10.3390u14138088

Chapter 6
Blockchain Technology in Healthcare Analytics

S. Karthigai Selvi

(iD) https://orcid.org/0000-0001-6249-2037
Galgotias University, India

R. Siva Shankar
Chiang Mai University, Thailand

K. Ezhilarasan
The Gandhigram Rural Institute, India

ABSTRACT

Blockchain is an exciting new technology that is being used to provide creative solutions in a number of industries, including the medical field. In the healthcare system, hospitals, labs, pharmacies, and doctors exchange and store patient data via a blockchain connected network. Blockchain-based software can reliably detect serious errors, including potentially harmful ones, in the medical domain. As a result, it can enhance the efficiency, security, and openness of medical data exchange within the healthcare system. Medical facilities can improve their understanding of patient care and obtain valuable insights from the use of this technology. This chapter discusses blockchain technology and its advantages, popular algorithms in blockchain technology, the current issues in medical data maintenance, and blockchain application fields in healthcare. Lastly, the study identifies and discusses the pros and cons of algorithms in medical data maintenance and key benefits of applied fields.

1. INTRODUCTION

Blockchain-based technologies have been added to the cryptocurrency industry to manage transactions and cut down on middlemen. The transaction details were

DOI: 10.4018/979-8-3693-1131-8.ch006

sent to several group members with the sender and receiver's information obscured, but the transaction ID was displayed. However, each transaction is recorded across a number of distributed servers, with the participants serving as witnesses. Each blockchain member has a complete copy of the blockchain, which is updated and synchronized continuously as new blocks are added. A node is a device, such as a computer or other electronic device, that provides access to or maintains a copy of the blockchain. Every record in a blockchain is accessible to every member of the blockchain network. Each blockchain member has a complete copy of the blockchain, which is updated and synchronized continuously as new blocks are added. A node is a computer or other gadget that keeps a copy of the blockchain on hand or grants access to it. Every participant in the blockchain network has access to every record in a blockchain. When a user adds a block to the chain, they must enter the transaction's details into a cryptographic hashing process that generates a code (a combination of letters and numbers) exclusive to that transaction (OECD, 2020). The network would be made aware of a potential case of data tampering if any portion of the data block were later changed since the hashing algorithm would generate a different code that would be incompatible with the other codes in that blockchain. Because a successful assault would necessitate breaking into several copies of the distributed ledger to update them all at once, the complexity of altering blocks increases with the number of users in a blockchain network (Miles, 2017).

'Append only' is the structure used by the majority of blockchains. In other words, the blockchain allows for the addition of new data, but once a block has been added, it cannot be changed or removed by any of the users. Each participant's copy of the blockchain is guaranteed to be consistent and legitimate thanks to this "append only" structure, which also enables users to confirm each new block added to the chain. A cryptographic hashing algorithm must be used each time a user adds a block to the chain to save information about the transaction. The sales transaction or medical history are saved as data in blocks of the block chain. Once a block's necessary data have been entered, it is added to the series of earlier blocks and a new block is created for the next data entry.

2. ADVANTAGES OF USING BLOCKCHAIN TECHNOLOGY

Blockchain technology produces several benefits to the society and are listed as follows:

- The digital signature function utilization ensures the fraud less operations. This facility made difficulties to change or corrupt the one individual's data by the others.

- With the help of changing programs, the systematic actions can be generated and made payments automatically.
- Earlier, the transactions made after getting the approval from the authorities such as government or bank. However, Blockchain technology safer, smoother, and faster the transactions by getting mutual agreement from users.

3. STRUCTURE AND DESIGN OF BLOCKCHAIN

At its basis, a blockchain is a chain of immutable, distributed, and decentralised blocks, where each block has a collection of data. The blocks are connected by means of cryptographic methods to create a logical chain of information. The consensus mechanism of a blockchain, which features a network of nodes that concur on the authenticity of transactions before adding them to the blockchain, is built to secure the security of data.

As seen in Figure 2, a structure of a block in a blockchain is made up of the following three elements:

- The header includes meta data, including the hash of the preceding block and a timestamp with a random integer used in the mining process.
- The hash is a distinct cryptographic number that serves as a representative of the entire block and is used for verification.

Figure 1. Layout of blockchain technology

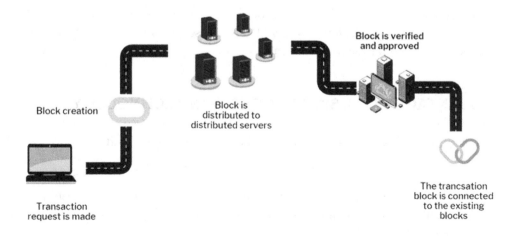

Figure 2. Block structure

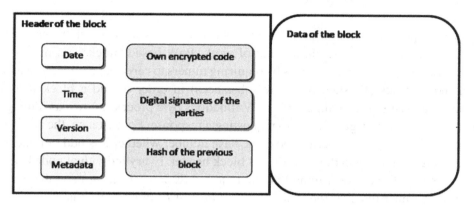

- The data section comprises the primary and actual information, such as transactions and smart contract agreements, which is kept in the block.

The time it takes to create a new block in a blockchain is referred to as block time. The intervals between blocks on different blockchains might varied from a few seconds to minutes or even hours. Longer block lengths may extend the timing for transaction approvals while decreasing the possibility of conflicts. Shorter block times may result in faster transaction approvals but with a greater possibility of conflicts.

3.1. Consensus Algorithms

Due to network consensus, the concept underlying Block-chain is ensured and trusted in engineering (Kombe C. et al., 2018). Because each domain has specific requirements, several consensus methods have already been implemented for explicit applications. For example, certain regions need little computation power, while others need trade preparation to happen more quickly. Consensus algorithms contains the outline of computation which is required to accept the confirmation of transaction blocks, are a crucial component of Blockchain innovation. In order to enable a greater majority of the diggers to make a decision, consensus algorithms aim to provide correspondence amongst excavators by assigning each one a similar load (Xiao, Y et al., 2020; Nguyen G.T. et al., 2018). By using decentralized consensus techniques, Blockchain maintains the integrity and correctness of knowledge. Consensus algorithm examples include

3.1.1. Proof of Work (PoW)

This concept is based on the premise that nodes are less likely to attack the network if they complete a significant amount of work. PoW-based Blockchain makes it nearly impossible for Sybil attacks by requiring miners to carry out computationally demanding tasks (finished by many substances) in order to add a block to the Blockchain (Ismail L. et al., 2019). PoW functions by a process known as mining; nodes will perform figures prior to requesting a response. For instance, the Bitcoin block chain's estimation period looks the hash number whether it is odd or none to get the high accuracy in the detection of block header. Every individual node bears the responsibility of confirming that the required response is accurate at the point where the miner resolves the issue. Because PoW uses more fuel, it is not a good choice for low-force applications.

3.1.2 Proof of Stake (PoS)

Security in the blockchain is divided across clients through PoS. Any node with a specific amount of stake in a given block chain can be considered a miner. This algorithm understands that a client with more stakes has less incentive to attack the network. Nodes share a minimal portion of their stake during mining (Xiao Y. et al., 2020). As a result, the network will maintain the amount in order to guarantee that a client is reliable and permitted to mine. PoS uses less energy than PoW because it requires less computing power. Because the wealthiest participants can claim a larger stake than individual nodes, the PoS problem stems from the way the blockchain mining cycle concentrates on them.

3.1.3 Delegated Proof of Stake (DPoS)

One further consensus algorithm that has been proposed to improve PoS is Delegated Proof of Stake. In this algorithm, those agents are in-charge of the plan rather than giving the partners the task of creating and approving blocks. Better exchange times due to fewer nodes being used are an advantage of this consensus technique. Additionally, the block size and intervals may be altered by the chosen nodes.

3.1.4 Transactions as Proof of Stake (TaPoS)

One further consensus algorithm that has been proposed to improve PoS is designated proof of Stake. In this algorithm, those agents are in charge of the plan rather than giving the partners the task of creating and approving blocks. Better exchange times due to fewer nodes being used are an advantage of this consensus technique. Additionally, the block size and intervals may be altered by the chosen nodes.

3.1.5 Practical Byzantine Fault Tolerance (PBFT)

For non-concurrent situation, PBFT is a suggested solution to the Byzantine Generals problem. It concurs that not just one third of the nodes are malignant, but more than two thirds of them are actual. A founding member is selected for each block age, and it is their duty to request exchanges. All things considered, the node's approval should aid in the addition of a node, at least two thirds. A BFT variant known as designated BFT (DBFT) uses distributed proof of stakes (DPoS) to authorize and generate blocks for a predetermined number of nodes.

4. BLOCKCHAIN TECHNOLOGY IN HEALTHCARE

In the past, medical records were kept manually. However, as the population grows, so does the number of medical books kept. Although it will require more room, manual maintenance will require more storage space and a longer diagnosis time. As a result, to manage the current situation, the clinical service makes use of telemedicine, cloud-based storage, and analytical software (Tahir A et al., 2020). The doctor is not the only one who can see patient data. Doctors, lab technicians, radiologists, nurses, accountants, chemists, legislators, and surgeons, among others, spread it. As a result, all data are transferred over the internet and stored in the cloud (Chow F et al. 2014). All individuals working in the medical field, as well as researchers, require access to patient data (Yao Q et al, 2014).

In the battle against malware and cyberthreats, the healthcare industry lags well behind other sectors. The primary cause of healthcare organizations' disregard for cyber security is the high cost of infrastructure security. A lot of big businesses continue to utilize outdated security apps and systems, which are more likely to be hacked, to break, and to need more regular patches. The more these systems are updated and improved, the more expensive it becomes to operate them. In terms of cyber security, 95% of health IT work is done by hand. Manual labour is risky and might result in errors. When vulnerabilities are manually patched on hundreds of servers, there's a greater chance that engineers will miss an important update, giving hackers a window of opportunity. Disjointed monitoring: System engineers look for security breaches by looking through the logs of individual servers or, even more harmful, apps. However, while the hacker destroys havoc on the surroundings, it might require hours to neutralize a threat.

Health insurance portability and accountability act fulfillment is not enough to shield your network and data. HIPAA establishes the norm for safeguarding private patient information, but the law isn't infallible when it comes to data security. Encryption is a prime illustration of this. HIPAA does not mandate encryption, however it is nonetheless advisable to maintain data protected to prevent data theft. In addition, hackers are now more sophisticated & strategic in their attacks. For their environments to be really secure, healthcare organizations must take security measures beyond the call of duty. Data about health is valuable. People's medical records are ten times more valuable than credit card information, according to Reuters. Numerous millions of medical records have already been taken by hackers, who profit handsomely from their sale on the underground market. Let's look at some of the other ways that hackers use healthcare data to generate revenue.

Data injection, breaching, and cloning are common effects of data transformation over the internet (Steve Alder et al., 2022). According to Steve Alder et al. (2022), 692 breaches occurred in the USA during the previous 12 months, from July 2021 to June 2022. The cloud management software included around 59224 records that were compromised in hacking and breaching activities. Eight unauthorized attempts to access the data have been discovered. The development of blockchain technology can help to securely transform digital data across the internet, which can help to resolve issues.

4.1. Blockchain Application Areas in Healthcare

Blockchain is seen as a multipurpose technology that is present and relevant in a number of industries, the most notable of which being healthcare (Agbo C.C et al, 2019). Because of the broad range of issues that can be resolved by the features and attributes provided by blockchain, the healthcare industry is vital and presents a number of chances for using this idea (Bell L. et al, 2018; Agbo C.C. et al., 2020). Decentralization is a key component of blockchain technology that is obviously advantageous for healthcare applications. It permits dispersed application deployment without depending on a centralized authority.

Patients and other healthcare stakeholders can be informed about how, by whom, and when their data is being utilized thanks to the transparency and openness created by the blockchain's replication of data across all network nodes (Agbo et al., 2019). Owing to its inherent characteristics, it can safeguard data against loss, corruption, or security breaches. Additionally, its immutability feature renders every record linked to the chain unchangeable, guaranteeing the authenticity and integrity of medical information. The security and privacy of the stored data are increased by employing cryptographic techniques to encrypt it, ensuring that only authorized users can decrypt it (Syed et al., 2019). Furthermore, as cryptographic keys are being employed and patient identities within the blockchain are pseudonyms, data about them can be shared among stakeholders without revealing their identity (Li X Jiang et al., 2017; Agbo C.C et al., 2019). A few writers discuss the potential uses of blockchain technology in the medical field (Agbo C.C. et al., 2020; Bell L. et al., 2018).

- **Electronic Medical Records**. Among the most common applications of blockchain in healthcare is the electronic medical record (EMR) management space. When creating, storing, and managing a patient's data, EMRs and PHRs used interchangeably. The patient can take control of their own health data management and determine how it is shared, processed, and used by putting a blockchain in place. With its decentralized, immutable, data provenance, strong, reliable, smart contract, security, and privacy features, blockchain technology is a good fit for managing and storing electronic medical records for patients.

- **Biomedical Research and Education**. Blockchain technology has additional applications in biomedical research and education. It aids in the eradication of data fabrication, underreporting, and the omission of unwanted clinical research findings from clinical studies. Because the data is automatically anonymized, patients find it simpler to consent to the use of their information (João Cunha et al., 2022). The immutability attribute ensures that the data obtained is authentic, and its open and transparent nature makes it easier to replicate research using blockchain-based data.

- **Drug/Pharmaceutical Supply Chain**. Healthcare supply chain management, particularly in the pharmaceutical sector, is another area where this technology can be used. Although the supply of phoney or inferior medications might have detrimental effects on the patient, this is a common issue. Decentralization, transparency, openness, immutability, data provenance, timestamping, and auditability are helpful attributes that help secure the containment of the counterfeit and dispersed medication issue. Every step of the prescription drug production, distribution, and delivery process is tracked, and all parties involved are kept informed.This allows for the detection of any malicious tampering or modification of the medication by any involved parties. This method makes the production and distribution of fake medications impossible. If a medication is registered at the time of creation, it is possible to track down the manufacturer of subpar products as well as stolen medications.

- **Equipment Tracking**. The monitoring of medical equipment from manufacture to decommissioning presents another potential for application. The financial savings that healthcare facilities realize are substantial. Comparing blockchain-based tracking solutions to conventional ones, there are a number of advantages. The two most notable ones are the inviolable and immutable attributes, which forbid changing or erasing the location history.

- **Health Data Analytics (HDA).** The application of blockchain technology presents a special chance to leverage the potential of other cutting-edge technologies, such machine learning and deep learning, to conduct predictive analytics on medical data and progress precision medicine research. Nevertheless, there are certain issues to take into account before implementing blockchain technology in the medical field. The first issue is one of secrecy and openness. This system has minimal confidentiality and extreme transparency because everyone can see anything. Generally speaking, transparency of information during a transaction is viewed as a restriction. Furthermore, utilizing hash values makes it possible to identify a user even if they are anonymous by looking through and evaluating the transaction data that is made publicly accessible on the network. This is a serious problem for healthcare applications since sensitive patient data is involved. Speed and scalability present the second difficulty. Depending on the protocol being utilized, transaction durations may be lengthy, and blockchain-based apps may not be able to scale due to speed limitations. In the process of creating scalable and real-time blockchain-based healthcare apps, this is a crucial problem. The threat of a 51% attack is the third and last challenge. This attack occurs when the network's consensus is tainted by an excessive number of malicious nodes relative to honest nodes. Healthcare applications need to be demanding when it comes to security, which makes this issue crucial.

5. HEALTHCARE USE CASES USING BLOCKCHAIN

5.1. Transparency in Supply chain

As in many other industries, establishing the origins of health care goods to verify its validity is a major difficulty for this kind of business. A blockchain-based tracking system allows customers to follow products from the start of manufacture to every step in the supply chain, giving them complete update and transparency over the purchasing products.

It is a major concern to the business, particularly in growing nations where tens of thousands of fatalities are brought on by fake prescription drugs every time. It is also suitable a lot crucial for health care gadgets, that are multiplying quickly used and, consequently, drawing the attention of unscrupulous individuals.

One of the best examples of a blockchain protocol is MediLedger, which permits the businesses in the suggested drug supply chain to verify the legitimacy of medications and additional essential data, such as expiration dates.

5.2. Health Records Based on Patients

Every country and area's healthcare systems be beset by the issue of data silos, which leaves patients' and their healthcare providers' views of each other's medical histories incomplete. Johns Hopkins University conducted a study in 2016 on medical errors. Their report resulted that the medical errors such as poor coordination care and lack in following therapeutical plan caused the numerous death rate in United States. They are shown in Figure 3.

The complete patient's data storage in block chain is impossible. Since, the real time data like their test result, treatment plan update by the doctor and the patients current health states are updated distinctly as blocks. Due to the time constraint,

Figure 3. The report of Johns Hopkins research
Source: National Center for Health Statistics, BMJ, https://www.bmj.com/content/353/bmj.i2139

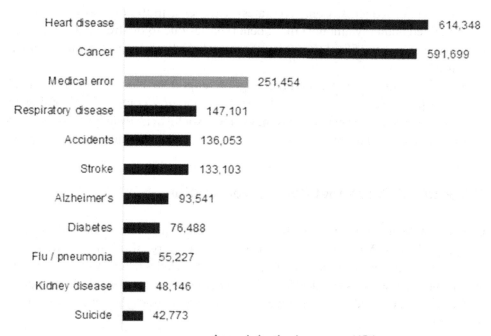

Annual deaths by cause, USA

each block gets different hash function which may like combination of characters. The distinct has function decoded with the permission of the data owner (patients).

In this case, each time a patient gives permission to share a portion of their medical record or a change is made to one, it is recorded as a transaction on the blockchain. One of the best examples of a information technology company collaborate with healthcare contributor to deploy blockchain-enabled EMRs is Medicalchain.

5.3. Insurance Settlement and Supply Chain

Blockchain systems enable different stakeholders in healthcare industry includes pharmaceutical companies, medical device suppliers, insurance company and healthcare providers to ensure their uniqueness as organizations. The supply chain technology maintains log details and tracking facility such as exchange of devices, services and the patient's payment details. Beyond supply chain management, this kind of environment allows insurance companies and business partners in the industry to implement digital automation and provides contract terms.

Rather than each party have different policies of contract with suppliers, manufacturer and organizations which provides health care services. It makes some disagreement between them over the claim of their payments, supplied goods, and prescriptions. Though, when using block chain technology each activity registered into blockchain ledger. Chronicled states that over a million of refund requests are generated annually amongst these beneficiaries due to the frequent changes in pricing schemes; over 5% of these claims are contested and need a laborious human resolution process.

Similar to this, digitized contract highly support to handle patient medical insurance policies, where 10% of claims are reportedly contested, according to Curisium. Insurance companies can employ more sophisticated analytics to improve health outcomes and costs once this data is digitalized and readily available, much like in other use cases.

5.4. Medical Personnel Record Verification

Blockchain technology enables to verify the medical professionals skills and their experiences. More trustworthy institutions and organizations record staffs' qualification, experiences and their activities. Blockchain technology supports the hiring organizations to track staffs history from the databases. A US company ProCredEx has created R3 Corda blockchain protocol to track the details of medical professions.

5.5. IoT Security for Remote Monitoring

The remote patient monitoring system uses several sensors to monitor the patients state and signs that provides greater insights into the patient conditions. It is now becoming a popular developing technology in healthcare. This allows for more proactive and preventative care. We've already discussed a number of exciting applications for edge computing and 5G in digital health that include remote monitoring. However, it leads a threat in patient's privacy and security. The poor performance of sensors may mislead the treatment planning. The supporting systems are more flexible or the sensors lost their sensing ability, in that situation patients care is very complicated.

6. DISCUSSION

The deep study of the blockchain algorithms witnessed to find several advantages and disadvantages that are depicted in Table1.

Key benefits of blockchain (paired with AI) are listed below

- Client confidence: Utilizing integration with manufacturers, wholesale, shipping, and other relevant parties, the consumer can follow every package's complete journey.

Table 1. List of algorithms and its advantages and disadvantages

Algorithm	Advantages	Drawbacks
PoW	• More stable connection between networks • Provides precise power and control decentralization in the network.	• High processing power (expensive); • Excessive electricity use; Little networks can be made weaker.
PoS	• Increased stakes and better incentives; • Enhanced resource efficiencyallows for speedier processing of transactions.	• A less secure network than proof of work (PoW); • A less decentralized network
DPoS	• Processes information faster than PoW and PoS; • Offers incentives more effectively. • Energy Efficiency. • Reduced hardware expenses	• Since there is less decentralization and less resilience, the network is more susceptible to attacks. • Wealthy individuals govern the network.
TaPos	• Greater security than PoS since every node in the network offers a streamlined PoS algorithm	• Reduced performance compared to DPoS due to • all nodes' inclusion not working properly during brief block-chain forks.
PBFT	• Significant reduction in electricity consumption. • Transactions such as PoW can be made without requiring confirmation.	• It is only effective in small consensus group sizes due to the high quantity of communication between nodes; • It is unable to prove the authenticity of a message to outside parties; • It is susceptible to Sybil attacks.

- Streamlining compliance: By combining supply chain data into a single system, manufacturers of medical devices and pharmaceuticals can reduce the amount of reporting required to ensure patient safety. One such system is FarmaTrust, whose blockchain-based system automatically notifies law enforcement when a problem is detected.

- Optimization of the supply chain: Based on centralized data, businesses utilize artificial intelligence (AI) to forecast demand more accurately and distribute resources optimally. Fig.4 contains a few screen grabs.

One of the most cutting-edge applications of blockchain technology and using supply chain management is Farma Trust's track and trace app. A notable example of this is the well-known collaboration between Walmart and IBM to guarantee food safety across the supply chain. It is anticipated that this will be the biggest immediate effect of blockchain on the healthcare sector because the technology and return on investment have already been shown.

The advantages of blockchain-enabled EMRs are listed below:

An accurate, single source of truth for medical records, improving interactions between patients and healthcare professionals. They allow patients the ability to explicitly consent to any sharing of their medical records with third parties or healthcare professionals, as well as to know when those records are changed. In

Figure 4. Healthcare tracking app using supply chain
Source: FarmaTrust

addition, patients have the option to designate time limitations for any third party to access their medical records and to share all or part of them with researchers.

Without the delay and expense of an intermediary, medical insurance can obtain instant, verifiable confirmation of healthcare services directly from patients. In addition to building blockchain for management of medical records, Medicalchain is also building a platform that will allow third parties to develop digital health solutions. These solutions allows to exchange or sell medical data of a patient by hiding their names and enables to transfer by Medtokens, which will be used to support the development of digital health applications like population-level analytics tools.

Advanced analytics will be fueled by the creation of considerably more comprehensive, digital, and shared patient health reports, which will have a significant effect on the healthcare sector. For instance, the absence of sufficient high-quality data is seriously impeding the development of personalized medicine, despite it being a very promising topic. Much more potent segmentation and analysis of targeted treatment results would be possible with access to more dependable and widely available population level data.

FarmaTrust provides supply chain solution for the above stated cases and also provides a supply chain solution to assist gen s addition to its supply chain solution; FarmaTrust has created a solution to assist for genomic treatments. Numerous research study initiatives are also investigating the potential of fusing blockchain technology with artificial intelligence to further personalized medicine (refer to these two examples)

Blockchain technology may be able to safeguard IoT devices being monitored remotely. The benefits are enumerated below.

Each data stored in blockchain has new hash function so it guarantees the security and enables to access authorized parties. The edited or updated source data immediately get and store with a new hash function. This function only executed by the persons who are having the particular set of cryptographic keys.

Patient data is nearly impossible to tamper by one because tempering requires all hash keys.

Since blockchain is decentralized, instead of passing through a centralized server, as most IoT connections, devices can communicate directly with one another. This makes DDoS and man-in-the-middle assaults highly complex to execute. Though, blockchain has the potential to improve IoT security in the healthcare industry, most of the IoT based applications are in initial stage only. The implementation of blockchain technology only provides the significant solution of those applications. Blockchain will more supportable to the remote health care companies by adopting several security plans.

CONCLUSION

This chapter discussed the significance of applying block chain in healthcare analytics, with popular algorithms and application areas. In the blockchain technology, medical records authorization, providers, data utilization related records, therapeutical data such as medicine information, insurance and current situation are recorded and managed through blockchain. Blockchain increases the data availability, improves efficiency of transformation, increases the transparence of data access over the internet. Thus, helps to access the medical history of an individual. Though the individual has more control over his data. The complete history of data avoids the more clinical trial. The tools of blockchain enables electronic data collection, aggregation and distribution of data over physician, researchers and pharmacist.

REFERENCES

Agbo, C. C., & Mahmoud, Q. H. (2020). Blockchain in healthcare opportunities, challenges, and possible solutions. *International Journal of Healthcare Information Systems and Informatics*, *15*(3), 82–97. doi:10.4018/IJHISI.2020070105

Agbo, C. C., Mahmoud, Q. H., & Eklund, J. M. (2019). Blockchain technology in healthcare: A systematic review. *Health Care*, *7*(2). PMID:30987333

Alder, S. (2022). June 2022 healthcare data breach report. *The HIPAA Journal*.

Bell, L., Buchanan, W. J., Cameron, J., & Lo, O. (2018). Applications of Blockchain Within Healthcare. *Blockchain in Healthcare Today*, *1*, 1–7. doi:10.30953/bhty.v1.8

Chow, F., Muftu, A., & Shorter, R. V. (2014). Virtualization and cloud computing in dentistry. *Journal of the Massachusetts Dental Society*, *63*(1), 14–75. PMID:24941546

Ismail, L., & Materwala, H. (2019). A review of blockchain architecture and consensus protocols: Use cases, challenges, and solutions. *Symmetry*, *11*(10), 1198. doi:10.3390ym11101198

Kombe, C., Ally, M., & Sam, A. (2018). A review on healthcare information systems and consensus protocols in blockchain technology. *Int. J. Adv. Technol. Eng. Explor.*, *5*(49), 473–483. doi:10.19101/IJATEE.2018.547023

Kuo, T. T., Kim, H. E., & Ohno-Machado, L. (2017). Blockchain distributed ledger technologies for biomedical and health care applications. *Journal of the American Medical Informatics Association : JAMIA*, *24*(6), 1211–1220. doi:10.1093/jamia/ocx068 PMID:29016974

Li, X., Jiang, P., Chen, T., Luo, X., & Wen, Q. (2017). A survey on the security of blockchain systems. *Future Generation Computer Systems*, *107*, 841–853. doi:10.1016/j.future.2017.08.020

Mayfield, C. A., Gigler, M. E., Snapper, L., Jose, J., Tynan, J., Scott, V. C., & Dulin, M. (2020). Using cloud-based, open-source technology to evaluate, improve, and rapidly disseminate community-based intervention data. *Journal of the American Medical Informatics Association : JAMIA*, *27*(11), 1741–1746. doi:10.1093/jamia/ocaa181 PMID:32940684

Syed, T., Alzahrani, A., Jan, S., Siddiqui, M., Nadeem, A., & Alghamdi, T. (2019). A comparative analysis of blockchain architecture and its applications: Problems and recommendations. *IEEE Access : Practical Innovations, Open Solutions*, *7*, 176838–176869. doi:10.1109/ACCESS.2019.2957660

Tahir, A., Chen, F., Khan, H. U., Ming, Z., Ahmad, A., Nazir, S., & Shafiq, M. (2020). A Systematic Review on Cloud Storage Mechanisms Concerning e-Healthcare Systems. *Sensors (Basel)*, *20*(18), 5392. doi:10.339020185392 PMID:32967094

Transform healthcare outcomes with the simplicity of IBM Blockchain. (2018). https://www.ibm.com/downloads/cas/DQPLDP8N

Xiao, Y., Zhang, N., Lou, W., & Hou, Y. T. (2020). A survey of distributed consensus protocols for blockchain networks. *IEEE Communications Surveys and Tutorials*, *22*(2), 1432–1465. doi:10.1109/COMST.2020.2969706

Yao, Q., Han, X., Ma, X. K., Xue, Y. F., Chen, Y. J., & Li, J. S. (2014). Cloud-based hospital information system as a service for grassroots healthcare institutions. *Journal of Medical Systems*, *38*(9), 104. doi:10.100710916-014-0104-3 PMID:25015761

Chapter 7
Endometrial Cancer Detection Using Pipeline Biopsies Through Machine Learning Techniques

Vemasani Varshini
 https://orcid.org/0009-0005-5295-3828
Vellore Institute of Technology, Chennai, India

Maheswari Raja
Vellore Institute of Technology, Chennai, India

Sharath Kumar Jagannathan
 https://orcid.org/0000-0003-2678-4133
Saint Peter's University, USA

ABSTRACT

Endometrial carcinoma (EC) is a common uterine cancer that leads to morbidity and death linked to cancer. Advanced EC diagnosis exhibits a subpar treatment response and requires a lot of time and money. Data scientists and oncologists focused on computational biology due to its explosive expansion and computer-aided cancer surveillance systems. Machine learning offers prospects for drug discovery, early cancer diagnosis, and efficient treatment. It may be pertinent to use ML techniques in EC diagnosis, treatments, and prognosis. Analysis of ML utility in EC may spur research in EC and help oncologists, molecular biologists, biomedical engineers, and bioinformaticians advance collaborative research in EC. It also leads to customised treatment and the growing trend of using ML approaches in cancer prediction and monitoring. An overview of EC, its risk factors, and diagnostic techniques are covered in this study. It concludes a thorough investigation of the prospective ML modalities for patient screening, diagnosis, prognosis, and the deep learning models, which gave the good accuracy.

DOI: 10.4018/979-8-3693-1131-8.ch007

1. INTRODUCTION

There are currently no clinically established EC screening methods; instead, the usual diagnostic procedure for EC is endometrial biopsy with dilatation and curettage. Women with atypical endometrial hyperplasia (AEH), a precancerous kind of endometrial lesion, or stage 1A EC without muscle penetration should receive progestin treatment. The majority of women with EC have good results with surgery alone; however, high-grade, recurring, and metastatic EC are linked to worse outcomes. Therefore, rather than just presenting symptoms, routine screening, early identification, and accurate prediction of recurrence or survival after oncotherapeutic regimens may increase the survival of EC patients. This review discusses machine learning (ML)-based approaches and methods that could help in EC prognostication and prediction (Kurman et al., 2014).

In oncology, ML methods (algorithms) have developed to improve the accuracy of predictions of cancer susceptibility, recurrence, and survival. A variety of statistical, probabilistic, and optimization techniques are combined in the discipline of machine learning (ML), a branch of artificial intelligence (AI), to help computers "learn" from the samples they have previously seen and spot intricate patterns in large, noisy, or complex datasets. AI makes it possible for machines to carry out "cognitive" tasks for people, like language understanding, reasoning, and problem-solving (Lee et al., 2017). Without the need for explicit instructions, computers can find patterns in datasets that are available and draw conclusions from the data by employing an appropriate AI system. At the moment, AI has primarily been used in healthcare for image identification jobs.

1.1. Context

Endometrial cancer (EC) has become a tedious task to detect and as discovering techniques to find it out helps the women and also the economy, this project will help patients to detect endometrial cancer in its early stages and get treated at the right time (Fader et al., 2009).

The surgical and pathological staging of EC is determined using the International Federation of Gynecology and Obstetrics (FIGO) staging system. The majority of EC patients receive an early diagnosis (80% in stage I), and they have the highest 5-year survival rate of all gynaecological tumours (95%). A good prognosis can be shown in those with early detection or EC that is less risky. There are few available prognostic or therapeutic options for people with higher stage EC who have experienced recurrence, with 5-year survival rates for these patients ranging from 47% to 58% for stage III EC patients and 15% to 17% for stage IV EC patients. Costly screening and a high rate of misdiagnosis are the main causes of high illness rates. There are generally four types of endometrial tissue namely the normal endometrium (NE),endometrial polyp (EP),endometrial hyperplasia (EH) and endometrioid adenocarcinoma (EA), where the NE category is having further 3 subtypes and the EH category is having 2 subtypes. With the rise of the endometrial cancer incidence and disease mortality represent a very impactful concern for the women, especially in the countries where the incidence rate of this cancer is highest.

Imaging tests including magnetic resonance imaging (MRI), computerised tomography (CT), or positron emission testing/CT may be performed to determine local extension and any metastatic disease. The detection of lymph node spread, which is seen in at least 90% of patients utilising microscopic-based techniques, is limited by imaging investigations. Accurately forecasting the course of an illness, however, is one of the more intriguing and challenging problems facing clinicians. In order to find patterns and connections related to diseases in huge datasets and to reliably forecast future illness risks and outcomes for specific patients, ML-based approaches are being used in research on a larger scale.

2. EXISTING LITERATURE AND LIMITATIONS

In affluent nations, endometrial cancer is the most prevalent gynecologic malignancy. For bettering patient outcomes and lowering death rates, early detection is essential. New endometrial cancer screening and diagnostic methods have attracted a lot of attention in recent years.

We will examine the most recent findings in endometrial cancer detection in this review of the literature.

1. Imaging methods: The most popular imaging modality for detecting endometrial cancer is transvaginal ultrasonography (TVUS). Its sensitivity and specificity, however, are constrained. TVUS is less precise than magnetic resonance imaging (MRI), which has shown potential in identifying early-stage endometrial cancer. The detection of metastatic or recurrent endometrial cancer may potentially be possible with positron emission tomography (PET) scans.

2. Biomarkers: The ability of many biomarkers to identify endometrial cancer has been researched. These include human epididymis protein 4, HE4, and CA-125. (HE4). Despite having some potential, these biomarkers are neither sensitive or specific enough to be utilised as standalone assays. The diagnostic precision of biomarkers may be increased by combining them with imaging methods.

3. Endometrial Biopsy: The most accurate way to diagnose endometrial cancer is through an endometrial biopsy. The operation can be carried out in an

outpatient environment and is less invasive. Endometrial biopsy does have some drawbacks, though, namely the chance for sampling error and the challenge of getting enough tissue samples.

4. Liquid Biopsy: A liquid biopsy involves searching for cancer-related biomarkers in blood or other bodily fluids. Although liquid biopsy has demonstrated potential in the identification of various cancers, its applicability in the detection of endometrial cancer is still under investigation.

5. AI: AI has the potential to revolutionise the detection of endometrial cancer. Large volumes of data from imaging and biomarker testing can be analysed by machine learning algorithms to find patterns that can point to the existence of cancer. Although this method has shown promise in a number of studies, additional study is required to confirm its accuracy and efficacy.

Table 1 summarize the survey and findings made through literature review made towards the Cancer detection techniques.

To sum up, there are a number of methods for detecting endometrial cancer, including imaging methods, biomarkers, endometrial biopsies, liquid biopsies, and AI. To increase diagnostic accuracy, a combination of these methods may be required since each strategy has benefits and drawbacks. To find the best method for early endometrial cancer screening, more study is required.

1) One of the research by M.Li et al on the auxiliary classification and diagnosis of the lung cancer subtypes based on the histopathological images and based on extracting the histopathological images and then perform the feature selection by selecting a subset of the features followed by the classification and comparison of the built model with the existing classification models, the accuracy was around 73.91% and then the feature selection was done using the relief algorithm and model building using the support vector machines, so advantage of this research is, as indicated by the AUC and ROC curve values the better at classifying the different lung cancer type and the limitations is over fitting due to the small data set (Li et al., 2021).

2) The lung cancer detection by Hatuwal, Bijaya and Thapa, Himal (2020) using the convolution neural network on histopathological images so this approach was based upon the data preprocessing feature extraction and model training using the four different convolutional neural network techniques, comparison by using the three layers of the network, the accuracy is found to be off 97.6%. The advantages of this techniques fine tuning of the hyper parameters leads to the better model fitting and the limitations is misclassifications pertaining to two lung cancer subtypes which are adenocarcinoma and squamous cell carcinoma (Hatuwal and Thapa, 2020).

Table 1. Summary of literature review on cancer detection techniques

Paper Title	Summary and Performance	Algorithms Used	Pros and Cons
M. Li et al., "Research on the Auxiliary Classification and Diagnosis of Lung Cancer Subtypes Based on Histopathological Images," in IEEE Access, vol. 9, pp. 53687-53707, 2021,	Approach: Extracted histopathological images, performed feature selection followed by classification and comparison of the built model with the existing classification models Accuracy: LUSC-ASC classification accuracy was 73.91%, the LUSC-SCLC classification accuracy was 83.91% and the ASC-SCLC classification accuracy was 73.67%	Feature selection using Relief algorithm and model building using SVM	**Pros:** As indicated by the AUC and ROC curve values, the Relief-SVM is better at classifying the different lung cancer types **Cons:** Overfitting due to small dataset
Hatuwal, Bijaya & Thapa, Himal. (2020). Lung Cancer Detection Using Convolutional Neural Network on Histopathological Images. International Journal of Computer Trends and Technology.	Approach: Data Preprocessing, Feature extraction and model training using 4 different CNN techniques and a comparison between the using triplet layer network Accuracy: VGG19 - accuracy, precision, recall and f1 score of 97.6% ResNet50 model- accuracy, precision, recall and f1 score of 96.2% Inception-ResNetv2 -test accuracy, precision, recall and f1 score is 97.04% DenseNet121-accuracy, precision, recall and F1score is 99%	CNN techniques-VCG19, ResNet50,Inception-ResNetv2 and DenseNet123, KNN for triplet network validation	**Pros:** Fine-tuning of hyperparameters leads to better model fitting **Cons:** Misclassifications pertaining to two lung cancer subtypes-adenocarcinoma and squamous cell carcinoma.
Qin, P., Chen, J., Zeng, J. et al. Large-scale tissue histopathology image segmentation based on feature pyramid. J Image Video Proc. 2018, 75 (2018).	**Approach:** Image resizing, oversampling, CNN for feature extraction and GICN to integrate multi-level features followed by the addition of GPP to include multi-scale semantic information to perform image segmentation **Accuracy:** The proposed algorithm achieved 63% of the average segmentation accuracy	Image semantic segmentation algorithm based on feature Pyramid (ResNet50- GICN-GPP)	**Pros:** Integration of multi-level features and an improvement in segmentation accuracy of 10-20% over existing algorithms **Cons:** Overall accuracy is low
Hui, S., Dong, L., Zhang, K. et al. Noninvasive identification of Benign and malignant eyelid tumours using clinical images via deep learning system. J Big Data 9, 84 (2022).	**Approach:** Image pre-processing, Dataset splitting into 2 sets using 4-fold cross validation, model building of 4 types of CNN models followed by their validation using prospective validation datasets **Accuracy:** The best model reached the accuracy, sensitivity, specificity, and AUC of 0.889 (95% CI 0.747–0.956), 0.933 (95% CI 0.702–0.988), 0.857 (95% CI 0.654–0.950), and 0.966 (95% CI 0.850–0.993), respectively	Convolutional Neural Networks	**Pros:** Model was successful in extracting the subtle features from eyelid tumours. **Cons:** Model may be biased and the model can lesions were identified only from 2- dimensional photographs without any additional clinical information.
Xu, Q., Wang, X. & Jiang, H. Convolutional neural network for breast cancer diagnosis using diffuse optical tomography. Vis. Computation. Ind. Biomed. Art 2, 1 (2019).	**Approach:** 75% Training and 25% testing data followed by classification using CNN model **Accuracy:** 0.80 specificity, 0.95 sensitivity, 90.2% accuracy, and 0.94 area under the receiver operating characteristic curve (AUC) on original dataset Sensitivity, specificity, accuracy, and AUC of 0.88, 0.96, 93.3%, and 0.95, respectively on augmented dataset	A CNN model consisting of 8 layers.	**Pros:** The proposed model attained high specificity and sensitivity **Cons:** The dataset used was small, so the model's attained performance metrics cannot be generalised

continued on following page

Table 1. Continued

Paper Title	Summary and Performance	Algorithms Used	Pros and Cons
G.S Jyothi et al, Study of the Efficacy of Pipelle Biopsy Technique to Diagnose Endometrial Diseases in Abnormal Uterine Bleeding	**Approach:** Data was analysed using statistical software version SPSS Inc. Age and duration were summarised in terms of the median with interquartile range since the data was not normally distributed. **Results:** The sensitivity, specificity, positive and negative predictive values, and accuracy of pipelle biopsy for endometrial carcinoma was 75%, 100%, 100%, 97.9%, and 98%, respectively.	McNemar's test	**Pros:** All the p values obtained were statistically significant. Pipelle biopsy has very high specificity and sensitivity for endometrial malignancy. **Cons:** For definitive diagnosis in case of polyps and focal endometrial lesions, we need a hysteroscopy dilation and curettage
Takahashi Y, Sone K, Noda K, et al. Automated system for diagnosing endometrial cancer by adopting deep-learning technology in hysteroscopy.	**Approach:** In this study, three distinct neural networks— Xception, MobileNetV2, and EfficientNetB0— were used to categorise the images that had been taken out of the video stream. These models were created using Keras based on TensorFlow, and they were trained using an Intel Core i7-9700 processor and an Nvidia GTX 1080ti graphics card. **Results:** While Xception required the largest learning period—roughly three times that of MobileNetV2—MobileNetV2 showed the fastest learning time.	Three distinct neural networks—Xception, MobileNetV2, and EfficientNetB0	**Pros:** a high accuracy for diagnosis of endometrial cancer can be obtained with such a small sample **Cons:** The accuracy rate of conventional diagnostic techniques, such as pathological diagnoses by curettage and cytology, is low, and screening for endometrial cancer has not been established.
Vinita Sarbhai et al, Histo-pathological study of endometrium by Pipelle sampling device versus Hysteroscopy guided biopsy in women with Abnormal Uterine Bleeding	**Approach:** Endometrial sampling by Pipelle was followed by hysteroscopic-directed biopsy in the premenstrual phase. The efficacy of Pipelle was determined by correlating the histopathological results obtained from it and the hysteroscopic-directed biopsy. **Results:** The histopathology of the endometrium obtained using Pipelle's curette has high specificity (100%) and positive predictive value (100%) for diagnosing endometrial pathology while sensitivity 25% and negative predictive value 76.32%.	Three distinct neural networks—Xception, MobileNetV2, and EfficientNetB0	**Pros:** none of the cases with premalignant or malignant lesions were missed on histopathology by endometrial aspiration biopsy. Endometrial aspiration biopsy is simple, cost effective, OPD procedure with 100% specificity and 100% positive predictive value for diagnosing the endometrial pathology **Cons:** It lacks specificity for focal intrauterine pathologies like polyps and fibroids.

continued on following page

Table 1. Continued

Paper Title	Summary and Performance	Algorithms Used	Pros and Cons
Sumaiya Dabeer, Maha Mohammed Khan, Saiful Islam, Cancer diagnosis in histopathological image: CNN based approach, Informatics in Medicine Unlocked, Volume 16, 2019, 100231, ISSN 2352-9148,	**Approach:** The CNN was trained using 2480 benign and 5429 malignant samples belonging to the RGB colour model. The proposed system provides an effective classification model for classifying breast tissue as being either benign or malignant. **Results:** Accuracy of 99.86%	CNN is used for feature extraction, and classification is done by using the fully connected Artificial Neural Network (ANN)	**Pros:** Extracting features through a convolutional neural network **Cons:** From image compression deep net is used for better performance autoencoder can be used
M. Muthu RamaKrishnan, Vikram Venkatraghavan, U. Rajendra Acharya, Mousumi Pal, Ranjan RashmiPaul, Lim Choo Min, Ajoy Kumar Ray, Jyotirmoy Chatterjee, Chandan Chakraborty; Automated oral cancer identification using histopathological images: A hybrid feature extraction paradigm;	**Approach:** Extracted these textural changes using Higher Order Spectra (HOS), Local Binary Pattern (LBP), and Laws Texture Energy (LTE) from the histopathological images **Results:** Accuracy 95.7%	Five different classifiers which were decision tree, Sugeno Fuzzy, Gaussian Mixture Model (GMM), K-Nearest Neighbour (K-NN), Radial Basis Probabilistic Neural Network (RBPNN)	**Pros:** Proposed a novel integrated index called Oral Malignancy Index (OMI) using the HOS, LBP, LTE features, to diagnose benign or malignant tissues **Cons:** High computational complexity

3) The large scale tissue histopathology images segmentation based on the feature pyramid by Qin, P., Chen, J.,Zeng, J.et al, this approach is based upon the resizing of the image over Sampling and convolutional neural network for feature extraction by GICN integrate features followed by the addition of GPP the multi scale semantic information and the accuracy of the proposed algorithm achieved 63% by using the image segmentation algorithm, the advantages is integration of the multilevel features but the overall accuracy is low (Qin et al., 2018).

4) The identification of benign and malignant eyelid tumours using the clinical images by the deep learning system by Hui, S., Dong, L.,Zhang .K.et.al., this approach is based upon the image preprocessing and the data set is been splitted into the two sets by using the 4 fold cross validation, the model is built upon the four types of the convolutional neural network models and validation using the prospective validation datasets, the accuracy curve was found to be the 88.9% the advantages of this model was successful in extracting the subtle features from eyelid tumours but the disadvantages are the model may be biassed and the model can be identified only from the two dimensional photographs without any additional clinical information (Qin et al., 2018).

5) The convolutional neural network for breast cancer diagnosis by Xu, Q., Wang, X. & Jiang, H. using the diffuse optical tomography and the approach followed is by splitting the data set into the 75% of the training data and 25% of the testing data followed by classification using convolutional neural network model, the accuracy achieved was 80% and the advantages of this algorithm is the proposed model attained high specificity and sensitivity but the disadvantages is the data set used was small so the models attained performance metrics cannot be generalised (Xu et al., 2019).

2.1 Objective of this Research

(i) Early Detection of Uterine Cancer

The prognosis of EC patients is severely hampered by the advanced stage of diagnosis and the restricted treatment options. Several studies have demonstrated that EC screening, early identification, monitoring, and prediction could greatly enhance patient prognosis. New and promising perspectives for the diagnosis and prediction of numerous malignancies, including breast, colorectal, and prostate cancer, are provided by advances in machine learning techniques (Kasius et al., 2021). Recently, ML has significantly influenced the creation of prospective computational tools for classifying, scoring, and predicting cancer patients in order to increase patient survival.

(ii) To Automate the Process of Detection Using CNN and Machine Learning Algorithms

By the use of artificial intelligence (AI), computers can carry out mental tasks including language comprehension, deductive reasoning, and problem solving on behalf of people. Machine learning is a cutting-edge method for creating AI models that is based on the scientific analysis of the statistical models and algorithms that computer systems employ to carry out tasks effectively. Without explicit instructions, computers can learn patterns in datasets that are available and draw conclusions from supplied data by using an appropriate AI model. Deep learning concepts can be realised with the help of the deep neural network (DNN). It is also a machine-learning technique that emphasises the utilisation of several layers of neural networks. A neural network is a network or circuit of artificial neurons or nodes from the standpoint of machine learning (Pecorelli, 2009).

A huge number of participants must be taken into account in order to train a model with the amount of data necessary to be extremely accurate. It is anticipated that as deep learning technology advances, accuracy rates will increase as sample sizes increase. A minimal number of samples must be used to analyse some disorders when deep learning is used in the medical industry. To improve accuracy with a limited number of samples, a system analysis approach must be developed, which is a difficulty for medical AI research. Also, utilising pathological images, ML has been successful in trying to predict tumour recurrence with a high degree of accuracy.

In order to increase the sensitivity and specificity of EC diagnosis and prognosis, ML-based techniques might be used and the process can be automated using the convolutional neural networks.

3. PROPOSED RESEARCH WORK

Used the convolutional neural network for feature extraction and training random forest classifiers, textual extraction methods for feature extraction and training different machine learning models.

Figure 1 depicts the process of implementing the CNN for the data set being collected for the research work.

Figure 2 represents the depiction of step-by-step processing of image which helps to accomplish the cancer detection through image processing.

Figure 3 indicates the process of implementing the various models such as SVM, Random Forest for the dataset collected for the research study.

The two promising picture of the image enhancement techniques and textual feature extraction is portrayed in Figure 4.

Figure 1. Process of implementing the CNN for the data

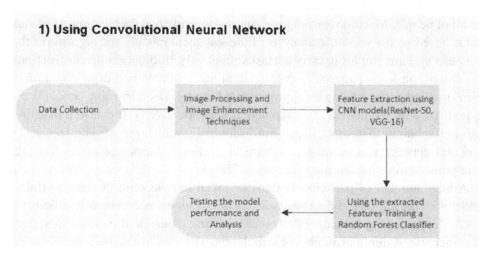

Figure 2. Depiction of step by step processing of image

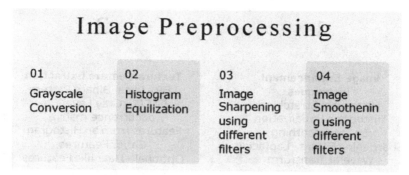

Figure 3. Process of implementing the various models such as SVM, random forest for the data

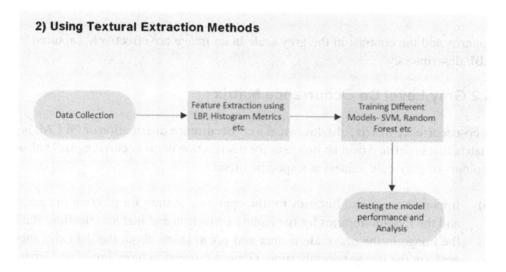

4. METHODOLOGY AND RESEARCH

As this endometrial cancer was to be detected from the images, we have to use the following features for the extraction of the features from the given data.

4.1 Local Binary Pattern

A useful texture descriptor for images is the Local Binary Pattern (LBP), which thresholds adjacent pixels based on the value of the current pixel. The local spatial

Figure 4. Picture of the image enhancement techniques and textual feature extraction

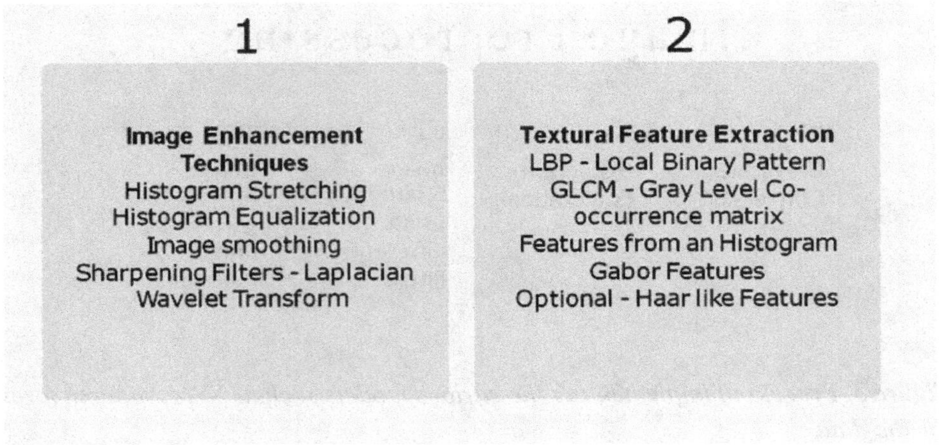

patterns and the contrast in the grey scale in an image are effectively captured by LBP descriptors.

4.2 Gray Level Co Occurrence Matrix

A co-occurrence matrix, also known as a co-occurrence distribution or GLCM, is a matrix that is defined over an image as the distribution of co-occurring pixel values (colours or grayscale values) at a specific offset.

(i)   Import the required libraries for the operating system for plotting the graph and the Python libraries for the feature extraction and feature selection. Read the image in the grayscale format and get to know about the data size then perform the image normalisation, Gamma correction, grey image, the image enhancement techniques such as histograms stretching, histogram equalisation, images smoothing and sharpening the filters using the Laplacian methods, wavelength transformation coming to the texture features they are local binary pattern, grey level co occurrence matrix, so here the features or selected from an histogram and the optional Haar like features are performed .

(ii) Compute the Local Binary Pattern representation of the image and then use it to build the histogram of the patterns, which is for normalising the histogram.

(iii) The Local Binary Pattern function has the parameters of radius, number of the points and histogram size.

(iv) Then compute the feature vector, finally for the histogram Matrix extraction there are various measures such as mean, variance, kurtosis, energy and entropy, pass all classes of the data to the Local Binary Pattern data generator function which will give the histogram then pass the image Matrix generator for the same parameters as the function.

(v) The next step is to equalise the histogram, perform the Laplacian function which have the parameters as the size and the depth of the image providing the source and the destination where the source is the Gaussian blur image and the destination is a Laplace in the kernel size as the parameter.

(v) Find the absolute distance using the Converse scale absolute method, then using the Haralick data generator for the optional Haar features, the histogram from that can be derived.

(vi) Start the training of the model, import all the necessary Python libraries and MAT plot library for plotting the graph and tensor flow Keras layers and Pandas as pd .Import the SK image library to import IV filters, feature, Restoration exposure, morphology and RGB pixels

(vii) Perform the oversampling of the images as there are four types of the endometrial tissue endometrial adenocarcinoma, EH Complex and simple, endometrial Polyp and NE follicular, luteal and menstrual.

(viii) Get dimensions using the shape function, for the equalisation of images repeat the axis. Use the train test split method to divide the data into the training data and the testing data.

Split the training and testing data in the ratio of 0.67 and 0.33 giving the random state as 42.

Divide the class labels and for the data augmentation, get it as a sequential model where the random flip is horizontal and the vertical, random rotation is 10 times, random translation with the factors parameters as width factor is equal to 0.2 and height factor is equal to 0.2.

(ix) Specify the input of the number of trees in random forest, number of the features to consider at every split such as auto and square root. Provide the maximum number of the levels in the tree, minimum number of the samples required to split a note and the minimum number of the samples required at each leaf node.

(x) Create the random grid and note the model with classify fully connected layers and make the loaded layers, this is important and there is a need to work with pretrained weights.

(xi) Use features from the convolutional neural network for the random forest and make use of the random grid to search for the best hyper parameters.

(xii) At first create the base model to tune the random forest, random search of the parameters using the three fold cross validation. Search across 100 different combinations and use all available cores and then tune the model on the training data, send the test data through some feature extracted process.

(xiii)   Now predict using the trained random forest model. Build the confusion Matrix which will verify the accuracy of each class in the given data set. Heat map also works to check accuracy on a few selected images.

(xiii)   Coming to the convolutional neural networks, use the CNN core models function and the CNN has got more of the accuracy.

5. RESULTS AND DISCUSSION FINDINGS AND THEIR SIGNIFICANCE

5. 1. Are the Results Expected or Different From Expectations and If Different, Why?

The results are as expected and got the highest accuracy for the convolutional neural networks and the random forest classifier.

5.2. Generalisation of the Results

Derived the accuracy for each of the models for the support vector machines, MLP, random forest classifier and the convolutional neural networks and the CNN has achieved the highest accuracy and similarly the random forest. Derived the confusion matrix so that we can get a clear picture of the precision and recall score.

5.3. Are the results different from the literature or the results of the previous studies?

The results were almost similar to the previous studies but the accuracy is highest in the random forest classifier and have given the different parameters such as ROC curve and AUC curve for the calculation of the accuracy for each model.

5.4. Possibility of Doing the Other Experiments, Which Could Be Done to Confirm the Results

Use the deep learning embedded convolutional neural networks and also the random forest so that the results can be more accurate.

5.5 The Results Support or Contradict Existing Theory/Practices/Algorithms/Technologies

The results derived are supporting the existing theory and the practices and in this research the process of the convolutional neural network models has been automated.

Figure 5 captures the screen shot of the implementation part through Support Vector Machines techniques.

In Figure 6, we see a screenshot of the section where Multi-Layer Perceptron approaches are put into practise.

The screen representation of the part of the implementation that uses Convolutional neural networks techniques is shown in Figure 7.

Figure 5. Implementation screenshot of support vector machines

Figure 6. Implementation screenshot of multi-layer perceptron approaches

Figure 7. Implementation screenshot of convolutional neural networks

```
cnn_models = [ResNet50, ResNet101, ResNet152, ResNet50V2, ResNet101V2, ResNet152V2, Xception, VGG16, VGG19, InceptionV3, InceptionResNetV2, DenseNet201, DenseNet121, DenseNet169]

cnn_models_400x = model_result(cnn_models)

<ipython-input-18-9671da1e6d95>:4: DeprecationWarning: The default dtype for empty Series will be 'object' instead of 'float64' in a future version. Specify a dtype explicitly to sile
  res_df["Convolution Model"] = pd.Series([])
<ipython-input-18-9671da1e6d95>:5: DeprecationWarning: The default dtype for empty Series will be 'object' instead of 'float64' in a future version. Specify a dtype explicitly to sile
  res_df["Accuracy"] = pd.Series([])
<ipython-input-18-9671da1e6d95>:6: DeprecationWarning: The default dtype for empty Series will be 'object' instead of 'float64' in a future version. Specify a dtype explicitly to sile
  res_df["True Negatives"] = pd.Series([])
<ipython-input-18-9671da1e6d95>:7: DeprecationWarning: The default dtype for empty Series will be 'object' instead of 'float64' in a future version. Specify a dtype explicitly to sile
  res_df["False Negatives"] = pd.Series([])
<ipython-input-18-9671da1e6d95>:8: DeprecationWarning: The default dtype for empty Series will be 'object' instead of 'float64' in a future version. Specify a dtype explicitly to sile
  res_df["True Positives"] = pd.Series([])
<ipython-input-18-9671da1e6d95>:9: DeprecationWarning: The default dtype for empty Series will be 'object' instead of 'float64' in a future version. Specify a dtype explicitly to sile
  res_df["False Positives"] = pd.Series([])
59/59 [==============================] - 14s 89ms/step
29/29 [==============================] - 3s 106ms/step
Accuracy =  0.579004329004329
Convolution Model    <function ResNet50 at 0x7f94c1f120d0>
Accuracy                     0.579004
True Negatives                   88.0
False Negatives                  18.0
True Positives                   95.0
False Positives                   7.0
Name: 0, dtype: object
1/1 [==============================] - 0s 331ms/step
The prediction for this image is:  5
The actual label for this image is:  1
Downloading data from https://storage.googleapis.com/tensorflow/keras-applications/resnet/resnet101_weights_tf_dim_ordering_tf_kernels_notop.h5
171446536/171446536 [==============================] - 1s 0us/step
59/59 [==============================] - 10s 139ms/step
29/29 [==============================] - 4s 141ms/step
Accuracy =  0.6147186147186147
Convolution Model    <function ResNet101 at 0x7f94c1f2160>
Accuracy                     0.614719
True Negatives                   92.0
False Negatives                  12.0
True Positives                   95.0
False Positives                   6.0
```

Figure 8 is a screenshot of the Random Forest Classifier techniques implementation section.

5.6 Summary

Imported the data, performed the image normalisation enhancement techniques and applied the Local Binary Pattern and Grey Level Co occurrence Matrix techniques for the histogram equalisation, from those numerical the different training models have been built and tested the accuracy of each model.

Figure 8. Implementation screenshot of random forest classifier

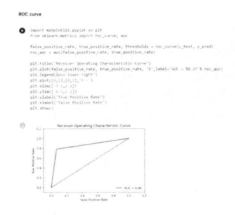

5.7 Contributions

Developed a wide range of machine learning models with the different types of parameters for the each model, performed the various preprocessing techniques such as reading the image in grayscale format, doing the image normalisation, gamma correction and then enhancing the image which was read in the grayscale format, then performing the ML models and training and then predict the test data accuracy for each of the model.

6. CONCLUSION

In this study, a methodology based on the analysis of histogram features and the Laplacian matrix to ascertain the presence of medical conditions within digital images has been employed. A significant achievement of research lies in the early detection of these conditions, facilitated by the use of diverse training models and automated algorithms. Furthermore, this approach offers the ability to discern subtypes within a particular class of medical conditions, thereby enhancing the precision of diagnosis. Beyond its primary focus, research indicates the potential for cross-condition applications, suggesting that the developed models may be adaptable to detect various medical conditions or diseases. Nevertheless, it is worth noting a limitation: this approach may be less effective when applied to images with substantial blurring, as clear and well-defined images are essential for accurate analysis. Future research endeavours may explore the development of advanced image enhancement techniques to further refine the capabilities of models and improve diagnostic accuracy.

REFERENCES

American Cancer Society. (n.d.). *Key Statistics for Endometrial Cancer*. Available at https://www.cancer.org/cancer/endometrial-cancer/about/key-statistics.html

Antonsen, S. L., Ulrich, L., & Hogdall, C. (2020). Overview of ACOG guidelines for management of endometrial cancer and the implications of molecular classification. *European Journal of Cancer*. Advance online publication. doi:10.1016/j.ejca.2020.04.007

Arechvo, A., Vargas-Hernández, V. M., & López-Cabanillas, J. L. (2015). Diagnostic utility of D&C in the detection of uterine sarcomas: Systematic review and meta-analysis. *Gynecologic Oncology*. Advance online publication. doi:10.1016/j. ygyno.2015.08.027

Aure, J. C., Hoeg, K., & Kolstad, P. (2015). Preoperative tumour size at MRI predicts deep myometrial invasion, lymph node metastases, and patient outcome in endometrial carcinomas. *International Journal of Gynecological Cancer*. Advance online publication. doi:10.1097/IGC.0000000000000333

Backes, F. J., Leon, M. E., Ivanov, I., Suarez, A., Frankel, W. L., Hampel, H., Fowler, J. M., Copeland, L. J., O'Malley, D. M., & Cohn, D. E. (2009). Prospective evaluation of DNA mismatch repair protein expression in primary endometrial cancer. *Gynecologic Oncology*, *114*(3), 486–490. Advance online publication. doi:10.1016/j. ygyno.2009.05.026 PMID:19515405

Bendifallah, S., Canlorbe, G., Collinet, P., Arsène, E., Huguet, F., Coutant, C., Hudry, D., Graesslin, O., Raimond, E., Touboul, C., Daraï, E., & Ballester, M. (2015). Just how accurate are the major risk stratification systems for early-stage endometrial cancer? *British Journal of Cancer*, *112*(5), 793–801. Advance online publication. doi:10.1038/bjc.2015.35 PMID:25675149

Bokhman, J. V. (1983). Two pathogenetic types of endometrial carcinoma. *Gynecologic Oncology*, *15*(1), 10–17. Advance online publication. doi:10.1016/0090-8258(83)90111-7 PMID:6822361

Clarke, B. A., & Gilks, C. B. (2010). Endometrial carcinoma: Controversies in histopathological assessment of grade and tumour cell type. *Journal of Clinical Pathology*, *63*(5), 410–415. Advance online publication. doi:10.1136/jcp.2009.071225 PMID:20418232

Colombo, N., Creutzberg, C., & Amant, F. (2016). ESMO-ESGO-ESTRO Consensus Conference on Endometrial Cancer: Diagnosis, Treatment and Follow-up. *Annals of Oncology*. DOI: 10.1093/annonc/mdw387

Creasman, W. T., Kohler, M. F., Odicino, F., Maisonneuve, P., & Boyle, P. (2004). Prognosis of papillary serous, clear cell, and grade 3 stage I carcinoma of the endometrium. *Gynecologic Oncology*, *95*(3), 593–596. Advance online publication. doi:10.1016/j.ygyno.2004.08.019 PMID:15581969

Dabeer, S., Khan, M. M., & Islam, S. (2019). Cancer diagnosis in histopathological image: CNN based approach. *Informatics in Medicine Unlocked, 16*. doi:10.1016/j. imu.2019.100231

Eltabbakh, G. H., Shamonki, M. I., Moody, J. M., & Garafano, L. L. (2000). Hysterectomy for obese women with endometrial cancer: Laparoscopy or laparotomy? *Gynecologic Oncology*, *78*(3), 329–335. Advance online publication. doi:10.1006/gyno.2000.5914 PMID:10985889

Fader, A. N., Arriba, L. N., Frasure, H. E., & von Gruenigen, V. E. (2009). Endometrial cancer and obesity: Epidemiology, biomarkers, prevention, and survivorship. *Gynecologic Oncology*, *114*(1), 121–127. Advance online publication. doi:10.1016/j.ygyno.2009.03.039 PMID:19406460

Hatuwal, B., & Thapa, H. (2020). Lung Cancer Detection Using Convolutional Neural Network on Histopathological Images. *International Journal of Computer Trends and Technology*, *68*(10), 21–24. doi:10.14445/22312803/IJCTT-V68I10P104

Hatuwal & Thapa. (2020). Lung Cancer Detection Using Convolutional Neural Network on Histopathological Images. *International Journal of Computer Trends and Technology*, *68*(10), 21-24. doi:10.14445/22312803/IJCTT-V68I10P104

Hui, S., Dong, L., Zhang, K., Nie, Z., Jiang, X., Li, H., Hou, Z., Ding, J., Wang, Y., & Li, D. (2022). Noninvasive identification of Benign and malignant eyelid tumours using clinical images via deep learning system. *Journal of Big Data*, *9*(1), 84. doi:10.118640537-022-00634-y

Hussein, Y. R., Broaddus, R., & Weigelt, B. (2020). The genomic heterogeneity of FIGO grade 3 endometrioid carcinoma impacts diagnostic accuracy and reproducibility. *International Journal of Gynaecological Pathology*. doi:10.1097/PGP.0000000000000627

Jyothi. (n.d.). *Study of the Efficacy of Pipelle Biopsy Technique to Diagnose Endometrial Diseases in Abnormal Uterine Bleeding*. Academic Press.

Kasius, J. C., Pijnenborg, J. M. A., Lindemann, K., Forsse, D., van Zwol, J., Kristensen, G. B., Krakstad, C., Werner, H. M. J., & Amant, F. (2021, November 22). Risk Stratification of Endometrial Cancer Patients: FIGO Stage, Biomarkers and Molecular Classification. *Cancers (Basel)*, *13*(22), 5848. doi:10.3390/cancers13225848 PMID:34831000

Kurman, R. J., Carcangiu, M. L., & Herrington, C. S. (2014). *WHO Classification of Tumours of Female Reproductive Organs*. IARC Press.

Lax, S. F., Kendall, B., & Tashiro, H. (2000). The frequency of p53, K-ras mutations, and microsatellite instability differs in uterine endometrioid and serous carcinoma: Evidence of distinct molecular genetic pathways. *The American Journal of Surgical Pathology*. Advance online publication. doi:10.1097/00000478-200010000-00003 PMID:10679651

Lee, C. K., Suh, D. H., & Kim, J. W. (2017). Accuracy of preoperative magnetic resonance imaging in predicting myometrial invasion of endometrial cancer: a systematic review and meta-analysis. *Journal of Obstetrics and Gynaecology Research*. doi:10.1111/jog.13321

Lee, Y. C., Lheureux, S., & Oza, A. M. (2017). Treatment strategies for endometrial cancer: Current practice and perspective. *Current Opinion in Obstetrics & Gynecology*, *29*(1), 47–58. Advance online publication. doi:10.1097/GCO.0000000000000338 PMID:27941361

Levine, D. A.Cancer Genome Atlas Research Network. (2013). Integrated genomic characterization of endometrial carcinoma. *Nature*, *497*(7447), 67–73. Advance online publication. doi:10.1038/nature12113 PMID:23636398

Lewin, S. N., Herzog, T. J., & Barrena Medel, N. I. (2010). Comparative Performance of the 2009 International Federation of Gynecology and Obstetrics' Staging System for Uterine Corpus Cancer. *Obstetrics and Gynecology*, *116*(5), 1141–1149. Advance online publication. doi:10.1097/AOG.0b013e3181f39849 PMID:20966700

Li, M., Ma, X., Chen, C., Yuan, Y., Zhang, S., Yan, Z., Chen, C., Chen, F., & Bai, Y. (2021). Research on the Auxiliary Classification and Diagnosis of Lung Cancer Subtypes Based on Histopathological Images. IEEE Access. doi:10.1109/ACCESS.2021.3071057

Li, M., Ma, X., Chen, C., Yuan, Y., Zhang, S., Yan, Z., Chen, C., Chen, F., Bai, Y., Zhou, P., Lv, X., & Ma, M. (2021). Research on the Auxiliary Classification and Diagnosis of Lung Cancer Subtypes Based on Histopathological Images. *IEEE Access : Practical Innovations, Open Solutions*, *9*, 53687–53707. doi:10.1109/ACCESS.2021.3071057

Muthu RamaKrishnan, Venkatraghavan, Acharya, Pal, RashmiPaul, Min, Ray, Chatterjee, & Chakraborty. (2012). *Automated oral cancer identification using histopathological images: A hybrid feature extraction paradigm*. doi:10.1016/j.micron.2011.09.016

Macdonald, G. M., Shafi, M. I., & Williams, A. R. (2001). Management of endometrial cancer: Issues and controversies. *European Journal of Gynaecological Oncology*.

Pecorelli, S. (2009). Revised FIGO staging for carcinoma of the vulva, cervix, and endometrium. *International Journal of Gynecology & Obstetrics.* . doi:10.1016/j. ijgo.2009.02.012

Qin, P., Chen, J., & Zeng, J. (2018). Large-scale tissue histopathology image segmentation based on feature pyramid. *J Image Video Proc., 75.* doi:10.1186/ s13640-018-0320-8

Snyder, A., & Mutch, D. G. (2019). Surgical staging of endometrial cancer: Time to move on? *American Journal of Obstetrics and Gynecology.* Advance online publication. doi:10.1016/j.ajog.2019.06.019

Takahashi, Y., Sone, K., & Noda, K. (n.d.). *Automated system for diagnosing endometrial cancer by adopting deep-learning technology in hysteroscopy.* Academic Press.

Thaker, P. H., Urbauer, D., & Frumovitz, M. (2014). Patterns of failure in patients with early stage uterine sarcoma. *Cancer.* Advance online publication. doi:10.1002/ cncr.28803

Xu, Q., Wang, X., & Jiang, H. (2019, May 8). Convolutional neural network for breast cancer diagnosis using diffuse optical tomography. *Visual Computing for Industry, Biomedicine, and Art, 2*(1), 1. doi:10.118642492-019-0012-y PMID:32240400

Xu, Q., Wang, X., & Jiang, H. (2019). Convolutional neural network for breast cancer diagnosis using diffuse optical tomography. *Visual Computing for Industry, Biomedicine, and Art, 2*(1), 1. doi:10.118642492-019-0012-y PMID:32240400

Zaino, R. J., Brady, M. F., Lele, S. M., Michael, H., Greer, B., & Bookman, M. A. (2011). Advanced stage mucinous adenocarcinoma of the ovary is both rare and highly lethal: A Gynecologic Oncology Group study. *Cancer, 117*(3), 554–562. Advance online publication. doi:10.1002/cncr.25460 PMID:20862744

Zaino, R. J., Kauderer, J., Trimble, C. L., Silverberg, S. G., Curtin, J. P., Lim, P. C., & Gallup, D. G. (2006). Reproducibility of the diagnosis of atypical endometrial hyperplasia: A Gynecologic Oncology Group study. *Cancer, 106*(4), 804–811. Advance online publication. doi:10.1002/cncr.21649 PMID:16400640

Chapter 8
Evaluating Antivirus Effectiveness Against Malware in Ascending Order for Increasing Blockchain Endpoint Protection

Humam Imad Wajeeh Al-Shahwani
University of Baghdad, Iraq

Maad M. Mijwil
iD https://orcid.org/0000-0002-2884-2504
*Baghdad College of Economic
Sciences University, Iraq*

Ruchi Doshi
iD https://orcid.org/0000-0002-7259-8481
Universidad Azteca, Mexico

Kamal Kant Hiran
*Sir Padampat Singhania University,
India*

Indu Bala
Lovely Professional University, India

ABSTRACT

Blockchain represents a new promising technology with a huge economic impact resulting from its uses in various fields such as digital currency and banking; malware represents a serious threat to users, and there are many differences in the effectiveness of antivirus software used to deal with the problem of malware. This chapter has developed a coefficient for measuring the effectiveness of antivirus software. This chapter evaluates the effectiveness of antivirus software by conducting tests on a group of protection programs using a folder containing an amount of data. These programs are applied to combat viruses contained in this folder. The study revealed that the effectiveness of antivirus software is as follows: AVG scored 0%, Advanced System Protector scored 20%, Avast scored 60%, and Malwarebytes scored 80%, respectively.
DOI: 10.4018/979-8-3693-1131-8.ch008

1. INTRODUCTION

Malware is a term that includes all types of malicious programs (Yang et al., 2019; Maniriho et al., 2022). In general, they all share that they are programs designed to cause harm to the user, whether it is an individual, a company, an institution, a government agency, or a technology as in our topic, which is (Blockchain) technology, but the difference between them is the way they cause (Unogwu et al., 2022; Kumar et al., 2019). This damage, due to the different purpose and benefit sought from its establishment, as well as the way it deals with anti-virus programs or anti-malware (Yang et al.,2023; Winter et al., 2022). Blockchain is an advanced database technology that allows information to be shared publicly within a network of dealers. A blockchain database stores data in blocks linked together in a chain (Santhi and Muthuswamy, 2022; Javaid et al., 2022). The data is temporally consistent because you cannot delete or modify the chain without consent from the network, and this is supposed to provide security within the chain as the blockchain network is a safe technology in itself, due to the consideration that it is almost impossible to lose data even if one of the blocks is exposed within the chain of hacking, the danger lies when ordinary users who use the endpoint of the network are compromised (Mustafa et al., 2022; Athanere and Thakur, 2022). There are many examples of well-planned (network endpoint in blockchain technology) malicious attacks that succeeded in achieving their goals, for example, targeting the user's email and then using the user's private data to finance their purposes.

The development and the complexity of the malicious software's founded on the other side a reflex development and complexity of the anti-viruses software's and tools, the anti-viruses software's and tools have a variation and differences between one and another be , on the other hand not all the users have enough knowledge of the anti-viruses software and application, there are many anti–virus that may not determine the infection or not scanning all the files within the folder or may take long time during the scanning process (Mijwil et al., 2023; Doshi et al., 2023; Kumar et al., 2022). Hence, the need of determine the level of effectiveness for the anti – virus software in practical environment according to a specific parameters that have impact effect of the anti- virus software and to the user interaction with those anti–viruses software, in this paper there are four major aspects the parameters determine to measure the level of the efficiency level of the anti – virus, then put the anti-virus under test in a practical environment to measure who far the anti-virus satisfy the parameters goals, the four major aspects of the parameters includes: Finding the infection, Scanning all the files, the time needed for scanning the required files and provide interface within local language of the users.

2. RELATED WORK

Blockchain Technology

Blockchain is a new technology that was formulated under the pseudonym (Satoshi Nakamoto) in October 2008 (Thangamayan et al., 2023; AlShamsi et al., 2022). Blockchain is a master ledger of transactions called (transaction ledger) and is available to the public. The contents of the ledger can be financing such as (balances, cryptocurrencies, shares, financial bonds) or real estate contents such as (title deeds for real estate such as houses, apartments, and farms) or it includes works (by creators in various fields or authors) who want to preserve the rights intellectual property. Figure 1 illustrates the mechanism of blockchain work.

Blockchain technology involves storing data permanently in a chain of blocks. Data cannot be changed or removed. Blocks are the data structure, and each block is linked to the previous block. These blocks are verified by the consensus algorithm,

Figure 1. The mechanism of blockchain work

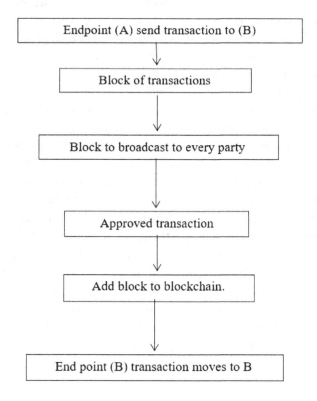

as a result of the foregoing, Blockchain technology is considered a safe technology to use, as it provides confidentiality through high-performance encryption techniques that are included in it, and reliability, because it is not possible to manipulate or change data after it is entered into the block. The advantages in performance in terms of confidentiality and reliability, in addition to the absence of a central authority controlling the work of the block chain, make it provide freedom and flexibility in dealing with commercial transactions and others, as it can be effective when applied in stock markets or government departments for real estate registration, banks, etc. And it is trading in cryptocurrencies, in short, the (Blockchain) can be considered as (a shared and immutable ledger that records transactions and tracks assets in a specific system in the network.

Malware

Malicious programs are programs that have been written with the intention of causing damage to devices or accessing data without authorization with the intent of exploiting or causing harm to people (Aslan et al., 2023; Yaacoub et al., 2023). Malware is categorized into many types such as viruses, Trojan horses, spyware, and worms. The authors of malicious programs may be either individuals or criminal organizations, and they sell their products to any party that pays them the required price, and the users of this type of program may also be individuals or organizations, and in some cases the authors of the programs are themselves the users of them, and in all cases there are individuals and organizations whose interest is to obtain prohibited data from computers or networks, or to destroy this data in order to reach its objectives, malware represents one of the most serious threats to computer security.

Antivirus Software

Virus detection systems play an important role in protecting computer systems from malicious attacks (Kumar et al., 2022; Vennam et al., 2021; Mijwil et al., 2022). Despite this, these systems can overlook different successful attacks, which can cause harmful results, because whenever there is a development in anti-virus systems, there is a greater development in malicious programs, and sometimes the opposite occurs, meaning more precisely that development occurs in malicious programs first and then it is The corresponding development in anti-virus programs to keep up with this development, but in practical experience the effectiveness of anti-virus programs differs from one to another as they do not all work at the same level of efficiency, and the level of knowledge of individuals varies as well as the extent of their effectiveness and how to use them optimally in terms of choosing the most effective types As well as constantly downloading updates for these types.

Table 1. Literature review with strengths and weaknesses

Weaknesses	Strengths	Explanation	Reference	no
The review did not, at this time, include industrial enforcement of the BCT and taking into account machine learning	The review shows that the use of (BCT) in the industry leads to integrity by ensuring data confidentiality and integrity and must be implemented to preserve data.	Classification the most important cyber-attacks that occurred in the last decade in the revolution Industry 4.0 based on four categories.	ElMamy et al., 2020	1
The sample opcodes are extracted using static analysis for malware only.	The proposed model achieved a detection accuracy of 98.7%. This model is better than many similar works	Use a template to detect malware run icons for malicious and benign executables as a feature. The proposed model uses an opcode extraction and counting Algorithm (OPEC) to prepare the opcode feature vector for the experiment.	Samantray and Tripathy, 2021	2
Some future challenges are likely to be explored in the field of IDS.	Provide a comprehensive survey of current trends in IDS research.	Reviews the different approaches to IDS, It compares them and provides a comparative analysis based on their advantages and disadvantages.	Bilaiya et al., 2021	3
There is a slight limitation in the absence of other types of malwares.	Discover that, on average, there are 86 major antivirus programs around the world capable of detecting 54.84%, 34.95%, 42.17%, and 16.82% of Portable Executable Files (PE), Java, JavaScript, and PHP malware, respectively.	Evaluation of the accuracy of conventional antiviruses.	Lima, 2021	4
There is a slight limitation in not addressing a broader range of threats.	Some notable cyber-attacks and cyber security solutions for the food and agricultural industry are concerned in detail.	A review of the main issue related to cyber threats and cyber security challenges for agriculture and food products.	Verma et al., 2023	5
There is a slight limitation in not dealing with a greater number of protocols, recommendations, and technology related to malicious software, hacking, and electronic piracy.	Some simplified measures and environments have been identified to enhance security. Thus, they highlight a few protocols, recommendations, and technologies that are essential as a solution to avoid endpoint exploitation on the part of the user.	Review vulnerabilities, hacking and associated risks.	Noor and Mustafa, 2023	6
There is a slight limitation of the research related to other security threats that have yet to be dealt with by the proposed framework.	Simulation of AVISPA framework authentication protocols. The results analysis shows that the proposed framework can efficiently deal with several security issues.	It uses the blockchain data structure to maintain the immutability of data. On the other hand, proposed protocols for authentication from users (people and devices) to the edge server and the edge server to the controller server. The proposed framework also provides access to users who use biometrics.	Islam et al., 2023	7

3. THE METHODS

The practical aim of the paper is to determine the effectiveness level of each one of the anti – virus software according to a specific parameters that covers important aspects of the anti-virus performance under experiment through particular environment, in order to achieve the particular aim of this paper, we chose windows environment and insert a malware with the size 269 KB the type of the file that carry the malware is zip file inside a folder contains many files of different types with the size of 7.47 GB. To assess the efficacy of antivirus software in real-world scenarios, follow these steps:

- Begin by placing a malicious program into a folder containing a substantial volume of data.
- Next, install the antivirus software of choice.
- Initiate a scan of the folder using the antivirus software to detect and isolate any threats. Record the scan results and parameters applied.
- Uninstall the antivirus software to prevent any potential conflicts or confusion with other antivirus programs.
- Repeat the entire process for each of the four antivirus programs until all have been evaluated.

Figure 2 and 3 shows the properties of each the file that carries the malware and the folder that contain the malware respectively.

This paper download and install the following four anti-virus:

- Malwarebytes
- Avast
- Advanced System Protector
- AVG

The procedure is when download and install each one of the anti – virus software, then applied the anti – virus software on the required folder, then the anti- virus being uninstall from the windows control panel, then deleted completely from the device, before downloading and install the next anti-virus, in order to avoid any intersection or confusion between the application of more than anti – virus software in the device . This paper assumes group of parameters all the related to the performance of the anti-virus software, the following parameters are:

1. Finding the infection (FI)
2. Determine the type of the infection (DTI)

Figure 2. The properties of the folder that contains the inserted malware

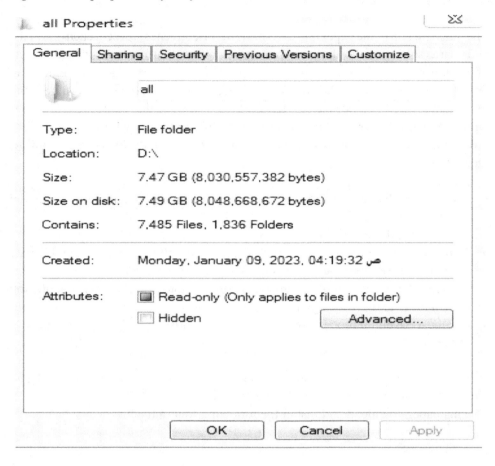

3.   Scanning all the required data (SRD)
4.   Time required for Scanning the Required data (TSRD)
5.   Interface of local language (IOLL)

If the anti – virus provide any one of the above parameters then the state vale related to this parameter it will be assigned to be (1), if the anti-virus does not provide any of the following parameter the state value related to this parameter it will be assigned to be (0), as the Table 2 show.

In order to determine the efficiency of anti-virus the paper apply the following equation (1):

Figure 3. The properties of the zip file that carry the malware

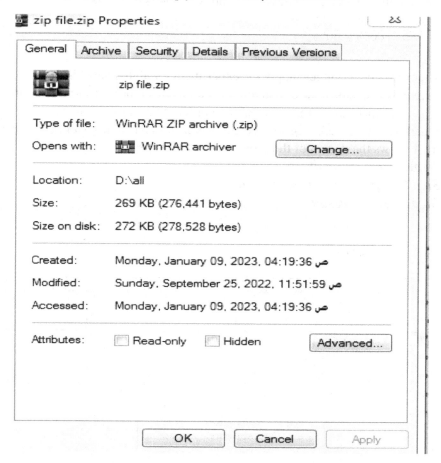

Table 2. Example of parameters value for a specific anti-virus

Parameters	Value of Parameters
FI	0
DTI	1
SRD	1
TSRD	0
IOII	1

$Rating\,(ER)\,of\,(anti-virus) = sum\ of\ the\ parameters\ /\ 5*100\%$

$$(1)$$

For example, the effectiveness of the above table is as follow:

$$ER = 3 / 5 * 100\% = 60\%$$

After the paper complete apply the experiment for all the anti-virus, and extract all the required results of the effectiveness of each one of the anti-virus software, the paper will compare the extracted results, in order to sorting the anti-virus software in ascending order according to their effectiveness as a final result of this paper. Figure 4 shows the design of the procedure of this paper.

Step1 : *insert the malware*

Step2 : *apply anti − virus software*

Step3 : *extract results for first anti − virus software*

Figure 4. The workflow

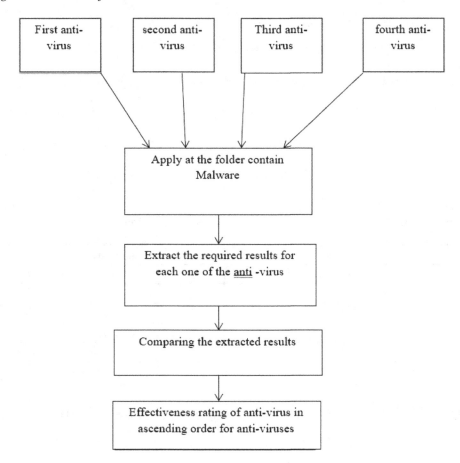

Step4 : *remove the anti − virus software*

Step5 : *repeat the step*(2,3,4)*until extract all the results for the four anti − virus software*

Step6 : *find the effectiveness of each one of the anti − virus due the equation*

Step7 : *compare the effectiveness of each one of the anti − virus in order to sort them in ascending order*

4. THE EFFECTS

Extracting the results from the experiment at the Malwarebytes. Table 3 shows the parameters value and Figure 5 shows the extracted results.

Figure 5. Virus detection by Malwarebytes software

Table 3. Parameters value for a Malwarebytes anti-virus

Parameters	Value of Parameters
FI	1
DTI	1
SRD	1
TSRD	1
IOLL	0

For example: $ER = 4/5*100\% = 80\%$

Figure 6. Virus detection by Avast software

Table 4. Parameters value for an Avast anti-virus

Parameters	Value of Parameters
FI	1
DTI	1
SRD	0
TSRD	0
IOLL	1
For example: $ER = 3 / 5 * 100\% = 60\%$.	

Extracting the results from the experiment at the Avast. Table 4 shows the parameters value and Figure 6 shows the extracted results.

Extracting the results from the experiment at the AVG. Table 5 shows the parameters value and Figure 7 shows the extracted results.

Extracting the results from the experiment at the Advanced system protector. Table 6 shows the parameters value and Figure 8 shows the extracted results.

Table 7 illustrates the conclusive results for the effectiveness rating of the anti-virus in ascending order (from worst to best performance):

Figure 7. Virus detection by AVG software

Table 5. Parameters value for a AVG anti-virus

Parameters	Value of Parameters
FI	0
DTI	0
SRD	0
TSRD	0
IOLL	0
For example: $ER = 0 / 0 * 100\% = 0\%$.	

5. CONCLUSIONS AND FUTURE WORK

Malware is malicious software that causes harm to users and devices and thus to the technology that is connected to these devices through the network. There are large types of malwares, and there are also large types of antivirus programs. This research issued parameters for measuring the effectiveness of a group of anti-virus programs in the framework of a practical experiment in order to arrange the effectiveness of these anti-virus programs in ascending order, and the final result of this research shows that the effectiveness classification is ascending in order as follows: Average 0%, Advanced System Protector 20% Avast 60%, Malwarebytes

Figure 8. Advanced system protector

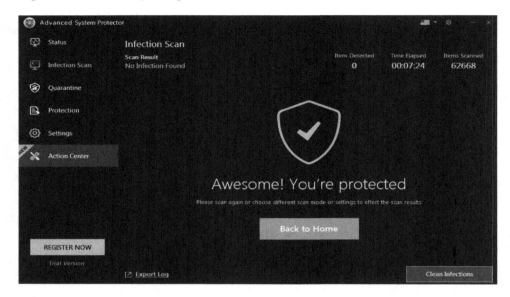

Table 6. Parameters value for an Advanced system protector anti-virus

Parameters	Value of Parameters
FI	0
DTI	0
SRD	0
TSRD	1
IOLL	0
For example: $ER = 1/5*100\% = 20\%$	

Table 7. Effectiveness rate of antivirus software

Software	Effectiveness Rate
AVG	0%
Advanced system protector	20%
Avast	60%
Malwarebytes	80%

80%. In the future, more studies will be conducted on blockchain while protecting computer systems.

Funding

None.

Conflicts of Interest

The authors have declared no conflict of interest.

REFERENCES

AlShamsi, M., Al-Emran, M., & Shaalan, K. (2022). A Systematic Review on Blockchain Adoption. *Applied Sciences (Basel, Switzerland)*, *12*(9), 1–18. doi:10.3390/app12094245 PMID:35685831

Aslan, Ö., Aktuğ, S. S., Ozkan-Okay, M., Yilmaz, A. A., & Akin, E. (2023). A Comprehensive Review of Cyber Security Vulnerabilities, Threats, Attacks, and Solutions. *Electronics (Basel)*, *12*(6), 1–42. doi:10.3390/electronics12061333

Athanere, S. & Thakur, R. (2022). Blockchain based hierarchical semi-decentralized approach using IPFS for secure and efficient data sharing. *Journal of King Saud University - Computer and Information Sciences*, *34*(4), 1523-1534. https://doi.org/doi:10.1016/j.jksuci.2022.01.019

Bilaiya, R., Ahlawat, P., & Bathla, R. (2021). Intrusion Detection Systems: Current Trends and Future Challenges. Handbook of Research on Machine Learning Techniques for Pattern Recognition and Information Security, 235-254. doi:10.4018/978-1-7998-3299-7.ch014

Doshi, R., Hiran, K. K., Mijwil, M. M., & Anand, D. (2023). To That of Artificial Intelligence, Passing Through Business Intelligence. Handbook of Research on AI and Knowledge Engineering for Real-Time Business Intelligence, 1-16. doi:10.4018/978-1-6684-6519-6.ch001

ElMamy, S. B., Mrabet, H., Gharbi, H., Jemai, A., & Trentesaux, D. (2020). A Survey on the Usage of Blockchain Technology for Cyber-Threats in the Context of Industry 4.0. *Sustainability (Basel)*, *12*(21), 1–19. doi:10.3390u12219179

Islam, E., Islam, R., Chetty, M., Lim, S., & Chadhar, M. (2023). User authentication and access control to blockchain-based forensic log data. *EURASIP Journal on Information Security*, *2023*(7), 1–24. doi:10.118613635-023-00142-3

Javaid, M., Haleem, A., Singh, R. P., Suman, R., & Khan, S. (2022). A review of Blockchain Technology applications for financial services. *BenchCouncil Transactions on Benchmarks. Standards and Evaluations*, *2*(3), 100073. doi:10.1016/j.tbench.2022.100073

Kumar, A., Dubey, K. K., Gupta, H., Lamba, S., Memoria, M., & Joshi, K. (2022). Keylogger Awareness and Use in Cyber Forensics. Rising Threats in Expert Applications and Solutions, 719-725. doi:10.1007/978-981-19-1122-4_75

Kumar, D. A., Das, S. K., & Sahoo, M. K. (2022). Malware Detection System Using API-Decision Tree. Advances in Data Science and Management, 511–517. doi:10.1007/978-981-16-5685-9_49

Kumar, R., Zhang, X., Wang, W., Khan, R. U., Kumar, J., & Sharif, A. (2019). A Multimodal Malware Detection Technique for Android IoT Devices Using Various Features. *IEEE Access : Practical Innovations, Open Solutions*, *7*, 64411–64430. doi:10.1109/ACCESS.2019.2916886

Lima, S. (2021). Limitation of COTS antiviruses: issues, controversies, and problems of COTS antiviruses. Handbook of Research on Cyber Crime and Information Privacy, 396-413. http://doi.org/ doi:10.4018/978-1-7998-5728-0.ch020

Maniriho, P., Mahmood, A. N., & Chowdhury, M. J. M. (2022). A study on malicious software behaviour analysis and detection techniques: Taxonomy, current trends and challenges. *Future Generation Computer Systems*, *130*, 1–18. doi:10.1016/j.future.2021.11.030

Mijwil, M. M., Gök, M., Doshi, R., Hiran, K. K., & Kösesoy, I. (2023). Utilizing Artificial Intelligence Techniques to Improve the Performance of Wireless Nodes. Applications of Artificial Intelligence in Wireless Communication Systems, 150-162. doi:10.4018/978-1-6684-7348-1.ch010

Mijwil, M. M., Sadıkoğlu, E., Cengiz, E., & Candan, H. (2022). Siber Güvenlikte Yapay Zekanın Rolü ve Önemi: Bir Derleme. *Veri Bilimi*, *5*(2), 97–105.

Mustafa, M., Alshare, M., Bhargava, D., Neware, R., Singh, B., & Ngulube, P. (2022). Perceived Security Risk Based on Moderating Factors for Blockchain Technology Applications in Cloud Storage to Achieve Secure Healthcare Systems. *Computational and Mathematical Methods in Medicine*, *2022*(6112815), 1–10. doi:10.1155/2022/6112815 PMID:35096132

Noor, M. A. F., & Mustafa, K. (2023). Protocols and Guidelines to Enhance the Endpoint Security of Blockchain at User's End. *Proceedings of International Conference on ICT for Digital, Smart, and Sustainable Development*. 10.4108/eai.24-3-2022.2318925

Samantray, O. P., & Tripathy, S. N. (2021). An Opcode-Based Malware Detection Model Using Supervised Learning Algorithms. *International Journal of Information Security and Privacy*, *15*(4), 18–30. doi:10.4018/IJISP.2021100102

Santhi, A. R., & Muthuswamy, P. (2022). Influence of Blockchain Technology in Manufacturing Supply Chain and Logistics. *Logistics*, *6*(1), 1–22. doi:10.3390/logistics6010015

Thangamayan, S., Pradhan, K., Loganathan, G. B., Sitender, S., Sivamani, S., & Tesema, M. (2023). Blockchain-Based Secure Traceable Scheme for Food Supply Chain. *Journal of Food Quality*, *2023*(4728840), 1–11. doi:10.1155/2023/4728840

Unogwu, O. J., Doshi, R., Hiran, K. K., & Mijwil, M. M. (2022). Introduction to Quantum-Resistant Blockchain. Advancements in Quantum Blockchain With Real-Time Applications, 36-55. doi:10.4018/978-1-6684-5072-7.ch002

Vennam, P., Pramod, T. C., Thippeswamy, B. M., Kim, Y., & Kumar, B. N. P. (2021). Attacks and Preventive Measures on Video Surveillance Systems: A Review. *Applied Sciences (Basel, Switzerland)*, *11*(12), 1–17. doi:10.3390/app11125571

Verma, H. C., Srivastava, S., Ahmed, T., & Usmani, N. A. (2023). Cyber Threats in Agriculture and the Food Industry: An Indian Perspective. Advances in Cyberology and the Advent of the Next-Gen Information Revolution, 109-124. doi:10.4018/978-1-6684-8133-2.ch006

Winter, R., Rosa, F. F., Shukla, P., & Kazemian, H. (2022). Brazil Method of Anti-Malware Evaluation and Cyber Defense Impacts. *Journal of Applied Security Research*, 1–17. doi:10.1080/19361610.2022.2104104

Yaacoub, J. A., Noura, H. N., Salman, O., & Chehab, A. (2023). Ethical hacking for IoT: Security issues, challenges, solutions and recommendations. *Internet of Things and Cyber-Physical Systems*, *3*, 280–308. doi:10.1016/j.iotcps.2023.04.002

Yang, H., Li, S., Wu, X., Lu, H., & Han, W. (2019). A Novel Solutions for Malicious Code Detection and Family Clustering Based on Machine Learning. *IEEE Access : Practical Innovations, Open Solutions*, *7*, 148853–148860. doi:10.1109/ACCESS.2019.2946482

Yang, Y., Lin, Y., Li, Z., Zhao, L., Yao, M., Lai, Y., & Li, P. (2023). GooseBt: A programmable malware detection framework based on process, file, registry, and COM monitoring. *Computer Communications*, *204*, 24–32. doi:10.1016/j. comcom.2023.03.011

Chapter 9
Leveraging Blockchain Technology and Smart Contracts for Intelligent Supply Chain Management

R. Elakya
Information Technology, Sri Venkateswara College of Engineering, India

R. Thanga Selvi
Vel Tech Rangarajan Dr. Sagunthala R&D Institute of Science and Technology, India

S. Girirajan
Computing Technologies, SRM Institute of Science and Technology, India

A. Vidhyavani
SRM Institute of Science and Technology, India

ABSTRACT

The current manual process of the traditional supply chain system, from raw material manufacturing to product delivery, lacks sufficient data and transaction security while being time-consuming. This outdated procedure is ineffective and unreliable for consumers. However, integrating blockchain and smart contract technologies into traditional supply chain management systems can significantly enhance data security, authenticity, time management, and transaction processes. By leveraging decentralized blockchain technology, the entire supply chain management (SCM) process becomes more trustworthy, ensuring consumer satisfaction. This study utilizes a peer-to-peer encrypted system in conjunction with smart contracts to ensure data immutability and prevent unauthorized access. Moreover, cryptographic methods are employed to enhance transaction security and address these issues. Ultimately, this chapter demonstrates how to maintain a highly secure, transparent, and efficient supply chain management process.

DOI: 10.4018/979-8-3693-1131-8.ch009

INTRODUCTION

Supply chain management (SCM) holds immense importance in today's global market, significantly influencing the global economy. SCM involves the movement of goods from producers to consumers and encompasses various stages (Swan, 2017). However, traditional supply chain management has limitations, especially in terms of facilitating customer reversals and ensuring the quality of supplied items. It primarily focuses on forward flows, i.e., the movement of products from senders to recipients (Zheng et al., 2021). However, supporting reverse flows and transactions for every consumer is equally crucial.

The advent of blockchain and smart contracts has the potential to disrupt traditional supply chain management systems (Croman et al., 2016). Blockchain's transparency and immutability can bring substantial benefits to the supply chain. By providing a secure mechanism for data collection and enabling the development and execution of programmed scripts or applications known as smart contracts, blockchain technology aids in modernizing the supply chain. Smart contracts empower supply chain managers to effectively track the origin and security of their products (Swan, 2017). We have addressed these issues and proposed a solution in our discussion.

The aim of this research is to create a conceptual framework for a supply chain management system that capitalizes on blockchain and smart contracts to facilitate safe transactions and ensure the delivery of high-quality products (Zyskind et al., 2015). By adopting this framework, customers will have the confidence to return products and receive refunds, leading to a trustworthy global market. Notably, our proposed paradigm will bring about a significant transformation in the entire supply chain management system (Panarello et al., 2018).

A blockchain is a dynamic collection of blocks that are cryptographically connected and secured, forming an unbroken chain of records. These blocks are cryptographically linked together, and they undergo validation by a majority of network nodes in the blockchain network. Once a block is verified, it becomes part of the shared chain that is accessible to all network nodes (Heilman et al., 2015). The processing of each piece of data on the blockchain involves significant computational effort and time to ensure its integrity. Blockchain systems offer distinct qualities that set them apart from other technologies. For example, data stored on the blockchain is immutable, resistant to tampering, and relies on a decentralized network. It is also safeguarded through encryption, making it challenging to compromise. In general, there are three main types of blockchains: public or permissionless, private or permissioned, and consortium blockchains. Each type has its own specific characteristics determined by the nature of the network participants and the geographical context in which it operates.

Smart contracts are coded software or script components written in high-level programming languages like Java, C++, NodeJS, Python, Go, Solidity, and others. Different blockchain systems make use of various programming languages for implementing smart contracts (Androulaki et al., 2018). For example, the Hyperledger manufacturing platform utilizes NodeJS and Python, while Ethereum employs the Solidity programming language, known for its reliability. Each peer in a blockchain network has access to copies of smart contracts. These smart contract scripts execute automatically, independently, and transparently (Zeng et al., 2019). They are executed within a secure environment to ensure the integrity and security of both the code and the data.

The fundamental concept of a cryptocurrency lies in its ability to be exchanged through transactions and added to new blocks in a highly secure manner. In the realm of cryptocurrencies, there are three key levels: technology, currency, and tokens. The prominent example of a cryptocurrency is Bitcoin, while the underlying technology that powers it is blockchain (which is more than just a currency; it is a set of rules). A protocol refers to a set of rules that govern how individuals interact within a network. It determines the usage of public keys and signatures for authentication in cryptocurrencies like Bitcoin and Ethereum (Kshetri, 2018).

The term "coin" refers to the built-in asset of the protocol that enables user interactions and serves as a reward for mining the blockchain and creating new blocks. Additionally, coins can be used for purchasing goods and services from others (Swan, 2014). On the other hand, tokens are associated with the usage of smart contracts. It's important to differentiate between tokens and coins. When someone invests in a coin, they are investing in the underlying protocol of that specific cryptocurrency. However, investing in a token means investing in the concept behind what is being built, as tokens represent assets or utility within a particular project or ecosystem.

Over time, the supply chain has undergone significant evolution due to the global market's influence (Tapscott & Tapscott, 2016). Supply chain management (SCM) has become increasingly crucial in today's world. However, numerous substantial challenges persist within supply chain management across various areas.

Trust between buyers and sellers is essential in the supply chain. Yet, in today's commercial landscape, complete trust is often lacking. Intermediaries within the supply chain hold considerable power and can manipulate market value without the knowledge of genuine supply chain members, benefiting at the expense of end consumers (Bonneau et al., 2015). Additionally, many businesses, hospitals, and other entities lack an encrypted mechanism to securely store individuals' private information, making the data vulnerable to cyberattacks and exposing sensitive public and private information.

Price transparency is also lacking due to intermediaries in the supply chain, creating a need for a direct link between buyers and vendors to enhance transaction transparency and trustworthiness (Szabo, 1997). In the current supply chain management system, the flow of commodities is unidirectional, placing the burden of defective products on customers who have limited options for recourse (Dinh et al., 2018). Manual paperwork is still prevalent at various stages, and the monitoring mechanisms in global transactions heavily rely on human intervention, making them more susceptible to errors and resulting in unjustified price increases and difficulties in tracing the source of issues (Ali et al., 2018).

These factors significantly impact the worldwide market and contribute to its instability. Flawless competition remains an elusive concept in the current state of the market. Addressing these challenges and improving supply chain management practices is essential for establishing a more transparent, trustworthy, and competitive global market.

Related Works

The author Yli-Huumo et al. (2016) provides a comprehensive overview of blockchain technology. It explores the fundamental characteristics of blockchain, including its decentralization, transparency, and immutability. The survey delves into various applications of blockchain across sectors such as finance, supply chain management, healthcare, and more. It also addresses the challenges and limitations of blockchain, such as scalability, energy consumption, and regulatory concerns. Additionally, the paper discusses emerging trends and future directions for blockchain technology, highlighting areas for further research and development. Overall, this survey serves as a valuable resource for understanding the potential, challenges, and future prospects of blockchain technology.

The systematic literature review conducted by Zheng et al. (2017) offers a comprehensive analysis of blockchain technology, focusing on its state-of-the-art advancements, applications, and challenges. Through an extensive examination of existing literature, the authors provide a thorough overview of blockchain technology and its implications across various domains. They explore the fundamental characteristics of blockchain, such as decentralization and immutability, and delve into the technical components that ensure the security and integrity of transactions, including distributed consensus mechanisms, cryptographic algorithms, and smart contracts. The review highlights the diverse applications of blockchain in sectors such as finance, supply chain management, healthcare, and government services, showcasing the potential benefits of increased transparency, improved efficiency, reduced costs, and enhanced trust. Additionally, the authors address the challenges associated with blockchain adoption, including scalability, energy consumption, regulatory and legal hurdles, interoperability, and the need for standardization. They discuss emerging trends, such as permissioned blockchains and hybrid approaches, that offer potential solutions to these challenges. Overall, the review serves as a valuable resource for researchers, practitioners, and organizations seeking a comprehensive understanding of the state-of-the-art advancements, applications, and challenges in the field of blockchain technology.

The survey paper by Dorri et al. (2017) comprehensively examines the security challenges and potential solutions in the realm of blockchain technology. Without the focus on the title, the paper explores key areas such as consensus protocols, privacy, scalability, and smart contracts. It discusses the vulnerabilities of consensus mechanisms, the risks to user privacy, and the scalability limitations faced by blockchain systems. The authors provide insights into potential solutions, including advanced consensus protocols, privacy-preserving techniques, and strategies to address scalability concerns. The paper also highlights the security considerations in smart contract implementation and proposes mitigation strategies. Overall, this survey paper serves as a valuable resource for understanding the security aspects of blockchain technology and offers potential solutions to ensure the robustness and reliability of blockchain systems.

The survey paper by Tschorsch and Scheuermann (2016) provides a comprehensive examination of consensus mechanisms and mining management in blockchain networks. It explores various algorithms, including Proof of Work (PoW), Proof of Stake (PoS), and Practical Byzantine Fault Tolerance (PBFT), and discusses their characteristics, advantages, and limitations. The authors emphasize the importance of consensus in ensuring the integrity of blockchain transactions and delve into the details of each mechanism, considering their computational requirements, security properties, and applicability in different contexts. The paper offers valuable insights for researchers and practitioners seeking a deeper understanding of consensus mechanisms and mining management in blockchain networks.

The research paper by Luthra et al. (2020) investigates the requirements and critical success factors for implementing blockchain-based supply chain traceability systems. It explores the benefits and challenges of utilizing blockchain technology in supply chain management. The authors emphasize the importance of traceability in supply chains and highlight the limitations of traditional systems. They discuss the business requirements for implementing blockchain-based traceability, including secure data storage, transparency, real-time visibility, and product tracking. The study identifies critical success factors such as stakeholder collaboration, data interoperability, standardization, scalability, and integration with existing IT infrastructure. It examines the benefits of blockchain in improving transparency, reducing counterfeiting, and enhancing product quality, while addressing challenges such as technical complexities and data privacy concerns. This research paper serves as a valuable resource for understanding the potential of blockchain in supply chain traceability and guiding the effective implementation of such systems.

The systematic literature review paper by Bello et al. (2020) provides an overview of blockchain-based smart contracts, examining their characteristics, applications, challenges, and potential future directions. The authors analyze a wide range of research papers and identify key themes and trends in the field of smart contracts on blockchain. They discuss the benefits of smart contracts, such as automation, transparency, and efficiency, and address challenges related to scalability, security, and legal implications. The paper concludes by highlighting potential research opportunities and areas for further exploration in the field.

The literature review paper by Xu et al. (2019) surveys the existing literature on blockchain technology, covering various aspects such as technical foundations, applications in different industries, challenges, and research trends. The authors analyze a comprehensive set of research articles and identify key themes and findings. They discuss the underlying concepts of blockchain, including distributed consensus and cryptographic techniques. The paper explores the applications of blockchain in industries such as finance, healthcare, supply chain, and government, highlighting the benefits and challenges associated with each domain. It also discusses emerging research directions and potential future developments in blockchain technology.

The comprehensive review paper by Conoscenti et al. (2016) explores the concepts and applications of blockchain technology and cryptocurrencies, covering topics such as decentralized consensus, smart contracts, security, and regulatory challenges. The authors provide an in-depth analysis of the technical foundations of blockchain, including cryptographic principles and consensus mechanisms. They examine the evolution of cryptocurrencies, such as Bitcoin, and discuss their impact on various industries. The paper also addresses security and privacy concerns associated with blockchain technology and explores potential regulatory frameworks to address these challenges. Overall, it provides a comprehensive understanding of the key concepts and applications of blockchain and cryptocurrencies.

The paper by Zheng et al. (2018) provides an overview of the principles and applications of blockchain technology, discussing its potential impact on various sectors, including finance, supply chain, healthcare, and energy. The authors explain the underlying principles of blockchain, such as distributed ledger, consensus mechanisms, and smart contracts. They explore the potential benefits of blockchain technology, such as improved transparency, efficiency, and trust in transactions. The paper examines real-world use cases of blockchain in different industries, highlighting the challenges and opportunities in each domain. It also discusses emerging research trends and future directions for the application of blockchain technology.

The paper by Beck et al. (2017) presents a comprehensive analysis of blockchain technology in the context of business and information systems research, examining its potential benefits, challenges, and future research directions. The authors discuss the key features of blockchain, including decentralization, immutability, and transparency, and explore its implications for business models and information systems. They examine various applications of blockchain, such as supply chain management, identity management, and financial services, highlighting the transformative potential of the technology. The paper also addresses the challenges and limitations of blockchain, including scalability, interoperability, and regulatory concerns. It concludes by discussing future research directions, such as governance models, standardization, and the integration of blockchain with emerging technologies.

MATERIALS AND METHODS

This section focuses on the methods and materials utilized to achieve the goal of modeling a cyber supply chain (SC) using blockchain technology. The modeling approach is based on the concept of the blockchain as a chain of information services that represents the operational fulfillment of the physical supply chain. The blockchain keeps a record of transaction activities, capturing the start and completion timings. In this context, the operations of logistics companies are considered information services provided to the blockchain architecture. The design of smart contracts can be seen as the computation of start and completion timings for these information services within a blockchain-driven cyber environment, mirroring real supply chain activities.

In Figure 1, the comprehensive structure of the blockchain and smart contract working mechanism is illustrated. The diagram showcases the various components and interactions involved in utilizing blockchain technology and smart contracts within the supply chain context. Logistics service providers are depicted as participants in the supply chain, undertaking specific operations that are sequentially organized as flow-oriented activities. These activities can include intermediaries, carriers, and other entities involved in the movement and management of goods throughout the supply chain. The blockchain and smart contract framework facilitate the secure and transparent execution of these activities, ensuring reliable and traceable transactions within the supply chain ecosystem.

The process of creating smart contracts within the context of supply chain management involves several steps. Firstly, logistics businesses are assigned specific tasks or operations within the supply chain. These tasks can include activities such as transportation, warehousing, inventory management, and order fulfillment. These assignments are then incorporated into the smart contracts, which serve as digital agreements between the parties involved.

Once the smart contracts are established, they are deployed on the blockchain network. The blockchain serves as a distributed ledger that records all the transactions and activities associated with the smart contracts. It provides a transparent and

173

Figure 1. Simple dataflow of the proposed model

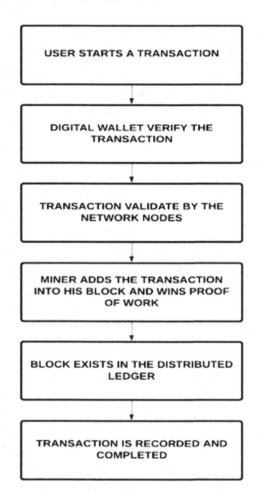

immutable record of the start and completion of the execution of the operations specified in the contracts.

As logistics firms carry out their assigned tasks, the progress and status of their activities are updated and recorded on the blockchain. This allows for real-time visibility and traceability of the supply chain operations, enabling stakeholders to monitor and track the movement of goods, verify the completion of tasks, and ensure compliance with contractual obligations.

The smart contract design, in this context, can be seen as the process of defining the parameters and conditions for the initiation and termination of information services within the blockchain-driven cyberspace. It involves specifying the criteria for triggering the start of a logistics operation and determining the conditions for its completion. This ensures that the execution of tasks aligns with the predefined rules and requirements set forth in the smart contracts.

By leveraging blockchain technology and smart contracts, the supply chain management process becomes more efficient, secure, and transparent. The decentralized nature of the blockchain ensures that all participants in the supply chain have access to the same information, reducing the need for intermediaries and streamlining the flow of data and transactions. Additionally, the immutability and tamper-resistant nature of the blockchain enhance trust and reliability in the supply chain ecosystem.

The system incorporates a permissioned blockchain at its core, which serves as the foundational layer. This blockchain records and stores all the transactions and events occurring within the supply chain network, ensuring an immutable and transparent ledger of activities.

Surrounding the blockchain layer are additional layers of infrastructure and services that support the seamless functioning of the supply chain. These layers include node infrastructure, which consists of the network of nodes or participants that maintain the blockchain network. These nodes contribute to the consensus mechanism and validate transactions, ensuring the integrity of the blockchain.

Another essential layer is the smart contract layer, which enables the execution of self-executing and self-enforcing contracts within the blockchain network. Smart contracts automate and streamline various processes in the supply chain, such as order fulfillment, payment settlements, and inventory management.

Together, these layers of infrastructure and services work in harmony to create a robust and efficient supply chain system. The blockchain layer acts as the backbone, recording and securing all transactions and events, while the other layers provide the necessary tools and functionalities to facilitate the smooth operation of the supply chain.

A blockchain-based architecture for food supply chain management in Figure 2 refers to the use of distributed ledger technology (DLT) to revolutionize the way the flow of food products is managed. By leveraging blockchain, a decentralized and immutable digital ledger, transparency, traceability, and efficiency are enhanced throughout the supply chain. This architecture allows for the secure and transparent tracking of food products from their origin to the end consumer.

Implementing a blockchain-based architecture involves recording each step of the food supply chain as a transaction on the blockchain. This includes important information such as the source of the food, quality certifications, transportation details, and storage conditions. These transactions are securely added to the blockchain, ensuring that the data remains unalterable and reliable.

Figure 2. Distributed ledger technology (DLT) for food supply chain management

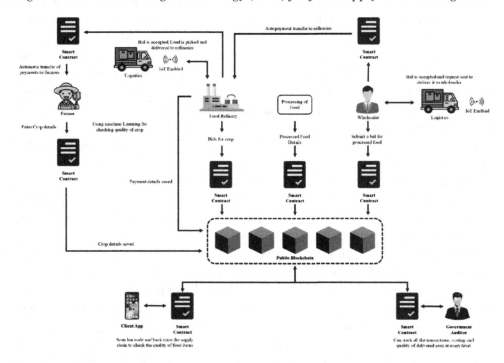

With this architecture, stakeholders can easily verify the authenticity and provenance of food products, monitor their quality and safety, and respond promptly to any issues or recalls. Smart contracts, embedded within the blockchain, can automate specific supply chain processes, streamlining operations and improving efficiency.

Overall, a blockchain-based architecture for food supply chain management offers significant benefits, including increased transparency, reduced risks of fraud and counterfeit products, enhanced food safety, and greater trust among supply chain participants and consumers. This approach transforms the sharing and accessibility of information within the food supply chain, leading to improved efficiency and accountability in ensuring the delivery of safe and high-quality food products.

Experiment and Results

The hardware specifications of a modern desktop computer can vary depending on the intended use and price range. However, there are some common specifications that can be found in typical modern desktop computers. The processor (CPU) is often an Intel Core i5 or i7, or an AMD Ryzen 5 or 7. These processors offer a good balance of performance and affordability for general computing tasks and moderate gaming. For memory (RAM), a typical configuration is 8 GB or 16 GB of DDR4 RAM. This provides sufficient memory for multitasking and running demanding applications smoothly. In terms of storage, modern desktop computers often come with a solid-state drive (SSD) with a capacity of 256 GB or 512 GB. SSDs offer faster data access and boot times compared to traditional hard disk drives. A dedicated graphics card (GPU) is commonly included, such as an Nvidia GeForce GTX or AMD Radeon RX. This is especially important for gaming or graphics-intensive tasks, providing better performance and visual quality. The motherboard should have an ATX or Micro-ATX form factor and support modern components. This ensures compatibility and future upgradability. A reliable power supply unit (PSU) with a capacity of 500W or 650W, certified as 80+ Bronze or Gold, is recommended to provide stable and efficient power to the system. The case should have an ATX or Micro-ATX form factor with good airflow and cable management options. This helps keep the components cool and organized. Additional peripherals typically include a keyboard, mouse, monitor, and speakers or headphones, depending on the user's preferences and requirements.

Algorithm for Smart Contract

```
Step 1: Begin
Step 2: Create the contract terms and conditions.
Step 3: Define variables and their types.
Step 4: Set buyerNegotiationState as false.
Step 5: Set sellerNegotiationState as false.
Step 6: Set dealState as false.
Step 7: Declare private string dealID.
Step 8: Create a function called initialization(msg) for the
smart contract.
Step 9: Set dealID as the value of msg.
Step 10: If sellerFlag exists, then:
- Set sellerNegotiationState as false.
- Send a message to the Seller to modify the sellerTerms.
- Else:
- Set sellerNegotiationState as true.
- End if.
Step 11: If buyerFlag is not equal to 1, then:
- Set buyerNegotiationState as false.
- Send a message to the Buyer to modify the buyerTerms.
- Else:
```

```
- Set buyerNegotiationState as true.
- End if.
Step 12: If buyerNegotiationState is true and
sellerNegotiationState is true, then:
- Set dealState as true.
- Send a message to the parent deal contract.
- Else:
- Declare "wait" as a variable to indicate the process is
waiting.
- End if.
Step 13: End.
```

Module 1: Product Lifecycle Management and Traceability

The Product Creation and Tracking module plays a crucial role in the supply chain management process by facilitating the seamless introduction of new products and providing comprehensive tracking capabilities. This module encompasses a range of functionalities that enable users to efficiently add and register new products, ensuring that each product is assigned a unique identifier. By recording vital information such as the product's current location and ownership, the module enables real-time monitoring of the product's movement throughout the supply chain.

One of the key tasks of this module is to verify the uniqueness of each product before its integration into the supply chain. By performing validation checks, the system ensures that duplicate products are not inadvertently included, enhancing data accuracy and preventing potential issues down the line.

Moreover, the module empowers authorized stakeholders to access timely and relevant information about the products. By leveraging tracking functionalities, users can effortlessly query the system to retrieve detailed insights into the status, whereabouts, and key milestones of a specific product at any given time. This level of transparency and visibility allows for enhanced decision-making, effective inventory management, and improved customer service.

Overall, the Product Creation and Tracking module serves as a fundamental component of the supply chain ecosystem, enabling efficient product introduction, reliable tracking, and accurate documentation. By streamlining these processes, it contributes to the optimization of supply chain operations, mitigates potential risks, and enhances the overall efficiency and effectiveness of the supply chain management system.

In Figure 3, we can observe the welcome page of the supply chain management system, which serves as the entry point for the system administrator. The administrator

Figure 3. Welcome page input of supply chain

is provided with an overview of the various actors involved in the supply chain, including manufacturers, distributors, and retailers. Additionally, both customers and administrators have the ability to access information about the products available on the website.

The website is designed with a user-friendly interface, ensuring ease of navigation and interaction for businesses. Within this interface, businesses have the functionality to create new products, transfer ownership of products, and access detailed product information. This empowers businesses to actively participate in the supply chain management process.

One of the key features of the website is the provision of real-time updates on the status of products within the supply chain. This includes information such as the current location of products, the quantity available, and the ownership details. These updates enable stakeholders to make informed decisions based on the most up-to-date information, ensuring efficient supply chain operations and effective inventory management.

Overall, the website serves as a central hub for supply chain management, offering a comprehensive set of features and functionalities to facilitate seamless collaboration and information sharing among the different actors involved. By providing a user-friendly interface and real-time updates, the website enhances transparency, efficiency, and decision-making capabilities within the supply chain ecosystem.

Module 2: Product Movement and Ownership Management

The Product Transfer and Ownership Management module serves as a critical component within the supply chain management system, specifically focusing on streamlining the transfer of product ownership between different entities. This module encompasses a range of functionalities that enable seamless and secure ownership transfers while maintaining data integrity and accuracy.

One of the primary functions of this module is to facilitate the specification of essential information such as the product ID, quantity, and the address of the new owner. By providing these details, the module ensures the precise identification and tracking of the products being transferred.

To ensure the legitimacy of ownership transfers, the module implements robust validation mechanisms. It verifies that the party initiating the transfer is indeed the current rightful owner of the product. By performing these verification checks, the module prevents unauthorized transfers and promotes trust among the participants in the supply chain.

Moreover, the module incorporates inventory management capabilities by checking the availability of the requested quantity of the product. This ensures that only valid transfers are executed, avoiding potential discrepancies or shortages in the supply chain.

Identity verification is another crucial aspect of this module. By implementing authentication protocols and security measures, the module ensures that the identities of the parties involved in the ownership transfer are verified. This helps prevent fraudulent activities and unauthorized access to the system, enhancing the overall security and integrity of the transfer process.

As ownership transfers occur, the module updates the relevant ownership records to accurately reflect the new owner and transfer details. This real-time updating of ownership records enhances transparency and accountability within the supply chain, enabling stakeholders to access reliable and up-to-date information regarding product ownership.

Overall, the Product Transfer and Ownership Management module plays a pivotal role in enabling efficient and secure ownership transfers within the supply chain. By enforcing validation checks, verifying identities, and maintaining accurate ownership records, the module ensures a reliable and transparent transfer process that fosters trust and integrity among the participants in the supply chain ecosystem.

Figure 4 showcases the transaction page within a smart contract-based supply chain management system that leverages the power of blockchain technology. This page serves as a comprehensive and transparent ledger, meticulously documenting all the transactions executed on the smart contract.

Figure 4. Transaction output of supply chain

By utilizing blockchain technology, the transaction page ensures the immutability and integrity of the recorded transactions. The decentralized nature of the blockchain network guarantees that once a transaction is recorded, it cannot be altered or manipulated, providing an unparalleled level of security and trust.

The transaction page plays a pivotal role in enhancing transparency and accountability within the supply chain process. It provides a centralized repository where all parties involved can view and access transactional data. This level of transparency fosters trust among stakeholders and enables them to verify and validate the transactions that have taken place, promoting a higher level of confidence in the system.

Each transaction is uniquely identified by a transaction ID, allowing for easy referencing, auditing, and tracking. This ID serves as a crucial identifier that facilitates the ability to trace a specific transaction back to its origin. By displaying the transaction ID on the transaction page, users can easily locate and retrieve the desired transaction, streamlining auditing processes and enabling efficient dispute resolution if needed.

Moreover, the transaction page acts as a valuable tool for monitoring and analyzing the supply chain process. It provides stakeholders with a consolidated view of all transactions, enabling them to assess the flow of goods, track the movement of products, and analyze transactional patterns. This real-time visibility empowers decision-makers to identify bottlenecks, optimize processes, and make informed strategic decisions based on accurate and up-to-date data.

Overall, the transaction page depicted in Figure 4 represents a crucial component within the smart contract-based supply chain management system. It serves as a reliable and transparent ledger that guarantees the integrity of transactions, enhances transparency and accountability, enables efficient auditing and tracking, and provides valuable insights for optimizing the supply chain process. By leveraging the capabilities of blockchain technology, the transaction page establishes a robust foundation for a secure, efficient, and trustworthy supply chain management ecosystem.

Module 3: Financial Transactions and Conflict Resolution

The Payment Processing and Dispute Resolution module is a critical component within the supply chain management system, responsible for managing the financial transactions and addressing any disputes that may arise during the supply chain process. This module plays a crucial role in ensuring smooth and secure payment processing and promoting fair and efficient dispute resolution.

One of the primary functions of this module is to handle the payment process between the buyer and seller. It includes features such as accepting payments from the buyer, verifying the legitimacy of the payment, and facilitating the secure transfer of funds to the seller. The module is designed to accommodate various payment methods, catering to both traditional options and emerging technologies like cryptocurrencies. By providing a secure and streamlined payment process, this module enhances financial transparency and facilitates timely transactions within the supply chain.

In addition to payment processing, the module incorporates mechanisms for effectively managing disputes that may occur during the supply chain journey. It provides a platform where parties can submit their disputes, present evidence, and engage in a structured resolution process. The module ensures fairness and impartiality by considering the evidence and arguments presented by all parties involved. By implementing clear rules and procedures, it strives to achieve equitable outcomes and maintain the trust and confidence of all stakeholders.

Furthermore, the module maintains a comprehensive record of payment transactions and dispute resolutions. This record serves as an audit trail, capturing crucial information such as payment details, timestamps, and resolution outcomes. The availability of this transparent and auditable record promotes accountability, facilitates traceability, and provides a basis for future reference or legal purposes.

To ensure the security and integrity of financial transactions and dispute resolution processes, the module incorporates robust authentication and authorization mechanisms. It employs encryption and access controls to safeguard sensitive financial and personal information, ensuring that only authorized individuals can participate in payment transactions and dispute resolution activities.

Overall, the Payment Processing and Dispute Resolution module is instrumental in promoting efficiency, transparency, and trust within the supply chain management system. By facilitating secure payment processing, fair dispute resolution, and maintaining comprehensive records, this module contributes to the overall effectiveness and reliability of the supply chain ecosystem.

Figure 5 presents the transaction page of a supply chain management system powered by blockchain technology, offering a detailed and comprehensive view of all transactions conducted on the smart contract. This page serves as a transparent and auditable ledger, providing stakeholders with a clear record of every transaction's occurrence, timestamp, and associated information.

Through the utilization of blockchain technology, the transaction page ensures the integrity and immutability of the recorded transactions. Each transaction is securely stored on the decentralized blockchain network, making it resistant to tampering or unauthorized modifications. This decentralized nature of the blockchain guarantees the reliability and trustworthiness of the transaction history.

The transaction page is designed to enhance transparency and accountability within the supply chain process. It enables authorized participants to access and review the details of each transaction, including the involved parties, transaction amounts, product information, and any additional relevant data. This level of transparency

Figure 5. Transaction output of supply chain

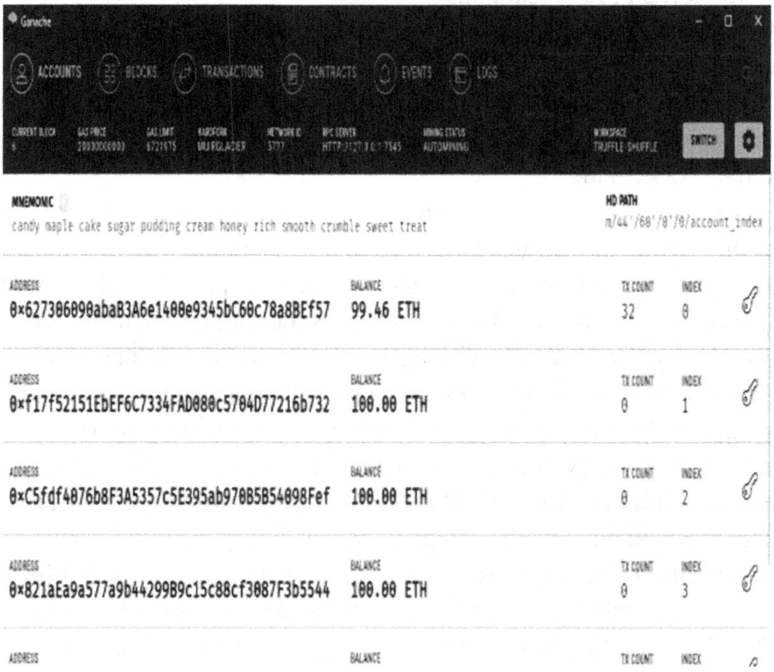

fosters trust among stakeholders, as they can independently verify and validate the accuracy of the recorded transactions.

Moreover, the transaction page provides a real-time and up-to-date overview of the supply chain process. It captures essential details such as the movement of goods, changes in ownership, and any associated documentation. This real-time visibility allows stakeholders to monitor the progress of transactions, track the location of goods, and identify potential bottlenecks or delays in the supply chain.

Furthermore, the transaction page serves as a valuable tool for auditing and compliance purposes. It enables auditors and regulatory bodies to verify the authenticity and accuracy of transactions, ensuring compliance with industry regulations and standards. The transparent nature of the blockchain-based transaction page streamlines the auditing process, reducing the time and effort required for manual reconciliation and verification.

Overall, the transaction page depicted in Figure 5 exemplifies the power of blockchain technology in revolutionizing supply chain management. By providing a detailed, transparent, and auditable ledger of transactions, it promotes trust, accountability, and efficiency in the supply chain ecosystem.

Figure 6 depicts the system terminal page, which provides a unique transaction ID for each transaction conducted within the supply chain management system. This transaction ID serves as a crucial identifier that enables easy tracking and auditing of the transaction on the blockchain.

By displaying the transaction ID on the transaction page, stakeholders can conveniently reference and access the specific transaction details associated with it. This ID acts as a reference point for auditing purposes, allowing auditors and authorized parties to verify the authenticity and accuracy of the transaction information stored on the blockchain.

The transaction ID plays a significant role in enhancing transparency and accountability within the supply chain. It enables stakeholders to trace the movement of goods, verify ownership transfers, and monitor the progress of the transaction. The unique ID also facilitates efficient record-keeping and retrieval, ensuring that transaction history can be easily accessed and referenced when needed.

Furthermore, the transaction ID serves as a valuable tool for auditing processes. Auditors can use the ID to identify and examine specific transactions, conduct in-depth analysis, and verify compliance with relevant regulations and policies. The presence of a unique transaction ID on the system terminal page streamlines the auditing process and ensures the integrity of the supply chain transactions.

Overall, Figure 6 illustrates the importance of the transaction ID in providing transparency, traceability, and accountability within the supply chain management system. By displaying this ID on the transaction page, stakeholders can conveniently

Figure 6. Terminal output of supply chain

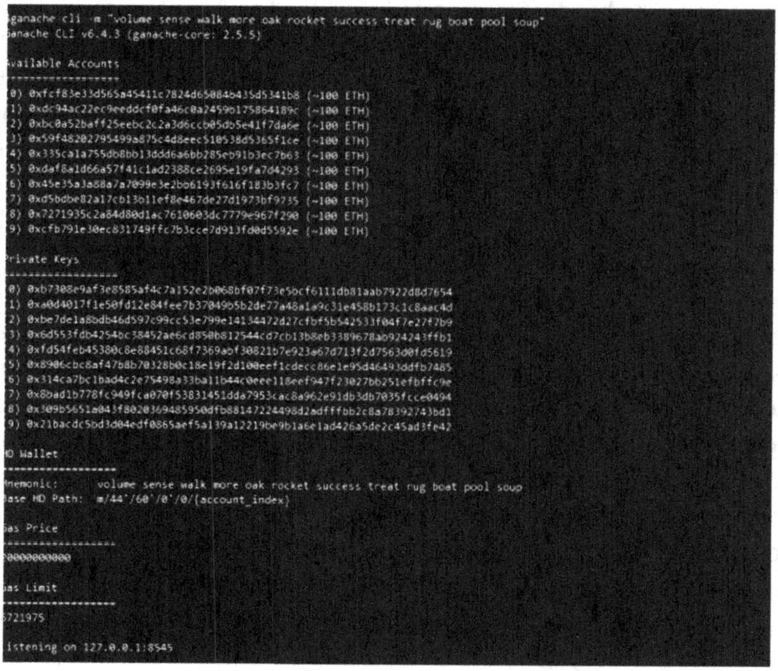

reference and audit transaction details, further enhancing trust and confidence in the system.

Testing

Testing is a crucial phase in the development and implementation of a blockchain-based supply chain management system. It involves a comprehensive evaluation of the system's functionality, reliability, and security to ensure its proper operation and effectiveness in supporting supply chain processes.

Functional testing assesses the system's core functionalities, such as product creation, tracking, and data sharing. It aims to validate that these functions operate as intended and meet the defined requirements. By conducting functional tests, potential issues or discrepancies can be identified and addressed, ensuring that the system performs its intended tasks accurately and efficiently.

Performance testing focuses on evaluating the system's performance under various conditions, such as different transaction volumes and network loads. This type of testing helps assess the system's responsiveness, scalability, and resource utilization. By simulating real-world scenarios and stress-testing the system, performance testing aims to identify any bottlenecks or performance limitations that may impact the system's ability to handle the expected workload and meet performance targets.

Security testing is of paramount importance in blockchain-based supply chain systems. It involves assessing the system's security measures and vulnerability to potential attacks or breaches. This includes testing for data protection, authentication mechanisms, encryption protocols, and access controls. By conducting security tests, any weaknesses or vulnerabilities can be identified, and appropriate measures can be implemented to mitigate risks and safeguard the integrity and confidentiality of supply chain data.

Integration testing verifies the interoperability and compatibility of the blockchain-based supply chain system with other existing systems or external entities. This includes testing data exchange, communication protocols, and integration points with external partners, such as suppliers, logistics providers, or regulatory agencies. Integration testing ensures that the system seamlessly interacts and shares information with relevant stakeholders, enabling smooth collaboration and data flow throughout the supply chain ecosystem.

Overall, testing in supply chain management for blockchain systems is a rigorous and iterative process that aims to identify and address any functional, performance, security, or integration issues. It plays a vital role in ensuring the system's reliability, functionality, and security, ultimately contributing to the successful implementation and operation of an efficient and transparent supply chain management system.

Figure 7 presents the results of unit testing, which offers valuable insights into the functionality and performance of the individual functions within the smart contract.

Figure 7. Unit testing result

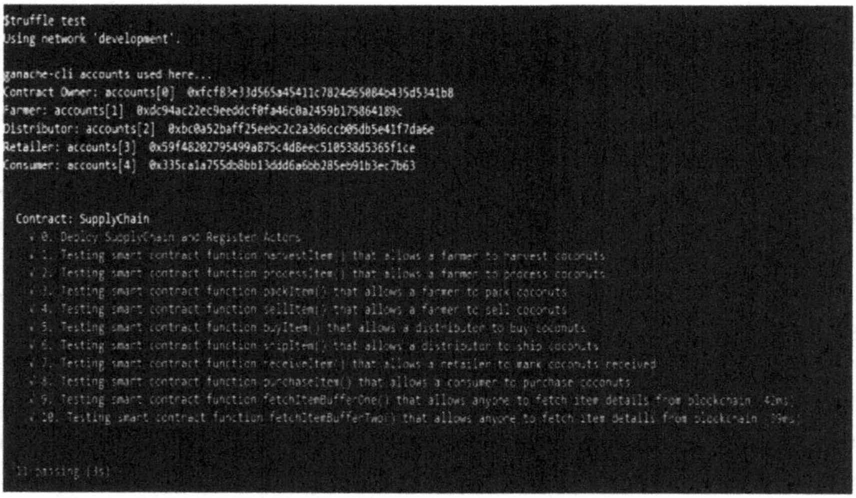

Unit testing is conducted to verify that each function operates as intended and meets the expected behavior. This testing process involves evaluating each function in isolation, utilizing different scenarios and inputs to ensure its proper execution. Unit testing also includes the examination of edge cases and potential error scenarios to identify any issues that may arise. By conducting comprehensive unit testing, any potential flaws or discrepancies in the smart contract's functions can be identified and resolved, ensuring the overall reliability and accuracy of the system.

Figure 8 depicts the results of integration testing, which offers valuable insights into the seamless interaction and performance of the different components within the system. Integration testing helps identify any potential issues or challenges that may arise when these components interact, ensuring the system functions as a cohesive whole and meets the user's requirements. This type of testing involves executing various scenarios, such as creating a new product, transferring ownership, and retrieving product details, to verify the smooth integration and functionality of these processes. By conducting integration testing, any inconsistencies or incompatibilities between system components can be identified and addressed, leading to a more robust and reliable supply chain management system.

Figure 9 illustrates the outcomes of system testing conducted on the smart contract supply chain management system utilizing blockchain technology. The testing encompasses various scenarios to validate the system's functionality and ensure it meets user requirements. These scenarios involve creating new products, transferring product ownership, and retrieving product details. By analyzing the testing results, valuable insights are gained regarding the system's performance and functionality.

Figure 8. Integration testing result

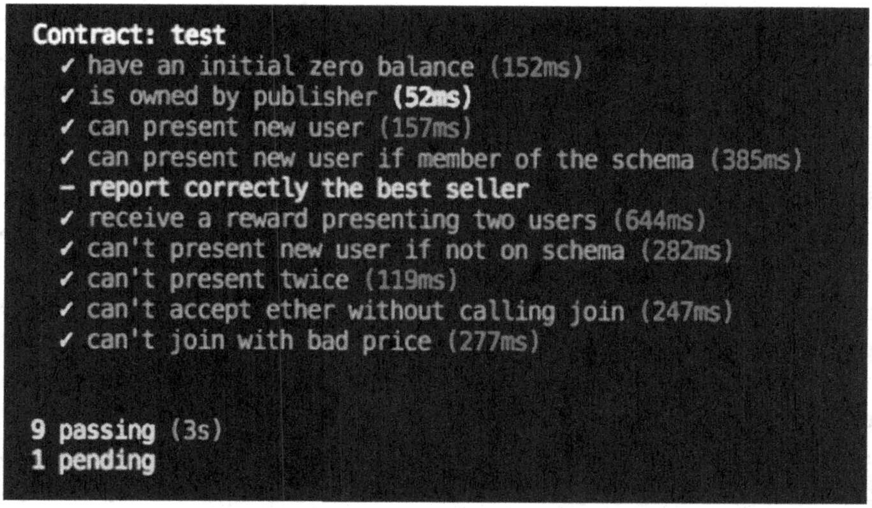

```
Contract: test
  ✓ have an initial zero balance (152ms)
  ✓ is owned by publisher (52ms)
  ✓ can present new user (157ms)
  ✓ can present new user if member of the schema (385ms)
  - report correctly the best seller
  ✓ receive a reward presenting two users (644ms)
  ✓ can't present new user if not on schema (282ms)
  ✓ can't present twice (119ms)
  ✓ can't accept ether without calling join (247ms)
  ✓ can't join with bad price (277ms)


9 passing (3s)
1 pending
```

Figure 9. System testing result

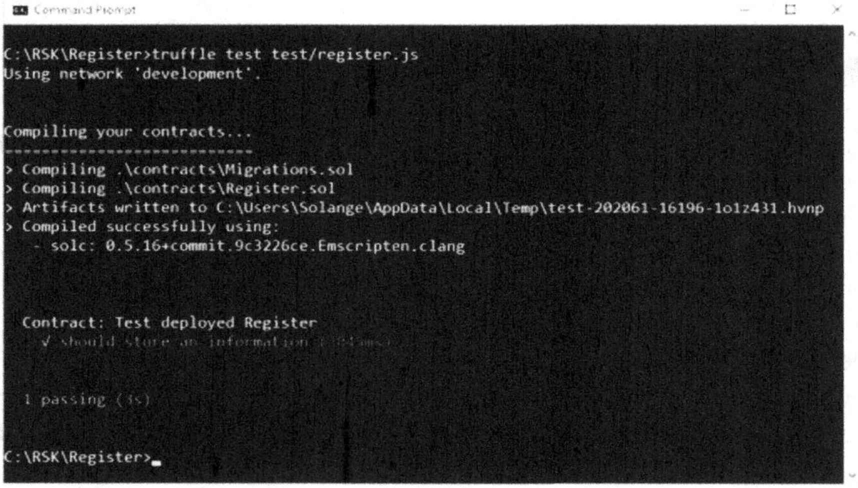

This information helps identify any issues or areas for improvement, enabling the system to be refined and optimized for seamless operation within the supply chain. The testing outcomes serve as a valuable tool for ensuring the system's reliability, accuracy, and efficiency in supporting supply chain management processes.

CONCLUSION

Blockchain technology has the potential to revolutionize supply chain management by offering increased efficiency, transparency, and accountability. The proposed project aims to leverage a smart contract for supply chain management using blockchain, which can offer numerous advantages. Firstly, the use of blockchain technology ensures the creation of an immutable and tamper-proof record of all transactions within the supply chain. This level of transparency and traceability enables stakeholders to track goods from their origin to the end consumer, promoting trust and authenticity. The smart contract automates and verifies transactions based on predefined criteria, eliminating the need for intermediaries and reducing costs. This leads to faster, more streamlined transactions with lower risks of errors or fraud. Secondly, smart contracts contribute to reducing disputes and enhancing accountability. The contract's terms and conditions are encoded and executed automatically, ensuring that all participants adhere to agreed-upon rules. This minimizes errors, disputes, and delays, leading to smoother supply chain operations. Additionally, blockchain technology fosters supply chain sustainability by enhancing transparency and traceability. The system can monitor the movement of goods and identify areas for waste reduction, emissions reduction, and other environmentally friendly practices. This enables improved environmental impact management, enhances supply chain resilience, and promotes corporate social responsibility. Overall, the integration of blockchain technology and smart contracts in supply chain management holds immense potential for optimizing operations, reducing risks, and promoting sustainable practices.

REFERENCES

Ali, R., Moura, L., & Albuquerque, C. (2018). Blockchain-Based Self-Sovereign Identity Management Systems: A Review. *IEEE Access : Practical Innovations, Open Solutions*, 6, 39907–39915.

Androulaki, E., Barger, A., Bortnikov, V., Cachin, C., Christidis, K., De Caro, A., . . . Muralidharan, S. (2018). Hyperledger Fabric: A Distributed Operating System for Permissioned Blockchains. In *Proceedings of the Thirteenth EuroSys Conference* (pp. 30:1-30:15). ACM. 10.1145/3190508.3190538

Bonneau, J., Miller, A., Clark, J., Narayanan, A., Kroll, J. A., & Felten, E. W. (2015). Sok: Research Perspectives and Challenges for Bitcoin and Cryptocurrencies. In *IEEE Symposium on Security and Privacy* (pp. 104-121). IEEE. 10.1109/SP.2015.14

Buterin, V. (2013). *Ethereum White Paper: A Next-Generation Smart Contract and Decentralized Application Platform*. Retrieved from https://ethereum.org/whitepaper/

Christidis, K., & Devetsikiotis, M. (2016). Blockchains and Smart Contracts for the Internet of Things. *IEEE Access : Practical Innovations, Open Solutions*, 4, 2292–2303. doi:10.1109/ACCESS.2016.2566339

Croman, K., Decker, C., Eyal, I., Gencer, A. E., Juels, A., Kosba, A., ... Song, D. (2016). On Scaling Decentralized Blockchains. In *International Conference on Financial Cryptography and Data Security* (pp. 106-125). Springer.

Dinh, T. T. A., Liu, D., Zhang, M., Chen, G., Ooi, B. C., & Wang, J. (2018). Untangling Blockchain: A Data Processing View of Blockchain Systems. *IEEE Transactions on Knowledge and Data Engineering*, 30(7), 1366–1385. doi:10.1109/TKDE.2017.2781227

Heilman, E., Kendler, A., Zohar, A., & Goldberg, S. (2015). Eclipse Attacks on Bitcoin's Peer-to-Peer Network. In *24th USENIX Security Symposium (USENIX Security 15)* (pp. 129-144). Academic Press.

Kosba, A., Miller, A., Shi, E., Wen, Z., & Papamanthou, C. (2016). Hawk: The Blockchain Model of Cryptography and Privacy-Preserving Smart Contracts. In *Proceedings of the 2016 ACM SIGSAC Conference on Computer and Communications Security* (pp. 839-851). ACM. 10.1109/SP.2016.55

Kshetri, N. (2018). Blockchain's Roles in Meeting Key Supply Chain Management Objectives. *International Journal of Information Management*, *39*, 80–89. doi:10.1016/j.ijinfomgt.2017.12.005

Luthra, S., Garg, D., & Haleem, A. (2020). Blockchain for Supply Chain Traceability: Business Requirements and Critical Success Factors. *International Journal of Information Management*, *52*, 101994.

Nakamoto, S. (2008). *Bitcoin: A Peer-to-Peer Electronic Cash System*. Retrieved from https://bitcoin.org/bitcoin.pdf

Panarello, A., Tapas, N., Merlino, G., Longo, F., & Puliafito, A. (2018). Blockchain and IoT Integration: A Systematic Survey. *Sensors (Basel)*, *18*(8), 2575. doi:10.339018082575 PMID:30082633

Swan, M. (2014). Blockchain: The New Technology of Trust. *Strategy and Leadership*, *42*(6), 6–11.

Swan, M. (2015). *Blockchain: Blueprint for a New Economy*. O'Reilly Media.

Swan, M. (2017a). *Blockchain: The Complete Guide to Understanding Blockchain Technology*. CreateSpace Independent Publishing Platform.

Swan, M. (2017b). *Blockchain: Blueprint for a New Economy*. O'Reilly Media.

Szabo, N. (1997). *The Idea of Smart Contracts. Nick Szabo's Papers and Concise Tutorials*. Retrieved from http://www.szabo.best.vwh.net/smart_contracts_idea.html

Tapscott, D., & Tapscott, A. (2016). *Blockchain Revolution: How the Technology Behind Bitcoin is Changing Money, Business, and the World*. Penguin.

Tschorsch, F., & Scheuermann, B. (2016). A Survey on Consensus Mechanisms and Mining Management in Blockchain Networks. *Business & Information Systems Engineering*, *58*(4), 371–384.

Yli-Huumo, J., Ko, D., Choi, S., Park, S., & Smolander, K. (2016). A Survey on Blockchain Technology: Usage, Challenges, and Future Directions. In *Proceedings of the 49th Hawaii International Conference on System Sciences (HICSS)* (pp. 4688-4697). IEEE.

Zeng, L., Wang, X., Xia, Q., Liu, K., & Liu, J. (2019). A Comprehensive Review of Blockchain Consensus Mechanisms: Proof of Work, Proof of Stake, and Beyond. *IEEE Access : Practical Innovations, Open Solutions*, 7, 22328–22370.

Zheng, Z., Cao, J., & Yu, R. (2018). Blockchain Challenges and Opportunities: A Survey. *International Journal of Web and Grid Services*, *14*(4), 352–375. doi:10.1504/IJWGS.2018.095647

Zheng, Z., Xie, S., Dai, H., Chen, X., & Wang, H. (2017). A Systematic Literature Review on Blockchain Technology: State-of-the-Art, Applications, and Challenges. *IEEE Access : Practical Innovations, Open Solutions*, 6, 28077–28096.

Zheng, Z., Xie, S., Li, H., Dai, H., & Wang, H. (2021). Blockchain Challenges and Opportunities: A Systematic Review. *Journal of Parallel and Distributed Computing*, *151*, 1–14.

Zyskind, G., Nathan, O., & Pentland, A. (2015). Decentralizing Privacy: Using Blockchain to Protect Personal Data. In Security and Privacy Workshops (pp. 180-184). IEEE.

Chapter 10
Optimization Techniques for Influenza Prediction in Biological Expert Systems

U. Vignesh
Vellore Institute of Technology, Chennai, India

Rahul Ratnakumar
Manipal Institute of Technology, India

ABSTRACT

Currently, the biggest challenge in the world is the detection of viral infection in various diseases, as par to the rapid spread of the disease. According to recent statistics, the number of people diagnosed with the Influenza virus is exponentially increasing day by day, with more than 2.5 million confirmed cases. The model proposed here analyses the Influenza virus by comparing different deep learning algorithms to bring out the best in terms of accuracy for detection and prediction. The models are trained using CT scan dataset comprising of both Influenza positive patients and negative patients. The results of algorithms are compared based on parameters such as train accuracy, test loss, etc. Some of the best models after training were, DenseNet-121 with accuracy of 96.28%, VGG-16 with accuracy of 95.75%, ResNet-50 with accuracy of 94.18%, etc. in detecting the virus from the CT scan dataset with the proposed ACDL algorithm. Thus, these models will be helpful and useful to the government and communities to initiate proper measures to control the outbreak of the Influenza virus in time.

1. INTRODUCTION

The human influenza A virus was discovered in 1933 soon after Shope succeeded in isolating swine influenza A virus in 1931. Since the discovery studies in the

DOI: 10.4018/979-8-3693-1131-8.ch010

influenza have made immense progress and have contributed greatly to not only virology but also immunology and molecular biology. The virus which is very similar to Influenza is the Corona virus. The SARS-CoV-2 originates from Wuhan, China, and got spread worldwide. This disease was identified as an epidemic by the World Health Organization on 03-11-20. The coronavirus is globally increasing at a very fast rate. As of now worldwide, there are 155,192,083 confirmed cases, 132,633,409 recoveries and 3,244,581 deaths. The ground-level symptoms include common cold, fever, tiredness, and feeling difficulty breathing. As per the World health organization, the pandemic is divided into different stages. The primary stage depicts cases of people who've been to already affected areas. The secondary stage depicts cases of people from the same family or place. The third stage is the most difficult one as the cases reported remains untraceable as it will be already spread to be public by the time. Such a scenario has only one solution which is the process of lockdown in both the cases and social distancing to decrease the spreading of the virus and control the virus among the public.

Normally, the RT-PCR test is done to spot or detect the presence of the virus and is treated as a standard test for the detection of the Influenza virus. Also, reports show that RT-PCR tests show variable sensitivity and may not be available in some regions, so currently, RT-PCR tests are not a prominent option for detection. Nowadays, X-rays and CT scans are used to detect the Influenza virus and for evaluating the disease from cases from different hospitals.

Also, CADx tools or Automated computer-aided diagnostic tools are being used to detect and segregate COVID-19 related differences from CXR and CT scans. Hence, this paper aims in doing a comparative study on different deep learning algorithms for the detection and prediction of the Influenza virus from CT scans. Firstly, all the algorithms are implemented by training and testing with the desired dataset and once it is done, the accuracy of all the algorithms can be computed. Hence, based on such parameters the comparison and prediction of the best models for Influenza analysis can be done.

2. RELATED WORK

Wang et al. (2020) used transfer learning and model integration based on the COVID-net model by Darwin-AL for identifying the COVID virus from Chest X-RAY images, the methodologies were implemented using ResNet-101 and ResNet-152 neural networks. Rajaraman et al. (2020) used iterative pruning for identifying pulmonary signs of the virus, for this they came up with a CNN and set of pre-trained models that have undergone training and evaluation based on Chest X-rays to learn about feature representations concerning modality. Hassan et al. (2020) came up with COVID-19 prediction system using deep learning on chest X-ray images. Mohammed et al. (2020) came up with a method for organizations in selecting a COVID-19 diagnosis system based on the multi-criteria decision-making (MCDM) method. Ko et al. (2020) used a 2D framework known as the FCO-net model, which is a technique to diagnose the virus from images based on CT and to segregate it from non–COVID-19 diseases and non-pneumonia diseases. Transfer learning is used to create the FCO-Net model with the help of four models which are VGG16, ResNet-50, Inception-v3, and Xception. Alazab et al. (2020) presented an artificial-intelligence technique based on CNN to detect COVID19 patients using CXR as a dataset. Punn et al. (2020) used DNN and RNN with the help of LSTM cells for predicting the number of recovered, confirmed, and death cases worldwide. Mahalle et al. (2020) made use of multimodal data for COVID-19 prediction.

In this study, a single dataset is used to implement (train and test) the necessary deep learning algorithms. A CT scan dataset comprising of Influenza patients and healthy persons is used (746 images in total).

Git is a distributed version control system which is free and open source, used to track changes in any set of files, and the authors of said changes. It is a very widely used software development collaboration tool, and is well known for its efficiency and speed regardless of the project size. It allows support for non-linear workflows on several branches running on multiple platforms and systems seamlessly. It is primarily used for maintaining a log of changes made to source-code over time by various editors. This log of changes is maintained by a diffing algorithm which is at the base of Git. This algorithm is able to compute the changes made to the source-code effectively.

Visual Studio is an integrated development environment (IDE) made by Microsoft. It comes packaged with a comprehensive set of tools to develop, build, debug and deploy .NET and C++ applications. This is thus useful for this project since the server-side component is made in the .NET Core framework. It also has support for other programming languages using plug-ins. Visual Studio has several tools which make the development process more streamlined and easier. For example, the code editor included in Visual Studio comes coupled with IntelliSense, which is a code-completion software which suggests code snippets based on the context. It also reduces typographical errors and displays hints for syntax errors. PGAdmin is a web-based management tool for PostgreSQL databases. It provides a graphical user interface (GUI) to interact with active sessions with the database. It provides a query tool to view entries in the database corresponding to the query. The GUI provides for ease of use when one wants to compare the query functioning between the server and the actual expected result from the database.

.NET Core is an open-source cross-platform developer framework which can be used for building various types of applications. It is free and multipurpose, being maintained by Microsoft. Its multiplatform nature allows for development of applications on web, desktop, Mac, mobile etc., making it extremely versatile as a framework. It provides support for modular architecture. Several packages and libraries can be readily found as per one's usage on the package manager called NuGet, which comes bundled with the .NET platform. NuGet allows developers to share their code which can be reused by others. Due to this, there is a sense of community among .NET developers and it is easier to find support when needed. It also allows for dependency injection, which is a programming technique, which decouples a class from its dependencies. This allows for more maintainable, decoupled and reusable code. .NET Core Framework for developing the server-side Application Programming Interface of the application.

The UI communicates with the API on the server to obtain the information. Several components from NuGet were used, most importantly EFCore, which allows for the connection between the server and the database. Angular is a free and open-source frontend framework, based in TypeScript, being maintained by Google. It is a design framework used to create the user interface and efficiently create single-page applications. It is able to create web applications with a consistent experience across mobile and web. It has several features to increase the speed and performance of the applications being developed, such as code-splitting (bundling code and components such that they can be loaded when needed) and universal code (performing serverside rendering of the webpage, instead of rendering in the browser). It also has several productivity tools such as Angular CLI and Templates. Angular being a TypeScript based framework, can run in the NodeJS runtime environment. It is used to create the webpage visible to the user (the UI). This webpage communicates with the API (made in .NET Core) to display the requested information in the webpage. PostgreSQL is an object-relational database which combines the SQL language with a number of additional capabilities to reliably store and access data. It is open-source and powerful, and can reliably scale even for the most challenging of data demands. The free and open-source nature of PostgreSQL makes it highly extensible. Thus, creation of new functions and specify your own data types without having to recompile your database in accordance to these new data types. It uses tables to represent data and their relationships, and allows transactions with ACID properties.

Some of the deep learning methodologies for Influenza detection were:

The first algorithm is based on transfer learning and model integration. Transfer learning uses the property of generalization on big datasets and then trains on small datasets (chest CXR). Here it makes use of two neural networks Relnet101 and Relnet152 to implement this methodology. The two models with the best outputs or results during the transfer learning process are combined for joint learning. Model Integration is the process of freezing the network parameters of both the models by providing extra weights to the outer layers and the weight which has the higher accuracy is taken. Next, transfer learning and model integration training is carried out using a CXR and RSNA pneumonia dataset. The structure of processes shown in figure. 1.

The results produced 96.1% accuracy in detecting the presence of the Influenza virus in the lungs compared to the RT-PCR test.

The second model is based upon iterative pruning. The iterative pruned deep learning model focuses on detecting signs of Influenza from CXR. The model evaluates the performance of a CNN and a combination of image net pre-trained models which are VGG-16, VGG-19 Inception-V3, Xception, Inception-ResNet-V2, MobileNet-V2, DenseNet-201, and NasNet-mobile. The top-performing CNN models are evaluated and the errors are corrected at their initial CNN layer which is then added with layers zero-padding, a stridden separable CNN, GAP layer, Dropout layer, and a layer that is dense based on softmax activation. The edited models are tuned to divide the CXR into normal or pneumonia based on bacteria or Influenza. The best-performing pruned models resulted in an accuracy of 99.01% in detecting the virus from chest X-Rays. The third model is based on the neural network ResNet-101 shown in figure. 2. Among these pre-trained models, ResNet-50 shows the best results with a sensitivity of 99.58%, specificity of 100.00%, and accuracy of 99.87%.

Figure 1. The structure of the process

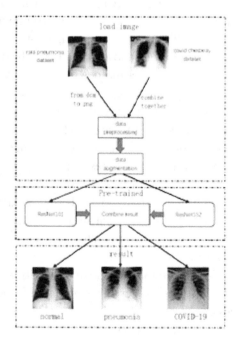

Table 1. Results of different CNN models

Methods	Accuracy	AUC	Sensitivity	Precision	F	MCC	Param.
User Custom	0.8674	0.8731	0.8323	0.8386	0.8354	0.7823	58997
VGG-16	0.8640	0.8808	0.9684	0.9812	0.975	0.9501	19436354
VGG-19	0.8606	0.8812	0.8606	0.8638	0.8605	0.8323	13635041
Inception-V	0.8572	0.8811	0.8473	0.8768	0.857	0.8264	30534683
Xception	0.8556	0.8785	0.8406	0.8700	0.8551	0.8227	20574283
DenseNet-201	0.8572	0.880	0.8523	0.8671	0.8566	0.826	12283004
MobileNet-V2	0.8564	0.8802	0.844	0.8604	0.8563	0.8240	13536123
NASNet- mobile	0.8500	0.8771	0.9584	0.8100	0.8505	0.8513	14857037

Figure 2. ResNet-101 architecture

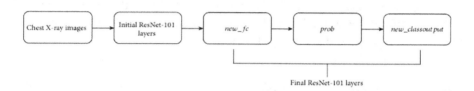

Table 2. Evaluation values for different models

Method and Item	Sensitivity	Specificity	Accuracy	AUC	P value
ResNet-50					<.000100
Influenza	100	99.7	99.5	0.99	
Other Viral Pne	98.1	98.9	98.9	1.00	
Non Pne	99.9	97.9	98.99	1.00	
VGG16					<.000100
Influenza	99.9	98.99	98.99	0.99	
Other Viral Pne	99.9	98.9	98.76	1.00	
Non Pne	99.9	98.91	98.67	1.00	
Xception					<.000100
Influenza	98.1	98.9	97.8	1.00	
Other Viral Pne	97.9	98.9	97.9	0.99	
Non Pne	99.9	99.9	99.9	0.99	
Inception-v3					<.000100
Influenza	89.1	96.9	95.1	0.96	
Other Viral Pne	93.2	96.11	93.11	0.97	
Non Pne	97.9	96.99	93.77	0.98	

From the computation, ResNet-50 shows excellent performance in identifying the virus from CT based images in the table. 1.

Firstly, the network is pre-trained based using a public dataset of CXR images. After that, except for prob, new_fc, and new_classoutput, the rates of learning of the rest of the layers are assigned to zero which refers to the classification of output layers and a fully connected softmax. Then the three layers are retrained again to distinguish the chest X-Ray images based on the opacity of airspace. Next, the network parameters are updated using stochastic gradient descent for momentum. This model produced an accuracy of 77.3% in detecting the Influenza virus from CXR.

The fourth model is based upon an Artificial Intelligence method to detect the virus from CT images and segregate it from non-Influenza pneumonia and non-pneumonia diseases. A 2D framework is developed known as the FCO-net(fast-track Influenza classification network). FCO-net is created by transfer learning one of the different models such as VGG16, ResNet-50, Inception-v3, and Xception. Then the training and testing of the FCO-net model are done, in the testing phase, the performance of the pre-trained models are compared based on the test parameters' sensitivity, specificity, and accuracy shown in table 2.

3. PROPOSED METHODOLOGY

Here, four different deep learning models are being implemented and compared for the detection and prediction of the COVID-19 virus from CT scans with the proposed algorithm named ACDL (Attribute Cluster Deep Learning).

1) Simple CNN (Convolutional Neural Network)

A Convolutional Neural Network (ConvNet/CNN) is a Deep Learning algorithm that takes input as an image, assign learnable weights and biases to various objects in the image, and will differentiate one from the other as shown in figure. 3.

After training, the model provides an accuracy of 93.84% in detecting the virus from the CT-scan dataset presented in figure. 4.

2) VGG-16

VGG-16 is a CNN network with 16 layers shown in figure. 5. It follows a more refined approach in order to leverage a pretrained network on a large dataset. The process of leveraging such features allows to provide better accuracy, hence VGG-16 can be an optimal choice for the CT scan dataset.

Figure 3. Different layers of CNN

```
Model: "sequential"

Layer (type)                    Output Shape           Param #
=================================================================
conv2d (Conv2D)                 (None, 300, 300, 32)   896

max_pooling2d (MaxPooling2D)    (None, 150, 150, 32)   0

conv2d_1 (Conv2D)               (None, 150, 150, 32)   9248

max_pooling2d_1 (MaxPooling2     (None, 75, 75, 32)     0

conv2d_2 (Conv2D)               (None, 75, 75, 32)     9248

max_pooling2d_2 (MaxPooling2     (None, 37, 37, 32)     0

conv2d_3 (Conv2D)               (None, 37, 37, 32)     9248

max_pooling2d_3 (MaxPooling2     (None, 18, 18, 32)     0

flatten (Flatten)               (None, 10368)          0

dropout (Dropout)               (None, 10368)          0

dense (Dense)                   (None, 256)            2654464

dense_1 (Dense)                 (None, 1)              257
=================================================================
Total params: 2,683,361
Trainable params: 2,683,361
Non-trainable params: 0
```

The model makes use of the bottleneck features while training. Figure 5 shows different layers of the model such as cov2d, maxpooling2d, etc. After training the model, an accuracy of 95.76% is computed in detecting the virus from the CT-scan dataset shown in figure. 6.

Figure 4. Graphs for training, validation accuracy, and loss

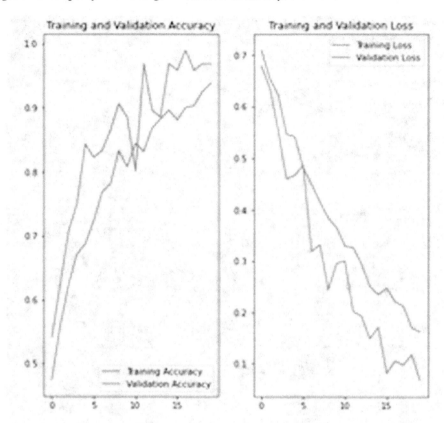

3) DenseNet-121

DenseNet-121 is a CNN network with 121 layers. Like all other networks, DenseNet also consists of all pooling and convolutional layers but what makes it different from other CNN networks is that it consists of dense blocks and transition layers. DenseNet-121 is a slow training network that is suitable for large datasets. The conceptual model and training prospects are shown in figure. 7 and figure. 8.

After training the model, an accuracy of 96.28% is computed in detecting the virus from the CT-scan dataset.

Figure 5. Different layers of VGG-16

```
Model: "vgg16"

Layer (type)                      Output Shape              Param #
==================================================================
input_3 (InputLayer)              [(None, 224, 224, 3)]     0

block1_conv1 (Conv2D)             (None, 224, 224, 64)      1792

block1_conv2 (Conv2D)             (None, 224, 224, 64)      36928

block1_pool (MaxPooling2D)        (None, 112, 112, 64)      0

block2_conv1 (Conv2D)             (None, 112, 112, 128)     73856

block2_conv2 (Conv2D)             (None, 112, 112, 128)     147584

block2_pool (MaxPooling2D)        (None, 56, 56, 128)       0

block3_conv1 (Conv2D)             (None, 56, 56, 256)       295168

block3_conv2 (Conv2D)             (None, 56, 56, 256)       590080

block3_conv3 (Conv2D)             (None, 56, 56, 256)       590080

block3_pool (MaxPooling2D)        (None, 28, 28, 256)       0

block4_conv1 (Conv2D)             (None, 28, 28, 512)       1180160

block4_conv2 (Conv2D)             (None, 28, 28, 512)       2359808

block4_conv3 (Conv2D)             (None, 28, 28, 512)       2359808

block4_pool (MaxPooling2D)        (None, 14, 14, 512)       0

block5_conv1 (Conv2D)             (None, 14, 14, 512)       2359808

block5_conv2 (Conv2D)             (None, 14, 14, 512)       2359808

block5_conv3 (Conv2D)             (None, 14, 14, 512)       2359808

block5_pool (MaxPooling2D)        (None, 7, 7, 512)         0
==================================================================
Total params: 14,714,688
Trainable params: 7,079,424
Non-trainable params: 7,635,264
```

4) ResNet-50

ResNet-50 is a CNN network with 50 layers. ResNet is a much simpler network when compared with other CNN networks and it also solves the problem of degrading

Figure 6. Graphs for training, validation accuracy, and loss

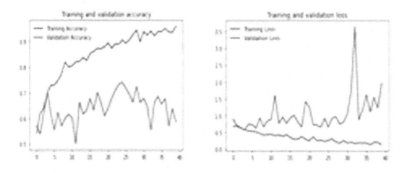

Figure 7. Different layers of DenseNet-121

```
Model: "model_3"
```

Layer (type)	Output Shape	Param #
input_6 (InputLayer)	(None, 64, 64, 3)	0
conv2d_3 (Conv2D)	(None, 64, 64, 3)	84
densenet121 (Model)	multiple	7037504
global_average_pooling2d_3 (	(None, 1024)	0
batch_normalization_5 (Batch	(None, 1024)	4096
dropout_5 (Dropout)	(None, 1024)	0
dense_3 (Dense)	(None, 256)	262400
batch_normalization_6 (Batch	(None, 256)	1024

accuracy shown in table. 3. ResNet also makes use of the skip connection method to transfer information from one layer to another. The accuracy results are shown in table 4.

4) ACDL Algorithm

The experiments conducted till now results the trained model prospects. The input for ACDL algorithm is remains the same as such of the other four deep learning model, which it finds repeated pattern with given length for prediction method. From this identified sequence, can't do analysis for the purpose of drug discovery since only one match takes more complexity instead this research work considered some protein sequences from suggested food items to find how the microorganism

Figure 8. Model training

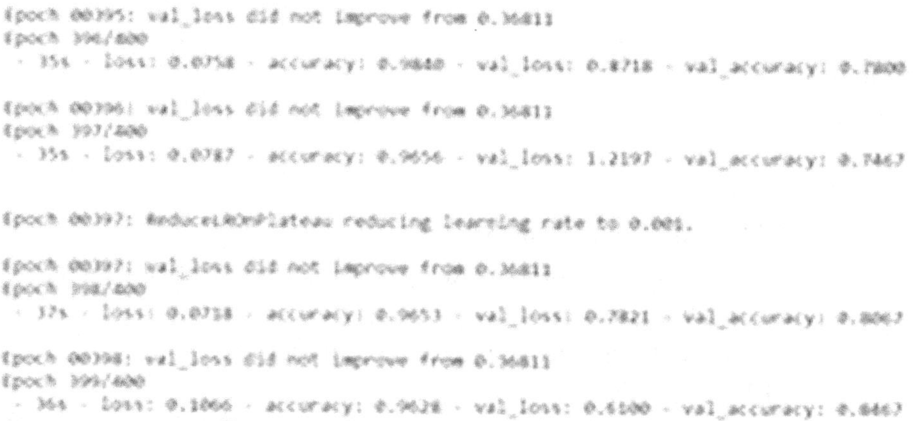

```
Epoch 00395: val_loss did not improve from 0.36811
Epoch 396/400
 - 35s - loss: 0.0758 - accuracy: 0.9840 - val_loss: 0.8718 - val_accuracy: 0.7800

Epoch 00396: val_loss did not improve from 0.36811
Epoch 397/400
 - 35s - loss: 0.0787 - accuracy: 0.9656 - val_loss: 1.2197 - val_accuracy: 0.7467

Epoch 00397: ReduceLROnPlateau reducing learning rate to 0.001.

Epoch 00397: val_loss did not improve from 0.36811
Epoch 398/400
 - 37s - loss: 0.0738 - accuracy: 0.9653 - val_loss: 0.7821 - val_accuracy: 0.8067

Epoch 00398: val_loss did not improve from 0.36811
Epoch 399/400
 - 36s - loss: 0.1066 - accuracy: 0.9628 - val_loss: 0.6500 - val_accuracy: 0.8467
```

Table 3. Model training

epoch	train_loss	valid_loss	error_rate	accuracy	time
0	1.433481	1.038275	0.529148	0.470852	04:41
1	1.354328	1.142244	0.591928	0.408072	04:40
2	1.284390	1.081527	0.533632	0.466368	04:33
3	1.238023	1.025250	0.488789	0.511211	04:34
4	1.219690	0.972281	0.479821	0.520179	04:38
5	1.207035	0.875177	0.426009	0.573991	04:29
6	1.168138	0.811662	0.394619	0.605381	04:31
7	1.092889	0.767507	0.349776	0.650224	04:38
8	1.039562	0.727893	0.340807	0.659193	04:36
9	0.959369	0.663496	0.322870	0.677130	04:31
10	0.914166	0.662281	0.295964	0.704036	04:39
11	0.804385	0.596793	0.264574	0.735426	04:32
12	0.807468	0.577464	0.242152	0.757848	04:28
13	0.814447	0.564449	0.237668	0.762332	04:18
14	0.774604	0.521672	0.206278	0.793722	04:14
15	0.705916	0.503392	0.197309	0.802691	04:09
18	n A77017	n 506568	210762	a 780238	04-10

pattern relates with those food products, so that a little concentration can be at the process of drug discovery regarding the medicine related to this type of disease analysis analysis in ACDL algorithm (Figure. 9). Considering these input sequences,

Figure 9. Algorithmic design

```
Input:
Sequences 'K'
Length 'P'
Process:
Fixed Value 'm'
    1.  Find the character count 'y'
            Compare y to the previous deep learning model attributes 'a'
            If y=y (any a)
                Training practices the prediction process 'I'
            Else
                Go for (y+1) and (y-1) up to 'm'
                If y=y (any a)
                    Training practices the prediction process 'I'
            All fails go to step 2
    2.  Compare the total count in all K
        If count(kk)=count(aa) in any K
            Training practices the prediction process 'I'
        All fails go to step 3
    3.  Perform alignment method
Output:
Disease Predicted 'D' in all 'K'
```

Table 4. Training outputs of different models

Model	Training Accuracy	Validation Accuracy	Training Loss	Validation Loss	Trainable Params	Non-Trainable Params
Simple CNN	0.93837535	0.96875	0.16265706317264492	0.06811186174551646	1,413,601	0
VGG-16	0.9575972	0.6328125	0.10559954847021574	2.47953138127923	13,502,465	7,635,264
DenseNet-121	0.9628	0.8467	0.1066	0.6100	7,219,414	86,208
ResNet-50	0.94187	0.8206	0.213624	0.187011	25,50,000	0
ACDL	0.929456	0.81345	0.13245	0.86754	14,30,000	0

algorithm calculates the index values – does the comparisons, if fails goes for the amino acids count – does the comparisons, if this also fails it selects the alignment methods or random selection method for forming the starting profile matrix. After training the model, an accuracy of 94.18% is computed in detecting the virus from the CT-scan dataset. The results and computations after training the four models trained with ACDL.

5. CONCLUSION

As the Influenza virus is increasing rapidly around the globe, the need for automated Influenza diagnosing systems is also being increasing. There are many different proposed models for Influenza analysis and the only question that arises is which model is the best for Influenza detection and prediction. Based on the work carried on this research, the simple CNN model provides an accuracy of 93.83%, VGG-16 provides an accuracy of 95.75%, DenseNet-121 provides an accuracy of 96.28%, and ResNet-50 with an accuracy of 94.18% in detecting the Influenza virus from CT-scan dataset. From the above-computed models, DenseNet-121 shows better and highest accuracy and less loss compared to other models. Hence this study acts as a reference model for government and health organizations to analyze the current Influenza situation.

REFERENCES

Alazab, M., Awajan, A., Mesleh, A., Abraham, A., Jatana, V., & Alhyari, S. (2020). Article. *International Journal of Computer Information Systems and Industrial Management Applications*, *12*, 168–181.

Hassan, Izzuddin, Tamrin, & Ali. (2020). Article. *International Journal of Biomedical Imaging*, 1-7.

Ko, H., Chung, H., Kang, W. S., Kim, K. W., Shin, Y., Kang, S. J., Lee, J. H., Kim, Y. J., & Kim, N. Y. (2020). Hyunseok JungJinseok Lee. *Journal of Medical Internet Research*, *22*, e19569. doi:10.2196/19569 PMID:32568730

Mahalle, Sable, Mahalle, & Shinde. (2020). Article. *Intelligent Systems and Methods to Combat Covid-19,* 1-10.

Mohammed, M. A., Abdulkareem, K. H., Al-Waisy, A. S., Mostafa, S. A., Al-Fahdawi, S., Dinar, A. M., Alhakami, W., Baz, A., Al-Mhiqani, M. N., Alhakami, H., Arbaiy, N., Maashi, M. S., Mutlag, A. A., Garcia-Zapirain, B., & De La Torre Diez, I. (2020). Benchmarking Methodology for Selection of Optimal COVID-19 Diagnostic Model Based on Entropy and TOPSIS Methods. *IEEE Access : Practical Innovations, Open Solutions*, 8, 99115–99131. doi:10.1109/ACCESS.2020.2995597

Punn, N. S., Sonbhadra, S. K., & Agarwal, S. (2020). *Article*. Cold Spring Harbor Laboratory Press.

Rajaraman, Siegelman, Alderson, Folio, Folio, & Antani. (2020). Article. *IEEE Access, 8*, 115041-115050.

Wang, N., Liu, H., & Xu, C. (2020). Article. *10th International Conference on Electronics Information and Emergency Communication (ICEIEC)*, 281-284.

Chapter 11
PayCrypto Analtcoin Minting Application as Interest to Cryptocurrencies

G. K. Sandhia
SRM Institute of Science and Technology, India

S. Girirajan
SRM Institute of Science and Technology, India

R. Vidhya
SRM Institute of Science and Technology, India

S. Nagadevi
SRM Institute of Science and Technology, India

K. R. Jansi
SRM Institute of Science and Technology, India

N. Ghuntupalli Manoj Kumar
SRM Institute of Science and Technology, India

R. Jeya
iD https://orcid.org/0000-0002-8650-3244
SRM Institute of Science and Technology, India

J. Ramaprabha
SRM Institute of Science and Technology, India

M. Gayathri
SRM Institute of Science and Technology, India

ABSTRACT

Blockchain is a distributed ledger. It stores transaction data in the form of a linked list combined with encryption algorithms to enhance the security and integrity of the data in each of the blocks. Any participant of the node can verify the correctness of a transaction and a block is created only after the majority of the participants of the network (51%) agree to the correctness of a transaction. The participants

DOI: 10.4018/979-8-3693-1131-8.ch011

reach a consensus on the transactions broadcast and the sequence in which these transactions occurred. At any point of time, all participants have an order of blocks of transactions they have accepted consensus on, and each participant has a set of unprocessed transactions it has in its pool. A block is then selected by one node on which validity of transactions is checked and then it is added to the blockchain. The main focus is to demonstrate the concept of staking cryptocurrencies on blockchains and how decentralized applications can be developed on the Ethereum network to deploy such applications.

INTRODUCTION

In the current fiat currency system, the citizens can submit (stake) their currency to regulated banks to earn some interest. The PayCrypto model tries to mimic the fiat system by leveraging the PoS model that helps validate transactions on a blockchain. This decentralized way of earning rewards for staking currency eliminates the fees required to maintain our transactions, overdraft fees etc.., charged by the centralized authorities. The prototype built uses two tokens deployed on a local blockchain to demonstrate the Defimodel. The user can interact with the smart contract using the metamask wallet to stake and un-stake crypto-currencies.

1.1 Blockchain

Blockchain is a distributed ledger. It stores transaction data in the form of a linked list combined with encryption algorithms (currently SHA-256) to enhance the security and integrity of the data in each of the blocks. Each block consists of a set of transactions (A Merkle tree and the root is kept in the block), a pointer to the previous block, and hash of the previous block.

The use of digital signatures implements the message authentication requirement of the security requirements. Only one person can sign but anyone can cross-check and the signature should be associated with a particular file i.e.., signature should not be copy pasted from one document to another.

While the proof-of-work takes care of such concerns, proof-of-stake implements all these security requirements without the strength of the security of a blockchain being dependent on the energy consumption (Mining).

1.2 Incentive Mechanisms

Incentive mechanisms make sure users participate in mining. This is done due to the dependency on the number of miners and the strength of the blockchain. The more people who can verify a transaction, the more honest a specific blockchain is. The incentive mechanisms currently in place are the block rewards and the transaction fees.

The participant that generates each block then includes a transaction in that block and that transaction is a coin generation transaction and the node can choose a recipient address of the transaction. This block reward is for any block proposed honest or otherwise.

Other than the block rewards, transaction fee can be imposed by the transaction initiator as a reward to mining his/her block. Generator of the transaction can select to create the output of the coin with output less than the input value. The difference is a transaction fee called gas fee is given to the block generator. This is purely optional.

1.3 Proof-of-Work

The PoW mechanism helps choose the block creator. To approximate choosing a random participant, choose a participant to a resource that no one can take control over. PoW chose the resource as computational power. PoS chose the resource as the amount of coins owned.

In PoW nodes compete against each other to solve a cryptographic hash puzzle. This hash function involves finding a nonce in a target space. Thus increasing the difficulty of computing the hash puzzle.

1.4 Consensus Mechanism

According to the consensus algorithm new transactions are broadcasted to all participants. Each participant compiles new transactions into a block. In each iteration a random participant gets to circulate the block. Other participant is agreeing to the block only if every transaction is authentic (unspent, valid signatures). Participants communicate their approval of the block by incorporating its hash in the next block they generate.

2. LITERATURE SURVEY

The following papers were studied and reviewed to help present views.

2.1 Bitcoin: A Peer-to-Peer Electronic Cash System

This paper coined the term blockchain in 2008. It introduces the concept of transferring digital currency directly from sender to receiver without the involvement of a third-party thus replacing the current trust-based system (Nakamoto S., 2008).

It talks about the PoW model that will help implement the said trustless system and how bitcoin demonstrates this PoW model.

2.2 A Hybrid POW-POS Implementation Against 51%Attack in Crypto-currency System

This paper discusses the approach of implementing PoW and PoS. While the PoW takes care of regulating the block generation time, PoS actually elects the user to validate and put the next block on the chain. And instead of a validating committee, all the participants validate each block. This helps in preventing the 51%attack (Kishor Datta Gupta, 2019).

2.3 PPCoin: Peer-to-Peer Crypto-Currency With Proof-of-Stake

This paper highlights the Security strengthening provided by the PoS mechanism while reducing the dependency of energy consumption on the same. It uses the coinage approach which is the product of the time a minter is a participant and the stake (Sunny King, 2012).

2.4 Blockchain Consensus: Analysis of Proof-of-Work and its applications

This paper demonstrates the PoW mechanism by building a decentralized application on the ethereum blockchain and quantifies the performance of PoW mechanism. This helps compare the PoW with other suggested algorithms to pick the most efficient and secure one.

2.5 Proof-of-Stake Consensus Mechanisms for Future Blockchain Networks: Fundamentals, Applications, and Opportunities

This paper demonstrates the PoS mechanism by building a decentralized application and quantifies the performance of PoS mechanism. This helps compare the PoS with other suggested algorithms to pick the most efficient and secure one.

2.6 Staking on Chains

This paper talks about the operational and technical challenges related to staking crypto-currencies. This concept of staking again introduces a slight centralization where the stakes give control of their coins to third party services (Raffael Huber, 2019).

2.7 Veros-Whitepaper

This paper mostly focuses on the use cases for blockchain mechanisms and scalability in said fields. Most fields it talks about involve gaming, Real estate, E-commerce platforms, ATMs, Public crypto-currency exchanges. The blockchain mechanism simplifies the ways of accepting payments locally and across borders due to the coins having one value worldwide (Veros, 2016).

2.8 Blockchain/Distributed Ledger Technology (DLT): What Impact on the Financial Sector?

This paper talks about the impact of distributed ledger technology and its influence on the finance space. The intermediation costs involved in the current centralized system and the replacement of such costs with the help of consensus mechanisms. The security aspect where centralized systems use firewalls for their server storage while blockchain uses cryptography. The single copy is maintained by centralized authorities while blockchain has multiple nodes retaining the same data. Blockchain implements a peer-to-peer network while data cannot be accessed by many clients in the current system and how blockchain is a trustless system.

2.9 Blockchain in Finance

This chapter talks about the Global Financial crisis of 2008 and how the blockchain mechanism could help prevent the occurrence of another such incident. This paper discusses "mainstream payment and settlement, securities issuance, clearing and settlement, derivatives and other financial instruments, trade repositories, credit bureaus, corporate governance."

2.10 Blockchain Application and Outlook in the Banking Industry

This chapter discusses the staking mechanism in current system and the interest rate impact on the stakers. "The banking industry in China is facing the impact of interest rate liberalization and profit decline caused by the narrowing interest-rate spread." This stake reward being common across nations due to the nature of block chains is another reason blockchain could be disruptive in the banking industry.

2.11 How Blockchain Is Changing Finance

This chapter talks about the cost to maintain the current centralized systems and how blockchain can mitigate these costs. "Cost through fees and delays, creating friction through redundant and onerous paper work, and opening up opportunities for fraud and crime."

The blockchain could bring a unified system of transaction thus reducing time to exchange value between 2 local individuals or 2 international corporate clients. The paper work is mitigated since all the data is stored in a blockchain forever (Data on a blockchain cannot be deleted by design). The centralized storage of data paves to data modification in one point. Decentralization removes this single point of attack (John P. Kelleher, 2021).

2.12 Ethereum White Paper: A Next Generation Smart Contract and Decentralized Application Platform

This paper talks about how blockchain can do beyond just acting as a form of currency. This paper talks about blockchain acting as Identity and reputation systems, Decentralized file storage, Smart multi-storage escrow, Cloud computing, Peer-to-peer gambling, On chain decentralized marketplaces (Veros, 2016).

2.13 Do You Need a Blockchain?

This chapter differentiates between permission less (e.g., Bitcoin/Ethereum) and permission (e.g. Hyperledger/Corda) blockchains and compare and contrast their features to those of a single node database and the difference between these two compared to a central storage. It also looks at 3 use cases for a blockchain, "Supply Chain Management, Interbank and International Payments, and Decentralized Autonomous Organizations."

3. PROPOSED SYSTEM

The chapter aims to build a staking mechanism utilizing the underlying cryptographic principles of a blockchain. The hash function and other cryptographic principles proposed in the blockchain system include

3.1. Collision Free

It should be not possible for two different inputs the hash function gives the same output.

$$H(x) = A => H(y)! = A$$

Application of this means if the hash output of two inputs are the same then we can assume that both the inputs are equal.

3.2 Hiding Property

The hash function is such that given the output hash, the input can not be found.

Given $H(x) = A => x$ cannot be found

Application of this implies with a given output alone, the input cannot be found.

3.3 Consensus Algorithm

The consensus algorithms helps protect against the double spend attack. The double spend attack is basically an attack where a single coin is spent in multiple transactions. Prevention against unauthentic transactions is cryptographic but imposed by the consensus algorithm.

3.4 Comparing Systems of Exchange of Value

In order for a currency to be successful, six key factors and how a specific type of currency performs against it is measured. Following history, the move to systems with increase in stability among these factors has been widely encouraged.

Fungible:

Current system can be exchanged for goods just as efficiently as a crypto-currency. With wider adaptation of crypto-currencies more and more exchanges can be made using the same.

Non-Consumable:

While some crypto-currencies have an exhaustive supply some can be minted forever. Both fiat currencies and crypto-currencies would never exactly have" depleted".

Portability:

Figure 1. Comparing systems of exchange of value

Traits of Money	Gold	Fiat (US Dollar)	Crypto (Bitcoin)
Fungible *(Interchangeable)*	High	High	High
Non-Consumable	High	High	High
Portability	Moderate	High	High
Durable	High	Moderate	High
Highly Divisible	Moderate	Moderate	High
Secure *(Cannot be counterfeited)*	Moderate	Moderate	High
Easily Transactable	Low	High	High
Scarce *(Predictable Supply)*	Moderate	Low	High
Sovereign *(Government Issued)*	Low	High	Low
Decentralized	Low	Low	High
Smart *(Programmable)*	Low	Low	High

Fiat currencies made of paper and also supporting digital transactions and crypto-currency that can be carried around in any smart device are both portable.

Durable:

While crypto-currencies are completely digital, paper could be torn anytime thus losing its value.

Highly divisible:

The US dollar is divisible upto 1/100 th of a dollar while bitcoin(a crypto-currency) is divisible upto 8 decimals. 1/100000000 of a bitcoin is the smallest amount of bitcoin and is called a "satoshi".

Secure:

Due to the decentralized way of data storage, the change of data would mean changing data in more than 51%(thus paving way to 51% attack) participant's copy of data which requires a computation power that is currently practically impossible.

Easily transactable:

Both fiat and crypto-currencies can be moved with digital transactions

Scarce:

While Fiat currencies can be issued after decisions made by the government, the supply of a crypto-currency are stipulated in the protocol.

Sovereign & decentralized:

While fiat currencies are controlled by a centralized authority, the crypto-currencies are decentralized. Thus the digital currency system has far more advantages than the current fiat system.

3.5 Comparison Between PoW and PoS

Proof-of-work helped implement the idea of blockchain in the real world, however the concept of PoW means that the digital coin is reliant on energy usage, thus involving serious cost up keep in the working of such mechanisms, which is paid by the users via a mix of coin price increase and gas fees. As the coin production rate slows in the Bitcoin chain, one day it could bring stress on increasing transaction/gas fees to maintain a certain level of security.

Do we really need humongous levels of energy usage to have a decentralized digital coin? Therefore it is crucial, both theoretically and technically, to find a way to maintain these networks such that the security of peer-to-peer digital coins does not have to rely on high energy usage.

Proof of stake method does not depend on the huge computation power thus less energy consumption. It performs based on the asset deposited into the chain. The more crypto-currency a node deposits, the higher probability it gets to be chosen as the next validator to put the next block on the chain and get the reward (Cong T. Nguyen, et.al, 2019).

"Coin age is a way to display how long a coin has been in one's possession in order to prioritize it for use in transactions or mining. It is calculated by multiplying the number of coins by the average amount of time in blocks they have been possessed." (Porat, A., Pratap, et.al, 2018)

The use of coinage assures that honest nodes are preferred to be chosen as the validator since holding stake over a long period of time implies that the node has not lost stake by wrongly approving transactions. As long as the reward for approving the transaction does not exceed the staked value, a node is forced to perform honest verifications. Thus a crypto-currency built using PoS can overcome the problem posed by both Fiat currencies and the energy consuming PoW mechanism.

4. PROPOSED SYSTEM

The various components of system architecture are discussed below:

Figure 2. System architecture

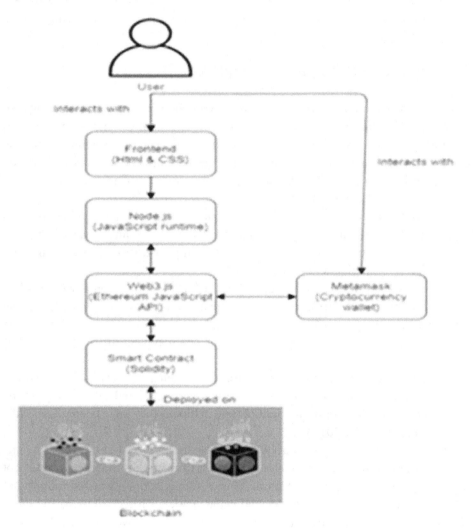

4.1 Blockchain

In this project the blockchain is where the transactions between the smart contract and the wallet are stored. A blockchain is a growing list of records, called blocks that are linked together using cryptography. Each block contains a cryptographic hash of the previous block, a timestamp, and transaction data (generally represented as a Merkle tree). The blockchain stores two types of data: the block list (a linked list) and the transaction list (a hash map).

It is in charge of: arriving block verification; arriving transaction verification; transaction list synchronisation; block list synchronisation.

The blockchain is a linked list in which the hash of the next block is calculated depending on the hash of the previous block as well as the data included within the block itself.

If any of the following conditions are met, a block is added to the list:

- The block is the final one (prior id + 1).
- The previous block is correct (prior hash == block.previousHash).
- The hash matches the data (estimated block hash == block.hash).
- The pow issue degree of difficulty is right (difficulty at blockchain index n block difficulty);
- All transactions within the block are legitimate.
- The total amount of output transactions equals the sum of input transactions plus 50 coins reflecting the block miner's payout;
- Examine the block to see if there is any double spending.

There is only 1 charge transaction and 1 incentive transaction.
A transaction within a block is valid if and only if

- The generated transaction hash equals transaction.hash.
- All input transactions have the correct signature (transaction data signature can be confirmed using the address's public key).
- When the number of input transactions exceeds the sum of output transactions, some room must be made for the transaction charge.
- The transaction has not yet been added to the blockchain. All input transactions are currently unspent in the blockchain.

Figure 3.

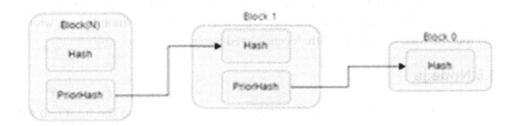

217

The timestamp proves that the transaction data existed when the block was published in order to get into its hash. Blocks form a chain, with each additional block reinforcing the ones before it.

Dataset: The study used cryptocurrency price information received from online sources, and 6 rows of data were gathered from every day's beginning, ending, the greatest, and worst prices, number of transactions, and price change. Subsequent gathering data, inappropriate data was removed, and the closing price of the next day, as the machine learning goal variable, was saved in a newly added column.

4.2 Smart Contract

The smart contract defines the logic of the application. In this case the smart contract tells the application to issue reward tokens when a specific amount of coin is staked. A smart contract is a self-executing contract with the terms of the agreement between buyer and seller being directly written into lines of code. The code and the agreements contained therein exist across a distributed, decentralized blockchain network

4.3 Web3.js

Web3.js is the JavaScript framework used to create functions that help interaction between the smart contract and the blockchain.web3. js is a collection of libraries which allows to interact with a local or remote ethereum node, using a HTTP or IPC connection. The web3 JavaScript library interacts with the Ethereum blockchain. It can retrieve user accounts, send transactions, interact with smart contracts, and more.

4.4 Metamask

Metamask is third-party wallet software used to connect to the user's wallet and enable interaction between the wallet and the smart contract. MetaMask is a software crypto-currency wallet used to interact with the Ethereum blockchain. It allows users to access their Ethereum wallet through a browser extension or mobile app, which can then be used to interact with decentralized applications.

4.5 Node.js

Node.js is the javascript runtime build environment used to run the front end for this application. Node.js is an open-source, cross-platform, back-end JavaScript runtime environment that runs on the V8 engine and executes JavaScript code outside a web browser.

4.6 Frontend

The front end is the portion the user interacts with. This is built using HTML &CSS. HTML and CSS are two pillars of web development; they are used to create web pages seen every day. HTML provides the structure to web page and CSS provides them the style to look better.

5. CONCLUSION

The PayCrypto model demonstrated the PoS model that helps validate transactions on a blockchain. The user can interact with the smart contract using the metamask wallet to stake and un-stake crypto-currencies. This model of staking will help widespread adoption of crypto-currencies.It is expected that the proof-of-stake model will evolve to be a more potentially competitive form of peer-to-peer crypto-currency over proof-of-work mechanisms due to the withdrawal of reliance on energy usage, therefore attaining lesser inflation/lesser gas fees at reasonable network security levels. This adoption of PoS over PoW can help build sustainable blockchains that can be adopted as a mode of exchange of value. The new decentralized transactional model made possible by DLT is likely to impact e-commerce significantly over the next decade. If one of the original points of application of the technology was payments and international transfers, we see in the flurry of initiatives - and of household names joining them - a clear signal that DLT is likely to prosper and have a deep impact on the economy, not just payment services.

6. FUTURE WORK

The model can be further developed to support multiple crypto-currencies. Since the value of different currencies differs, weights could be introduced to award tokens proportionately. This could be deployed as a private blockchain for specific applications say gaming, reward air miles etc.., or could be deployed as a public crypto-currency leveraging the PoS mechanism.

REFERENCES

Bitflyer. (2018). https://bitflyer.com/en-eu/glossary/coin_age

Gupta, Rahman, Poudyal, Huda, & Mahmud. (2019). A Hybrid POW-POS Implementation Against 51% Attack in Cryptocurrency System. *IEEE International Conference on Cloud Computing Technology and Science (CloudCom).*

Huber, Hays, & Valek. (2019). *Staking on Chains.* Bitcoin, Suisse AG, Decrypt.

Kelleher, J. P. (2021). *Why Do Bitcoins Have Value?* Investopedia.

King & Nadal. (2012). *PPCoin: Peer-to-Peer Crypto-Currency with Proof-of-Stake.* Academic Press.

Nakamoto, S. (2008). *Bitcoin: A peer-to-peer electronic cash system.* Academic Press.

Nguyen, C. T., Hoang, D. T., Nguyen, D. N., Niyato, D., Nguyen, H. T., & Dutkiewicz, E. (2019). Proof-of-Stake Consensus Mechanisms for Future Blockchain Networks: Fundamentals, Applications and Opportunities. *IEEE Access : Practical Innovations, Open Solutions*, *7*, 85727–85745. doi:10.1109/ACCESS.2019.2925010

Porat, A., Pratap, A., Shah, P., & Adkhar, V. (2018). Blockchain Consensus: An analysis of Proof-of-Work and its applications. Stanford.

Veros. (2016). *Whitepaper: Ethereum Blockchain.* Author.

Chapter 12
Recent Trends in Big Data:
Challenges and Opportunities

Kannadhasan Suriyan
https://orcid.org/0000-0001-6443-9993
Study World College of Engineering, India

Kanagaraj Venusamy
Rajalakshmi Engineering College, India

R. Nagarajan
https://orcid.org/0000-0002-4990-5869
Gnanamani College of Technology, India

ABSTRACT

Using big data and algorithmic techniques, not all of the data gathered in this way is relevant for analysis or decision-making. To be more specific, the chapter addresses issues that arise during the fine tuning of large data sets, presenting open research questions that can aid in the processing of large data sets and the extraction of valuable information from them, as well as providing an overview of big data tools and techniques that can be used to address these issues. Healthcare, public administration, retail, and other multidisciplinary scientific inquiries are only few of the areas where boundaries might be blurred. Big data is mostly derived from social computing, internet text and document storage, and internet search indexing. Online communities, recommendation systems, reputation systems, and prediction markets are all examples of social computing. Internet search indexing includes ISI, IEEE Xplorer, Scopus, Thomson Reuters, etc.

1. INTRODUCTION

Fast digital technology transitions provide the data source, resulting in an explosion of large amounts of data. Traditional database administration systems and data

DOI: 10.4018/979-8-3693-1131-8.ch012

processing programs are unable to handle the enormous datasets generated by these devices. Petabytes and beyond are not uncommon for various types of data. Structured, unstructured, or semi-structured are all possible options. Such data are technically defined by the 3Vs (Volume, Velocity, and Variety). To put it another way: volume refers to an enormous amount of information that is being generated every day; velocity measures how quickly that information can be gathered and processed. There is a lot of variety in the types of data that may be found in a variety. V stands for truthfulness and refers to the fact that it is both accessible and accountable. For big data analysis, the primary goal is to process large amounts of data in a variety of traditional and non-traditional ways. Even though photos and video can be stored and displayed, they are not semantically annotated or searchable because they are not naturally in a structured format like tweets and blogs. converting this information into a logically organized format Any subsequent analysis will be extremely difficult to perform effectively. The next generation of information technology industries will be well-served by the strength of big data. There are a number of IT companies that relate to big data, cloud computing, the internet of things, and social media as a means of solving deliberate problems.

Despite the fact that data warehouses are used to manage datasets, obtaining knowledge data from the available big data is a time-consuming procedure. When dealing with extremely huge datasets, it is impossible to use data mining techniques. This lack of coordination between database systems and analysis tools like data mining and statistical analysis is a major issue in the study of large amounts of data. It's difficult to discover new information in these scenarios. It is imperative that data be presented in a way that can be used in real-world scenarios. In explaining the data revolution, there is a need to consider its epistemological implications (Kitchin, 2014). As a result, the research on complexity theory of big data will help us understand the key characteristics and development of complex patterns in big data, simplify its representation, gain better knowledge abstraction, and lead the design of computer models. There isn't a single field in which big data is associated. It is highly likely that 4G will not be able to meet the increasing demands of manufacturing and industrial automation technology in the age of M2M, IoT, Big Data, and Smart Factories. Based on cyber-physical manufacturing systems, "smart manufacturing" has become a global development trend (CPMS). Automation, collaboration, real-time monitoring, and smart linked control are all hallmarks of Industrial IoT (IIoT), which is one of the significant difficulties resulting from the CPSM trend's development. The use of advanced manufacturing technology has resulted in the creation of a vast volume of data. There is a barrier to CPMS advancement because current mobile technologies, including 3G and 4G, can't deliver on the high dependability, fast data transfer and low latency required by the CPMS standard. Innovation in diverse industrial processes is required to ensure efficiency and ongoing improvement in these markets. Automated robotics or warehouse transportation activities, for example, may necessitate improved data transferability from the system in the near future The standardization of 5G, which is currently underway, could be crucial in meeting these needs in the manufacturing sector (Del, 2014; Jin et al., 2015; Kakhani et al., 2015; Kitchin, 2014; Kuo et al., 2014). Manufacturers and telecommunications providers will be able to exploit cutting-edge technology and preserve their competitiveness and profitability with the 5G network. If stakeholders' aspirations for 5G are met, the future of many aspects of daily life would be drastically altered. It is now possible to develop Smart Factories and use new technologies like artificial intelligence, automation, the Internet of Things (IoT), or augmented reality to solve problems. M2M will also benefit from the 5G network. Extreme low latency is one of the most critical 5G needs, along with high availability and low data error probability (and response time). A good network security system, a high density of connections, and high bandwidth are also essential. Real-time control of manufacturing processes and the ability to maintain real-time connectivity across operating locations, if necessary, will be provided by the 5G network and has a large potential to boost IIoT and CPMS.

An indoor and an outside (macro) system are two types of mobile services. Because of issues with field strength, capacity, or quality, an indoor system is necessary when macro base station cells are unable to meet a facility's needs. Mobile connectivity in manufacturing plants is ensured by indoor base stations, which contain individual indoor antenna systems and other equipment. If a large building has a high demand for mobile network capacity, then these indoor solutions should be built to ensure that there is sufficient coverage and capacity on all 3G and 4G networks. Manufacturers utilize these systems for mobile communication since they rely on fixed-line networks throughout the manufacturing process, but these fixed infrastructures are not flexible enough and are also deemed expensive. In addition to 4G's ability to deliver high data rates, industrial stakeholders must also weigh the benefits of using wired technology. Three key components make up the radio base station, or access network. The first component is the so-called Base Band Unit (BBU), which contains the necessary hardware and software for uplink and downlink baseband processing. The RRU (Remote Radio Unit) is a radio frequency transmitter and receiver used in the system. An optical fiber connects the amplifier to the BBU, which is in charge of making sure it gets enough juice. The "jumper" wire connects the RRU to the passive antenna via coaxial cable. Antennas emit radio waves with the required qualities for the supplied technology. To put it another way, big data refers to a collection of data that is so large that it necessitates the use of new technologies and architectures in order to extract any value from it (Bologa et al., 2013; Brown et al., 2011; Halevi & Moed, 2012; Helland, 2013; Huang, 1997).

Location-specific data derived from traffic management is one of the newest types of big data. As a result of the monitoring of individual electronic devices like Smartphones. Because we live in a world that increasingly relies on data-intensive technologies, Big Data has evolved. With such a massive amount of data, it is impossible to do effective analysis with the current methods available. There are numerous obstacles and issues that need to be understood while implementing and adjusting to the new technology of Big Data, which is a relatively new phenomenon in the market. The term "Big Data" refers to datasets that continue to increase in size so rapidly that current database administration concepts and techniques are no longer able to keep up with them. Data capture, storage, search, sharing, analytics, and visualization are just a few of the potential stumbling blocks. Many problems arise as a result of the sheer amount, speed, diversity, variability, value, and complexity of big data. Scalability, unstructured data, accessibility, real-time analytics, fault tolerance, and many more are some of the issues addressed in huge data management. Diverse sectors generate and store data in very different ways, whether it's encoded video, pictures, audio, or text/numerical information. This is because the amount of data stored varies per sector.

Most of the processes have been digitized and new social networks, blogs, sensors, hand-held gadgets, wearable devices, and the growth of the Internet have resulted in an ever-increasing volume of data that is constantly being generated. There is no denying the impact of the Internet on business, government, education, and people's daily lives. The rate at which data is being generated and the type of data being generated have both surpassed the capacity of current data storage solutions, and this trend is now in a revolutionary stage. The advent and widespread use of the Internet has resulted in data carrying far more information than in the past. There has been a massive increase in data over the previous two decades. This is a general trend that can be found practically everywhere. Data analysts at International Data Corporation (IDC) predict a 35-trillion-gigabyte increase in digital data volume between 2012 and 2020. One gigabyte is comparable to 40 (four-drawer) file cabinets of text or two music CDs, according to IDC. It was at this time that social media and the cloud (via multi-core CPUs and graphics cards) first began to play major roles in the growth of big data. Currently, Facebook has 1.04 billion daily active users, 934 million mobile daily active users, 125 billion friend connections, 205 billion images published every day, and 70 languages available to its users. There are 30 billion pieces of content on Facebook, 2.7 billion likes and comments, and an average of 130 friends for each user (Facebook, 2015). There are new avenues to research social and cultural processes as a result of this development. It is possible for a company to gain a competitive edge by making sense of the massive amounts of data it has at its disposal. Relational Data Base Management Systems (RDBMS) and simple data analysis tools like Structured Query Language (SQL) were utilized by enterprises in their day-to-day operations that helped them make and plan decisions. Even Nevertheless, as data volumes continue to grow, it has become nearly difficult to analyse these data using current storage strategies and simple queries. For example, consumer reviews of their Facebook sites or tweets.

An overview of big data, from its sources to dimensions, is provided in this chapter. Existing ways to data processing have limitations, which need the use of big data analytics and the creation of new methods for storing and processing large amounts of data. There will be a discussion of the Big Data Value Chain, which is a collection of operations ranging from data collection to data analysis. Conclusions address limits of big data analytics and point researchers in the right path for future study. It's difficult to store and retrieve large amounts of structured and unstructured data in a reasonable length of time. A few of these constraints to handling and processing massive amounts of data using the old storage strategies led to the creation of the term "Big Data." Despite the fact that the Internet's rise has drawn attention to big data, the two cannot be compared. However, the Internet facilitates the collection and exchange of raw data as well as knowledge. With the advent of Big Data, it is now possible to anticipate the future course of action with high precision and an acceptable time delay by storing, processing, and comprehending vast amounts of previously unstructured data.

Marketers and insurance companies concentrate on customer-specific insurance plans, while healthcare professionals concentrate on providing patients with high-quality, low-cost care. Despite advances in data storage, collection, analysis, and algorithms related to predicting human behavior, it is important to understand the underlying driving and regulating factors (market, law, social norms, and architecture) that can help in developing robust models that can handle big data while still yielding high prediction accuracy. For big data analytics, classic techniques like rule-based systems, pattern mining, and decision trees are being explored in order to construct business rules on enormous data sets more quickly and effectively. Either distributed data storage methods, in-memory computation, or cluster computing can be used to accomplish this. In the past, grid computing was used to perform these tasks, but cloud computing has recently superseded it (Bizer et al., 2012; Manyika et al., 2011; Sagiroglu & Sinanc, 2013; Yunan, 2012; Zaslavsky et al., 2013).

2. BIG DATA

The term "Big Data" has recently become a catchphrase. Academics and industry specialists alike are taking advantage of it. Literature provides a wide range of definitions for the term. Relational database management system (RDBMS) companies introduced data warehouse technology in the late 1980s, which is commonly classified as online analytical processing (OLAP).In order to assist in the making of business decisions and the gathering of business information. In the beginning, it was intended to keep production databases light and fast by archiving a lot of data and keeping them lean and mean. Various copies of data are stored in a data mart on multiple database servers. You can have a standalone data mart, as well as a corporate data mart. Two analytical data marts were populated with the extracted data. To carry out their duties, the data analysts construct algorithms in this location. Data marts linked to a business user and a statistical analyst. In spite of the fact that detailed reporting based on complicated statistical modeling has not failed in delivering business value, it is difficult to continually transport data across the network and takes a long time to produce results. Additionally, the amount of data that can be saved on the system is constrained. Big data processing is made more challenging by the fact that new data is constantly being created. As of late, big data has received a great deal of interest from government agencies as well as industries such as healthcare and finance. As a result, the volume of data generated in these fields is huge, and it is impossible to classify it into a relational database management system.

It is therefore imperative that companies, industries, and other business sectors devise effective methods for managing and processing this massive amount of data in order to assure timely and accurate decision-making. There have been recent developments and implementations of big data and business analytics methodologies to examine a vast volume of data created by various business enterprises. For businesses, it is essential to have access to ever-increasing amounts of transactional data more quickly. This enables enterprises observe the past and predict the future by analyzing data in real time Therein lies the allure of real-time analytics, which gives us the ability to see what has occurred, why it has occurred, what might happen in the future, and, most importantly, what we can do about it (prescriptive). We discuss the four analytics flavors that have enormous commercial value, but they are more challenging to adopt and apply. Increasing operational effectiveness is not the sole benefit of utilizing large amounts of big data. Economic development and a rise in the level of living are also possible outcomes.

Big data analytics can be used in a variety of ways to improve the performance of businesses and sectors. Improved health care, education, national security, and excellent governance (Huang, 1997; Kuo et al., 2014) are only a few examples. There is a lot of promise in this technology for assisting policymakers in creating safe playgrounds for businesses, helping waste managers find out what type of garbage is generated in a particular area, and providing insight into the sharing of waste collection materials. Educator performance can be evaluated and improved through the use of big data and business analytics by education monitoring agencies. This data can also be utilized to minimize traffic congestion in large cities or better organize the public transportation system by analyzing the position of mobile networks. It is the purpose of this research to conduct a complete inquiry into big data and business analytics methodologies for improved business decision making, technology approaches, applications, and open research questions. Big data has provided enormous benefits for businesses in industrialized countries, and this study aims at highlighting the potential for indigenous businesses to profit from the same technology. According to a new report, big data analytics faces a number of issues in terms of securing and managing data as well as ensuring regulatory compliance. For more than a decade, researchers and businesses have been studying and implementing big data analytics. This is because big data is being used in so many fields, including healthcare, business, education, network optimization, travel estimates, and finance. Big data analytics, implementations, and associated technologies have been the subject of several studies and evaluations in recent years. Research by Sing et al. Examined the hardware and software factors needed to achieve effective big data analytics. The taxonomy and confluence of cloud computing and big data analytics was also described. Big data in the cloud, software and hardware aspects such as data availability, scalability and data size were the focus of these investigations, however. Big data analytics tools were not included in the studies since they were not discussed in depth. Reviews of big data analytics, open source tools for big data implementation, and iterative clustering techniques for large data analysis were recently published. Described methods for data mining and knowledge discovery in the context of big data analytics. Big data analytics can benefit from the authors' data mining algorithm, which was principally described in the paper. Despite this, big data analytics difficulties, applications, existing technologies, and data sources were not thoroughly covered.

The merits and disadvantages of open source tools for big data analytics were discussed. Although the assessment focuses on tools, other aspects of efficient big data application are not adequately addressed. Recently released a similar survey that examined big data technology, applications, and open source tools for big data analytics. In contrast, our research differs from theirs in a number of areas. In the first place, this evaluation focuses on the most current developments in big data and business analytics. Secondly, we talked about the many platforms and open source tools available, as well as their pros and cons. Big data success criteria for analytic teams, as well as hurdles for implementing analytics in enterprises, are presented in this paper. For the fourth time, big data and business analytics can take advantage of newly discovered data sources and applications. A last section of this review focuses on big data and analytics open research directions. The review comes at a good time. Laney used a 3Vs model to address the challenges of big data and business analytics with increasing data (2001). The term "big data" is used by academics to describe the massive amounts of unstructured data generated by a wide variety of high-performance heterogeneous applications, ranging from social networking to scientific computing. Existing data management technologies are incapable of handling datasets that are so large that they can't be analyzed in any meaningful way. Despite the fact that big data has been characterized in a variety of ways, no single definition exists. Only a few people have defined what it does, and even fewer have concentrated on what it is. The 3Vs-based concept of big data is arbitrary. As the definition of big data may change over time, how can we know what it is? For example, today's enormous data could be stored in the future because to improvements in storage technology. Defining big data is only the beginning of the challenge of utilizing this data to its fullest potential and generating actionable insights for business operations and strategy.

When it comes to dealing with massive amounts of data, the term "Big Data" has been coined to describe it. Despite its novelty, the term "Big Data" will be further explored in the coming literature. In the beginning, the subject's concept, qualities, and the two primary techniques to dealing with it are discussed. Further, the comprehensive report explains how Big Data may be used in every facet of the business and human being. The use of Big Data Analytics after combining it with digital capabilities to secure corporate growth and its visualization to make it accessible to the technically-trained business analysts have been discussed in detail. Big Data can be used to improve population health, banking, telecom, food, and food business, as well as fraud detection, sentiment analysis, and sentiment mapping. The report goes into great detail about the obstacles that are preventing the growth of Big Data Analytics. On one, there are practical issues to consider, and on the other, there are theoretical problems to consider. In addition to the difficulties of safeguarding and democratizing data, there are many additional issues that must be overcome, such as a lack of skilled data experts and software that can handle data quickly. The article's authors hope to explain the concepts in a clear and concise manner by incorporating various examples and examples within the text. The proliferation of big data in the digital age is due in large part to the proliferation of data generated by numerous technologies. With the acquisition of massive datasets, it enables evolutionary breakthroughs in numerous domains. Traditional database administration tools and data processing software are unable to handle huge and complicated datasets. Unstructured and semi-structured data in petabytes and more is available. It is characterized as a range of three to four volts.

Volume, velocity, and variety are the 3Vs. To put it another way: volume refers to an enormous amount of information that is being generated every day; velocity measures how quickly that information can be gathered and processed. Structured, unstructured, and semi-structured data, for example, are all sorts of variety. Veracity, which incorporates availability and responsibility, is the fourth V. When it comes to analyzing large amounts of data, the most important goal is to use numerous traditional and computationally intelligent ways (Kakhani et al., 2015) to do so. The definition of big data can be found in the figure below. However, the precise concept of big data is not specified, and it is believed to be problem-specific by some people. We will be able to make better decisions, discover new insights, and optimize our processes while being inventive and cost-effective.

By the end of 2015, big data is predicted to have grown to 25 billion records. From an information and communication technology standpoint, big data is a strong motivator for the next generation of information technology companies, which are mostly based on the third platform and include big data, cloud computing and the internet of things. This lack of coordination between database systems and analysis tools like data mining and statistical analysis is a major issue in the study of large amounts of data. These issues typically arise when we attempt to uncover and express information for use in real-world applications. There is a fundamental challenge in describing the core aspects of huge data quantitatively. It is hoped that the study of the complexity theory of big data will also help to better understand the essential characteristics and formation of complex patterns in large datasets, as well as to simplify their representation, improve knowledge abstraction, and guide computer model and algorithm design. Big data and its trends have been studied extensively by a number of scholars. Big data concerns, their research issues, and numerous techniques linked with them are the primary focus of this work. As a result, this article serves as a starting point for further exploration of big data. In addition, we list unresolved difficulties in big data research.

Large data sets have proliferated in recent years thanks to a variety of technologies, including mobile devices, sensor technologies, remote sensing, and readers for radio frequency identification (RFID). When there isn't enough room to retain all of these records, they are either ignored or erased due of the high expense of storing them. As a result, the first hurdle for large data analysis is the storage mediums and faster input/output speed. Such situations necessitate that data accessibility be at the top of the knowledge discovery and representation priority list. The primary reason is that material must be quickly and easily available for further investigation. Analysts have been using hard disk drives for data storage for decades, but random input/output performance is slower than sequential input/output on hard disk drives than in the past. The notion of solid state drive (SSD) and phrase change memory (PCM) were introduced to solve this issue. There are, however, no storage solutions that can meet the demands of processing large amounts of data.

Another problem with Big Data analysis is the ever-increasing number of datasets, which necessitates more data mining jobs. Additionally, when dealing with huge datasets, data reduction, data selection, and feature selection are critical. Researchers have an unparalleled difficulty in tackling this problem. When dealing with high-dimensional data, traditional algorithms may not always be capable of responding quickly enough. In recent years, the automation of this process and the development of new machine learning algorithms to assure consistency has been a key challenge. to name only a few Clustering of vast numbers of objects.

The primary focus should be on datasets that aid in the analysis of large data. Large amounts of semi-structured and unstructured data may now be collected in a reasonable amount of time thanks to new technologies like Hadoop and MapReduce. The most difficult problem for engineers to solve is how to effectively evaluate these data in order to better understand the situation. Designing storage systems and enhancing effective data analysis tools that guarantee results when data comes from a variety of sources will be a big problem in this situation Data analysis and data management, as well as archiving, management, preservation, information retrieval and representation can all benefit from better machine learning algorithm design. In order to deal with real-world issues, a wide variety of hybridized methodologies are being created. All of these methods are depending on the specific issue at hand. A sequential computer that can handle big datasets. While some of the strategies have high scalability over parallel computers, there are others that do not. Currently available methods may not be able to process big data efficiently enough to acquire useful information, given how rapidly its quantity is growing. When dealing with enormous datasets, the most common strategy is to employ data warehouses and data marts.

Computational complexity increase while dealing with enormous datasets. Managing the dataset's discrepancies and uncertainties is the main challenge. Computational complexity is typically modelled using systematic methods. Developing a thorough mathematical system that can be used to Big Data may seem tough at first. The complexity of a single domain can be easily understood, however, to do domain-specific data analytics. It is possible that a series of such developments could imitate big data analytics in several fields. Machine learning approaches that require the least amount of memory have been extensively researched and surveyed in this area.

Scalability and security are two of the most pressing issues facing big data analysis methodologies. In the last few decades, academics have focused on speeding up data analysis and processing, as Moore's Law has predicted. Sample, on-line and multiresolution analytic approaches must be developed for the latter. When it comes to analyzing large amounts of data, incremental strategies are ideal. There is a natural dramatic shift in processor technology incorporated with an increasing number of cores when the data size grows faster than CPU speeds. Parallel computing is a result of this transition in processors. For real-time applications like navigation, social networks, financial markets, the internet search and timeliness, parallel computing is necessary. To summarize, big data has created numerous challenges for hardware and software developers working on parallel computing, clouds, distributed computing, data visualization, and scaling. Using more mathematical models in conjunction with computer science can help us overcome this problem.

Global interrelations, the art of business, cultural revolutions and an incredible number of personal traits have been restructured by the Internet. In the near future, machines will be able to use the internet to control an enormous number of autonomous devices, resulting in the Internet of Things (IoT). Appliances, like human web browsers, are now users of the internet. For its most promising opportunities and challenges, the Internet of Things is attracting a growing number of researchers. It has a significant impact on the development of information, network, and communication technology in the future. Everything will eventually be connected and intelligently managed in the future. Due to the emergence of mobile devices, embedded and ubiquitous communication technologies, cloud computing, and data analytics, the IoT idea is becoming more relevant to the actual world. In addition, the Internet of Things creates hurdles in terms of volume, velocity, and variety. In a broader sense, Internet of Things allows devices to exist in a variety of places and supports applications ranging from the trivial to the vital, just like the internet. IoT definitions, content, and differences from other comparable concepts are all still a mystery. Big data and artificial intelligence can be combined to improve data management and knowledge discovery in large-scale automation applications.

Big data professionals have the hardest difficulty of all when it comes to extracting knowledge from IoT data. Because of this, it is imperative to build an infrastructure for IoT data analysis. Machine learning techniques can be used to extract useful information from the constant streams of data generated by an IoT device. Understanding and analyzing these streams of data created by IoT devices is a complex problem that requires big data analytics. From an IoT perspective, the only way to deal with big data is through machine learning algorithms and computational intelligence techniques. In addition, many academic publications explore IoT-related technology. Frames, rules, tagging, and other theories of human information processing have inspired the development of knowledge exploration systems.

There are four main parts to this process: acquiring knowledge, building a knowledge base, disseminating that knowledge, and putting that knowledge to use. Knowledge acquisition is a process in which various traditional and computational intelligence techniques are used to discover new information, which is then stored in knowledge bases and used to build expert systems.

3. CONCLUSION

Disseminating relevant information from the knowledge base and developing expert systems is critical to the success of these systems. Dissemination of knowledge is critical to obtaining useful data from a body of existing knowledge. The process of extracting information from papers, knowledge contained within those documents, and knowledge bases is known as knowledge extraction. To conclude, new knowledge is put to use in a variety of contexts. It is the pinnacle of all research. In order to get the best results, the knowledge exploration process must be iterated over and over again. There are several topics, debates, and investigations in this area of scientific inquiry.

REFERENCES

Bizer, C., Boncz, P., Brodie, M. L., & Erling, O. (2012). The meaningful use of Big Data: Four perspectives—four challenges. *SIGMOD Record, 40*(4), 56–60. doi:10.1145/2094114.2094129

Bologa, A.-R., Bologa, R., & Florea, A. (2013). Big Data and Specific Analysis Methods for Insurance Fraud Detection. *Database Systems Journal, 4,* 30–39.

Brown, B., Chui, M., & Manyika, J. (2011). Are you ready for the era of 'Big Data'. *The McKinsey Quarterly, 4,* 24–35.

Del, S. (2014). On the use of mapreduce for imbalanced big data using random forest. *Information Sciences, 285,* 112–137. doi:10.1016/j.ins.2014.03.043

Halevi, G., & Moed, H. (2012). The evolution of Big Data as a research and scientific topic: Overview of the literature. *Research Trends, Special Issue on Big Data, 30,* 3–6.

Helland, P. (2013). Condos and clouds. *Communications of the ACM, 56*(1), 50–59. doi:10.1145/2398356.2398374

Huang, Z. (1997). A fast clustering algorithm to cluster very large categorical data sets in data mining. *SIGMOD Workshop on Research Issues on Data Mining and Knowledge Discovery.*

Jin, X., Wah, B. W., Cheng, X., & Wang, Y. (2015). Significance and challenges of big data research. *Big Data Research, 2*(2), 59–64. doi:10.1016/j.bdr.2015.01.006

Kakhani, M. K., Kakhani, S., & Biradar, S. R. (2015). Research issues in big data analytics. *International Journal of Application or Innovation in Engineering & Management, 2*(8), 228–232.

Kitchin, R. (2014). Big Data, new epistemologies and paradigm shifts. *Big Data & Society*, *1*(1), 1–12. doi:10.1177/2053951714528481

Kuo, M. H., Sahama, T., Kushniruk, A. W., Borycki, E. M., & Grunwell, D. K. (2014). Health big data analytics: Current perspectives, challenges and potential solutions. *International Journal of Big Data Intelligence*, *1*(1/2), 114–126. doi:10.1504/IJBDI.2014.063835

Manyika, J., Chui, M., Brown, B., Bughin, J., Dobbs, R., Roxburgh, C., & Byers, A. H. (2011). *Big Data: The next frontier for innovation, competition, and productivity. Technical report*. McKinsey Global Institute.

Sagiroglu, S., & Sinanc, D. (2013). Big Data: A review. *Collaboration Technologies and Systems (CTS), 2013 International Conference on, 42-47.*

Yunan. (2012). *What is Big Data's role in helping companies achieve competitive advantage through analytics*. Academic Press.

Zaslavsky, A., Perera, C., & Georgakopoulos, D. (2013). *Sensing as a service and Big Data*. arXiv preprint arXiv:1301.0159.

Compilation of References

Abd El-Moghith, I. A., & Darwish, S. M. (2021). Towards designing a trusted routing scheme in wireless sensor networks: A new deep blockchain approach. *IEEE Access : Practical Innovations, Open Solutions*, 9, 103822–103834. doi:10.1109/ACCESS.2021.3098933

Adarsh, S., Anoop, V. S., & Asharaf, S. (2022, September). Distributed Consensus Mechanism with Novelty Classification Using Proof of Immune Algorithm. *International Conference on Innovative Computing and Communications Proceedings of ICICC*, 2, 173–183.

Agbo, C. C., & Mahmoud, Q. H. (2020). Blockchain in healthcare opportunities, challenges, and possible solutions. *International Journal of Healthcare Information Systems and Informatics*, 15(3), 82–97. doi:10.4018/IJHISI.2020070105

Agbo, C. C., Mahmoud, Q. H., & Eklund, J. M. (2019). Blockchain technology in healthcare: A systematic review. *Health Care*, 7(2). PMID:30987333

Akhavan, P., & Attaran, M. (2020). Blockchain technology for secure and privacy-preserving applications in healthcare: A comprehensive survey. *Journal of Medical Systems*, 44(8), 142.

Akkar, H. A. R., & Salman, S. A. (2020). Detection of biomedical images by using bio-inspired artificial intelligent. *Engineering and Technology Journal*, 38(2), 255–264. doi:10.30684/etj. v38i2A.319

Akyildiz, I. F., Lee, A., Vuran, M. C., & Mohanty, S. (2019). A survey on blockchain technology for securing IoT networks. *IEEE Communications Surveys and Tutorials*, 20(4), 3684–3711.

Alazab, M., Awajan, A., Mesleh, A., Abraham, A., Jatana, V., & Alhyari, S. (2020). Article. *International Journal of Computer Information Systems and Industrial Management Applications*, 12, 168–181.

Alder, S. (2022). June 2022 healthcare data breach report. *The HIPAA Journal*.

Alfandi. (2020). Blockchain technology in healthcare: A systematic literature review and taxonomy-based research agenda. *Health Information Science and Systems, 8*.

Ali, M. H. (2019). Blockchain technology for electronic health records. Academic Press.

Ali, M., El-Moghith, A., Ibrahim, A., El-Derini, M. N., & Darwish, S. M. (2022). Wireless Sensor Networks Routing Attacks Prevention with Blockchain and Deep Neural Network. *Computers, Materials & Continua, 70*(3). Advance online publication. doi:10.32604/cmc.2022.021305

Ali, R., Moura, L., & Albuquerque, C. (2018). Blockchain-Based Self-Sovereign Identity Management Systems: A Review. *IEEE Access : Practical Innovations, Open Solutions, 6,* 39907–39915.

Alqahtani. (2021). A Verification Approach for Functional Requirements of Interacting Smart Contracts in Blockchain-Based Supply Chain Management Systems. *IEEE Access, 9.*

Alroobaea, R., Arul, R., Rubaiee, S., Alharithi, F. S., Tariq, U., & Fan, X. (2022). AI-assisted bio-inspired algorithm for secure IoT communication networks. *Cluster Computing, 25*(3), 1805–1816. doi:10.100710586-021-03520-z

Alshamrani, S. S., & Basha, A. F. (2021). IoT data security with DNA-genetic algorithm using blockchain technology. *International Journal of Computer Applications in Technology, 65*(2), 150–159. doi:10.1504/IJCAT.2021.114988

AlShamsi, M., Al-Emran, M., & Shaalan, K. (2022). A Systematic Review on Blockchain Adoption. *Applied Sciences (Basel, Switzerland), 12*(9), 1–18. doi:10.3390/app12094245 PMID:35685831

American Cancer Society. (n.d.). *Key Statistics for Endometrial Cancer.* Available at https://www.cancer.org/cancer/endometrial-cancer/about/key-statistics.html

Androulaki, E., Barger, A., Bortnikov, V., Cachin, C., Christidis, K., De Caro, A., . . . Muralidharan, S. (2018). Hyperledger Fabric: A Distributed Operating System for Permissioned Blockchains. In *Proceedings of the Thirteenth EuroSys Conference* (pp. 30:1-30:15). ACM. 10.1145/3190508.3190538

Anguraj, D. K., Thirugnanasambandam, K., Raghav, R. S., Sudha, S. V., & Saravanan, D. (2021). Enriched cluster head selection using augmented bifold cuckoo search algorithm for edge-based internet of medical things. *Journal of Digital Applications in Cardiology, 34*(9), e4817. doi:10.1002/dac.4817

Antonsen, S. L., Ulrich, L., & Hogdall, C. (2020). Overview of ACOG guidelines for management of endometrial cancer and the implications of molecular classification. *European Journal of Cancer.* Advance online publication. doi:10.1016/j.ejca.2020.04.007

Arechvo, A., Vargas-Hernández, V. M., & López-Cabanillas, J. L. (2015). Diagnostic utility of D&C in the detection of uterine sarcomas: Systematic review and meta-analysis. *Gynecologic Oncology.* Advance online publication. doi:10.1016/j.ygyno.2015.08.027

Ashour, A., Samanta, S., Dey, N., Kausar, N., Abdessalemkaraa, W., & Hassanien, A. (2015). Computed Tomography Image Enhancement Using Cuckoo Search: A Log Transform Based Approach. *Journal of Signal and Information Processing, 6*(3), 244–257. doi:10.4236/jsip.2015.63023

Aslan, Ö., Aktuğ, S. S., Ozkan-Okay, M., Yilmaz, A. A., & Akin, E. (2023). A Comprehensive Review of Cyber Security Vulnerabilities, Threats, Attacks, and Solutions. *Electronics (Basel)*, *12*(6), 1–42. doi:10.3390/electronics12061333

Athanere, S. & Thakur, R. (2022). Blockchain based hierarchical semi-decentralized approach using IPFS for secure and efficient data sharing. *Journal of King Saud University - Computer and Information Sciences*, *34*(4), 1523-1534. https://doi.org/ doi:10.1016/j.jksuci.2022.01.019

Atkinson, D. (2023). Virtual Modeling and Immersive Holographic Imaging Technologies, Cloud-based Digital Twin Manufacturing and Visual Perceptive Systems, and Bio-inspired Computational Intelligence and Context Awareness Algorithms in the Industrial Metaverse. *Journal of Self-Governance and Management Economics*, *11*(1), 73–88.

Aure, J. C., Hoeg, K., & Kolstad, P. (2015). Preoperative tumour size at MRI predicts deep myometrial invasion, lymph node metastases, and patient outcome in endometrial carcinomas. *International Journal of Gynecological Cancer*. Advance online publication. doi:10.1097/IGC.0000000000000333

Azaria, E. (2016). MedRec: Using Blockchain for Medical Data Access and Permission Management. Academic Press.

Backes, F. J., Leon, M. E., Ivanov, I., Suarez, A., Frankel, W. L., Hampel, H., Fowler, J. M., Copeland, L. J., O'Malley, D. M., & Cohn, D. E. (2009). Prospective evaluation of DNA mismatch repair protein expression in primary endometrial cancer. *Gynecologic Oncology*, *114*(3), 486–490. Advance online publication. doi:10.1016/j.ygyno.2009.05.026 PMID:19515405

Bai, C., & Sarkis, J. (2020). A supply chain transparency and sustainability technology appraisal model for blockchain technology. *International Journal of Production Research*, *58*(7), 2142–2162. doi:10.1080/00207543.2019.1708989

Basiri, M. E., Ghasem-Aghaee, N., & Aghdam, M. H. (2013). Efficient ant colony optimization for image feature selection. *Signal Processing*, *93*(1), 1–14. doi:10.1016/j.sigpro.2012.06.019

Bell, L., Buchanan, W. J., Cameron, J., & Lo, O. (2018). Applications of Blockchain Within Healthcare. *Blockchain in Healthcare Today*, *1*, 1–7. doi:10.30953/bhty.v1.8

Bendifallah, S., Canlorbe, G., Collinet, P., Arsène, E., Huguet, F., Coutant, C., Hudry, D., Graesslin, O., Raimond, E., Touboul, C., Daraï, E., & Ballester, M. (2015). Just how accurate are the major risk stratification systems for early-stage endometrial cancer? *British Journal of Cancer*, *112*(5), 793–801. Advance online publication. doi:10.1038/bjc.2015.35 PMID:25675149

Bhattacharya, S., Sarker, R., Khan, M. M., & Abbass, H. A. (2019). Blockchain-inspired optimization algorithms: A systematic review. *IEEE Access : Practical Innovations, Open Solutions*, *7*, 123033–123051.

Bhoware, A., Jajulwar, K., Deshmukh, A., Dabhekar, K., Ghodmare, S., & Gulghane, A. (2023, April). Performance Analysis of Network Security System Using Bioinspired-Blockchain Technique for IP Networks. In *2023 11th International Conference on Emerging Trends in Engineering & Technology-Signal and Information Processing (ICETET-SIP)* (pp. 1-6). IEEE. 10.1109/ICETET-SIP58143.2023.10151475

Bilaiya, R., Ahlawat, P., & Bathla, R. (2021). Intrusion Detection Systems: Current Trends and Future Challenges. Handbook of Research on Machine Learning Techniques for Pattern Recognition and Information Security, 235-254. doi:10.4018/978-1-7998-3299-7.ch014

Biswas, K., & Misra, S. (2021). Blockchain-based applications in smart grids: A review. *IEEE Transactions on Industrial Informatics, 17*(2), 1332–1341.

Bitflyer. (2018). https://bitflyer.com/en-eu/glossary/coin_age

Bizer, C., Boncz, P., Brodie, M. L., & Erling, O. (2012). The meaningful use of Big Data: Four perspectives—four challenges. *SIGMOD Record, 40*(4), 56–60. doi:10.1145/2094114.2094129

Bokhman, J. V. (1983). Two pathogenetic types of endometrial carcinoma. *Gynecologic Oncology, 15*(1), 10–17. Advance online publication. doi:10.1016/0090-8258(83)90111-7 PMID:6822361

Bologa, A.-R., Bologa, R., & Florea, A. (2013). Big Data and Specific Analysis Methods for Insurance Fraud Detection. *Database Systems Journal, 4*, 30–39.

Bonneau, J., Miller, A., Clark, J., Narayanan, A., Kroll, J. A., & Felten, E. W. (2015). Sok: Research Perspectives and Challenges for Bitcoin and Cryptocurrencies. In *IEEE Symposium on Security and Privacy* (pp. 104-121). IEEE. 10.1109/SP.2015.14

Brown, B., Chui, M., & Manyika, J. (2011). Are you ready for the era of 'Big Data'. *The McKinsey Quarterly, 4*, 24–35.

Buterin, V. (2013). *Ethereum White Paper: A Next-Generation Smart Contract and Decentralized Application Platform*. Retrieved from https://ethereum.org/whitepaper/

Buterin, V. (2013). *Ethereum: A Next-Generation Smart Contract and Decentralized Application Platform*. Academic Press.

Chakraborty, S., Chatterjee, S., Dey, N., Ashour, A. S., Ashour, A. S., Shi, F., & Mali, K. (2020). Modified cuckoo search algorithm in microscopic image segmentation of hippocampus. *Journal of Ambient Intelligence and Humanized Computing, 11*(7), 2925–2937. doi:10.100712652-019-01311-5

Chanal, P. M., Kakkasageri, M. S., & Manvi, S. K. S. (2021). *Security and privacy in the internet of things: computational intelligent techniques-based approaches. In Recent Trends in Computational Intelligence Enabled Research*. Academic Press.

Chaouchi, H., & Qadir, J. (2020). Blockchain technology and internet of things: A systematic review. *Journal of Network and Computer Applications, 168*, 102715.

Chawla, R., Beram, S. M., Murthy, C. R., Thiruvenkadam, T., Bhavani, N. P. G., Saravanakumar, R., & Sathishkumar, P. J. (2022). *Brain tumor recognition using an integrated bat algorithm with a convolutional neural network approach*. doi:10.1016/j.measen.2022.100426

Chen, L. X., Lee, W. K., Chang, C. C., Choo, K. K. R., & Zhang, N. (2020). Blockchain based searchable encryption for electronic health record sharing. Academic Press.

Chen, Y. (2020). A blockchain-based decentralized authentication scheme for medical products in the Internet of Medical Things. Academic Press.

Chen, G., Xu, B., Lu, M., & Chen, N. S. (2018). Exploring blockchain technology and its potential applications for education. *Smart Learning Environments*, *5*(1), 1–10. doi:10.118640561-017-0050-x

Chen, J., Wang, H., Xiong, L., Zeng, Z., & Wang, X. (2019). Blockchain-based secure and efficient algorithm for demand response management in smart grid. *IEEE Transactions on Industrial Informatics*, *15*(6), 3700–3709.

Chow, F., Muftu, A., & Shorter, R. V. (2014). Virtualization and cloud computing in dentistry. *Journal of the Massachusetts Dental Society*, *63*(1), 14–75. PMID:24941546

Christidis, K., & Devetsikiotis, M. (2016). Blockchains and Smart Contracts for the Internet of Things. *IEEE Access : Practical Innovations, Open Solutions*, *4*, 2292–2303. doi:10.1109/ACCESS.2016.2566339

Clarke, B. A., & Gilks, C. B. (2010). Endometrial carcinoma: Controversies in histopathological assessment of grade and tumour cell type. *Journal of Clinical Pathology*, *63*(5), 410–415. Advance online publication. doi:10.1136/jcp.2009.071225 PMID:20418232

Colombo, N., Creutzberg, C., & Amant, F. (2016). ESMO-ESGO-ESTRO Consensus Conference on Endometrial Cancer: Diagnosis, Treatment and Follow-up. *Annals of Oncology*. DOI: 10.1093/annonc/mdw387

Creasman, W. T., Kohler, M. F., Odicino, F., Maisonneuve, P., & Boyle, P. (2004). Prognosis of papillary serous, clear cell, and grade 3 stage I carcinoma of the endometrium. *Gynecologic Oncology*, *95*(3), 593–596. Advance online publication. doi:10.1016/j.ygyno.2004.08.019 PMID:15581969

Croman, K., Decker, C., Eyal, I., Gencer, A. E., Juels, A., Kosba, A., ... Song, D. (2016). On Scaling Decentralized Blockchains. In *International Conference on Financial Cryptography and Data Security* (pp. 106-125). Springer.

Crosby, M., Pattanayak, P., Verma, S., & Kalyanaraman, V. (2016). Blockchain technology: Beyond bitcoin. *Applied Innovation*, *2*(6-10), 71–81.

Cui, L., Su, X., Ming, Z., Chen, Z., Yang, S., Zhou, Y., & Xiao, W. (2020). CREAT: Blockchain-assisted compression algorithm of federated learning for content caching in edge computing. *IEEE Internet of Things Journal*, *9*(16), 14151–14161. doi:10.1109/JIOT.2020.3014370

Dabeer, S., Khan, M. M., & Islam, S. (2019). Cancer diagnosis in histopathological image: CNN based approach. *Informatics in Medicine Unlocked, 16.* doi:10.1016/j.imu.2019.100231

De Angelis, A. (2020). Blockchain and the General Data Protection Regulation: Can they coexist? Academic Press.

de Vos, B. D., Berendsen, F. F., Viergever, M. A., Sokooti, H., Staring, M., & Išgum, I. (2019). A deep learning framework for unsupervised affine and deformable image registration. *Medical Image Analysis, 52*, 128-143. doi:10.1016/j.media.2018.11.010

De, K. (2019). Secure and Privacy-Preserving Patient-Centric Data Sharing via Blockchain. Academic Press.

Del, S. (2014). On the use of mapreduce for imbalanced big data using random forest. *Information Sciences, 285*, 112–137. doi:10.1016/j.ins.2014.03.043

Dhasarathan, C., Kumar, M., Srivastava, A. K., Al-Turjman, F., Shankar, A., & Kumar, M. (2021). A bio-inspired privacy-preserving framework for healthcare systems. *The Journal of Supercomputing, 77*(10), 11099–11134. doi:10.100711227-021-03720-9

Dinh, T. T. A., Liu, D., Zhang, M., Chen, G., Ooi, B. C., & Wang, J. (2018). Untangling Blockchain: A Data Processing View of Blockchain Systems. *IEEE Transactions on Knowledge and Data Engineering, 30*(7), 1366–1385. doi:10.1109/TKDE.2017.2781227

Doshi, R., Hiran, K. K., Mijwil, M. M., & Anand, D. (2023). To That of Artificial Intelligence, Passing Through Business Intelligence. Handbook of Research on AI and Knowledge Engineering for Real-Time Business Intelligence, 1-16. doi:10.4018/978-1-6684-6519-6.ch001

Dwivedi, S. (2022). Blockchain Technology for Telemedicine and Healthcare IoT: A Comprehensive Review. Academic Press.

ElMamy, S. B., Mrabet, H., Gharbi, H., Jemai, A., & Trentesaux, D. (2020). A Survey on the Usage of Blockchain Technology for Cyber-Threats in the Context of Industry 4.0. *Sustainability (Basel), 12*(21), 1–19. doi:10.3390u12219179

Eltabbakh, G. H., Shamonki, M. I., Moody, J. M., & Garafano, L. L. (2000). Hysterectomy for obese women with endometrial cancer: Laparoscopy or laparotomy? *Gynecologic Oncology, 78*(3), 329–335. Advance online publication. doi:10.1006/gyno.2000.5914 PMID:10985889

Enireddy, V., & Kumar, R. K. (2015). Improved cuckoo search with particle swarm optimization for classification of compressed images. *Sadhana, 40*(8), 2271–2285. doi:10.100712046-015-0440-0

Fader, A. N., Arriba, L. N., Frasure, H. E., & von Gruenigen, V. E. (2009). Endometrial cancer and obesity: Epidemiology, biomarkers, prevention, and survivorship. *Gynecologic Oncology, 114*(1), 121–127. Advance online publication. doi:10.1016/j.ygyno.2009.03.039 PMID:19406460

Fernández-Caramés, T. M., & Fraga-Lamas, P. (2019). A Review on the Use of Blockchain for the Internet of Things. *IEEE Access : Practical Innovations, Open Solutions, 7*, 39409–39431.

Fu, Y., Lei, Y., Wang, T., Curran, W. J., Liu, T., & Yang, X. (2020). Deep learning in medical image registration: A review. *Physics in Medicine and Biology*, *65*(20), 20TR01. Advance online publication. doi:10.1088/1361-6560/ab843e PMID:32217829

Geetha, K., Anitha, V., Elhoseny, M., Kathiresan, S., Shamsolmoali, P., & Selim, M. M. (2021). An evolutionary lion optimization algorithm-based image compression technique for biomedical applications. *Expert Systems: International Journal of Knowledge Engineering and Neural Networks*, *38*(1), e12508. doi:10.1111/exsy.12508

Gill, S. S., & Buyya, R. (2019). Bio-inspired algorithms for big data analytics: a survey, taxonomy, and open challenges. In *Big data analytics for intelligent healthcare management* (pp. 1–17). Academic Press. doi:10.1016/B978-0-12-818146-1.00001-5

Gudmundsson, M., El-Kwae, E. A., & Kabuka, M. R. (1998). Edge detection in medical images using a genetic algorithm. *IEEE Transactions on Medical Imaging*, *17*(3), 469–475. doi:10.1109/42.712136 PMID:9735910

Gupta, Rahman, Poudyal, Huda, & Mahmud. (2019). A Hybrid POW-POS Implementation Against 51% Attack in Cryptocurrency System. *IEEE International Conference on Cloud Computing Technology and Science (CloudCom)*.

Gupta, V., & Bibhu, V. (2023). Deep residual network based brain tumor segmentation and detection with MRI using improved invasive bat algorithm. *Multimedia Tools and Applications*, *82*(8), 12445–12467. doi:10.100711042-022-13769-0

Halevi, G., & Moed, H. (2012). The evolution of Big Data as a research and scientific topic: Overview of the literature. *Research Trends, Special Issue on Big Data*, *30*, 3–6.

Han, L., Wang, Y., & Yan, W. (2019). A Blockchain-Based Framework for Transparent Control and Traceability of Bioinspired Algorithms in Edge Computing. *IEEE Internet of Things Journal*, *6*(4), 7121–7133.

Han, X., Zhang, R., Liu, X., & Jiang, F. (2020, October). Biologically inspired smart contract: A blockchain-based DDoS detection system. In *2020 IEEE International Conference on Networking, Sensing and Control (ICNSC)* (pp. 1-6). IEEE. 10.1109/ICNSC48988.2020.9238104

Hassan, Izzuddin, Tamrin, & Ali. (2020). Article. *International Journal of Biomedical Imaging*, 1-7.

Hastig, S. M., & Sodhi, M. M. S. (2019). Blockchain for supply chain traceability: Business requirements and critical success factors. *Production and Operations Management*, *29*(4), 935–954. doi:10.1111/poms.13147

Hatuwal, B., & Thapa, H. (2020). Lung Cancer Detection Using Convolutional Neural Network on Histopathological Images. *International Journal of Computer Trends and Technology*, *68*(10), 21–24. doi:10.14445/22312803/IJCTT-V68I10P104

He, D., & Xu, X. (2019). Blockchain and swarm intelligence-inspired optimization algorithms. In *Swarm Intelligence Based Optimization* (pp. 425–435). Springer.

Heilman, E., Kendler, A., Zohar, A., & Goldberg, S. (2015). Eclipse Attacks on Bitcoin's Peer-to-Peer Network. In *24th USENIX Security Symposium (USENIX Security 15)* (pp. 129-144). Academic Press.

Helland, P. (2013). Condos and clouds. *Communications of the ACM, 56*(1), 50–59. doi:10.1145/2398356.2398374

Huang, Z. (1997). A fast clustering algorithm to cluster very large categorical data sets in data mining. *SIGMOD Workshop on Research Issues on Data Mining and Knowledge Discovery.*

Huber, Hays, & Valek. (2019). *Staking on Chains.* Bitcoin, Suisse AG, Decrypt.

Huddiniah, E. R., & Er, M. (2019). Product Variety, Supply Chain Complexity and the Needs for Information Technology: A Framework Based on Literature Review, Operations and Supply Chain Management. *International Journal (Toronto, Ont.), 12*(4), 245–255.

Hui, S., Dong, L., Zhang, K., Nie, Z., Jiang, X., Li, H., Hou, Z., Ding, J., Wang, Y., & Li, D. (2022). Noninvasive identification of Benign and malignant eyelid tumours using clinical images via deep learning system. *Journal of Big Data, 9*(1), 84. doi:10.118640537-022-00634-y

Hussein, Y. R., Broaddus, R., & Weigelt, B. (2020). The genomic heterogeneity of FIGO grade 3 endometrioid carcinoma impacts diagnostic accuracy and reproducibility. *International Journal of Gynaecological Pathology.* doi:10.1097/PGP.0000000000000627

IBSR. (2023). *Internet Brain Segmentation Repository (IBSR).* https://www.nitrc.org/projects/ibsr

Islam, E., Islam, R., Chetty, M., Lim, S., & Chadhar, M. (2023). User authentication and access control to blockchain-based forensic log data. *EURASIP Journal on Information Security, 2023*(7), 1–24. doi:10.118613635-023-00142-3

Ismail, L., & Materwala, H. (2019). A review of blockchain architecture and consensus protocols: Use cases, challenges, and solutions. *Symmetry, 11*(10), 1198. doi:10.3390ym11101198

Jauhar, S. K. (2018). Blockchain-Based Smart Contract for Supply Chain Transactions. *International Journal of Supply Chain Management, 7*(2).

Javaid, M., Haleem, A., Singh, R. P., Suman, R., & Khan, S. (2022). A review of Blockchain Technology applications for financial services. *BenchCouncil Transactions on Benchmarks. Standards and Evaluations, 2*(3), 100073. doi:10.1016/j.tbench.2022.100073

Jin, X., Wah, B. W., Cheng, X., & Wang, Y. (2015). Significance and challenges of big data research. *Big Data Research, 2*(2), 59–64. doi:10.1016/j.bdr.2015.01.006

Joo, S., Yang, Y. S., Moon, W. K., & Kim, H. C. (2004). Computer-aided diagnosis of solid breast nodules: Use of an artificial neural network based on multiple sonographic features. *IEEE Transactions on Medical Imaging, 23*(10), 1292–1300. doi:10.1109/TMI.2004.834617 PMID:15493696

Jyothi. (n.d.). *Study of the Efficacy of Pipelle Biopsy Technique to Diagnose Endometrial Diseases in Abnormal Uterine Bleeding*. Academic Press.

Kakhani, M. K., Kakhani, S., & Biradar, S. R. (2015). Research issues in big data analytics. *International Journal of Application or Innovation in Engineering & Management*, *2*(8), 228–232.

Kasius, J. C., Pijnenborg, J. M. A., Lindemann, K., Forsse, D., van Zwol, J., Kristensen, G. B., Krakstad, C., Werner, H. M. J., & Amant, F. (2021, November 22). Risk Stratification of Endometrial Cancer Patients: FIGO Stage, Biomarkers and Molecular Classification. *Cancers (Basel)*, *13*(22), 5848. doi:10.3390/cancers13225848 PMID:34831000

Kaur. (2018). Integration of Blockchain and Internet of Things for Food Supply Chain Management. *2018 5th International Conference on Internet of Things: Smart Innovation and Usages (IoT-SIU)*.

Kaur, I., Kumar, Y., & Sandhu, A. K. (2021, November). A Comprehensive Survey of AI, Blockchain Technology and Big Data Applications in Medical Field and Global Health. In *2021 International Conference on Technological Advancements and Innovations (ICTAI)* (pp. 593-598). IEEE. 10.1109/ICTAI53825.2021.9673285

Kavitha, C. T., & Chellamuthu, C. (2014). Medical image fusion based on hybrid intelligence. *Applied Soft Computing, 20*, 83-94. doi:10.1016/j.asoc.2013.10.034

Kelleher, J. P. (2021). *Why Do Bitcoins Have Value?* Investopedia.

Khandelwal, S., Bhatnagar, S., Mungale, N., & Jain, R. (2022). Design of a Blockchain-Powered Biometric Template Security Framework using Augmented sharding. In *Advances in data mining and database management book series* (pp. 80–101). IGI Global., doi:10.4018/978-1-6684-5072-7.ch004

Khan, M. A., AlZubi, A. F. S., & Zomaya, A. Y. (2021). Blockchain-Driven Bio-Inspired Resource Management in Internet of Things. *IEEE Transactions on Services Computing*, *14*(2), 429–442.

Khattak, H. A., Tehreem, K., Almogren, A., Ameer, Z., Din, I. U., & Adnan, M. (2020). Dynamic pricing in industrial internet of things: Blockchain application for energy management in smart cities. *Journal of Information Security and Applications*, *55*, 102615. doi:10.1016/j.jisa.2020.102615

King & Nadal. (2012). *PPCoin: Peer-to-Peer Crypto-Currency with Proof-of-Stake*. Academic Press.

Kitchin, R. (2014). Big Data, new epistemologies and paradigm shifts. *Big Data & Society*, *1*(1), 1–12. doi:10.1177/2053951714528481

Ko, H., Chung, H., Kang, W. S., Kim, K. W., Shin, Y., Kang, S. J., Lee, J. H., Kim, Y. J., & Kim, N. Y. (2020). Hyunseok JungJinseok Lee. *Journal of Medical Internet Research*, *22*, e19569. doi:10.2196/19569 PMID:32568730

Kombe, C., Ally, M., & Sam, A. (2018). A review on healthcare information systems and consensus protocols in blockchain technology. *Int. J. Adv. Technol. Eng. Explor.*, *5*(49), 473–483. doi:10.19101/IJATEE.2018.547023

Kosba, A., Miller, A., Shi, E., Wen, Z., & Papamanthou, C. (2016). Hawk: The Blockchain Model of Cryptography and Privacy-Preserving Smart Contracts. In *Proceedings of the 2016 ACM SIGSAC Conference on Computer and Communications Security* (pp. 839-851). ACM. 10.1109/SP.2016.55

Kshetri, P. S. (2017). Can blockchain strengthen the Internet of Things? Academic Press.

Kshetri, N. (2018). Blockchain's Roles in Meeting Key Supply Chain Management Objectives. *International Journal of Information Management, 39*, 80–89. doi:10.1016/j.ijinfomgt.2017.12.005

Kumar, A., Dubey, K. K., Gupta, H., Lamba, S., Memoria, M., & Joshi, K. (2022). Keylogger Awareness and Use in Cyber Forensics. Rising Threats in Expert Applications and Solutions, 719-725. doi:10.1007/978-981-19-1122-4_75

Kumar, D. A., Das, S. K., & Sahoo, M. K. (2022). Malware Detection System Using API-Decision Tree. Advances in Data Science and Management, 511–517. doi:10.1007/978-981-16-5685-9_49

Kumar, R., Zhang, X., Wang, W., Khan, R. U., Kumar, J., & Sharif, A. (2019). A Multimodal Malware Detection Technique for Android IoT Devices Using Various Features. *IEEE Access : Practical Innovations, Open Solutions, 7*, 64411–64430. doi:10.1109/ACCESS.2019.2916886

Kuo, M. H., Sahama, T., Kushniruk, A. W., Borycki, E. M., & Grunwell, D. K. (2014). Health big data analytics: Current perspectives, challenges and potential solutions. *International Journal of Big Data Intelligence, 1*(1/2), 114–126. doi:10.1504/IJBDI.2014.063835

Kuo, T. T., Kim, H. E., & Ohno-Machado, L. (2017). Blockchain distributed ledger technologies for biomedical and health care applications. *Journal of the American Medical Informatics Association : JAMIA, 24*(6), 1211–1220. doi:10.1093/jamia/ocx068 PMID:29016974

Kurman, R. J., Carcangiu, M. L., & Herrington, C. S. (2014). *WHO Classification of Tumours of Female Reproductive Organs*. IARC Press.

Lai, C., Yan, Y., & Sui, Y. (2020). Research on application of blockchain technology in energy Internet. *Energy Procedia, 165*, 20–27.

Lax, S. F., Kendall, B., & Tashiro, H. (2000). The frequency of p53, K-ras mutations, and microsatellite instability differs in uterine endometrioid and serous carcinoma: Evidence of distinct molecular genetic pathways. *The American Journal of Surgical Pathology*. Advance online publication. doi:10.1097/00000478-200010000-00003 PMID:10679651

Lee, C. K., Suh, D. H., & Kim, J. W. (2017). Accuracy of preoperative magnetic resonance imaging in predicting myometrial invasion of endometrial cancer: a systematic review and meta-analysis. *Journal of Obstetrics and Gynaecology Research*. doi:10.1111/jog.13321

Lee, Y. C., Lheureux, S., & Oza, A. M. (2017). Treatment strategies for endometrial cancer: Current practice and perspective. *Current Opinion in Obstetrics & Gynecology, 29*(1), 47–58. Advance online publication. doi:10.1097/GCO.0000000000000338 PMID:27941361

Levine, D. A. Cancer Genome Atlas Research Network. (2013). Integrated genomic characterization of endometrial carcinoma. *Nature*, *497*(7447), 67–73. Advance online publication. doi:10.1038/nature12113 PMID:23636398

Lewin, S. N., Herzog, T. J., & Barrena Medel, N. I. (2010). Comparative Performance of the 2009 International Federation of Gynecology and Obstetrics' Staging System for Uterine Corpus Cancer. *Obstetrics and Gynecology*, *116*(5), 1141–1149. Advance online publication. doi:10.1097/AOG.0b013e3181f39849 PMID:20966700

Liang, X., Shetty, S., Tosh, D., Kamhoua, C., Kwiat, K., & Njilla, L. (2018). Integrating Blockchain for Data Sharing and Collaboration in Mobile Healthcare Applications. *IEEE Access : Practical Innovations, Open Solutions*, *6*, 14707–14718.

Liao, X., Xiong, N., Zhang, X., & Zhang, W. (2018). A blockchain-based algorithm for secure and efficient task scheduling in crowdsensing. *IEEE Transactions on Computational Social Systems*, *5*(3), 759–769.

Li, M., Ma, X., Chen, C., Yuan, Y., Zhang, S., Yan, Z., Chen, C., Chen, F., & Bai, Y. (2021). Research on the Auxiliary Classification and Diagnosis of Lung Cancer Subtypes Based on Histopathological Images. IEEE Access. doi:10.1109/ACCESS.2021.3071057

Lima, S. (2021). Limitation of COTS antiviruses: issues, controversies, and problems of COTS antiviruses. Handbook of Research on Cyber Crime and Information Privacy, 396-413. http://doi.org/ doi:10.4018/978-1-7998-5728-0.ch020

Liu, H., Zhang, S., Zhang, P., Zhou, X., Shao, X., Pu, G., & Zhang, Y. (2021). Blockchain and federated learning for collaborative intrusion detection in vehicular edge computing. *IEEE Transactions on Vehicular Technology*, *70*(6), 6073–6084. doi:10.1109/TVT.2021.3076780

Li, X., Jiang, P., Chen, T., Luo, X., & Wen, Q. (2017). A survey on the security of blockchain systems. *Future Generation Computer Systems*, *107*, 841–853. doi:10.1016/j.future.2017.08.020

Li, X., Jiang, P., Chen, T., Luo, X., & Wen, Q. (2017). A Survey on the Security of Blockchain Systems. *Future Generation Computer Systems*, *82*, 395–411.

Luthra, S., Garg, D., & Haleem, A. (2020). Blockchain for Supply Chain Traceability: Business Requirements and Critical Success Factors. *International Journal of Information Management*, *52*, 101994.

Lu, Y. (2018). Blockchain and the related issues: A review of current research topics. *J. Manag. Anal.*, *5*(4), 231–255. doi:10.1080/23270012.2018.1516523

Lv, Q., Li, C., Zhu, Y., & Cao, G. (2020). A blockchain-based algorithm for vehicle assignment in intelligent transportation systems. *IEEE Transactions on Intelligent Transportation Systems*, *21*(9), 3836–3845.

Macdonald, G. M., Shafi, M. I., & Williams, A. R. (2001). Management of endometrial cancer: Issues and controversies. *European Journal of Gynaecological Oncology*.

Mahalle, Sable, Mahalle, & Shinde. (2020). Article. *Intelligent Systems and Methods to Combat Covid-19*, 1-10.

Mancilla, N. O. (2017). Analysis of Information Distortion Upstream Concerning Consumers' Quality Perceptions in Agro-Food Supply Chain. *International Journal on Food System Dynamics*, *8*(3).

Mancilla, N. O., & Sepulveda, W. S. (2021). Upstream information distortion in the agro- ´ food supply chain. *Supply Chain Management*, *142*(267), 411–423.

Maniriho, P., Mahmood, A. N., & Chowdhury, M. J. M. (2022). A study on malicious software behaviour analysis and detection techniques: Taxonomy, current trends and challenges. *Future Generation Computer Systems*, *130*, 1–18. doi:10.1016/j.future.2021.11.030

Mansour, R. F. (2022). Artificial intelligence-based optimization with deep learning model for blockchain-enabled intrusion detection in CPS environment. *Scientific Reports*, *12*(1), 12937. doi:10.103841598-022-17043-z PMID:35902617

Manyika, J., Chui, M., Brown, B., Bughin, J., Dobbs, R., Roxburgh, C., & Byers, A. H. (2011). *Big Data: The next frontier for innovation, competition, and productivity. Technical report.* McKinsey Global Institute.

Mary Shanthi Rani, M., Chitra, P., Lakshmanan, S., Kalpana Devi, M., Sangeetha, R., & Nithya, S. (2022). DeepCompNet: A novel neural net model compression architecture. *Computational Intelligence and Neuroscience*, *2022*, 2022. doi:10.1155/2022/2213273 PMID:35242176

Masoumi, H., Behrad, A., Pourmina, M. A., & Roosta, A. (2012). Automatic liver segmentation in MRI images using an iterative watershed algorithm and artificial neural network. *Biomedical Signal Processing and Control*, *7*(5), 429–437. doi:10.1016/j.bspc.2012.01.002

Mayfield, C. A., Gigler, M. E., Snapper, L., Jose, J., Tynan, J., Scott, V. C., & Dulin, M. (2020). Using cloud-based, open-source technology to evaluate, improve, and rapidly disseminate community-based intervention data. *Journal of the American Medical Informatics Association : JAMIA*, *27*(11), 1741–1746. doi:10.1093/jamia/ocaa181 PMID:32940684

Meidute-Kavaliauskiene, I., Yıldız, B., Çiğdem, Ş., & Činčikaitė, R. (2021). An Integrated Impact of Blockchain on Supply Chain Applications. *Logistics*, *5*(2), 33. doi:10.3390/logistics5020033

Mijwil, M. M., Gök, M., Doshi, R., Hiran, K. K., & Kösesoy, I. (2023). Utilizing Artificial Intelligence Techniques to Improve the Performance of Wireless Nodes. Applications of Artificial Intelligence in Wireless Communication Systems, 150-162. doi:10.4018/978-1-6684-7348-1.ch010

Mijwil, M. M., Sadıkoğlu, E., Cengiz, E., & Candan, H. (2022). Siber Güvenlikte Yapay Zekanın Rolü ve Önemi: Bir Derleme. *Veri Bilimi*, *5*(2), 97–105.

Mohammed, M. A., Ibrahim, D. A., & Abdulkareem, K. H. (2021). Bio-inspired robotics-enabled schemes in blockchain-fog-cloud assisted IoMT environment. *Journal of King Saud University-Computer and Information Sciences*.

Mohammed, M. A., Abdulkareem, K. H., Al-Waisy, A. S., Mostafa, S. A., Al-Fahdawi, S., Dinar, A. M., Alhakami, W., Baz, A., Al-Mhiqani, M. N., Alhakami, H., Arbaiy, N., Maashi, M. S., Mutlag, A. A., Garcia-Zapirain, B., & De La Torre Diez, I. (2020). Benchmarking Methodology for Selection of Optimal COVID-19 Diagnostic Model Based on Entropy and TOPSIS Methods. *IEEE Access : Practical Innovations, Open Solutions*, 8, 99115–99131. doi:10.1109/ACCESS.2020.2995597

Monti, M., & Rasmussen, S. (2017). RAIN: A bio-inspired communication and data storage infrastructure. *Artificial Life*, 23(4), 552–557. doi:10.1162/ARTL_a_00247 PMID:28985116

Möser, M., & Böhme, R. (2017). The Economics of Bitcoin Transaction Fees. In *Decision Economics for Global Supply Chain Management* (pp. 357-382). Academic Press.

Mougayar, W. (2016). The Business Blockchain: Promise, Practice, and Application of the Next Internet Technology. Academic Press.

Mustafa, M., Alshare, M., Bhargava, D., Neware, R., Singh, B., & Ngulube, P. (2022). Perceived Security Risk Based on Moderating Factors for Blockchain Technology Applications in Cloud Storage to Achieve Secure Healthcare Systems. *Computational and Mathematical Methods in Medicine*, 2022(6112815), 1–10. doi:10.1155/2022/6112815 PMID:35096132

Muthu RamaKrishnan, Venkatraghavan, Acharya, Pal, RashmiPaul, Min, Ray, Chatterjee, & Chakraborty. (2012). *Automated oral cancer identification using histopathological images: A hybrid feature extraction paradigm.* doi:10.1016/j.micron.2011.09.016

Nagarajan, G., Minu, R. I., Muthukumar, B., Vedanarayanan, V., & Sundarsingh, S. D. (2016). Hybrid Genetic Algorithm for Medical Image Feature Extraction and Selection. *Procedia Computer Science, 85*, 455-462. doi:10.1016/j.procs.2016.05.192

Nakamoto, S. (2008). *Bitcoin: A peer-to-peer electronic cash system.* Academic Press.

Nakamoto, S. (2008). *Bitcoin: A Peer-to-Peer Electronic Cash System.* Academic Press.

Nakamoto, S. (2008). *Bitcoin: A Peer-to-Peer Electronic Cash System.* Retrieved from https://bitcoin.org/bitcoin.pdf

Narayanan, A., Chandrasekaran, K., & Palanisamy, V. (2018). Blockchain-based bio-inspired computing: A survey. *IEEE Access : Practical Innovations, Open Solutions*, 6, 42405–42418.

Natanelov. (2021). Blockchain and Smart Contracts for Supply Chain Finance: Potential Applications in Cross-Border Beef Supply Chains. *Frontiers in Blockchain, 4*.

Ng, D. K. (2018). Blockchain and consent in the electronic health record. Academic Press.

Nguyen, C. T., Hoang, D. T., Nguyen, D. N., Niyato, D., Nguyen, H. T., & Dutkiewicz, E. (2019). Proof-of-Stake Consensus Mechanisms for Future Blockchain Networks: Fundamentals, Applications and Opportunities. *IEEE Access : Practical Innovations, Open Solutions, 7*, 85727–85745. doi:10.1109/ACCESS.2019.2925010

Noor, M. A. F., & Mustafa, K. (2023). Protocols and Guidelines to Enhance the Endpoint Security of Blockchain at User's End. *Proceedings of International Conference on ICT for Digital, Smart, and Sustainable Development.* 10.4108/eai.24-3-2022.2318925

Padmapriya, M. K., & Eric, P. V. (2022). Bio-Inspired Multi-Level Hybrid Crypto System. *International Journal of Software Innovation, 10*(1), 1–16.

Panarello, A., Tapas, N., Merlino, G., Longo, F., & Puliafito, A. (2018). Blockchain and IoT Integration: A Systematic Survey. *Sensors (Basel), 18*(8), 2575. doi:10.339018082575 PMID:30082633

Pecorelli, S. (2009). Revised FIGO staging for carcinoma of the vulva, cervix, and endometrium. *International Journal of Gynecology & Obstetrics.* . doi:10.1016/j.ijgo.2009.02.012

Porat, A., Pratap, A., Shah, P., & Adkhar, V. (2018). Blockchain Consensus: An analysis of Proof-of-Work and its applications. Stanford.

Prasetyo, J., De Masi, G., Zakir, R., Alkilabi, M., Tuci, E., & Ferrante, E. (2021, June). A bio-inspired spatial defense strategy for collective decision-making in self-organized swarms. In *Proceedings of the Genetic and Evolutionary Computation Conference* (pp. 49-56). 10.1145/3449639.3459356

Priyadharshini, F. R. A., Hariprasad, N., Asvitha, S., Anandhi, V., & Swetha Priyadarshini, A. P. (2018). *An approach to segment computed tomography images using bat algorithm.* Retrieved from https://ieeexplore.ieee.org/document/8632347

Punn, N. S., Sonbhadra, S. K., & Agarwal, S. (2020). *Article.* Cold Spring Harbor Laboratory Press.

Qin, P., Chen, J., & Zeng, J. (2018). Large-scale tissue histopathology image segmentation based on feature pyramid. *J Image Video Proc., 75.* doi:10.1186/s13640-018-0320-8

Rahaman, S. M. M., & Chang, V. (2019). Biometric data management on blockchain: An integrated model and research directions. *Journal of Information Security and Applications, 49,* 102406.

Rahebi, J., & Tajik, H. R. (2011). Biomedical Image Edge Detection using an Ant Colony Optimization Based on Artificial Neural Networks. *International Journal of Engineering Science and Technology, 3*(12), 8217–8222.

Rajaraman, Siegelman, Alderson, Folio, Folio, & Antani. (2020). Article. *IEEE Access, 8,* 115041-115050.

Rani, M. M. S., & Chitra, P. (2016, October). A novel hybrid method of haar-wavelet and residual vector quantization for compressing medical images. In *2016 IEEE International Conference on Advances in Computer Applications (ICACA)* (pp. 321-326). IEEE. 10.1109/ICACA.2016.7887974

Sabir, Z., & Amine, A. (2022). BIoVN: A Novel Blockchain-Based System for Securing Internet of Vehicles Over NDN Using Bioinspired HoneyGuide. In *Advances in Blockchain Technology for Cyber Physical Systems* (pp. 177–192). Springer International Publishing. doi:10.1007/978-3-030-93646-4_8

Sagiroglu, S., & Sinanc, D. (2013). Big Data: A review. *Collaboration Technologies and Systems (CTS), 2013 International Conference on*, 42-47.

Salim, F. D., Huang, X., & An, S. (2018). Blockchain technology in healthcare: A systematic review. *Healthcare Informatics Research*, 24(4), 277–286.

Samantray, O. P., & Tripathy, S. N. (2021). An Opcode-Based Malware Detection Model Using Supervised Learning Algorithms. *International Journal of Information Security and Privacy*, 15(4), 18–30. doi:10.4018/IJISP.2021100102

Santhi, A. R., & Muthuswamy, P. (2022). Influence of Blockchain Technology in Manufacturing Supply Chain and Logistics. *Logistics*, 6(1), 1–22. doi:10.3390/logistics6010015

Seyedhosseini, M., Meddeb, A., & Ghannay, S. (2019). Blockchain-based optimization for the Internet of Things: A systematic literature review. *IEEE Access : Practical Innovations, Open Solutions*, 7, 97172–97185.

Shahdoosti, H. R., & Tabatabaei, Z. (2019). MRI and PET/SPECT image fusion at feature level using ant colony based segmentation. *Biomedical Signal Processing and Control*, 47, 63-74. doi:10.1016/j.bspc.2018.08.017

Shah, Z., Shah, G. A., Shah, M. A., & Badshah, M. (2019). A blockchain-based adaptive particle swarm optimization algorithm for secure IoT environments. *Sensors (Basel)*, 19(10), 2283. PMID:31108929

Shanmugavadivu, P., Chitra, P., Lakshmanan, S., Nagaraja, P., & Vignesh, U. (2022). Bio-Optimization of Deep Learning Network Architectures. *Security and Communication Networks*, ●●●, 2022.

Shetty, S., Rane, S., Jain, S., & Mukherjee, S. (2020). Blockchain-enabled swarm intelligence: A review. *Swarm and Evolutionary Computation*, 57, 100690.

Singh, G., Tripathi, A., & Raw, R. S. (2020). Blockchain technology: A survey on its security challenges and privacy issues in the healthcare sector. *Journal of Information Security and Applications*, 53, 102566.

Snyder, A., & Mutch, D. G. (2019). Surgical staging of endometrial cancer: Time to move on? *American Journal of Obstetrics and Gynecology*. Advance online publication. doi:10.1016/j.ajog.2019.06.019

Soleimani, V., & Heidari Vincheh, F. (2013). *Improving ant colony optimization for brain MRI image segmentation and brain tumor diagnosis*. IEEE. https://ieeexplore.ieee.org/document/6601866

Somasundaram, K., & Ezhilarasan, K. (2013). A Fully Automatic Scheme for Skull Stripping from MRI of Head Scans Using Morphological Neck Breaking Operations. In M. S. Kumar (Ed.), *Proceedings of the Fourth International Conference on Signal and Image Processing 2012* (ICSIP 2012) (Lecture Notes in Electrical Engineering, Vol. 222). Springer. 10.1007/978-81-322-1000-9_25

Somasundaram, K., & Ezhilarasan, K. (2012). Edge detection in MRI of head scans using fuzzy logic. In *2012 IEEE International Conference on Advanced Communication Control and Computing Technologies (ICACCCT)* (pp. 131-135). 10.1109/ICACCCT.2012.6320756

Sonavane, S. M., Prashantha, G. R., Deshmukh, J. Y., Salunke, M. D., Jadhav, H. B., & Nikam, P. D. (2023). Design of a Blockchain-Based Access Control Model with QoS-Awareness Via Bioinspired Computing Techniques. *International Journal of Intelligent Systems and Applications in Engineering*, *11*(7s), 631–639.

Sreekanth, G. R., Alrasheedi, A. F., Venkatachalam, K., Abouhawwash, M., & Askar, S. S. (2022). Extreme Learning Bat Algorithm in Brain Tumor Classification. *Intelligent Automation & Soft Computing*, *34*(1). Advance online publication. doi:10.32604/iasc.2022.024538

Srivastava. (2021). Application of blockchain in agri-food supply chain: A systematic literature review. *Computers in Industry, 123*.

Sun, Y., Wen, Y., & Wen, X. (2020). Towards a Blockchain-Based Bioinspired Artificial Intelligence Framework for Large-Scale Medical Data Sharing. *Journal of Healthcare Engineering*, *2020*, 1–10. doi:10.1155/2020/7289648

Swan, M. (2015). *Blockchain: Blueprint for a New Economy*. Academic Press.

Swan, M. (2014). Blockchain: The New Technology of Trust. *Strategy and Leadership*, *42*(6), 6–11.

Swan, M. (2015). *Blockchain: Blueprint for a New Economy*. O'Reilly Media.

Swan, M. (2017a). *Blockchain: The Complete Guide to Understanding Blockchain Technology*. CreateSpace Independent Publishing Platform.

Syed, T., Alzahrani, A., Jan, S., Siddiqui, M., Nadeem, A., & Alghamdi, T. (2019). A comparative analysis of blockchain architecture and its applications: Problems and recommendations. *IEEE Access : Practical Innovations, Open Solutions*, *7*, 176838–176869. doi:10.1109/ACCESS.2019.2957660

Szabo, N. (1997). *The Idea of Smart Contracts. Nick Szabo's Papers and Concise Tutorials*. Retrieved from http://www.szabo.best.vwh.net/smart_contracts_idea.html

Taherdangkoo, M., Bagheri, M. H., Yazdi, M., & Andriole, K. P. (2013). An effective method for segmentation of MR brain images using the Ant Colony Optimization Algorithm. *Journal of Digital Imaging*, *26*(6), 1116–1123. doi:10.100710278-013-9596-5 PMID:23563793

Tahir, A., Chen, F., Khan, H. U., Ming, Z., Ahmad, A., Nazir, S., & Shafiq, M. (2020). A Systematic Review on Cloud Storage Mechanisms Concerning e-Healthcare Systems. *Sensors (Basel)*, *20*(18), 5392. doi:10.339020185392 PMID:32967094

Takahashi, Y., Sone, K., & Noda, K. (n.d.). *Automated system for diagnosing endometrial cancer by adopting deep-learning technology in hysteroscopy*. Academic Press.

Tan. (2021). *A blockchain-based solution for secure pharmaceutical supply chain management?* Academic Press.

Tapscott, D., & Tapscott, A. (2016). *Blockchain revolution: how the technology behind bitcoin is changing money, business, and the world.* Academic Press.

Tapscott, D., & Tapscott, A. (2016). *Blockchain Revolution: How the Technology Behind Bitcoin is Changing Money, Business, and the World.* Penguin.

Tavares, R. P., & Guerreiro, S. I. (2019). A blockchain-based architecture for collaborative machine learning with bio-inspired optimization. In *International Conference on Bio-Inspired Systems and Signal Processing* (pp. 457-464). Springer.

Thaker, P. H., Urbauer, D., & Frumovitz, M. (2014). Patterns of failure in patients with early stage uterine sarcoma. *Cancer.* Advance online publication. doi:10.1002/cncr.28803

Thangamayan, S., Pradhan, K., Loganathan, G. B., Sitender, S., Sivamani, S., & Tesema, M. (2023). Blockchain-Based Secure Traceable Scheme for Food Supply Chain. *Journal of Food Quality*, *2023*(4728840), 1–11. doi:10.1155/2023/4728840

Transform healthcare outcomes with the simplicity of IBM Blockchain. (2018). https://www.ibm.com/downloads/cas/DQPLDP8N

Treleaven, H. (2019). Blockchains for health and wellness: A systematic review. Academic Press.

Tschorsch, F., & Scheuermann, B. (2016). A Survey on Consensus Mechanisms and Mining Management in Blockchain Networks. *Business & Information Systems Engineering*, *58*(4), 371–384.

Unogwu, O. J., Doshi, R., Hiran, K. K., & Mijwil, M. M. (2022). Introduction to Quantum-Resistant Blockchain. Advancements in Quantum Blockchain With Real-Time Applications, 36-55. doi:10.4018/978-1-6684-5072-7.ch002

Vennam, P., Pramod, T. C., Thippeswamy, B. M., Kim, Y., & Kumar, B. N. P. (2021). Attacks and Preventive Measures on Video Surveillance Systems: A Review. *Applied Sciences (Basel, Switzerland)*, *11*(12), 1–17. doi:10.3390/app11125571

Verma, H. C., Srivastava, S., Ahmed, T., & Usmani, N. A. (2023). Cyber Threats in Agriculture and the Food Industry: An Indian Perspective. Advances in Cyberology and the Advent of the Next-Gen Information Revolution, 109-124. doi:10.4018/978-1-6684-8133-2.ch006

Veros. (2016). *Whitepaper: Ethereum Blockchain.* Author.

Wang, N., Liu, H., & Xu, C. (2020). Article. *10th International Conference on Electronics Information and Emergency Communication (ICEIEC)*, 281-284.

Wang, G., & Cao, J. (2020). Blockchain and evolutionary computation: A comprehensive review. *IEEE Transactions on Evolutionary Computation*, *24*(2), 293–308.

Wang, H., Tang, Y., Hu, J., Li, X., & Li, Z. (2020). Blockchain and bio-inspired algorithms for secure and efficient data sharing in mobile healthcare social networks. *IEEE Access : Practical Innovations, Open Solutions, 8*, 156130–156141.

Wang, X., Luo, K., & Xu, H. (2019). Blockchain Meets Artificial Intelligence: Challenges and Opportunities. *ACM Transactions on Internet Technology, 19*(3), 23.

Wang, Y., Singgih, M., Wang, J., & Rit, M. (2019). Making sense of blockchain technology: How will it transform supply chains? *International Journal of Production Economics, 211*, 221–236. doi:10.1016/j.ijpe.2019.02.002

Wang, Z., Li, Y., & Zhang, Y. (2020). A blockchain-based bio-inspired optimization algorithm for secure and efficient data fusion in edge computing. *IEEE Transactions on Computational Social Systems, 7*(3), 732–742.

Winter, R., Rosa, F. F., Shukla, P., & Kazemian, H. (2022). Brazil Method of Anti-Malware Evaluation and Cyber Defense Impacts. *Journal of Applied Security Research*, 1–17. doi:10.10 80/19361610.2022.2104104

Wood, G. (2014). *Ethereum: A Secure Decentralized Generalized Transaction Ledger*. Academic Press.

Xiao, Y., Zhang, N., Lou, W., & Hou, Y. T. (2020). A survey of distributed consensus protocols for blockchain networks. *IEEE Communications Surveys and Tutorials, 22*(2), 1432–1465. doi:10.1109/COMST.2020.2969706

Xiong, J., Chen, S., Chen, X., Wu, F., Liang, W., & He, J. (2019). Blockchain-based bio-inspired optimization for Internet of Things. *IEEE Internet of Things Journal, 7*(11), 11224–11235.

Xu, P., Lee, J., Barth, J., & Richey, R. (2021). Blockchain as supply chain technology: Considering transparency and security. *International Journal of Physical Distribution & Logistics Management, 51*(3), 305–324. doi:10.1108/IJPDLM-08-2019-0234

Xu, Q., Wang, X., & Jiang, H. (2019, May 8). Convolutional neural network for breast cancer diagnosis using diffuse optical tomography. *Visual Computing for Industry, Biomedicine, and Art, 2*(1), 1. doi:10.118642492-019-0012-y PMID:32240400

Xu, X., Wang, Y., Wang, Q., & Zhang, W. (2020). Blockchain and swarm intelligence-based particle filter algorithm for energy management in smart grid. *Energies, 13*(9), 2417.

Yaacoub, J. A., Noura, H. N., Salman, O., & Chehab, A. (2023). Ethical hacking for IoT: Security issues, challenges, solutions and recommendations. *Internet of Things and Cyber-Physical Systems, 3*, 280–308. doi:10.1016/j.iotcps.2023.04.002

Yang, H., Li, S., Wu, X., Lu, H., & Han, W. (2019). A Novel Solutions for Malicious Code Detection and Family Clustering Based on Machine Learning. *IEEE Access : Practical Innovations, Open Solutions, 7*, 148853–148860. doi:10.1109/ACCESS.2019.2946482

Yang, Y., Lin, Y., Li, Z., Zhao, L., Yao, M., Lai, Y., & Li, P. (2023). GooseBt: A programmable malware detection framework based on process, file, registry, and COM monitoring. *Computer Communications*, *204*, 24–32. doi:10.1016/j.comcom.2023.03.011

Yan, J., Zhang, C., Li, J., & Li, W. (2020). Blockchain-inspired bio-inspired optimization algorithm for service composition in edge computing. *IEEE Transactions on Network Science and Engineering*, *7*(1), 480–492.

Yao, Q., Han, X., Ma, X. K., Xue, Y. F., Chen, Y. J., & Li, J. S. (2014). Cloud-based hospital information system as a service for grassroots healthcare institutions. *Journal of Medical Systems*, *38*(9), 104. doi:10.100710916-014-0104-3 PMID:25015761

Yli-Huumo, J., Ko, D., Choi, S., Park, S., & Smolander, K. (2016). A Survey on Blockchain Technology: Usage, Challenges, and Future Directions. In *Proceedings of the 49th Hawaii International Conference on System Sciences (HICSS)* (pp. 4688-4697). IEEE.

Yunan. (2012). *What is Big Data's role in helping companies achieve competitive advantage through analytics*. Academic Press.

Zaino, R. J., Brady, M. F., Lele, S. M., Michael, H., Greer, B., & Bookman, M. A. (2011). Advanced stage mucinous adenocarcinoma of the ovary is both rare and highly lethal: A Gynecologic Oncology Group study. *Cancer*, *117*(3), 554–562. Advance online publication. doi:10.1002/cncr.25460 PMID:20862744

Zaino, R. J., Kauderer, J., Trimble, C. L., Silverberg, S. G., Curtin, J. P., Lim, P. C., & Gallup, D. G. (2006). Reproducibility of the diagnosis of atypical endometrial hyperplasia: A Gynecologic Oncology Group study. *Cancer*, *106*(4), 804–811. Advance online publication. doi:10.1002/cncr.21649 PMID:16400640

Zaslavsky, A., Perera, C., & Georgakopoulos, D. (2013). *Sensing as a service and Big Data*. arXiv preprint arXiv:1301.0159.

Zeng, L., Wang, X., Xia, Q., Liu, K., & Liu, J. (2019). A Comprehensive Review of Blockchain Consensus Mechanisms: Proof of Work, Proof of Stake, and Beyond. *IEEE Access : Practical Innovations, Open Solutions*, *7*, 22328–22370.

Zhang, G., Yu, H., Ma, C., & Guan, Y. (2019). Blockchain-based optimization: Opportunities, challenges, and solutions. *IEEE Transactions on Industrial Informatics*, *15*(6), 3690–3700.

Zhang, J., Zhang, H., Yan, L., & Cao, J. (2019). Blockchain-Based Privacy-Preserving Method for ECG Data in Mobile Healthcare Applications. *Sensors (Basel)*, *19*(19), 4253. PMID:31575009

Zheng, X., Zhang, Y., Yang, F., & Xu, F. (2022). Resource allocation on blockchain-enabled mobile edge computing system. *Electronics (Basel)*, *11*(12), 1869. doi:10.3390/electronics11121869

Zheng, Z., Cao, J., & Yu, R. (2018). Blockchain Challenges and Opportunities: A Survey. *International Journal of Web and Grid Services*, *14*(4), 352–375. doi:10.1504/IJWGS.2018.095647

Compilation of References

Zheng, Z., Xie, S., Dai, H., Chen, X., & Wang, H. (2017). A Systematic Literature Review on Blockchain Technology: State-of-the-Art, Applications, and Challenges. *IEEE Access : Practical Innovations, Open Solutions*, *6*, 28077–28096.

Zheng, Z., Xie, S., Li, H., Dai, H., & Wang, H. (2021). Blockchain Challenges and Opportunities: A Systematic Review. *Journal of Parallel and Distributed Computing*, *151*, 1–14.

Zhou, F. (2021). Blockchain-Enabled Cross-Border E-Commerce Supply Chain Management: A Bibliometric Data-Driven Analysis. *Sustainability*, *13*(13). Advance online publication. doi:10.3390u14138088

Zhou, H., Li, H., & Zhou, W. (2020). Bioinspired Computing Meets Blockchain: A Comprehensive Survey. *IEEE Access : Practical Innovations, Open Solutions*, *8*, 70750–70770.

Zohar, A. (2015). Bitcoin: Under the Hood. *Communications of the ACM*, *58*(9), 104–113. doi:10.1145/2701411

Zyskind, G., Nathan, O., & Pentland, A. (2015). Decentralizing Privacy: Using Blockchain to Protect Personal Data. In Security and Privacy Workshops (pp. 180-184). IEEE.

Related References

To continue our tradition of advancing information science and technology research, we have compiled a list of recommended IGI Global readings. These references will provide additional information and guidance to further enrich your knowledge and assist you with your own research and future publications.

Aasi, P., Rusu, L., & Vieru, D. (2017). The Role of Culture in IT Governance Five Focus Areas: A Literature Review. *International Journal of IT/Business Alignment and Governance, 8*(2), 42-61. https://doi.org/ doi:10.4018/IJITBAG.2017070103

Abdrabo, A. A. (2018). Egypt's Knowledge-Based Development: Opportunities, Challenges, and Future Possibilities. In A. Alraouf (Ed.), *Knowledge-Based Urban Development in the Middle East* (pp. 80–101). Hershey, PA: IGI Global. doi:10.4018/978-1-5225-3734-2.ch005

Abu Doush, I., & Alhami, I. (2018). Evaluating the Accessibility of Computer Laboratories, Libraries, and Websites in Jordanian Universities and Colleges. *International Journal of Information Systems and Social Change, 9*(2), 44–60. doi:10.4018/IJISSC.2018040104

Adegbore, A. M., Quadri, M. O., & Oyewo, O. R. (2018). A Theoretical Approach to the Adoption of Electronic Resource Management Systems (ERMS) in Nigerian University Libraries. In A. Tella & T. Kwanya (Eds.), *Handbook of Research on Managing Intellectual Property in Digital Libraries* (pp. 292–311). Hershey, PA: IGI Global. doi:10.4018/978-1-5225-3093-0.ch015

Afolabi, O. A. (2018). Myths and Challenges of Building an Effective Digital Library in Developing Nations: An African Perspective. In A. Tella & T. Kwanya (Eds.), *Handbook of Research on Managing Intellectual Property in Digital Libraries* (pp. 51–79). Hershey, PA: IGI Global. doi:10.4018/978-1-5225-3093-0.ch004

Agarwal, P., Kurian, R., & Gupta, R. K. (2022). Additive Manufacturing Feature Taxonomy and Placement of Parts in AM Enclosure. In S. Salunkhe, H. Hussein, & J. Davim (Eds.), *Applications of Artificial Intelligence in Additive Manufacturing* (pp. 138–176). IGI Global. https://doi.org/10.4018/978-1-7998-8516-0.ch007

Al-Alawi, A. I., Al-Hammam, A. H., Al-Alawi, S. S., & AlAlawi, E. I. (2021). The Adoption of E-Wallets: Current Trends and Future Outlook. In Y. Albastaki, A. Razzaque, & A. Sarea (Eds.), *Innovative Strategies for Implementing FinTech in Banking* (pp. 242–262). IGI Global. https://doi.org/10.4018/978-1-7998-3257-7.ch015

Alsharo, M. (2017). Attitudes Towards Cloud Computing Adoption in Emerging Economies. *International Journal of Cloud Applications and Computing*, 7(3), 44–58. doi:10.4018/IJCAC.2017070102

Amer, T. S., & Johnson, T. L. (2017). Information Technology Progress Indicators: Research Employing Psychological Frameworks. In A. Mesquita (Ed.), *Research Paradigms and Contemporary Perspectives on Human-Technology Interaction* (pp. 168–186). Hershey, PA: IGI Global. doi:10.4018/978-1-5225-1868-6.ch008

Andreeva, A., & Yolova, G. (2021). Liability in Labor Legislation: New Challenges Related to the Use of Artificial Intelligence. In B. Vassileva & M. Zwilling (Eds.), *Responsible AI and Ethical Issues for Businesses and Governments* (pp. 214–232). IGI Global. https://doi.org/10.4018/978-1-7998-4285-9.ch012

Anohah, E. (2017). Paradigm and Architecture of Computing Augmented Learning Management System for Computer Science Education. *International Journal of Online Pedagogy and Course Design*, 7(2), 60–70. doi:10.4018/IJOPCD.2017040105

Anohah, E., & Suhonen, J. (2017). Trends of Mobile Learning in Computing Education from 2006 to 2014: A Systematic Review of Research Publications. *International Journal of Mobile and Blended Learning*, 9(1), 16–33. doi:10.4018/IJMBL.2017010102

Arbaiza, C. S., Huerta, H. V., & Rodriguez, C. R. (2021). Contributions to the Technological Adoption Model for the Peruvian Agro-Export Sector. *International Journal of E-Adoption*, 13(1), 1–17. https://doi.org/10.4018/IJEA.2021010101

Bailey, E. K. (2017). Applying Learning Theories to Computer Technology Supported Instruction. In M. Grassetti & S. Brookby (Eds.), *Advancing Next-Generation Teacher Education through Digital Tools and Applications* (pp. 61–81). Hershey, PA: IGI Global. doi:10.4018/978-1-5225-0965-3.ch004

Baker, J. D. (2021). Introduction to Machine Learning as a New Methodological Framework for Performance Assessment. In M. Bocarnea, B. Winston, & D. Dean (Eds.), *Handbook of Research on Advancements in Organizational Data Collection and Measurements: Strategies for Addressing Attitudes, Beliefs, and Behaviors* (pp. 326–342). IGI Global. https://doi.org/10.4018/978-1-7998-7665-6.ch021

Banerjee, S., Sing, T. Y., Chowdhury, A. R., & Anwar, H. (2018). Let's Go Green: Towards a Taxonomy of Green Computing Enablers for Business Sustainability. In M. Khosrow-Pour (Ed.), *Green Computing Strategies for Competitive Advantage and Business Sustainability* (pp. 89–109). Hershey, PA: IGI Global. doi:10.4018/978-1-5225-5017-4.ch005

Basham, R. (2018). Information Science and Technology in Crisis Response and Management. In M. Khosrow-Pour, D.B.A. (Ed.), Encyclopedia of Information Science and Technology, Fourth Edition (pp. 1407-1418). Hershey, PA: IGI Global. doi:10.4018/978-1-5225-2255-3.ch121

Batyashe, T., & Iyamu, T. (2018). Architectural Framework for the Implementation of Information Technology Governance in Organisations. In M. Khosrow-Pour, D.B.A. (Ed.), Encyclopedia of Information Science and Technology, Fourth Edition (pp. 810-819). Hershey, PA: IGI Global. doi:10.4018/978-1-5225-2255-3.ch070

Bekleyen, N., & Çelik, S. (2017). Attitudes of Adult EFL Learners towards Preparing for a Language Test via CALL. In D. Tafazoli & M. Romero (Eds.), *Multiculturalism and Technology-Enhanced Language Learning* (pp. 214–229). Hershey, PA: IGI Global. doi:10.4018/978-1-5225-1882-2.ch013

Bergeron, F., Croteau, A., Uwizeyemungu, S., & Raymond, L. (2017). A Framework for Research on Information Technology Governance in SMEs. In S. De Haes & W. Van Grembergen (Eds.), *Strategic IT Governance and Alignment in Business Settings* (pp. 53–81). Hershey, PA: IGI Global. doi:10.4018/978-1-5225-0861-8.ch003

Bhardwaj, M., Shukla, N., & Sharma, A. (2021). Improvement and Reduction of Clustering Overhead in Mobile Ad Hoc Network With Optimum Stable Bunching Algorithm. In S. Kumar, M. Trivedi, P. Ranjan, & A. Punhani (Eds.), *Evolution of Software-Defined Networking Foundations for IoT and 5G Mobile Networks* (pp. 139–158). IGI Global. https://doi.org/10.4018/978-1-7998-4685-7.ch008

Bhatt, G. D., Wang, Z., & Rodger, J. A. (2017). Information Systems Capabilities and Their Effects on Competitive Advantages: A Study of Chinese Companies. *Information Resources Management Journal*, *30*(3), 41–57. doi:10.4018/IRMJ.2017070103

Bhattacharya, A. (2021). Blockchain, Cybersecurity, and Industry 4.0. In A. Tyagi, G. Rekha, & N. Sreenath (Eds.), *Opportunities and Challenges for Blockchain Technology in Autonomous Vehicles* (pp. 210–244). IGI Global. https://doi.org/10.4018/978-1-7998-3295-9.ch013

Bhyan, P., Shrivastava, B., & Kumar, N. (2022). Requisite Sustainable Development Contemplating Buildings: Economic and Environmental Sustainability. In A. Hussain, K. Tiwari, & A. Gupta (Eds.), *Addressing Environmental Challenges Through Spatial Planning* (pp. 269–288). IGI Global. https://doi.org/10.4018/978-1-7998-8331-9.ch014

Boido, C., Davico, P., & Spallone, R. (2021). Digital Tools Aimed to Represent Urban Survey. In M. Khosrow-Pour D.B.A. (Ed.), *Encyclopedia of Information Science and Technology, Fifth Edition* (pp. 1181-1195). IGI Global. https://doi.org/10.4018/978-1-7998-3479-3.ch082

Borkar, P. S., Chanana, P. U., Atwal, S. K., Londe, T. G., & Dalal, Y. D. (2021). The Replacement of HMI (Human-Machine Interface) in Industry Using Single Interface Through IoT. In R. Raut & A. Mihovska (Eds.), *Examining the Impact of Deep Learning and IoT on Multi-Industry Applications* (pp. 195–208). IGI Global. https://doi.org/10.4018/978-1-7998-7511-6.ch011

Brahmane, A. V., & Krishna, C. B. (2021). Rider Chaotic Biography Optimization-driven Deep Stacked Auto-encoder for Big Data Classification Using Spark Architecture: Rider Chaotic Biography Optimization. *International Journal of Web Services Research*, *18*(3), 42–62. https://doi.org/10.4018/ijwsr.2021070103

Burcoff, A., & Shamir, L. (2017). Computer Analysis of Pablo Picasso's Artistic Style. *International Journal of Art, Culture and Design Technologies*, *6*(1), 1–18. doi:10.4018/IJACDT.2017010101

Byker, E. J. (2017). I Play I Learn: Introducing Technological Play Theory. In C. Martin & D. Polly (Eds.), *Handbook of Research on Teacher Education and Professional Development* (pp. 297–306). Hershey, PA: IGI Global. doi:10.4018/978-1-5225-1067-3.ch016

Calongne, C. M., Stricker, A. G., Truman, B., & Arenas, F. J. (2017). Cognitive Apprenticeship and Computer Science Education in Cyberspace: Reimagining the Past. In A. Stricker, C. Calongne, B. Truman, & F. Arenas (Eds.), *Integrating an Awareness of Selfhood and Society into Virtual Learning* (pp. 180–197). Hershey, PA: IGI Global. doi:10.4018/978-1-5225-2182-2.ch013

Carneiro, A. D. (2017). Defending Information Networks in Cyberspace: Some Notes on Security Needs. In M. Dawson, D. Kisku, P. Gupta, J. Sing, & W. Li (Eds.), Developing Next-Generation Countermeasures for Homeland Security Threat Prevention (pp. 354-375). Hershey, PA: IGI Global. https://doi.org/ doi:10.4018/978-1-5225-0703-1.ch016

Carvalho, W. F., & Zarate, L. (2021). Causal Feature Selection. In A. Azevedo & M. Santos (Eds.), *Integration Challenges for Analytics, Business Intelligence, and Data Mining* (pp. 145-160). IGI Global. https://doi.org/10.4018/978-1-7998-5781-5.ch007

Chase, J. P., & Yan, Z. (2017). Affect in Statistics Cognition. In *Assessing and Measuring Statistics Cognition in Higher Education Online Environments: Emerging Research and Opportunities* (pp. 144–187). Hershey, PA: IGI Global. doi:10.4018/978-1-5225-2420-5.ch005

Chatterjee, A., Roy, S., & Shrivastava, R. (2021). A Machine Learning Approach to Prevent Cancer. In G. Rani & P. Tiwari (Eds.), *Handbook of Research on Disease Prediction Through Data Analytics and Machine Learning* (pp. 112–141). IGI Global. https://doi.org/10.4018/978-1-7998-2742-9.ch007

Cifci, M. A. (2021). Optimizing WSNs for CPS Using Machine Learning Techniques. In A. Luhach & A. Elçi (Eds.), *Artificial Intelligence Paradigms for Smart Cyber-Physical Systems* (pp. 204–228). IGI Global. https://doi.org/10.4018/978-1-7998-5101-1.ch010

Cimermanova, I. (2017). Computer-Assisted Learning in Slovakia. In D. Tafazoli & M. Romero (Eds.), *Multiculturalism and Technology-Enhanced Language Learning* (pp. 252–270). Hershey, PA: IGI Global. doi:10.4018/978-1-5225-1882-2.ch015

Cipolla-Ficarra, F. V., & Cipolla-Ficarra, M. (2018). Computer Animation for Ingenious Revival. In F. Cipolla-Ficarra, M. Ficarra, M. Cipolla-Ficarra, A. Quiroga, J. Alma, & J. Carré (Eds.), *Technology-Enhanced Human Interaction in Modern Society* (pp. 159–181). Hershey, PA: IGI Global. doi:10.4018/978-1-5225-3437-2.ch008

Cockrell, S., Damron, T. S., Melton, A. M., & Smith, A. D. (2018). Offshoring IT. In M. Khosrow-Pour, D.B.A. (Ed.), Encyclopedia of Information Science and Technology, Fourth Edition (pp. 5476-5489). Hershey, PA: IGI Global. https://doi.org/ doi:10.4018/978-1-5225-2255-3.ch476

Coffey, J. W. (2018). Logic and Proof in Computer Science: Categories and Limits of Proof Techniques. In J. Horne (Ed.), *Philosophical Perceptions on Logic and Order* (pp. 218–240). Hershey, PA: IGI Global. doi:10.4018/978-1-5225-2443-4.ch007

Dale, M. (2017). Re-Thinking the Challenges of Enterprise Architecture Implementation. In M. Tavana (Ed.), *Enterprise Information Systems and the Digitalization of Business Functions* (pp. 205–221). Hershey, PA: IGI Global. doi:10.4018/978-1-5225-2382-6.ch009

Das, A., & Mohanty, M. N. (2021). An Useful Review on Optical Character Recognition for Smart Era Generation. In A. Tyagi (Ed.), *Multimedia and Sensory Input for Augmented, Mixed, and Virtual Reality* (pp. 1–41). IGI Global. https://doi.org/10.4018/978-1-7998-4703-8.ch001

Dash, A. K., & Mohapatra, P. (2021). A Survey on Prematurity Detection of Diabetic Retinopathy Based on Fundus Images Using Deep Learning Techniques. In S. Saxena & S. Paul (Eds.), *Deep Learning Applications in Medical Imaging* (pp. 140–155). IGI Global. https://doi.org/10.4018/978-1-7998-5071-7.ch006

De Maere, K., De Haes, S., & von Kutzschenbach, M. (2017). CIO Perspectives on Organizational Learning within the Context of IT Governance. *International Journal of IT/Business Alignment and Governance, 8*(1), 32-47. https://doi.org/doi:10.4018/IJITBAG.2017010103

Demir, K., Çaka, C., Yaman, N. D., İslamoğlu, H., & Kuzu, A. (2018). Examining the Current Definitions of Computational Thinking. In H. Ozcinar, G. Wong, & H. Ozturk (Eds.), *Teaching Computational Thinking in Primary Education* (pp. 36–64). Hershey, PA: IGI Global. doi:10.4018/978-1-5225-3200-2.ch003

Deng, X., Hung, Y., & Lin, C. D. (2017). Design and Analysis of Computer Experiments. In S. Saha, A. Mandal, A. Narasimhamurthy, S. V, & S. Sangam (Eds.), Handbook of Research on Applied Cybernetics and Systems Science (pp. 264-279). Hershey, PA: IGI Global. doi:10.4018/978-1-5225-2498-4.ch013

Denner, J., Martinez, J., & Thiry, H. (2017). Strategies for Engaging Hispanic/Latino Youth in the US in Computer Science. In Y. Rankin & J. Thomas (Eds.), *Moving Students of Color from Consumers to Producers of Technology* (pp. 24–48). Hershey, PA: IGI Global. doi:10.4018/978-1-5225-2005-4.ch002

Devi, A. (2017). Cyber Crime and Cyber Security: A Quick Glance. In R. Kumar, P. Pattnaik, & P. Pandey (Eds.), *Detecting and Mitigating Robotic Cyber Security Risks* (pp. 160–171). Hershey, PA: IGI Global. doi:10.4018/978-1-5225-2154-9.ch011

Dhaya, R., & Kanthavel, R. (2022). Futuristic Research Perspectives of IoT Platforms. In D. Jeya Mala (Ed.), *Integrating AI in IoT Analytics on the Cloud for Healthcare Applications* (pp. 258–275). IGI Global. doi:10.4018/978-1-7998-9132-1.ch015

Doyle, D. J., & Fahy, P. J. (2018). Interactivity in Distance Education and Computer-Aided Learning, With Medical Education Examples. In M. Khosrow-Pour, D.B.A. (Ed.), Encyclopedia of Information Science and Technology, Fourth Edition (pp. 5829-5840). Hershey, PA: IGI Global. https://doi.org/ doi:10.4018/978-1-5225-2255-3.ch507

Eklund, P. (2021). Reinforcement Learning in Social Media Marketing. In B. Christiansen & T. Škrinjarić (Eds.), *Handbook of Research on Applied AI for International Business and Marketing Applications* (pp. 30–48). IGI Global. https://doi.org/10.4018/978-1-7998-5077-9.ch003

El Ghandour, N., Benaissa, M., & Lebbah, Y. (2021). An Integer Linear Programming-Based Method for the Extraction of Ontology Alignment. *International Journal of Information Technology and Web Engineering*, *16*(2), 25–44. https://doi.org/10.4018/IJITWE.2021040102

Elias, N. I., & Walker, T. W. (2017). Factors that Contribute to Continued Use of E-Training among Healthcare Professionals. In F. Topor (Ed.), *Handbook of Research on Individualism and Identity in the Globalized Digital Age* (pp. 403–429). Hershey, PA: IGI Global. doi:10.4018/978-1-5225-0522-8.ch018

Fisher, R. L. (2018). Computer-Assisted Indian Matrimonial Services. In M. Khosrow-Pour, D.B.A. (Ed.), Encyclopedia of Information Science and Technology, Fourth Edition (pp. 4136-4145). Hershey, PA: IGI Global. doi:10.4018/978-1-5225-2255-3.ch358

Galiautdinov, R. (2021). Nonlinear Filtering in Artificial Neural Network Applications in Business and Engineering. In Q. Do (Ed.), *Artificial Neural Network Applications in Business and Engineering* (pp. 1–23). IGI Global. https://doi.org/10.4018/978-1-7998-3238-6.ch001

Gardner-McCune, C., & Jimenez, Y. (2017). Historical App Developers: Integrating CS into K-12 through Cross-Disciplinary Projects. In Y. Rankin & J. Thomas (Eds.), *Moving Students of Color from Consumers to Producers of Technology* (pp. 85–112). Hershey, PA: IGI Global. doi:10.4018/978-1-5225-2005-4.ch005

Garg, P. K. (2021). The Internet of Things-Based Technologies. In S. Kumar, M. Trivedi, P. Ranjan, & A. Punhani (Eds.), *Evolution of Software-Defined Networking Foundations for IoT and 5G Mobile Networks* (pp. 37–65). IGI Global. https://doi.org/10.4018/978-1-7998-4685-7.ch003

Garg, T., & Bharti, M. (2021). Congestion Control Protocols for UWSNs. In N. Goyal, L. Sapra, & J. Sandhu (Eds.), *Energy-Efficient Underwater Wireless Communications and Networking* (pp. 85–100). IGI Global. https://doi.org/10.4018/978-1-7998-3640-7.ch006

Gauttier, S. (2021). A Primer on Q-Method and the Study of Technology. In M. Khosrow-Pour D.B.A. (Eds.), *Encyclopedia of Information Science and Technology, Fifth Edition* (pp. 1746-1756). IGI Global. https://doi.org/10.4018/978-1-7998-3479-3.ch120

Ghafele, R., & Gibert, B. (2018). Open Growth: The Economic Impact of Open Source Software in the USA. In M. Khosrow-Pour (Ed.), *Optimizing Contemporary Application and Processes in Open Source Software* (pp. 164–197). Hershey, PA: IGI Global. doi:10.4018/978-1-5225-5314-4.ch007

Ghobakhloo, M., & Azar, A. (2018). Information Technology Resources, the Organizational Capability of Lean-Agile Manufacturing, and Business Performance. *Information Resources Management Journal*, *31*(2), 47–74. doi:10.4018/IRMJ.2018040103

Gikandi, J. W. (2017). Computer-Supported Collaborative Learning and Assessment: A Strategy for Developing Online Learning Communities in Continuing Education. In J. Keengwe & G. Onchwari (Eds.), *Handbook of Research on Learner-Centered Pedagogy in Teacher Education and Professional Development* (pp. 309–333). Hershey, PA: IGI Global. doi:10.4018/978-1-5225-0892-2.ch017

Gokhale, A. A., & Machina, K. F. (2017). Development of a Scale to Measure Attitudes toward Information Technology. In L. Tomei (Ed.), *Exploring the New Era of Technology-Infused Education* (pp. 49–64). Hershey, PA: IGI Global. doi:10.4018/978-1-5225-1709-2.ch004

Goswami, J. K., Jalal, S., Negi, C. S., & Jalal, A. S. (2022). A Texture Features-Based Robust Facial Expression Recognition. *International Journal of Computer Vision and Image Processing*, *12*(1), 1–15. https://doi.org/10.4018/IJCVIP.2022010103

Hafeez-Baig, A., Gururajan, R., & Wickramasinghe, N. (2017). Readiness as a Novel Construct of Readiness Acceptance Model (RAM) for the Wireless Handheld Technology. In N. Wickramasinghe (Ed.), *Handbook of Research on Healthcare Administration and Management* (pp. 578–595). Hershey, PA: IGI Global. doi:10.4018/978-1-5225-0920-2.ch035

Hanafizadeh, P., Ghandchi, S., & Asgarimehr, M. (2017). Impact of Information Technology on Lifestyle: A Literature Review and Classification. *International Journal of Virtual Communities and Social Networking*, 9(2), 1–23. doi:10.4018/IJVCSN.2017040101

Haseski, H. İ., Ilic, U., & Tuğtekin, U. (2018). Computational Thinking in Educational Digital Games: An Assessment Tool Proposal. In H. Ozcinar, G. Wong, & H. Ozturk (Eds.), *Teaching Computational Thinking in Primary Education* (pp. 256–287). Hershey, PA: IGI Global. doi:10.4018/978-1-5225-3200-2.ch013

Hee, W. J., Jalleh, G., Lai, H., & Lin, C. (2017). E-Commerce and IT Projects: Evaluation and Management Issues in Australian and Taiwanese Hospitals. *International Journal of Public Health Management and Ethics*, 2(1), 69–90. doi:10.4018/IJPHME.2017010104

Hernandez, A. A. (2017). Green Information Technology Usage: Awareness and Practices of Philippine IT Professionals. *International Journal of Enterprise Information Systems*, 13(4), 90–103. doi:10.4018/IJEIS.2017100106

Hernandez, M. A., Marin, E. C., Garcia-Rodriguez, J., Azorin-Lopez, J., & Cazorla, M. (2017). Automatic Learning Improves Human-Robot Interaction in Productive Environments: A Review. *International Journal of Computer Vision and Image Processing*, 7(3), 65–75. doi:10.4018/IJCVIP.2017070106

Hirota, A. (2021). Design of Narrative Creation in Innovation: "Signature Story" and Two Types of Pivots. In T. Ogata & J. Ono (Eds.), *Bridging the Gap Between AI, Cognitive Science, and Narratology With Narrative Generation* (pp. 363–376). IGI Global. https://doi.org/10.4018/978-1-7998-4864-6.ch012

Hond, D., Asgari, H., Jeffery, D., & Newman, M. (2021). An Integrated Process for Verifying Deep Learning Classifiers Using Dataset Dissimilarity Measures. *International Journal of Artificial Intelligence and Machine Learning*, 11(2), 1–21. https://doi.org/10.4018/IJAIML.289536

Horne-Popp, L. M., Tessone, E. B., & Welker, J. (2018). If You Build It, They Will Come: Creating a Library Statistics Dashboard for Decision-Making. In L. Costello & M. Powers (Eds.), *Developing In-House Digital Tools in Library Spaces* (pp. 177–203). Hershey, PA: IGI Global. doi:10.4018/978-1-5225-2676-6.ch009

Hu, H., Hu, P. J., & Al-Gahtani, S. S. (2017). User Acceptance of Computer Technology at Work in Arabian Culture: A Model Comparison Approach. In M. Khosrow-Pour (Ed.), *Handbook of Research on Technology Adoption, Social Policy, and Global Integration* (pp. 205–228). Hershey, PA: IGI Global. doi:10.4018/978-1-5225-2668-1.ch011

Huang, C., Sun, Y., & Fuh, C. (2022). Vehicle License Plate Recognition With Deep Learning. In C. Chen, W. Yang, & L. Chen (Eds.), *Technologies to Advance Automation in Forensic Science and Criminal Investigation* (pp. 161-219). IGI Global. https://doi.org/10.4018/978-1-7998-8386-9.ch009

Ifinedo, P. (2017). Using an Extended Theory of Planned Behavior to Study Nurses' Adoption of Healthcare Information Systems in Nova Scotia. *International Journal of Technology Diffusion, 8*(1), 1–17. doi:10.4018/IJTD.2017010101

Ilie, V., & Sneha, S. (2018). A Three Country Study for Understanding Physicians' Engagement With Electronic Information Resources Pre and Post System Implementation. *Journal of Global Information Management, 26*(2), 48–73. doi:10.4018/JGIM.2018040103

Ilo, P. I., Nkiko, C., Ugwu, C. I., Ekere, J. N., Izuagbe, R., & Fagbohun, M. O. (2021). Prospects and Challenges of Web 3.0 Technologies Application in the Provision of Library Services. In M. Khosrow-Pour D.B.A. (Ed.), *Encyclopedia of Information Science and Technology, Fifth Edition* (pp. 1767-1781). IGI Global. https://doi.org/10.4018/978-1-7998-3479-3.ch122

Inoue-Smith, Y. (2017). Perceived Ease in Using Technology Predicts Teacher Candidates' Preferences for Online Resources. *International Journal of Online Pedagogy and Course Design, 7*(3), 17–28. doi:10.4018/IJOPCD.2017070102

Islam, A. Y. (2017). Technology Satisfaction in an Academic Context: Moderating Effect of Gender. In A. Mesquita (Ed.), *Research Paradigms and Contemporary Perspectives on Human-Technology Interaction* (pp. 187–211). Hershey, PA: IGI Global. doi:10.4018/978-1-5225-1868-6.ch009

Jagdale, S. C., Hable, A. A., & Chabukswar, A. R. (2021). Protocol Development in Clinical Trials for Healthcare Management. In M. Khosrow-Pour D.B.A. (Ed.), *Encyclopedia of Information Science and Technology, Fifth Edition* (pp. 1797-1814). IGI Global. https://doi.org/10.4018/978-1-7998-3479-3.ch124

Jamil, G. L., & Jamil, C. C. (2017). Information and Knowledge Management Perspective Contributions for Fashion Studies: Observing Logistics and Supply Chain Management Processes. In G. Jamil, A. Soares, & C. Pessoa (Eds.), *Handbook of Research on Information Management for Effective Logistics and Supply Chains* (pp. 199–221). Hershey, PA: IGI Global. doi:10.4018/978-1-5225-0973-8.ch011

Jamil, M. I., & Almunawar, M. N. (2021). Importance of Digital Literacy and Hindrance Brought About by Digital Divide. In M. Khosrow-Pour D.B.A. (Ed.), *Encyclopedia of Information Science and Technology, Fifth Edition* (pp. 1683-1698). IGI Global. https://doi.org/10.4018/978-1-7998-3479-3.ch116

Janakova, M. (2018). Big Data and Simulations for the Solution of Controversies in Small Businesses. In M. Khosrow-Pour, D.B.A. (Ed.), Encyclopedia of Information Science and Technology, Fourth Edition (pp. 6907-6915). Hershey, PA: IGI Global. doi:10.4018/978-1-5225-2255-3.ch598

Jhawar, A., & Garg, S. K. (2018). Logistics Improvement by Investment in Information Technology Using System Dynamics. In A. Azar & S. Vaidyanathan (Eds.), *Advances in System Dynamics and Control* (pp. 528–567). Hershey, PA: IGI Global. doi:10.4018/978-1-5225-4077-9.ch017

Kalelioğlu, F., Gülbahar, Y., & Doğan, D. (2018). Teaching How to Think Like a Programmer: Emerging Insights. In H. Ozcinar, G. Wong, & H. Ozturk (Eds.), *Teaching Computational Thinking in Primary Education* (pp. 18–35). Hershey, PA: IGI Global. doi:10.4018/978-1-5225-3200-2.ch002

Kamberi, S. (2017). A Girls-Only Online Virtual World Environment and its Implications for Game-Based Learning. In A. Stricker, C. Calongne, B. Truman, & F. Arenas (Eds.), *Integrating an Awareness of Selfhood and Society into Virtual Learning* (pp. 74–95). Hershey, PA: IGI Global. doi:10.4018/978-1-5225-2182-2.ch006

Kamel, S., & Rizk, N. (2017). ICT Strategy Development: From Design to Implementation – Case of Egypt. In C. Howard & K. Hargiss (Eds.), *Strategic Information Systems and Technologies in Modern Organizations* (pp. 239–257). Hershey, PA: IGI Global. doi:10.4018/978-1-5225-1680-4.ch010

Kamel, S. H. (2018). The Potential Role of the Software Industry in Supporting Economic Development. In M. Khosrow-Pour, D.B.A. (Ed.), Encyclopedia of Information Science and Technology, Fourth Edition (pp. 7259-7269). Hershey, PA: IGI Global. doi:10.4018/978-1-5225-2255-3.ch631

Kang, H., Kang, Y., & Kim, J. (2022). Improved Fall Detection Model on GRU Using PoseNet. *International Journal of Software Innovation*, *10*(2), 1–11. https://doi.org/10.4018/IJSI.289600

Kankam, P. K. (2021). Employing Case Study and Survey Designs in Information Research. *Journal of Information Technology Research*, *14*(1), 167–177. https://doi.org/10.4018/JITR.2021010110

Karas, V., & Schuller, B. W. (2021). Deep Learning for Sentiment Analysis: An Overview and Perspectives. In F. Pinarbasi & M. Taskiran (Eds.), *Natural Language Processing for Global and Local Business* (pp. 97–132). IGI Global. https://doi.org/10.4018/978-1-7998-4240-8.ch005

Kaufman, L. M. (2022). Reimagining the Magic of the Workshop Model. In T. Driscoll III, (Ed.), *Designing Effective Distance and Blended Learning Environments in K-12* (pp. 89–109). IGI Global. https://doi.org/10.4018/978-1-7998-6829-3.ch007

Kawata, S. (2018). Computer-Assisted Parallel Program Generation. In M. Khosrow-Pour, D.B.A. (Ed.), Encyclopedia of Information Science and Technology, Fourth Edition (pp. 4583-4593). Hershey, PA: IGI Global. doi:10.4018/978-1-5225-2255-3. ch398

Kharb, L., & Singh, P. (2021). Role of Machine Learning in Modern Education and Teaching. In S. Verma & P. Tomar (Ed.), *Impact of AI Technologies on Teaching, Learning, and Research in Higher Education* (pp. 99-123). IGI Global. https://doi.org/10.4018/978-1-7998-4763-2.ch006

Khari, M., Shrivastava, G., Gupta, S., & Gupta, R. (2017). Role of Cyber Security in Today's Scenario. In R. Kumar, P. Pattnaik, & P. Pandey (Eds.), *Detecting and Mitigating Robotic Cyber Security Risks* (pp. 177–191). Hershey, PA: IGI Global. doi:10.4018/978-1-5225-2154-9.ch013

Khekare, G., & Sheikh, S. (2021). Autonomous Navigation Using Deep Reinforcement Learning in ROS. *International Journal of Artificial Intelligence and Machine Learning, 11*(2), 63–70. https://doi.org/10.4018/IJAIML.20210701.oa4

Khouja, M., Rodriguez, I. B., Ben Halima, Y., & Moalla, S. (2018). IT Governance in Higher Education Institutions: A Systematic Literature Review. *International Journal of Human Capital and Information Technology Professionals, 9*(2), 52–67. doi:10.4018/IJHCITP.2018040104

Kiourt, C., Pavlidis, G., Koutsoudis, A., & Kalles, D. (2017). Realistic Simulation of Cultural Heritage. *International Journal of Computational Methods in Heritage Science, 1*(1), 10–40. doi:10.4018/IJCMHS.2017010102

Köse, U. (2017). An Augmented-Reality-Based Intelligent Mobile Application for Open Computer Education. In G. Kurubacak & H. Altinpulluk (Eds.), *Mobile Technologies and Augmented Reality in Open Education* (pp. 154–174). Hershey, PA: IGI Global. doi:10.4018/978-1-5225-2110-5.ch008

Lahmiri, S. (2018). Information Technology Outsourcing Risk Factors and Provider Selection. In M. Gupta, R. Sharman, J. Walp, & P. Mulgund (Eds.), *Information Technology Risk Management and Compliance in Modern Organizations* (pp. 214–228). Hershey, PA: IGI Global. doi:10.4018/978-1-5225-2604-9.ch008

Lakkad, A. K., Bhadaniya, R. D., Shah, V. N., & Lavanya, K. (2021). Complex Events Processing on Live News Events Using Apache Kafka and Clustering Techniques. *International Journal of Intelligent Information Technologies*, *17*(1), 39–52. https://doi.org/10.4018/IJIIT.2021010103

Landriscina, F. (2017). Computer-Supported Imagination: The Interplay Between Computer and Mental Simulation in Understanding Scientific Concepts. In I. Levin & D. Tsybulsky (Eds.), *Digital Tools and Solutions for Inquiry-Based STEM Learning* (pp. 33–60). Hershey, PA: IGI Global. doi:10.4018/978-1-5225-2525-7.ch002

Lara López, G. (2021). Virtual Reality in Object Location. In A. Negrón & M. Muñoz (Eds.), *Latin American Women and Research Contributions to the IT Field* (pp. 307–324). IGI Global. https://doi.org/10.4018/978-1-7998-7552-9.ch014

Lee, W. W. (2018). Ethical Computing Continues From Problem to Solution. In M. Khosrow-Pour, D.B.A. (Ed.), Encyclopedia of Information Science and Technology, Fourth Edition (pp. 4884-4897). Hershey, PA: IGI Global. doi:10.4018/978-1-5225-2255-3.ch423

Lin, S., Chen, S., & Chuang, S. (2017). Perceived Innovation and Quick Response Codes in an Online-to-Offline E-Commerce Service Model. *International Journal of E-Adoption*, *9*(2), 1–16. doi:10.4018/IJEA.2017070101

Liu, M., Wang, Y., Xu, W., & Liu, L. (2017). Automated Scoring of Chinese Engineering Students' English Essays. *International Journal of Distance Education Technologies*, *15*(1), 52–68. doi:10.4018/IJDET.2017010104

Ma, X., Li, X., Zhong, B., Huang, Y., Gu, Y., Wu, M., Liu, Y., & Zhang, M. (2021). A Detector and Evaluation Framework of Abnormal Bidding Behavior Based on Supplier Portrait. *International Journal of Information Technology and Web Engineering*, *16*(2), 58–74. https://doi.org/10.4018/IJITWE.2021040104

Mabe, L. K., & Oladele, O. I. (2017). Application of Information Communication Technologies for Agricultural Development through Extension Services: A Review. In T. Tossy (Ed.), *Information Technology Integration for Socio-Economic Development* (pp. 52–101). Hershey, PA: IGI Global. doi:10.4018/978-1-5225-0539-6.ch003

Mahboub, S. A., Sayed Ali Ahmed, E., & Saeed, R. A. (2021). Smart IDS and IPS for Cyber-Physical Systems. In A. Luhach & A. Elçi (Eds.), *Artificial Intelligence Paradigms for Smart Cyber-Physical Systems* (pp. 109–136). IGI Global. https://doi.org/10.4018/978-1-7998-5101-1.ch006

Manogaran, G., Thota, C., & Lopez, D. (2018). Human-Computer Interaction With Big Data Analytics. In D. Lopez & M. Durai (Eds.), *HCI Challenges and Privacy Preservation in Big Data Security* (pp. 1–22). Hershey, PA: IGI Global. doi:10.4018/978-1-5225-2863-0.ch001

Margolis, J., Goode, J., & Flapan, J. (2017). A Critical Crossroads for Computer Science for All: "Identifying Talent" or "Building Talent," and What Difference Does It Make? In Y. Rankin & J. Thomas (Eds.), *Moving Students of Color from Consumers to Producers of Technology* (pp. 1–23). Hershey, PA: IGI Global. doi:10.4018/978-1-5225-2005-4.ch001

Mazzù, M. F., Benetton, A., Baccelloni, A., & Lavini, L. (2022). A Milk Blockchain-Enabled Supply Chain: Evidence From Leading Italian Farms. In P. De Giovanni (Ed.), *Blockchain Technology Applications in Businesses and Organizations* (pp. 73–98). IGI Global. https://doi.org/10.4018/978-1-7998-8014-1.ch004

Mbale, J. (2018). Computer Centres Resource Cloud Elasticity-Scalability (CRECES): Copperbelt University Case Study. In S. Aljawarneh & M. Malhotra (Eds.), *Critical Research on Scalability and Security Issues in Virtual Cloud Environments* (pp. 48–70). Hershey, PA: IGI Global. doi:10.4018/978-1-5225-3029-9.ch003

McKee, J. (2018). The Right Information: The Key to Effective Business Planning. In *Business Architectures for Risk Assessment and Strategic Planning: Emerging Research and Opportunities* (pp. 38–52). Hershey, PA: IGI Global. doi:10.4018/978-1-5225-3392-4.ch003

Meddah, I. H., Remil, N. E., & Meddah, H. N. (2021). Novel Approach for Mining Patterns. *International Journal of Applied Evolutionary Computation*, *12*(1), 27–42. https://doi.org/10.4018/IJAEC.2021010103

Mensah, I. K., & Mi, J. (2018). Determinants of Intention to Use Local E-Government Services in Ghana: The Perspective of Local Government Workers. *International Journal of Technology Diffusion*, *9*(2), 41–60. doi:10.4018/IJTD.2018040103

Mohamed, J. H. (2018). Scientograph-Based Visualization of Computer Forensics Research Literature. In J. Jeyasekar & P. Saravanan (Eds.), *Innovations in Measuring and Evaluating Scientific Information* (pp. 148–162). Hershey, PA: IGI Global. doi:10.4018/978-1-5225-3457-0.ch010

Montañés-Del Río, M. Á., Cornejo, V. R., Rodríguez, M. R., & Ortiz, J. S. (2021). Gamification of University Subjects: A Case Study for Operations Management. *Journal of Information Technology Research*, *14*(2), 1–29. https://doi.org/10.4018/JITR.2021040101

Moore, R. L., & Johnson, N. (2017). Earning a Seat at the Table: How IT Departments Can Partner in Organizational Change and Innovation. *International Journal of Knowledge-Based Organizations, 7*(2), 1–12. doi:10.4018/IJKBO.2017040101

Mukul, M. K., & Bhattaharyya, S. (2017). Brain-Machine Interface: Human-Computer Interaction. In E. Noughabi, B. Raahemi, A. Albadvi, & B. Far (Eds.), *Handbook of Research on Data Science for Effective Healthcare Practice and Administration* (pp. 417–443). Hershey, PA: IGI Global. doi:10.4018/978-1-5225-2515-8.ch018

Na, L. (2017). Library and Information Science Education and Graduate Programs in Academic Libraries. In L. Ruan, Q. Zhu, & Y. Ye (Eds.), *Academic Library Development and Administration in China* (pp. 218–229). Hershey, PA: IGI Global. doi:10.4018/978-1-5225-0550-1.ch013

Nagpal, G., Bishnoi, G. K., Dhami, H. S., & Vijayvargia, A. (2021). Use of Data Analytics to Increase the Efficiency of Last Mile Logistics for Ecommerce Deliveries. In B. Patil & M. Vohra (Eds.), *Handbook of Research on Engineering, Business, and Healthcare Applications of Data Science and Analytics* (pp. 167–180). IGI Global. https://doi.org/10.4018/978-1-7998-3053-5.ch009

Nair, S. M., Ramesh, V., & Tyagi, A. K. (2021). Issues and Challenges (Privacy, Security, and Trust) in Blockchain-Based Applications. In A. Tyagi, G. Rekha, & N. Sreenath (Eds.), *Opportunities and Challenges for Blockchain Technology in Autonomous Vehicles* (pp. 196–209). IGI Global. https://doi.org/10.4018/978-1-7998-3295-9.ch012

Naomi, J. F. M., K., & V., S. (2021). Machine and Deep Learning Techniques in IoT and Cloud. In S. Velayutham (Ed.), *Challenges and Opportunities for the Convergence of IoT, Big Data, and Cloud Computing* (pp. 225-247). IGI Global. https://doi.org/10.4018/978-1-7998-3111-2.ch013

Nath, R., & Murthy, V. N. (2018). What Accounts for the Differences in Internet Diffusion Rates Around the World? In M. Khosrow-Pour, D.B.A. (Ed.), Encyclopedia of Information Science and Technology, Fourth Edition (pp. 8095-8104). Hershey, PA: IGI Global. https://doi.org/ doi:10.4018/978-1-5225-2255-3.ch705

Nedelko, Z., & Potocan, V. (2018). The Role of Emerging Information Technologies for Supporting Supply Chain Management. In M. Khosrow-Pour, D.B.A. (Ed.), Encyclopedia of Information Science and Technology, Fourth Edition (pp. 5559-5569). Hershey, PA: IGI Global. doi:10.4018/978-1-5225-2255-3.ch483

Related References

Negrini, L., Giang, C., & Bonnet, E. (2022). Designing Tools and Activities for Educational Robotics in Online Learning. In N. Eteokleous & E. Nisiforou (Eds.), *Designing, Constructing, and Programming Robots for Learning* (pp. 202–222). IGI Global. https://doi.org/10.4018/978-1-7998-7443-0.ch010

Ngafeeson, M. N. (2018). User Resistance to Health Information Technology. In M. Khosrow-Pour, D.B.A. (Ed.), Encyclopedia of Information Science and Technology, Fourth Edition (pp. 3816-3825). Hershey, PA: IGI Global. doi:10.4018/978-1-5225-2255-3.ch331

Nguyen, T. T., Giang, N. L., Tran, D. T., Nguyen, T. T., Nguyen, H. Q., Pham, A. V., & Vu, T. D. (2021). A Novel Filter-Wrapper Algorithm on Intuitionistic Fuzzy Set for Attribute Reduction From Decision Tables. *International Journal of Data Warehousing and Mining*, *17*(4), 67–100. https://doi.org/10.4018/IJDWM.2021100104

Nigam, A., & Dewani, P. P. (2022). Consumer Engagement Through Conditional Promotions: An Exploratory Study. *Journal of Global Information Management*, *30*(5), 1–19. https://doi.org/10.4018/JGIM.290364

Odagiri, K. (2017). Introduction of Individual Technology to Constitute the Current Internet. In *Strategic Policy-Based Network Management in Contemporary Organizations* (pp. 20–96). Hershey, PA: IGI Global. doi:10.4018/978-1-68318-003-6.ch003

Odia, J. O., & Akpata, O. T. (2021). Role of Data Science and Data Analytics in Forensic Accounting and Fraud Detection. In B. Patil & M. Vohra (Eds.), *Handbook of Research on Engineering, Business, and Healthcare Applications of Data Science and Analytics* (pp. 203–227). IGI Global. https://doi.org/10.4018/978-1-7998-3053-5.ch011

Okike, E. U. (2018). Computer Science and Prison Education. In I. Biao (Ed.), *Strategic Learning Ideologies in Prison Education Programs* (pp. 246–264). Hershey, PA: IGI Global. doi:10.4018/978-1-5225-2909-5.ch012

Olelewe, C. J., & Nwafor, I. P. (2017). Level of Computer Appreciation Skills Acquired for Sustainable Development by Secondary School Students in Nsukka LGA of Enugu State, Nigeria. In C. Ayo & V. Mbarika (Eds.), *Sustainable ICT Adoption and Integration for Socio-Economic Development* (pp. 214–233). Hershey, PA: IGI Global. doi:10.4018/978-1-5225-2565-3.ch010

Oliveira, M., Maçada, A. C., Curado, C., & Nodari, F. (2017). Infrastructure Profiles and Knowledge Sharing. *International Journal of Technology and Human Interaction*, *13*(3), 1–12. doi:10.4018/IJTHI.2017070101

Otarkhani, A., Shokouhyar, S., & Pour, S. S. (2017). Analyzing the Impact of Governance of Enterprise IT on Hospital Performance: Tehran's (Iran) Hospitals – A Case Study. *International Journal of Healthcare Information Systems and Informatics*, *12*(3), 1–20. doi:10.4018/IJHISI.2017070101

Otunla, A. O., & Amuda, C. O. (2018). Nigerian Undergraduate Students' Computer Competencies and Use of Information Technology Tools and Resources for Study Skills and Habits' Enhancement. In M. Khosrow-Pour, D.B.A. (Ed.), Encyclopedia of Information Science and Technology, Fourth Edition (pp. 2303-2313). Hershey, PA: IGI Global. https://doi.org/ doi:10.4018/978-1-5225-2255-3.ch200

Özçınar, H. (2018). A Brief Discussion on Incentives and Barriers to Computational Thinking Education. In H. Ozcinar, G. Wong, & H. Ozturk (Eds.), *Teaching Computational Thinking in Primary Education* (pp. 1–17). Hershey, PA: IGI Global. doi:10.4018/978-1-5225-3200-2.ch001

Pandey, J. M., Garg, S., Mishra, P., & Mishra, B. P. (2017). Computer Based Psychological Interventions: Subject to the Efficacy of Psychological Services. *International Journal of Computers in Clinical Practice*, *2*(1), 25–33. doi:10.4018/IJCCP.2017010102

Pandkar, S. D., & Paatil, S. D. (2021). Big Data and Knowledge Resource Centre. In S. Dhamdhere (Ed.), *Big Data Applications for Improving Library Services* (pp. 90–106). IGI Global. https://doi.org/10.4018/978-1-7998-3049-8.ch007

Patro, C. (2017). Impulsion of Information Technology on Human Resource Practices. In P. Ordóñez de Pablos (Ed.), *Managerial Strategies and Solutions for Business Success in Asia* (pp. 231–254). Hershey, PA: IGI Global. doi:10.4018/978-1-5225-1886-0.ch013

Patro, C. S., & Raghunath, K. M. (2017). Information Technology Paraphernalia for Supply Chain Management Decisions. In M. Tavana (Ed.), *Enterprise Information Systems and the Digitalization of Business Functions* (pp. 294–320). Hershey, PA: IGI Global. doi:10.4018/978-1-5225-2382-6.ch014

Paul, P. K. (2018). The Context of IST for Solid Information Retrieval and Infrastructure Building: Study of Developing Country. *International Journal of Information Retrieval Research*, *8*(1), 86–100. doi:10.4018/IJIRR.2018010106

Paul, P. K., & Chatterjee, D. (2018). iSchools Promoting "Information Science and Technology" (IST) Domain Towards Community, Business, and Society With Contemporary Worldwide Trend and Emerging Potentialities in India. In M. Khosrow-Pour, D.B.A. (Ed.), Encyclopedia of Information Science and Technology, Fourth Edition (pp. 4723-4735). Hershey, PA: IGI Global. https://doi.org/ doi:10.4018/978-1-5225-2255-3.ch410

Pessoa, C. R., & Marques, M. E. (2017). Information Technology and Communication Management in Supply Chain Management. In G. Jamil, A. Soares, & C. Pessoa (Eds.), *Handbook of Research on Information Management for Effective Logistics and Supply Chains* (pp. 23–33). Hershey, PA: IGI Global. doi:10.4018/978-1-5225-0973-8.ch002

Pineda, R. G. (2018). Remediating Interaction: Towards a Philosophy of Human-Computer Relationship. In M. Khosrow-Pour (Ed.), *Enhancing Art, Culture, and Design With Technological Integration* (pp. 75–98). Hershey, PA: IGI Global. doi:10.4018/978-1-5225-5023-5.ch004

Prabha, V. D., & R., R. (2021). Clinical Decision Support Systems: Decision-Making System for Clinical Data. In G. Rani & P. Tiwari (Eds.), *Handbook of Research on Disease Prediction Through Data Analytics and Machine Learning* (pp. 268-280). IGI Global. https://doi.org/10.4018/978-1-7998-2742-9.ch014

Pushpa, R., & Siddappa, M. (2021). An Optimal Way of VM Placement Strategy in Cloud Computing Platform Using ABCS Algorithm. *International Journal of Ambient Computing and Intelligence*, *12*(3), 16–38. https://doi.org/10.4018/IJACI.2021070102

Qian, Y. (2017). Computer Simulation in Higher Education: Affordances, Opportunities, and Outcomes. In P. Vu, S. Fredrickson, & C. Moore (Eds.), *Handbook of Research on Innovative Pedagogies and Technologies for Online Learning in Higher Education* (pp. 236–262). Hershey, PA: IGI Global. doi:10.4018/978-1-5225-1851-8.ch011

Rahman, N. (2017). Lessons from a Successful Data Warehousing Project Management. *International Journal of Information Technology Project Management*, *8*(4), 30–45. doi:10.4018/IJITPM.2017100103

Rahman, N. (2018). Environmental Sustainability in the Computer Industry for Competitive Advantage. In M. Khosrow-Pour (Ed.), *Green Computing Strategies for Competitive Advantage and Business Sustainability* (pp. 110–130). Hershey, PA: IGI Global. doi:10.4018/978-1-5225-5017-4.ch006

Rajh, A., & Pavetic, T. (2017). Computer Generated Description as the Required Digital Competence in Archival Profession. *International Journal of Digital Literacy and Digital Competence*, *8*(1), 36–49. doi:10.4018/IJDLDC.2017010103

Raman, A., & Goyal, D. P. (2017). Extending IMPLEMENT Framework for Enterprise Information Systems Implementation to Information System Innovation. In M. Tavana (Ed.), *Enterprise Information Systems and the Digitalization of Business Functions* (pp. 137–177). Hershey, PA: IGI Global. doi:10.4018/978-1-5225-2382-6.ch007

Rao, A. P., & Reddy, K. S. (2021). Automated Soil Residue Levels Detecting Device With IoT Interface. In V. Sathiyamoorthi & A. Elci (Eds.), *Challenges and Applications of Data Analytics in Social Perspectives* (Vol. S, pp. 123–135). IGI Global. https://doi.org/10.4018/978-1-7998-2566-1.ch007

Rao, Y. S., Rauta, A. K., Saini, H., & Panda, T. C. (2017). Mathematical Model for Cyber Attack in Computer Network. *International Journal of Business Data Communications and Networking*, *13*(1), 58–65. doi:10.4018/IJBDCN.2017010105

Rapaport, W. J. (2018). Syntactic Semantics and the Proper Treatment of Computationalism. In M. Danesi (Ed.), *Empirical Research on Semiotics and Visual Rhetoric* (pp. 128–176). Hershey, PA: IGI Global. doi:10.4018/978-1-5225-5622-0.ch007

Raut, R., Priyadarshinee, P., & Jha, M. (2017). Understanding the Mediation Effect of Cloud Computing Adoption in Indian Organization: Integrating TAM-TOE- Risk Model. *International Journal of Service Science, Management, Engineering, and Technology*, *8*(3), 40–59. doi:10.4018/IJSSMET.2017070103

Rezaie, S., Mirabedini, S. J., & Abtahi, A. (2018). Designing a Model for Implementation of Business Intelligence in the Banking Industry. *International Journal of Enterprise Information Systems*, *14*(1), 77–103. doi:10.4018/IJEIS.2018010105

Rezende, D. A. (2018). Strategic Digital City Projects: Innovative Information and Public Services Offered by Chicago (USA) and Curitiba (Brazil). In M. Lytras, L. Daniela, & A. Visvizi (Eds.), *Enhancing Knowledge Discovery and Innovation in the Digital Era* (pp. 204–223). Hershey, PA: IGI Global. doi:10.4018/978-1-5225-4191-2.ch012

Rodriguez, A., Rico-Diaz, A. J., Rabuñal, J. R., & Gestal, M. (2017). Fish Tracking with Computer Vision Techniques: An Application to Vertical Slot Fishways. In M. S., & V. V. (Eds.), Multi-Core Computer Vision and Image Processing for Intelligent Applications (pp. 74-104). Hershey, PA: IGI Global. https://doi.org/doi:10.4018/978-1-5225-0889-2.ch003

Related References

Romero, J. A. (2018). Sustainable Advantages of Business Value of Information Technology. In M. Khosrow-Pour, D.B.A. (Ed.), Encyclopedia of Information Science and Technology, Fourth Edition (pp. 923-929). Hershey, PA: IGI Global. doi:10.4018/978-1-5225-2255-3.ch079

Romero, J. A. (2018). The Always-On Business Model and Competitive Advantage. In N. Bajgoric (Ed.), *Always-On Enterprise Information Systems for Modern Organizations* (pp. 23–40). Hershey, PA: IGI Global. doi:10.4018/978-1-5225-3704-5.ch002

Rosen, Y. (2018). Computer Agent Technologies in Collaborative Learning and Assessment. In M. Khosrow-Pour, D.B.A. (Ed.), Encyclopedia of Information Science and Technology, Fourth Edition (pp. 2402-2410). Hershey, PA: IGI Global. doi:10.4018/978-1-5225-2255-3.ch209

Roy, D. (2018). Success Factors of Adoption of Mobile Applications in Rural India: Effect of Service Characteristics on Conceptual Model. In M. Khosrow-Pour (Ed.), *Green Computing Strategies for Competitive Advantage and Business Sustainability* (pp. 211–238). Hershey, PA: IGI Global. doi:10.4018/978-1-5225-5017-4.ch010

Ruffin, T. R., & Hawkins, D. P. (2018). Trends in Health Care Information Technology and Informatics. In M. Khosrow-Pour, D.B.A. (Ed.), Encyclopedia of Information Science and Technology, Fourth Edition (pp. 3805-3815). Hershey, PA: IGI Global. doi:10.4018/978-1-5225-2255-3.ch330

Sadasivam, U. M., & Ganesan, N. (2021). Detecting Fake News Using Deep Learning and NLP. In S. Misra, C. Arumugam, S. Jaganathan, & S. S. (Eds.), *Confluence of AI, Machine, and Deep Learning in Cyber Forensics* (pp. 117-133). IGI Global. https://doi.org/10.4018/978-1-7998-4900-1.ch007

Safari, M. R., & Jiang, Q. (2018). The Theory and Practice of IT Governance Maturity and Strategies Alignment: Evidence From Banking Industry. *Journal of Global Information Management*, 26(2), 127–146. doi:10.4018/JGIM.2018040106

Sahin, H. B., & Anagun, S. S. (2018). Educational Computer Games in Math Teaching: A Learning Culture. In E. Toprak & E. Kumtepe (Eds.), *Supporting Multiculturalism in Open and Distance Learning Spaces* (pp. 249–280). Hershey, PA: IGI Global. doi:10.4018/978-1-5225-3076-3.ch013

Sakalle, A., Tomar, P., Bhardwaj, H., & Sharma, U. (2021). Impact and Latest Trends of Intelligent Learning With Artificial Intelligence. In S. Verma & P. Tomar (Eds.), *Impact of AI Technologies on Teaching, Learning, and Research in Higher Education* (pp. 172-189). IGI Global. https://doi.org/10.4018/978-1-7998-4763-2.ch011

Sala, N. (2021). Virtual Reality, Augmented Reality, and Mixed Reality in Education: A Brief Overview. In D. Choi, A. Dailey-Hebert, & J. Estes (Eds.), *Current and Prospective Applications of Virtual Reality in Higher Education* (pp. 48–73). IGI Global. https://doi.org/10.4018/978-1-7998-4960-5.ch003

Salunkhe, S., Kanagachidambaresan, G., Rajkumar, C., & Jayanthi, K. (2022). Online Detection and Prediction of Fused Deposition Modelled Parts Using Artificial Intelligence. In S. Salunkhe, H. Hussein, & J. Davim (Eds.), *Applications of Artificial Intelligence in Additive Manufacturing* (pp. 194–209). IGI Global. https://doi.org/10.4018/978-1-7998-8516-0.ch009

Samy, V. S., Pramanick, K., Thenkanidiyoor, V., & Victor, J. (2021). Data Analysis and Visualization in Python for Polar Meteorological Data. *International Journal of Data Analytics*, 2(1), 32–60. https://doi.org/10.4018/IJDA.2021010102

Sanna, A., & Valpreda, F. (2017). An Assessment of the Impact of a Collaborative Didactic Approach and Students' Background in Teaching Computer Animation. *International Journal of Information and Communication Technology Education*, 13(4), 1–16. doi:10.4018/IJICTE.2017100101

Sarivougioukas, J., & Vagelatos, A. (2022). Fused Contextual Data With Threading Technology to Accelerate Processing in Home UbiHealth. *International Journal of Software Science and Computational Intelligence*, 14(1), 1–14. https://doi.org/10.4018/IJSSCI.285590

Scott, A., Martin, A., & McAlear, F. (2017). Enhancing Participation in Computer Science among Girls of Color: An Examination of a Preparatory AP Computer Science Intervention. In Y. Rankin & J. Thomas (Eds.), *Moving Students of Color from Consumers to Producers of Technology* (pp. 62–84). Hershey, PA: IGI Global. doi:10.4018/978-1-5225-2005-4.ch004

Shanmugam, M., Ibrahim, N., Gorment, N. Z., Sugu, R., Dandarawi, T. N., & Ahmad, N. A. (2022). Towards an Integrated Omni-Channel Strategy Framework for Improved Customer Interaction. In P. Lai (Ed.), *Handbook of Research on Social Impacts of E-Payment and Blockchain Technology* (pp. 409–427). IGI Global. https://doi.org/10.4018/978-1-7998-9035-5.ch022

Sharma, A., & Kumar, S. (2021). Network Slicing and the Role of 5G in IoT Applications. In S. Kumar, M. Trivedi, P. Ranjan, & A. Punhani (Eds.), *Evolution of Software-Defined Networking Foundations for IoT and 5G Mobile Networks* (pp. 172–190). IGI Global. https://doi.org/10.4018/978-1-7998-4685-7.ch010

Siddoo, V., & Wongsai, N. (2017). Factors Influencing the Adoption of ISO/IEC 29110 in Thai Government Projects: A Case Study. *International Journal of Information Technologies and Systems Approach*, *10*(1), 22–44. doi:10.4018/IJITSA.2017010102

Silveira, C., Hir, M. E., & Chaves, H. K. (2022). An Approach to Information Management as a Subsidy of Global Health Actions: A Case Study of Big Data in Health for Dengue, Zika, and Chikungunya. In J. Lima de Magalhães, Z. Hartz, G. Jamil, H. Silveira, & L. Jamil (Eds.), *Handbook of Research on Essential Information Approaches to Aiding Global Health in the One Health Context* (pp. 219–234). IGI Global. https://doi.org/10.4018/978-1-7998-8011-0.ch012

Simões, A. (2017). Using Game Frameworks to Teach Computer Programming. In R. Alexandre Peixoto de Queirós & M. Pinto (Eds.), *Gamification-Based E-Learning Strategies for Computer Programming Education* (pp. 221–236). Hershey, PA: IGI Global. doi:10.4018/978-1-5225-1034-5.ch010

Simões de Almeida, R., & da Silva, T. (2022). AI Chatbots in Mental Health: Are We There Yet? In A. Marques & R. Queirós (Eds.), *Digital Therapies in Psychosocial Rehabilitation and Mental Health* (pp. 226–243). IGI Global. https://doi.org/10.4018/978-1-7998-8634-1.ch011

Singh, L. K., Khanna, M., Thawkar, S., & Gopal, J. (2021). Robustness for Authentication of the Human Using Face, Ear, and Gait Multimodal Biometric System. *International Journal of Information System Modeling and Design*, *12*(1), 39–72. https://doi.org/10.4018/IJISMD.2021010103

Sllame, A. M. (2017). Integrating LAB Work With Classes in Computer Network Courses. In H. Alphin Jr, R. Chan, & J. Lavine (Eds.), *The Future of Accessibility in International Higher Education* (pp. 253–275). Hershey, PA: IGI Global. doi:10.4018/978-1-5225-2560-8.ch015

Smirnov, A., Ponomarev, A., Shilov, N., Kashevnik, A., & Teslya, N. (2018). Ontology-Based Human-Computer Cloud for Decision Support: Architecture and Applications in Tourism. *International Journal of Embedded and Real-Time Communication Systems*, *9*(1), 1–19. doi:10.4018/IJERTCS.2018010101

Smith-Ditizio, A. A., & Smith, A. D. (2018). Computer Fraud Challenges and Its Legal Implications. In M. Khosrow-Pour, D.B.A. (Ed.), Encyclopedia of Information Science and Technology, Fourth Edition (pp. 4837-4848). Hershey, PA: IGI Global. doi:10.4018/978-1-5225-2255-3.ch419

Sosnin, P. (2018). Figuratively Semantic Support of Human-Computer Interactions. In *Experience-Based Human-Computer Interactions: Emerging Research and Opportunities* (pp. 244–272). Hershey, PA: IGI Global. doi:10.4018/978-1-5225-2987-3.ch008

Srilakshmi, R., & Jaya Bhaskar, M. (2021). An Adaptable Secure Scheme in Mobile Ad hoc Network to Protect the Communication Channel From Malicious Behaviours. *International Journal of Information Technology and Web Engineering*, *16*(3), 54–73. https://doi.org/10.4018/IJITWE.2021070104

Sukhwani, N., Kagita, V. R., Kumar, V., & Panda, S. K. (2021). Efficient Computation of Top-K Skyline Objects in Data Set With Uncertain Preferences. *International Journal of Data Warehousing and Mining*, *17*(3), 68–80. https://doi.org/10.4018/IJDWM.2021070104

Susanto, H., Yie, L. F., Setiana, D., Asih, Y., Yoganingrum, A., Riyanto, S., & Saputra, F. A. (2021). Digital Ecosystem Security Issues for Organizations and Governments: Digital Ethics and Privacy. In Z. Mahmood (Ed.), *Web 2.0 and Cloud Technologies for Implementing Connected Government* (pp. 204–228). IGI Global. https://doi.org/10.4018/978-1-7998-4570-6.ch010

Syväjärvi, A., Leinonen, J., Kivivirta, V., & Kesti, M. (2017). The Latitude of Information Management in Local Government: Views of Local Government Managers. *International Journal of Electronic Government Research*, *13*(1), 69–85. doi:10.4018/IJEGR.2017010105

Tanque, M., & Foxwell, H. J. (2018). Big Data and Cloud Computing: A Review of Supply Chain Capabilities and Challenges. In A. Prasad (Ed.), *Exploring the Convergence of Big Data and the Internet of Things* (pp. 1–28). Hershey, PA: IGI Global. doi:10.4018/978-1-5225-2947-7.ch001

Teixeira, A., Gomes, A., & Orvalho, J. G. (2017). Auditory Feedback in a Computer Game for Blind People. In T. Issa, P. Kommers, T. Issa, P. Isaías, & T. Issa (Eds.), *Smart Technology Applications in Business Environments* (pp. 134–158). Hershey, PA: IGI Global. doi:10.4018/978-1-5225-2492-2.ch007

Tewari, P., Tiwari, P., & Goel, R. (2022). Information Technology in Supply Chain Management. In V. Garg & R. Goel (Eds.), *Handbook of Research on Innovative Management Using AI in Industry 5.0* (pp. 165–178). IGI Global. https://doi.org/10.4018/978-1-7998-8497-2.ch011

Related References

Thompson, N., McGill, T., & Murray, D. (2018). Affect-Sensitive Computer Systems. In M. Khosrow-Pour, D.B.A. (Ed.), Encyclopedia of Information Science and Technology, Fourth Edition (pp. 4124-4135). Hershey, PA: IGI Global. doi:10.4018/978-1-5225-2255-3.ch357

Triberti, S., Brivio, E., & Galimberti, C. (2018). On Social Presence: Theories, Methodologies, and Guidelines for the Innovative Contexts of Computer-Mediated Learning. In M. Marmon (Ed.), *Enhancing Social Presence in Online Learning Environments* (pp. 20–41). Hershey, PA: IGI Global. doi:10.4018/978-1-5225-3229-3.ch002

Tripathy, B. K. T. R., S., & Mohanty, R. K. (2018). Memetic Algorithms and Their Applications in Computer Science. In S. Dash, B. Tripathy, & A. Rahman (Eds.), Handbook of Research on Modeling, Analysis, and Application of Nature-Inspired Metaheuristic Algorithms (pp. 73-93). Hershey, PA: IGI Global. https://doi.org/doi:10.4018/978-1-5225-2857-9.ch004

Turulja, L., & Bajgoric, N. (2017). Human Resource Management IT and Global Economy Perspective: Global Human Resource Information Systems. In M. Khosrow-Pour (Ed.), *Handbook of Research on Technology Adoption, Social Policy, and Global Integration* (pp. 377–394). Hershey, PA: IGI Global. doi:10.4018/978-1-5225-2668-1.ch018

Unwin, D. W., Sanzogni, L., & Sandhu, K. (2017). Developing and Measuring the Business Case for Health Information Technology. In K. Moahi, K. Bwalya, & P. Sebina (Eds.), *Health Information Systems and the Advancement of Medical Practice in Developing Countries* (pp. 262–290). Hershey, PA: IGI Global. doi:10.4018/978-1-5225-2262-1.ch015

Usharani, B. (2022). House Plant Leaf Disease Detection and Classification Using Machine Learning. In M. Mundada, S. Seema, S. K.G., & M. Shilpa (Eds.), *Deep Learning Applications for Cyber-Physical Systems* (pp. 17-26). IGI Global. https://doi.org/10.4018/978-1-7998-8161-2.ch002

Vadhanam, B. R. S., M., Sugumaran, V., V., V., & Ramalingam, V. V. (2017). Computer Vision Based Classification on Commercial Videos. In M. S., & V. V. (Eds.), Multi-Core Computer Vision and Image Processing for Intelligent Applications (pp. 105-135). Hershey, PA: IGI Global. https://doi.org/ doi:10.4018/978-1-5225-0889-2.ch004

Vairinho, S. (2022). Innovation Dynamics Through the Encouragement of Knowledge Spin-Off From Touristic Destinations. In C. Ramos, S. Quinteiro, & A. Gonçalves (Eds.), *ICT as Innovator Between Tourism and Culture* (pp. 170–190). IGI Global. https://doi.org/10.4018/978-1-7998-8165-0.ch011

Valverde, R., Torres, B., & Motaghi, H. (2018). A Quantum NeuroIS Data Analytics Architecture for the Usability Evaluation of Learning Management Systems. In S. Bhattacharyya (Ed.), *Quantum-Inspired Intelligent Systems for Multimedia Data Analysis* (pp. 277–299). Hershey, PA: IGI Global. doi:10.4018/978-1-5225-5219-2.ch009

Vassilis, E. (2018). Learning and Teaching Methodology: "1:1 Educational Computing. In K. Koutsopoulos, K. Doukas, & Y. Kotsanis (Eds.), *Handbook of Research on Educational Design and Cloud Computing in Modern Classroom Settings* (pp. 122–155). Hershey, PA: IGI Global. doi:10.4018/978-1-5225-3053-4.ch007

Verma, S., & Jain, A. K. (2022). A Survey on Sentiment Analysis Techniques for Twitter. In B. Gupta, D. Peraković, A. Abd El-Latif, & D. Gupta (Eds.), *Data Mining Approaches for Big Data and Sentiment Analysis in Social Media* (pp. 57–90). IGI Global. https://doi.org/10.4018/978-1-7998-8413-2.ch003

Wang, H., Huang, P., & Chen, X. (2021). Research and Application of a Multidimensional Association Rules Mining Method Based on OLAP. *International Journal of Information Technology and Web Engineering*, *16*(1), 75–94. https://doi.org/10.4018/IJITWE.2021010104

Wexler, B. E. (2017). Computer-Presented and Physical Brain-Training Exercises for School Children: Improving Executive Functions and Learning. In B. Dubbels (Ed.), *Transforming Gaming and Computer Simulation Technologies across Industries* (pp. 206–224). Hershey, PA: IGI Global. doi:10.4018/978-1-5225-1817-4.ch012

Wimble, M., Singh, H., & Phillips, B. (2018). Understanding Cross-Level Interactions of Firm-Level Information Technology and Industry Environment: A Multilevel Model of Business Value. *Information Resources Management Journal*, *31*(1), 1–20. doi:10.4018/IRMJ.2018010101

Wimmer, H., Powell, L., Kilgus, L., & Force, C. (2017). Improving Course Assessment via Web-based Homework. *International Journal of Online Pedagogy and Course Design*, *7*(2), 1–19. doi:10.4018/IJOPCD.2017040101

Wong, S. (2021). Gendering Information and Communication Technologies in Climate Change. In M. Khosrow-Pour D.B.A. (Eds.), *Encyclopedia of Information Science and Technology, Fifth Edition* (pp. 1408-1422). IGI Global. https://doi.org/10.4018/978-1-7998-3479-3.ch096

Related References

Wong, Y. L., & Siu, K. W. (2018). Assessing Computer-Aided Design Skills. In M. Khosrow-Pour, D.B.A. (Ed.), Encyclopedia of Information Science and Technology, Fourth Edition (pp. 7382-7391). Hershey, PA: IGI Global. doi:10.4018/978-1-5225-2255-3.ch642

Wongsurawat, W., & Shrestha, V. (2018). Information Technology, Globalization, and Local Conditions: Implications for Entrepreneurs in Southeast Asia. In P. Ordóñez de Pablos (Ed.), *Management Strategies and Technology Fluidity in the Asian Business Sector* (pp. 163–176). Hershey, PA: IGI Global. doi:10.4018/978-1-5225-4056-4.ch010

Yamada, H. (2021). Homogenization of Japanese Industrial Technology From the Perspective of R&D Expenses. *International Journal of Systems and Service-Oriented Engineering, 11*(2), 24–51. doi:10.4018/IJSSOE.2021070102

Yang, Y., Zhu, X., Jin, C., & Li, J. J. (2018). Reforming Classroom Education Through a QQ Group: A Pilot Experiment at a Primary School in Shanghai. In H. Spires (Ed.), *Digital Transformation and Innovation in Chinese Education* (pp. 211–231). Hershey, PA: IGI Global. doi:10.4018/978-1-5225-2924-8.ch012

Yilmaz, R., Sezgin, A., Kurnaz, S., & Arslan, Y. Z. (2018). Object-Oriented Programming in Computer Science. In M. Khosrow-Pour, D.B.A. (Ed.), Encyclopedia of Information Science and Technology, Fourth Edition (pp. 7470-7480). Hershey, PA: IGI Global. doi:10.4018/978-1-5225-2255-3.ch650

Yu, L. (2018). From Teaching Software Engineering Locally and Globally to Devising an Internationalized Computer Science Curriculum. In S. Dikli, B. Etheridge, & R. Rawls (Eds.), *Curriculum Internationalization and the Future of Education* (pp. 293–320). Hershey, PA: IGI Global. doi:10.4018/978-1-5225-2791-6.ch016

Yuhua, F. (2018). Computer Information Library Clusters. In M. Khosrow-Pour, D.B.A. (Ed.), Encyclopedia of Information Science and Technology, Fourth Edition (pp. 4399-4403). Hershey, PA: IGI Global. doi:10.4018/978-1-5225-2255-3.ch382

Zakaria, R. B., Zainuddin, M. N., & Mohamad, A. H. (2022). Distilling Blockchain: Complexity, Barriers, and Opportunities. In P. Lai (Ed.), *Handbook of Research on Social Impacts of E-Payment and Blockchain Technology* (pp. 89–114). IGI Global. https://doi.org/10.4018/978-1-7998-9035-5.ch007

Zhang, Z., Ma, J., & Cui, X. (2021). Genetic Algorithm With Three-Dimensional Population Dominance Strategy for University Course Timetabling Problem. *International Journal of Grid and High Performance Computing, 13*(2), 56–69. https://doi.org/10.4018/IJGHPC.2021040104

About the Contributors

U. Vignesh is currently an Assistant Professor Senior Grade 2 in School of Computer Science and Engineering, Vellore Institute of Technology (VIT) - Chennai. Prior to his recent appointment at the VIT, he was a Post-Doctoral Fellow in National Institute of Technology (NIT), Trichy – India. Dr. Vignesh received his undergraduate degree in B.Tech (IT) as well as his M.Tech (IT) degree from Anna University - Chennai, and his PhD in Computer Science and Engineering from VIT University - Chennai. Dr. Vignesh published several papers in preferred Journals, patents and chapters in books, and participated in a range of forums on computer science, social science, etc. He also presented various academic as well as research-based papers at several national and international conferences. His research activities are currently twofold: while the first research activity is set to explore the developmental role that society needs with technology such as, Artificial Intelligence; the second major research theme that he is pursuing is focused on the bioinformatics and data mining.

Ruchi Doshi is having more than 16 years of academic, research and software development experience in Asia and Africa. Currently she is working as research supervisor at the Azteca University, Mexico and Adjunct Professor at the Jyoti Vidyapeeth Women's University, Jaipur, Rajasthan, India. She worked in the BlueCrest University College, Liberia, West Africa as Registrar and Head, Examination; BlueCrest University College, Ghana, Africa; Amity University, Rajasthan, India; Trimax IT Infrastructure & Services, Udaipur, India. She worked as a Founder Chair, Women in Engineering (WIE) and Secretary Position in the IEEE Liberia Subsection. She worked with Ministry of Higher Education (MoHE) in Liberia and Ghana for the Degree approvals and accreditations processes. She is interested in the field of Machine Learning and Cloud computing framework development. She has published numerous research papers in peer-reviewed international journals and conferences. She is a Reviewer, Advisor, Ambassador and Editorial board member of various reputed International Journals and Conferences.

* * *

Jeevarekha A. received her Bachelor of Science from Fatima College, Madurai, Tamil Nadu, India, in 2010 and Master of Science degree from Bharathiar University, Coimbatore,. Tamil Nadu, India, in 2012. She is a gold medalist in MSc. In 2018, she received her Ph.D. from Bharathidasan University, Tamil Nadu, India. She got INSPIRE Fellowship from the Department of Science and Technologies for her doctoral study. Her area of specialization is Nonlinear Dynamics. She has published her research works in highly reputed national and international journals.

Kande Archana is an Assistant Professor in the Department of CSE at Malla Reddy Institute of Engineering and Technology. She focuses on research in the area of Image Processing, Network Security, Signal Processing and Data Mining. She studied BTech and MTech degree in Department of CSE from Jawaharlal Nehru Technological University, Hyderabad, and currently pursuing PhD from Jawaharlal Nehru Technological University, Hyderabad. She has conducted and participated in various Workshops, Webinars, STTP, Seminars, faculty development programs and International Conferences held by various colleges. She is working as Reviewer for various International Journals and Conferences. She is Guiding BTech and M Tech students in their seminars and project dissertations. Published 40+ papers in International Journals and International & National Conferences.

M. Ashok is a technocrat with exposure to academics and Research. He has obtained PhD in Computer Science and Technology from Sri Krishna Devaraya University in Digital Image Processing in the year 2012. He has done his M.Tech. in Computer Science from JNTU, Anantapur and B.Tech. in Electronics and Communication Engineering from Sri Krishna Devaraya University. At Academic end, he worked in Institutions like Malla Reddy Institute of Engineering and Technology and Sri Sai Jyothi Engineering College, in various capacities from Assistant Professor to Professor and Principal. Has organized many Conferences, Workshops and FDPs. Presently Guiding Three PhD Scholars under JNTUH and guided many M.Tech Students in JNTUH; Materialized many MOUs between Academic Institutes and Industries, established Laboratories and Services. He has been invited to various colleges to deliver lectures and keynote addresses. His research interest is in the field of Image Processing, Data Mining and OS. He is an Editorial Board Member and Reviewer of ICETETS, NCARSE - International Conference and published 50+ research papers in many reputed Journals and Conferences. He is a Professional Member of IETE – India, ISTE-India, CSI-India, IAENG-Hong Kong.

Sandhia G. K. obtained her B.Tech Degree in Information Technology and M.E.in Computer Science and Engineering in the year 2005 and 2007 respectively. She completed her Ph.D in Computer Science and Engineering in the year 2021. She has 19 years of Experience in the field of Education and continues her research in the field of Cryptography, Network Security, Blockchain and quantum computing. She has published more than 20 research papers in indexed Journals and conferences.

Sharath Kumar Jagannathan is currently working as Assistant Professor at Saint Peters University, USA. He obtained his undergraduate degree in computer science (2000) from Madras University, India. He then pursued his master's degree in software systems engineering from University of Melbourne Australia in 2005. Sharath worked as an Associate Professor from 2011 to 2021 (10 years) at VIT University India and during this tenure he received his doctoral degree in the area of social network privacy preservation in 2020. Sharath has over 15 journal publications, one International Conference and an Indian patent till date. His research Interests include machine learning, Deep Learning and anonymization techniques.

Ezhilarasan K. is currently working as a Guest Faculty in Centre for Geoinformatics, Gandhigram Rural Institute (Deemed to be University), Dindigul, Tamil Nadu, India Since 2016. He worked as Project Fellow under UGC-Major Research Project from July 2010 to Jan 2013. He received BEST paper award in International Conference on Signal and Image Processing (ICSIP-2012) at Coimbatore. He also got fellowship from Jawharlal Nehru Memorial Fund for Doctoral Studies (JNMF) from Jan 2014 to June 2015. His main research work focuses on Medical Image Processing and Satellite Image Processing. He has published his research work in National and International conferences and Journals. He has published book chapters and published by reputed publishers. He is also a life time member of Indian Society For Technical Education (ISTE). He has guided PG students for their dessertation.

Somasundaram K. was born in 1953. He was the Professor and Head Department of Computer Science and Applications, at Gndhigram Rural Institute, India, from 1996 to 2018. He was the Head of the Computer Centre from 1989 to 2014. He has served as Registrar and Controller of Examinations. He served as Professor of Physics for the same institute from 976 to 1999. He obtained his M.Sc. in Physics degree from Madras University in 1976. He obtained his Post Graduate Diploma in Computer Methods from Madurai Karmaraj University in 1989. He obtained his Ph.D degree in theoretical MHD waves from the Indian Institute of Science, Bengaluru in 1984. He has guided 18 Ph.D candidates and completed four research projects funded by the Department of Science and Technology, Government of India, University Grants Commission, Government of India, Association of Commonwealth

Universities, UK. He is a life member of the Indian Society for Technical Education, India, the Telemedicine Society of India, and an annual member of IEEE, USA. He has published about 200 articles in journals and conferences. His areas of interest are Magnetic Resonance Image(MRI) processing, image segmentation, image computer, computer simulation for kosava yield, brain image processing and brain extraction from MRI of human head, and tumor detection.

Jansi K. R. obtained her B.Tech Degree in Information Technology and M.Tech Degree in Computer Science and Engineering in the year 2004 and 2008 respectively. She completed her Ph.D in Computer Science and Engineering in the year 2021. She has 19 years of Experience in the field of Education and continues her research in the field of Wireless Network, Security and Privacy, Blockchain and has published more than 20 research papers in indexed Journals and conferences.

Maad M. Mijwil is an Iraqi Academician; he was born in Baghdad, Iraq, in 1987. He received his B.Sc. degree in software engineering from Baghdad college of economic sciences university, Iraq, in 2009. He received a M.Sc. degree in 2015 from the computer science department, university of Baghdad in the field of wireless sensor networks, Iraq. Currently, he is working as a Lecturer and an academic member of staff in the computer techniques engineering department at Baghdad college of economic sciences university, Iraq. He has over ten years of experience in teaching and guiding projects for undergraduates. He has authored more than 100 publications, including papers/ chapters(published 75 peer reviewed papers in national/international conferences and journals), preprints, presentations, and posters. He is also an editor in more than 10 international/national journals and a reviewer in more than 100 international/national journals. He has served on technical program committees for many prestigious conferences. Also, he graduated from Publons academy as a peer reviewer. His Google citations are over 1000 mark.

R. Nagarajan received his B.E. in Electrical and Electronics Engineering from Madurai Kamarajar University, Madurai, India, in 1997. He received his M.E. in Power Electronics and Drives from Anna University, Chennai, India, in 2008. He received his Ph.D in Electrical Engineering from Anna University, Chennai, India, in 2014. He has worked in the industry as an Electrical Engineer. He is currently working as Professor of Electrical and Electronics Engineering at Gnanamani College of Technology, Namakkal, and Tamilnadu, India. His current research interest includes Power Electronics, Power System, Soft Computing Techniques and Renewable Energy Sources. He is published more than ninety research papers in various referred international journal.

Chitra P. has completed her Doctoral Degree in Computer Science and Applications in 2019 and she has also finished her PDF in the year 2021. She is a vibrant researcher in the field of Image compression, Machine learning and deep learning. She has a good number of publications in journals, Book chapters, and National and international conferences. She is currently working on AI-based techniques.

Elakya R. is an Assistant Professor in Department of Information Technology at Sri Venkateswara College of Engineering, Sriperumbudur-602117, Tamil Nadu, India.

Jeya R. obtained her M.Tech Degree in Computer Science and Engineering from Manonmaniam Sundaranar University, Tirunelveli, India in the year 2005. After completing her postgraduation, she joined as a Lecturer in the Department of Information Technology at Sri Krishna College of Engineering, Coimbatore during June 2005 to November 2006. Later, She Joined as an Assistant Professor in the Department of Computer Science and Engineering, SRMIST, Chennai. She has 15 years of Experience in the field of Education; She continues her research in the field of Wireless Communication and completed Ph.D in SRM institute of science and Technology in 2021. She has published more than 25 research papers in Conferences and Journals.

Siva Shankar Ramasamy did Master of Computer Applications and Doctoral degree from Gandhigram Rural Institute [Ministry of Human Resource Development-India], Tamil Nadu, India. He worked in the National Institute of Technology-Trichy., and Madanapalle Institute of Technology & Science, India. He is a Life Member of "Computer Society of India" and "International Association of Engineers". He is currently working in the International College of Digital Innovation-Chiang Mai University, Thailand. His contributions are associated with 3 Research Patents, 25 International research articles and 2 national level Projects. He is currently doing research in the areas of Sustainability Development, Medical Image Segmentation, IoT, Rural Reconstruction, Cross Border E-Commerce, Digital Business and Blue Economy.

Rahul Ratnakumar received his Bachelor's degree from College of Engineering Trivandrum, University of Kerala in Electrical and Electronics Engineering in 2009. He obtained Master of Engineering degree from Birla Institute of Technology and Science (BITS), Pilani with a specialization in Microelectronics in 2012. He worked on the project- Interface circuit design for a MEMS Vibratory Gyroscope, with the Analog and Mixed Signal Design group of CSIR-CEERI Pilani. He is completed his doctoral work in Malaviya National Institute of Technology (MNIT), Jaipur in the topic of VLSI implementation of Clustering Algorithms. He has a post-doctoral fellowship from the Department of Systems and Computer Engineering at Carleton University, Canada in the field of Autonomous Vehicles. His field of Interests are Computer Architecture, Digital VLSI design, Image Processing, soft computing and data mining. Currently he is working in Manipal University, Karnataka.

Karthigai Selvi S. is serving as an Assistant Professor in the School of Computer Science and Engineering, Galgotias University, Uttar Pradesh. She had been worked as a Guest Teacher in the Department of Computer Science and Applications, The Gandhigram Rural Institute – Deemed to be University, India for five years. She did her UG (B.Sc. Mathematics) and Ph.D (Full-time) in The Gandhigram Rural Institute – Deemed to be University. She has more than Ten years Teaching experiences, One year corporate experience like Programmer and served as Project Consultant in Mother Teresa Women's University, India. Her research work focuses on Human Brain Image Processing and Sustainable Development. She bagged a National Award in Student Research Convention held on 2013. She has published more than thirty papers in reputed journals (SCI, Scopus and Web of Science), International and National Conferences. She has served as a Resource Person in Universities and Colleges.

V. Sivakumar is associate professor in Asia Pacific University of Technology and Innovation (APU) with 25 years of experience in Education. He had served as Faculty at Senior Positions in Several Public Universities of India, Ethiopia & Libya. He bagged Gold Medal in his Masters. He is a passionate educator and researcher. He is a SME in the field of Artificial Intelligence. He is an active member of Asia Pacific Center of Analytics, APU. He has got over 50 publications in Scopus, Web of Science and reputed peer-reviewed journals and as book chapters. He has participated and presented his research articles in several International Conferences. He is actively contributing for several referred journals as referee and editorial board member.

Praveenkumar Somasundaram was born in the year 1985, in India. He got his Bachelor of Engineering (B.E.) in electrical and electronics from Anna University, India in the Year 2006. He got his Master of Science in Electrical Engineering from Oklahoma State University, USA in 2010 and Master of Science in Electrical Engineering from University of Southern California in the year 2013. In 2010, he was an intern in Qualcomm, San Diego. From 2013-2016, he was a verification Engineer at Seagate, Fremont, USA. From 2017-2018, he was Verification Engineer at Aricent Technologies Inc, Bangalore, India. From 2018 to Mar 2019, he was Member of Technical Staff at Mirafra Inc, USA. During April 2019- March 2022, he was a Staff Engineer at Qualcomm Atheros, California, USA. From April 2022 onwards he is working as Staff Engineer at Qualcomm Technologies Inc. at San Diego, USA. He has published ten research articles, six in peer reviewed Journals and four in international conferences. His research interest are in brain extraction from MRI of human head scans, brain tumor detection using MRI and image compression using DCT. He has received a best researcher award. He has served as reviewer for several International Conferences. He is a member of IEEE.

Kamakshi Prasad Valurouthu is currently serving as a Senior Professor of Computer Science & Engineering at JNTUH College of Engineering Science & Technology in Hyderabad, has 31 years of teaching and research experience. He obtained his B.Tech., M.Tech., and Ph.D. degrees from KLCE, Andhra University College of Engineering, and IIT Madras, respectively. He joined JNTU as an Assistant Professor in 1992 and was subsequently promoted to the positions of Associate Professor, Professor, and Senior Professor in 2003, 2006, and 2016, respectively. Throughout his tenure, he has held various administrative roles within the University, including Additional Controller of Exams, Coordinator of TEQIP-II, Head of the Department of CSE, Controller of Exams, Director of Innovative Technologies, Director of Evaluation, and currently serves as the Chairperson of the Board of Studies for CSE and CSE allied branches. Additionally, he is actively involved as a member of the Board of Studies, Academic Councils, and Governing Bodies of several autonomous and non-autonomous colleges affiliated with JNTUH and other Universities. He has also served as the Visitor's (President of India) nominee for the Executive Council of MANUU, Hyderabad and as a board member of the School of Computer and Information Sciences (SCIS) at Hyderabad Central University. In recognition of his contributions, he received the Telangana Government's state teacher award for the year 2020. His research interests encompass a wide range of areas, including Quantum Computing, Machine Learning, Data Mining, Speech & Image Processing, and Theoretical Computer Science. He has successfully supervised 29 Ph.D. candidates and 3 MS degree holders, while currently guiding 8 more Ph.D. research scholars.

Index

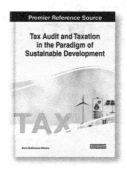   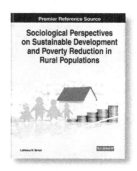

Printed in the United States
by Baker & Taylor Publisher Services